Transactions

The Interplay Between
Individual, Family, and Society

Transactions

The Interplay Between Individual, Family, and Society

by John Spiegel, M.D.

Edited by John Papajohn, Ph.D.

Science House

The author is grateful for permission to use, in whole or in part, material of his which previously appeared in the following:

Collective Violence, edited by James F. Short, Jr. and Marvin E. Wolfgang, Chicago: Aldine-Atherton, 1970. Chapter Fourteen
Integration and Conflict in Family Behavior, report no. 27, Topeka, Kansas: Group for the Advancement of Psychiatry, 1954. Chapter Five
The International Journal of Group Tensions, Jan.-Mar., 1971. Chapter Twelve
Psychoanalytic Review, vol. 57 (1970), no. 3. Chapter Thirteen
Psychiatry, XVII (1954). Chapter Nine
Science and Psychoanalysis, Volume II: Individual and Familial Dynamics, edited by Jules H. Masserman, M.D., New York: Grune and Stratton, 1959. Chapter Ten
Zygon: A Journal of Religion and Science, 4:3 (Sept. 1969). Chicago: The University of Chicago Press. © 1969
The University of Chicago. Chapter Eleven

Designed by Gordon Lander

Library of Congress Catalog Card Number: 74-173283
Standard Book Number: 87668-050-3

Manufactured in the United States of America

To our co-workers in community mental health.

Contents

Author's Preface

An author owes so much to so many people who have influenced or helped him in the course of his work that a complete account would require an autobiography. In a brief summary suitable to this collection of papers selected from a lifetime of research, omissions cannot be avoided.

First, I would like to thank John Papajohn, without whose energy and dedication this book would never have appeared. A colleague and co-worker in family research over many years, he conceived the idea of organizing for publication a series of published and unpublished papers written for diverse purposes. The format he devised has provided the coherence which is so often lacking in volumes of collected papers.

Reaching far back in time, I want to express my gratitude for the support I received from my first colleague, Roy R. Grinker, Sr. Following upon our mutual studies of the war neuroses during World War II, he encouraged me to pursue my nascent interest in the field that has come to be known as social psychiatry. In the late forties and early fifties a psychoanalytically trained psychiatrist who undertook further training in the social sciences proceeded at his own risk. Most psychoanalysts regarded such a venture as foolhardy, and, viewing my efforts more in sorrow than in anger, wondered why I should want to waste my time on such a fruitless diversion.

Equally important to the development of my perspective on research was the combined interest of Florence and Clyde Kluckhohn, Talcott Parsons, and Samuel Stauffer, all members in the early fifties of the Department of Social Relations at Harvard University. What skills I have acquired in the social sciences is due mainly to their efforts. The influence of Florence Kluckhohn's theoretical approach to the sources of variation in human behavior is evident in many of the papers included in this volume, and she was chiefly responsible for the design and methods of the family studies reported herein. But what impressed me when I joined the Social Relations faculty at Harvard in 1954 was the reversal of the attitude previously expressed by my psychoanalytic colleagues. None of my new associates thought it peculiar or wasteful for a psychoanalyst to try to integrate his insights and methods with the procedures of social science.

Another important source of support at Harvard was George Gardner, Director of the Judge Baker Guidance Center and of the Department of Psychiatry at the Children's Hospital Medical Center in Boston. Both a psychoanalyst and a clinical psychologist, Dr. Gardner not only served as an important intellectual bridge for me and many others between the Department of Social Relations and the Harvard Medical School, but he also provided the facilities for the clinical studies of family interaction which Florence Kluckhohn and I co-directed. The Chairman of the Department of Social Relations, David McClellan, also provided a great wealth of administrative and personal support.

Finally, among those whose concern and foresight promoted the development of my own research interests, Abram Sachar played a prominent role. As the first president of Brandeis University, it was Dr. Sachar who initially sensed the need for more intensive research on violent behavior and then persuaded me to organize the Lemberg Center for the Study of Violence at Brandeis. His sympathetic understanding of interdisciplinary research and of exploratory studies enabled the Lemberg Center to move ahead despite questions in various quarters as to the academic respectability of research on violence. In this endeavor, Charles Schottland, then Dean of the Florence Heller School for Advanced Studies in Social Welfare, now president of Brandeis University, provided the organizational context for the establishment and growth of the Lemberg Center. In addition, Samuel Lemberg, long a member of the Board of Trustees of Brandeis, supplied the financial support which has enabled the Center to navigate amidst the shifting currents of private and public research grants.

Foundations and their executives rarely receive the credit due them for supporting studies of unpredictable value. For example, when in 1950 John Gardner of the Carnegie Corporation provided a grant for the support of a conference, organized by Roy Grinker, Jurgen Ruesch, David Shakow, Lawrence Frank, and myself, to discuss the topic of "A Unified Theory of Human Behavior," no one could have predicted that anything would come of it. Yet, out of this conference, which struggled manfully with its resisting subject matter for several years, emerged the well-known book, edited by Roy Grinker, entitled, *Toward a Unified Theory of Human Behavior*. It was also under the extraordinary stimulation of this conference that I prepared the previously unpublished first two chapters of this book on transactional inquiry and the transactional field.

The National Institute of Mental Health (H.E.W.) made substantial contributions to the research undertaken by Florence Kluckhohn and myself, entitled, "Family Transactions in Mental Health and Illness," and its executive staff, particularly Philip Sapir, gave us support and personal attention whenever it was required. The family case histories, which form Chapters Seven and Eight of this volume, were originally written as position papers for this research project and have not been previously published.

Another previously unpublished contribution to this research is to be found in Chapter Three on the structure and function of social roles. The subject matter of this chapter was originally delivered in the form of two lectures on Social Psychiatry given at Tulane University in 1958 under the sponsorship of the Department of Psychiatry and Neurology and the Department of Sociology and Anthropology, with the help of a grant from the Mona Bronfman Scheckman Foundation. Dr. Harold Lief and Professor Forrest Laviolette were co-chairmen of this series of lectures.

The National Institute of Mental Health and the Ford Foundation made major contributions to the research undertaken by the Lemberg Center on urban collective violence. I am much indebted to Edward Flynn of the N.I.M.H. for the spirit of cooperation and encouragement which he provided in the course of our work. The Pauline and Louis G. Cowan Foundation of New York also provided support for various aspects of the studies reported herein, as did the Marcus Foundation of Chicago.

The sort of interdisciplinary research to which this book is addressed could not have taken place without the help of co-workers and research associates from a variety of backgrounds. Although it is not possible to mention all those who have participated, I would like to express my gratitude for the contributions of Norman Bell, Ezra Vogel, Helen Friedman, and Albert Treischman to the family research. Similarly, I am indebted to Lemberg Center staff associates Ralph Lewis, Marie Lyons, Terry Knopf, Richard Fischer, Joyce Hartweg, and Lester McCullough for collaboration in the violence research.

Finally, it would not be possible to complete the list of those who have woven their way through the fabric of research reported here without mentioning the enormous help and stimulation provided by the Group for the Advancement of Psychiatry, generally, and its Committee on the Family, specifically. Members of the Committee on the Family participated intensely in the preparation of the report which appears as Chapter Five of this book. It is indeed remarkable that there exists an organization whose members are willing to take so much time and trouble criticizing and encouraging each other's work, and I regard myself as fortunate to have been a member of GAP. One of its guiding principles has been of special relevance to my own work. This is the notion that, although professional training within the boundaries of a particular discipline is essential, this is only the first step. The boundaries of a discipline diminish in significance unless one is willing to cross them for the sake of collaborating with those trained in other professions and points of view in the effort to increase our knowledge of human behavior.

John Spiegel

Editor's Preface

The extensive contributions of John Spiegel span a broad range of subject matter and problem areas. At an earlier time he focused his theoretical and research efforts on the war neuroses, and then on the family, systems theory, and ethnic groups; at present he is writing about violence. The main developmental outlines, however, of his theoretical approach have become somewhat obscure. The internal consistency that characterizes the broadening of his theoretical perspectives — the integration of earlier theoretical formulations with later ones — is lost to the reader who, by virtue of his interest in a given problem area, limits his reading.

The specific choice of papers included in this volume and the order in which they are presented are intended to bring into sharp relief the main course of Spiegel's thinking and its application to different problems within the field of mental health.

His early work on the war neuroses is not included since it was largely limited to the use of traditional psychoanalytic theory. It was this work, however, that stimulated him to search for a broader theoretical base that could encompass those social and cultural variables that he became increasingly convinced needed to be included in a comprehensive understanding of the origins of neuroses in men undergoing the stresses of combat. This effort eventually led him to an intensive study of Dewey and Bentley and to the formulation of transactional systems theory.

In Chapter One, Transactional Inquiry: The Description of Systems, which has not been published previously, he traces the course of his thinking in formulating his theory. In Chapter Two, "The Transactional Field," (also appearing for the first time in this volume), he applies his theory in an innovative way to research problems in mental health. This transactional systems theory constitutes the foundation of his subsequent work. It provides an integrating framework within which psychological, social, and cultural theoretical constructs can be employed in a comprehensive ordering of human behavior. In the psychological domain, psychoanalytic theory remains for Spiegel the preferred psychological model. In the social domain, his development of the social role concept is a unique contribution. This concept is presented in Chapters Three and Four, "Structure of Social Roles" and "Function of Social Roles." These chapters constitute an edited version of two addresses delivered at Tulane University in 1954 and have not appeared in print before. In the cultural domain, Spiegel adopted the concept of value orientation as formulated by Kluckhohn; it is outlined in Chapter Five, "Integration and Conflict in Family Behavior," which he co-authored with Florence Kluckhohn. In this paper the transactionally ordered interrelationship among intrapsychic process (psychoanalytically conceived), social role structure and functioning, and cultural value orientations (as they are played out in the context of the family) is described.

This primarily theoretical paper is followed by Chapter Six, "A Functional Theory of Family Process," which presents a detailed analysis of the dynamics of the interpersonal process within an ethnic family as it faces the stresses of culture change in the United States. Chapters Seven and Eight round out Part III through an in-depth study of two Italian-American families, one of which has a high degree of conflict and the other substantially less. These studies breathe life into the theoretical formulations presented earlier and dramatically illustrate the wealth of clinical insight that this framework provides. In analyzing the first family, the Tondis, the social role concept is the primary theoretical tool; while in analyzing the second family, the Sirrentis, the focus shifts to value orientation theory. Psychoanalytic formulations are used in both family studies.

This alternating shift in focus from social role to value orientation with the concomitant use of psychoanalytic theory appears in the two subsequent chapters on psychotherapy. In Chapter Nine, social role is employed as the key analytic concept, while in Chapter

Ten, the emphasis is on cultural value orientation. This alternating shift in focus in dealing with a single problem area is consistent with the transactional system assumptions outlined in Part I. Only one dimension of the field of transacting events is discussed at a given time with the appropriate theoretical construct.

In Chapter Eleven, "Toward a Theory of Collective Violence," the major thrust is on the use of value orientation theory in ordering the events related to violence, while in Chapter Twelve, social role theory is used to analyze those same events. The same shift in emphasis from social role to value orientations appears in Chapters Thirteen and Fourteen where the campus becomes the locus of social conflict.

In Part III Spiegel concentrates on the family as a subsystem of society. In Part IV he deals with the individual as a participant in a one-to-one relationship with a doctor in psychotherapy. In Part V his focus broadens again to encompass those macroscopic events that constitute social conflict.

A basic editorial problem in compiling these papers was the question of whether the summary of social role theory and value orientation theory that appears in each paper of Parts IV and V should be deleted since both theories are presented in detail in Chapters Three, Four, and Five. It was decided not to do so for two reasons: first, the summaries constitute an integral part of each paper; and second, these recapitulations of theory underscore a central theme of this book — the alternating shift of foci and the theoretical constructs that order events in a transacting system of reverberating processes.

As a student of John Spiegel's, I had been aware of the unpublished papers in this volume for many years. Jason Aronson of Science House had also known of Spiegel's work through seminars that the latter had offered in the psychiatry department of the Massachusetts General Hospital in 1958. We share a strong conviction that these unpublished papers are especially relevant today now that the emphasis in mental health is shifting from the individual to the community. Abortive efforts to apply traditional psychological models in conceptualizing complex community mental health problems indicate a need for new directions. John Spiegel's transactional systems theory provides a bridge from traditional psychoanalytic theory to those social and cultural factors that must be included in a comprehensive approach to community mental health issues. Traditionally trained mental health workers should be able to use this theory in order to move from the familiar ways of conceptualizing individual pathology to new ways of ordering those phenomena that they are now being called upon to understand and to relate to.

The executive editor of the Violence Institute at Brandeis University, Robert Erwin, has made a significant contribution to the preparation of this volume. He copyedited the first draft of these papers and guided me through the complex maze of editorial requirements, thereby facilitating completion of this work.

Nancy Dreyer's research assistance and diligent handling of the multiple secretarial tasks required to assemble this volume are very much appreciated.

I would also like to acknowledge my gratitude to the Marcus Foundation of Chicago, whose generous financial support enabled me to bring this book to completion.

John Papajohn

Transactions

The Interplay Between
Individual, Family, and Society

Part I

Transactional Theory

In Chapter One John Spiegel describes transactional systems theory in terms of its philosophical underpinnings. The limitations of the Aristotelian assumptions upon which modern scientific thought is based are reviewed in the light of Dewey and Bentley's writings. It is concluded that Aristotelian assumptions of linear causality in which events are connected by cause-and-effect relationships delimits the range of variables that can be examined at one time. The alternate assumption — that events constitute a field of transacting processes in which change in one part is related to change in the others — is explicated. This assumption makes possible the utilization of a broad number of parameters which are traditionally grouped within different scientific disciplines or "systems" such as biology, sociology, psychology, and cultural anthropology. The interrelationships that characterize these parameters can now be examined as reverberating processes in a field of transactionally related events.

In Chapter Two the transactional field model is applied to the events traditionally subsumed under different mental health disciplines. The limitations and distortions of the linear model in which events are conceptualized as independent and dependent variables within each of these disciplines are discussed.

ONE

Transactional Inquiry: Description of Systems

Since we cannot be universal and know all that is to be known of everything, we ought to know a little about everything. For it is better to know something about everything than to know all about one thing. This universality is the best. If we can have both, still better; but if we must choose, we ought to choose the former. And the world feels this and does so; for the world is often a good judge.

If a man made himself the first object of study, he would see how incapable he is of going further. How can a part know the whole? But he may aspire to know at least the parts to which he bears some proportion. But the parts of the world are all so related and linked to one another that I believe it impossible to know one without the other and without the whole.

It is not in Montaigne, but in myself, that I find all that I see in him.

Pascal, Pensées

How everything is connected with everything else is the problem, *par excellence*, of philosophy. It is also of concern to scientists, at least in their more self-conscious, holistic moods. Programs for the unity of the sciences show the desire among scientists for some kind of togetherness in the face of their innumerable, noncommunicating specialties. The need to grasp interconnections makes itself felt if one takes a hard look at almost any subject, no matter how specialized or "applied." *(See Behan and Hirschfeld 1963.)* The

1

trouble with most such programs, however, is that they are built around the operations of the separate disciplines. They usually come to grief when the participants begin to argue about which discipline is higher, broader, more general, more basic, or more "real." Claims are made for a hierarchial organization of the sciences, each disci-pline occurring at some predetermined level in relation to the others. Those at higher levels then have a tendency to swallow up those at lower levels on the assumption that those ranked higher are more inclusive or general. On the other hand, those lower down on the hierarchy are apt to bite back and attempt to swallow those higher up on the principle of being more "basic." The basic sciences, like physics and chemistry, claim that the virtue of their lowly position is that, in the end, all other sciences will be reduced to — that is, explained in terms of — physics and chemistry. The "higher ups," such as sociology and psychology, counter-attack with the claim that physics and chemistry *as sciences* are types of social and psycho-logical behavior which they will willingly "explain" to the socio-logically and psychologically ignorant.

Such claims for territorial dominance appear to be aspects of the disciplines rather than of the personnel populating them. Indi-vidual scientists and some university departments are continuously crossing disciplinary boundaries. But disputes can break out with special virulence in neighboring disciplines, where they are compli-cated by "the narcissism of small differences."[1] Left to their own devices, the disciplines seem unable to transcend themselves. The situation would seem to require the services of an umpire — some-one not so embedded in a discipline as to leap to its defense against all encroachers and poachers. For such purposes we turn to the philosopher, with his long experience of looking at human affairs *sub specie aeternitatis*.

Philosophy, however, has more to offer us than its role of referee. Establishing ground-rules and keeping all players in some sort of reasonable order is only one of its functions. More important is the role of philosophy as the purveyor of a certain freshness to the scientific scene. The separate disciplines are likely after a time, either to go stale or else to produce breakthroughs — great leaps

---

[1] I have listened to a psychologist with a psychoanalytic background attempt to explain to a sociologist the unconscious, irrational, and emotional "reasons" for the latter's emphasis on social factors in the motivation of behavior. The sociologist's immediate response was to expound the socio-logical origin of the psychoanalytic theories the psychologist was using to make the explanation in the first place!

2

forward which take a long time to digest. Philosophy finds its way through the staleness and the novelty to a perspective within which the sciences and the various branches of learning can reassemble for fresh starts. So it is to philosophy that we look for possible aid.

In the appeal to philosophy, it is natural for me to turn to the two men who have had the most influence on my own thinking: Alfred North Whitehead and John Dewey. Philosophers generally have been concerned with what we know and how we know it, but among recent philosophers these two men have been most clearly preoccupied with the relation between systems of behavior.[2] It must be recognized, of course, that far reaches of philosophic thought lie behind, to the side, and in front of these two men. I use Whitehead and Dewey, therefore, as much as rallying points for certain issues as for their specific contributions. I do not use them — and would not be technically competent to do so — for a general discussion of philosophic issues and controversies.

With regard to systems theory, Whitehead is of importance on a number of grounds. In the first place, he chose to pry apart scientific generalizations, even those most sacrosanct, in order to examine the meanings behind or within them. He was skeptical toward the "laws" of science — more than a little doubtful of the notion that the cosmos contained a legislature with nothing to do but pass and repeal these laws. He was also scornful toward human logic, or, rather, toward logical systems framed by men as if they were the last word on the method for arriving at truth.[3] These attitudes of

---

[2] Two other recent scientific and philosophical points of view have been concerned with this problem: Communications Theory and General Systems Theory. Since it is not the purpose in this chapter to review all the approaches from which aid might have been elicited, but only those actually drawn upon, they will not be dealt with here. Both General Systems Theory and Communications Theory have something in common with the trans-actional approach which I use. All three approaches attempt to frame a way of organizing the data of behavior so that they will not be imprisoned by the specialized disciplines and yet can be related to them for technical purposes. All three try to make a place for openness and change, for novelty and creativity as well as for sameness and continuity over time, within a consistent if not "unified" framework. They differ in the conceptual materials and technical resources which they use for the organization of the data. At this point in time, it cannot be said which approach is more useful or valid.

[3] An example of scorn: "The conclusion is that Logic, conceived as an adequate analysis of the advance of thought, is a fake. It is a superb instrument, but it requires a background of common sense . . . [for] the final outlook of Philosophic thought cannot be based upon the exact statements which form the basis of special sciences. The exactness is a fake." (From the Ingersoll Lecture, entitled "Immortality," in Whitehead 1948, p. 104.)

3

nondeference toward the scientific and philosophic establishment were not adopted out of any disrespect for science or philosophy. His attack was merely against taking the particular methods, findings, and generalizations of a science at a particular point of time (our time) too seriously, as having ultimate truth or value. He summarized his attack on the error of taking scientific abstractions as concrete fact in the slogan: "The Fallacy of Misplaced Concreteness." The error comes about when we take a theoretical generalization — like the theory of mechanics in physics — as having the status of a fact in the annals of truth. In actuality, they can be considered "true" only in a qualified, limited sense — limited to the modes of abstraction of the scientific speciality in which they arise and by the degree of progress it has made at the time.[4]

A second way in which Whitehead is important to us comes about through his insistence on the relativity and mutual interrelatedness of both scientific generalizations and empirical facts, coming out of the separate disciplines. In emphasizing the significance of a "mode of abstraction," he continually pointed out that, in order to abstract, one must, of necessity, leave out a lot of information not usable in the particular system of abstraction employed by a particular discipline.[5] He was interested in what happened to the

---

[4] "Thus one aim of philosophy is to challenge the half-truths constituting the scientific first principles. The systematization of science cannot be conducted in water tight compartments. All general truths condition each other; and the limits of their application cannot be adequately defined apart from their correlation by yet wider generalities. The criticism of principles must chiefly take the form of determining the proper meanings to be assigned to the fundamental notions of the various sciences, when these notions are considered in respect to their status relatively to each other. The determination of this status requires a generality transcending any special subject-matter." *(From "Process and Reality," in Northrup and Gross (eds.) 1953, p. 576.)*

[5] "The disadvantage of exclusive attention to a group of abstractions, however well-founded, is that, by the nature of the case, you have abstracted from the remainder of things. Insofar as the excluded things are important in your experience, your modes of thought are not fitted to deal with them. You cannot think without abstractions; accordingly, it is of the utmost importance to be vigilant in critically revising your *modes* of abstraction. It is here that philosophy finds its niche as essential to the healthy progress of society. It is the critic of abstractions. A civilization which cannot burst through its current abstractions is doomed to sterility after a very limited period of progress. An active school of philosophy is quite as important for the locomotion of ideas as an active school of railway engineers is for the locomotion of fuel." *(From "Science and the Modern World," in Northrup and Gross (eds.) 1953, p. 416.)*

4

information which dropped out. He appealed to the common, everyday experience of humans, which cannot be fitted so neatly into the scientific modes of abstraction. Ordinary people, even scientists in ordinary walks of life, have to use the excluded information in some way in order to get along in a more complex world with more disorderly information than is permitted to enter the halls of science. This appeal on behalf of the bewildered — those lost in the wilds of civil chaos *and* of scientific generalization — was made as much for the sake of the scientist as for the ordinary man.

Where science is concerned, Whitehead proposed a method, philosophical and conceptual but nevertheless a method, for viewing the information which drops out of one system of abstractions so that it appears within a second system as an "aspect" of the first one. He usually said this in a rather complicated way, using a special vocabulary specifically invented for the demonstration of this principle and employing little concrete illustration. As a result, the net effect in a large part of his writing is a sort of obscurantism, like listening to someone talking philosophical Esperanto. Whitehead nevertheless had his reasons for talking in this manner. It is important to keep in mind that vagueness of expression was not in his opinion as great an error as a pretended precision in wording and phrasing and handling of data which goes beyond what we know.[6]

That the information which drops out of one system of abstractions becomes essential to another system of abstraction is not such a startling thought. What is significant, however, is that Whitehead used the disjunction of knowledge produced by the process of abstraction to reconnect what had been pulled apart and isolated. He did this by stating that the information which has dropped out of the first system and which is of the essence of the second reappears, from the standpoint of the second system, as an *aspect* of the first one. In this fashion, by switching back and forth between the two systems, we connect up and put together what we have just rendered asunder through the process of abstraction. We thereby restore to the world and to ourselves a potential unity or organization which

---

[6] "Philosophy in its advance must involve obscurity of expression, and novel phrases. The permanent, essential factors governing the nature of things lie in the dim background of our conscious experience . . . The besetting sin of philosophers is that, being merely men, they endeavour to survey the universe from the standpoint of gods. There is a pretence at adequate clarity of fundamental ideas. We can never disengage our measure of clarity from a pragmatic sufficiency within occasions of ill-defined limitations. Clarity always means 'clear enough.'" *(From "Analysis of Meaning," in Whitehead 1948, pp. 131-32.)*

the very effort to order our thoughts and investigations had destroyed. The key to the reunification, which Whitehead called "prehension," is the switching back and forth between the "perspectives" provided by each mode of abstraction, so that what is lost in one is recovered in the other and restored by it to the first (and vice versa).

Suppose, for example, we consider a sunset in terms of physics and astronomy. We come across such matters as the rotation of the earth on its axis and around the sun, the transmission and speed of light and its spectrum of colors, and how the spectrum of color is selectively filtered by the dust in the atmosphere to produce the gorgeous salmons, pinks, and oranges in the sky. "Gorgeous," however, is not in the vocabulary or in the system of abstractions of physics and astronomy. Instead, impressions of spectacular color fit, though not too neatly, into the psychological abstractions which we can use to explain our appreciative response. In the psychological system, we can, if we wish, talk about the amount of primitive or sexual energy which has been neutralized, sublimated, and placed at the disposal of the ego for cathexis with just such a substitute set of objects as we are seeing in the sky. What the colorful objects — sun, sky, clouds, horizon — are substitutes for is, of course, indeterminate and varied in the individual case, but presumably the particular response has been shifted from some much earlier, much valued object like a parent or some other person loved and hated in childhood.[7]

Whatever set of scientific abstractions is used to explain the psychological "aspects" of our behavior — and there could be many others — the point is that our raw experience is of the sunset we watch: a unified event. It is only when we come to science that the experience is fragmented. But, according to Whitehead, even in science the unity can be restored — with the help of philosophy, of course. Science uses analysis, which is division of behavior into parts. Philosophy, reviewing the behavior of the scientists, recombines what has been divided by showing us that the "gorgeous" which has been lost to physics reappears from the standpoint of psychology. It can even go a step further and demonstrate how "gorgeous" is not only restored to the sunset but also becomes a part of our response to the physical and astronomic principles themselves.

---

[7] In one of the books of the French convict Jean Genet is the passage: "I am tired of satisfying my desire for murder stealthily by admiring the imperial pomp of sunsets. My eyes have bathed enough in them. Let's get to my hands." (Genet 1963, p. 130)

How extraordinary of nature to have arranged these effects through the laws of gravitation, electro-magnetic radiation, and all the rest of its precision mechanics. Such efficiency! Such aesthetic sensibility! All these reactions, which become "aspects" of the physical systems themselves, can be explained by psychology.

Through this way of getting at the behavior of scientists and the relation of this behavior to everyday or "naïve" experience, Whitehead accomplished an important thing. He accepted the validity of "the ideally isolated system," which is the standard object of scientific investigation. But he insisted that there was also a scientific and equally valid way of *studying combinations of systems* and that, indeed, this must be done. We can count on the probability that the poets and artists will do it, will assemble systems and aspects of behavior in new combinations and patterns; they always have, and there is no reason to expect that they will abandon their role. In some ways, their job is easier because they are not supposed to be precise. The scientist should always set up his procedures so that he can check his errors and their sources. But if this is not done by scientists for combinations of systems, then science can never come completely to grips with human experience in the world.[8] It is the underlining of this necessity that, in my opinion, constitutes Whitehead's crucial contribution.

We now come to Whitehead's method for achieving the synthesis, and here we begin to branch off somewhat from his approach. He raised the knotty question of the location of experience, pinpointing a metaphysical problem of honorable pedigree but of doubtful current status. Where is the beautiful sunset: in the mind, in the sky, or in both? The answers correspond to the three metaphysical positions meant to deal with the question of ultimate reality, or what is really real.

Those who say that the sunset is in the mind hold that ideas and thoughts are the only reality, matter being merely an illusion, a creation of the mind. These are the metaphysical idealists. Those

---

[8] The wording "human experience in the world" will undoubtedly remind some readers of a branch of philosophy which has come into prominence since Whitehead's day. We refer to Existentialism, both in philosophy and in psychology. We believe that Existentialism is concerned with the same problems which we have been discussing. But its opposition to the analysis of experience is so severe and fanatical, its determination to dismiss the vocabularies and abstractions of the separate disciplines so rigid and complete, its dedication to the subjective description of the phenomenon-as-it-occurs so far-reaching, that, as a program, it has lost its usefulness to science.

who say the sunset is really in the sky believe that the sun and the light emitted from it are the locus of reality; the mind is capable merely of a subjective transient and insubstantial registration of the external reality. These are the metaphysical materialists. Both sorts of answers are from the monists among the metaphysicians. The dualists say that the sunset is both in the sky *and* in the mind. Accordingly, there are two different kinds of reality, mental and physical, subjective and objective, ideal and material.

Whitehead dismissed all three sorts of answers as inadequate. He demonstrated that these answers necessarily followed from the way the question was posed: what is the real and where is it located? He showed how the question was determined by forms of thought which had been handed down from Aristotelian notions of substance and essence and from the classical mechanics of the 17th century. If one thinks of matter as a material substance of which qualities are predicated, then it must have both location and extension in space and time. Reality was treated as if it were a substance of some kind — either material or spiritual (ideational) — which had to exist somewhere in space. But since the work of Maxwell on electro-magnetic radiation and of Einstein on the theory of relativity, our notions of matter and of location in space have changed greatly. Matter has become interchangeable with energy and can no longer be conceived as a substance or an entity characterized by simple location. Space is no longer an empty container of positioned matter but must now be thought of as a space-time continuum — a field with regions and a varied structure. Matter has become a part of the space-time field itself, a part of its structure, no longer accountable on the basis of simple location. The data on the basis of which we estimate location now depend wholly on the position of the observer, relative to what is observed, in the space-time continuum. Thus whatever we say reality is must depend upon complex interrelations between the observers, the space-time continuum, and the part of the continuum (matter or energy) which is being observed.

On the basis of these new physical concepts, Whitehead postulated that reality could not have a simple location and could be identified neither with a thing-like entity (a piece of matter) nor with a thought-like entity (an idea). In a brilliant demonstration, he showed how our definitions of matter, which had made matter seem so reliable and concrete, were themselves an illustration of the fallacy of misplaced concreteness. What we took to be the ultimate and most simple reality of things — their location in time and space — were merely our own abstractions, our ways of thinking about things.

In preparing the way for a new approach to a reality which would be neither thing-like nor thought-like, Whitehead believed that it was necessary to soften some ancient dichotomies. The antithesis between man and nature, mind and matter, living organisms and inanimate objects was put, he held, too sharply, the distinctions nailed down in too hard-and-fast a manner. The boundaries between each of the oppositions, he claimed, were indeterminate, allowing for a high degree of overlap and melting into each other. The distinctions were a matter of perspective and focus; sometimes they applied, sometimes they didn't. This indeterminate status of mind and matter, man and nature became an important part of his solution of the problem of reality — the metaphysical problem.

In formulating his solution of the problem he relied heavily upon the concept of process. Reality is neither a thing-like entity nor a thought-like entity but is the concrete result in a particular event of a process going on between them. It was for the sake of describing how the process worked that he invented his special language. Process refers to *a realization* in a concrete event — a "concrescence" in his language — of interaction between thing and thing and between thoughts and things. But, because of the indeterminateness which he believed it necessary to introduce into the process, the shading off between man and nature, organic and inorganic, mind and matter, and because of his preoccupation with the problem of location, it becomes difficult in reading him to decide anything at all about where process is and who is doing what in space-time. Process is everywhere and nowhere, a part of space-time itself. In Whitehead's hands the world becomes an organism, over-unified, too much connected up, so that even little electrons become like thinking beings, joining up with like-minded electrons and protons to "create" an atom.

It is here that we part company with him. So many distinctions between the behavior of different species and different categories have been erased that it is difficult to see how one could set up any observational procedure to investigate how process takes place. Unification is achieved by sheer determination and verbal fireworks, brilliant but too indefinite for use. When we recover from the brilliance, we don't know where to go next. It is hard to see how Whitehead, who cleared up so many muddles, got himself into this one. The answer is too complex for us to trace out, but one aspect of it is of importance to us. We must recall that he started out to overcome intellectual discontinuities and contradictions which were partly of historical origin and partly the result of the procedures within the scientific specialities. He wanted to lay down a conceptual apparatus that would be at least as unified and as self-consistent as our ordinary experience and that would abolish philosophical antitheses which did not correspond with common sense. He went a long distance down this road, but in a sense he kept putting up erroneous signposts as he went along. He thought the road was called "Reality" and that he was broadening it into a highway and filling in metaphysical potholes. At the end of the road — a receding terminus which he did not claim to have reached — there would be the discovery of the true nature of the world.

Our point is that he should have called this road "Knowledge." He was not investigating reality, for reality is not the kind of thing that a philosopher can investigate. It requires specialized techniques, and it is a matter for science and scholarship, joined in partnership. What the philosopher can and does study, what Whitehead was actually working on, is the status of our knowledge about it and the adequacy of our tools for investigating it. If the philosopher sticks to the investigation of what we know and how well we know it, and all the problems involved in this enterprise, then he has his hands full. He also has a definite subject matter to deal with — epistemology. This is a road without a terminus, endless, because knowledge, adequate and inadequate, keeps stretching out. Reality is not a road at all but a territory to be explored, vast and without visible bounds. Knowledge is the road — or rather the highway and byway system of roads — which we have built for its exploration. In the process of exploring, we change the landscape, so that whatever reality is, it is probably not what it would have been or might have been without our activity. This leaves room for a certain amount of indefiniteness and indeterminateness, in addition to creativity, around the topic of reality. There are things we cannot know scientifically — namely, what the world would have been like had we not been around to investigate it.

Though we now have left room for indefiniteness, it is within human limits. If knowledge is exploration, and if exploring is human behavior, then a study of knowledge is also a study of human behavior. One of the reasons Whitehead got into his muddle is that he was too much the Platonist, conducting a love affair with ideas. They held for him an independent existence as "eternal objects." In the same way, percepts floated around in space and time as "prehensions." Prehension was a good word for Whitehead's purposes. It eliminates the anxiety and ambiguity from the word "apprehension" and exhibits the movement of thought in grasping the object so that the result — the realization — of process is of *both* thought *and* object. The result of the process, however, became so convincing a reality to him that it became separated from the behavior of man — a disembodied process.

This tendency to detach consciousness from behavior has troubled philosophy as well as everyday thinking ever since Plato introduced the notion of eternal forms. It is important for us to put it in its proper place — this disembodiment — lest its unresolved status contaminate the points we wish to make in this chapter. My own position is that of behaviorism in a broad sense and so what I have to say about the interrelations between the different systems of behavior ought to be consistent with this orientation. Yet the disembodiment of an idea and its tendency to float around as if it had an independent existence or constituted a separate realm of reality is so general a phenomenon in the history of human affairs that it must be taken into account. If we define behaviorism as the assumption that there is no phenomenon or part of reality which we can study, scientifically, apart from the behavior of the men doing the investigating, whether their own behavior, that of plants and animals, or that of nonliving objects and processes, then how are we to account for the generality of the phenomenon of thought as a spiritual substance, an eternal object, or an influential force supposedly divorced from the men who formulated it?

Here, again, we come up against a question which is too complex for us to handle without oversimplifying. We can deal only with certain aspects of it. We assume that it is clear enough, and requires no further discussion here, that thought and action are completely different but related forms of behavior. Without clearly defining the difference between them, psychoanalysis and other ways of studying *mental function* could not be justified as disciplines separate from social psychology and sociology. The whole question of what is externalized and what is internalized in human behavior would disappear, without justification. Without clearly defining both thought and action as parts of human behavior subject to experimental investigation, we could not bring either of them into the sphere of operations of science. However, we are still left with the question of why thought but not action tends to float away from behavior.

I would like to suggest two answers and one solution. The

first answer has to do with the time dimension and its function. Time brings up the phenomena of becoming, being, and perishing, appearance and disappearance, origins and ends, permanence and change. If we can understand time as part of the structure of the space-time continuum, determined in part by the position of the observer in that structure, then these matters become behavorial events related to what position a particular observer has in the continuum. However, if we understand time as a container enclosing successive moments (or hours, or years, or centuries) wholly separate from space, then these divisions chop up the event and give it a hardness and discreteness which it does not present when viewed in the framework of the space-time continuum. This is especially true of events viewed as occurring in the distant past. They come to have a discrete quality which makes them like a package, split off and discontinuous with reference to the present. This is the first answer: that both idea and act, when viewed in the past, become over-hardened, distorted way beyond the fluid nature of the event itself. When encountering them in the present as representatives of the past, we are likely to say, "Oh, how interesting; that's just what we think now" instead of "still think;" or we may say, "What a peculiar idea they had then" instead of contemplating the continuous, slow process of the development of ideas. This is the first way in which they become detached from behavior; behavior seems to refer mainly to the context of present experience, to that which is immediately at hand.[9]

The second answer has to do with the difference between thoughts and actions as systems of behavior. Thoughts or ideas can be more easily systematized than actions, more densely packed, and more easily reviewed. This is a function of language, especially recorded language. The word is stronger than the deed. Actions speak louder than words only over short time spans. The word, as thought and idea, is more persistent, if for no other reason than the fact that it can more easily be recorded, stored, and reproduced.

---

[9] To take an extreme example, when we are told by astronomers that a smudge on a photograph taken through a telescope represents an explosion in a distant galaxy which took place ten billion years ago, it is hard to believe in the reality of this event. We can't see how to make the mental connection between the photograph and the behavior of the galaxy over that span of time. It is just a statement of empty words, signifying little if anything beyond the way an astronomer is likely to talk. Of course, we believe in the astronomer's procedures; so we won't deny him his fact, if he says so.

Thus it is more easily packaged, distributed, and redistributed. Actions as systems of behavior are always more extended or spread out in space-time, more fluid, and less easily recorded and reviewed. The information we need to discern action is more easily lost. As a result of this difference, a system of thought or a system of belief — an ideology — presents itself as more discrete than a system of action.

Now, if we bear in mind the densely packed character of systems of thought as well as the package-like character assumed by anything recorded from the past, then we can understand how ideas from the past, especially if they have persisted, can so easily be perceived as segregated from behavior, eternal and disembodied.

It is probably obvious that we have come across another instance of the fallacy of misplaced concreteness, pointed out by Whitehead. But we would like to rephrase Whitehead's formula. The error is not the result of substituting the abstract for the concrete. All perceptions of phenomena, no matter how concrete-appearing, are abstractions from the data of observation; something is always excluded from any percept or construct. The relevant distinction is between the handling of data which refer to a system of behavior and those which refer to a behaving object. The subject matter of observation is different in the two cases, and the procedures of observation are different. A system is spread out or extended in space-time in a different pattern than an object, and the definition of its boundaries presents an entirely different problem.

Since we need to deal with the subject of the interrelation between systems, this distinction is of great importance. The confusion between system and object has been of trouble elsewhere in science and philosophy. The concept of "a mind" makes an object out of a behavioral system; it was pushed to absurd limits in the concept of a "group mind." Some anthropologists would like to treat culture as an independent and self-sufficient entity — an organism. There would seem to be ample evidence that treating systems as entities, bodies, or isolated objects leads to our conceiving of them as floating off into space, waving wanly at the behavior from which they have departed hence. But once turned loose in space, as independent entities, they spring into action and become capable of "causing" everything else to happen the way it happens. So it is with "mind," which can thus become the ultimate cause, the fundamental ground of experience, or matter, or "God," or politics, or economics, depending upon whether one is an idealist, a materialist, a theist, a Hobesian, or a Marxian.

If we define reality as the behavior that we are interested in exploring, provided we can acquire reliable data about it, and if we decide that behavior is related to our position as observers in the multidimensional space-time continuum, then behavior that is referred to the operation of systems will not float off into space, and we will no longer attribute such omnipotent effects to any one system. Instead, we will investigate the nature of behavior within and between systems. There will then be no ultimates, no final causes, no absolutes; no system will be more basic or fundamental than any other. Such terms are the effects of linear patterns, based on two-dimensional physical models. We do not say that the surface of a sphere is eternal or infinite just because we can walk about on it without coming to an end.

But we are getting ahead of our story. Mention of the fact that such words as ultimate, absolute, and final are terms — that is, names for aspects of phenomena — brings us to a problem which we have only touched upon: the adequacy of our terms for dealing with the behavior which we wish to deal with. This problem lies in the province of philosophy in much the same way as the problem of reality. It is shared by philosophy with linguistics and psychology, but philosophy takes in a wider area of observations relevant to the problem. Whether under the guise of semantics, the analysis of meaning, logic, or epistemology, the philosopher has recently concerned himself with the function of words, sentences, propositions, and postulates in the formulation of knowledge.

For those not trained in technical philosophy, this terrain is tricky. It is easy to lose one's footing. Above all, one must watch one's words, because everything hangs upon the proper use of words and definitions. In appealing to philosophy for aid in this realm, we have taken a risk. This makes it all the more necessary to choose one philosopher and let him be our guide. I have chosen John Dewey, or, rather, the combined scouting talents of Dewey and Arthur Bentley, as exhibited in their book *Knowing and the Known. (Dewey and Bentley 1949)*

There are several reasons for this choice. Dewey and Bentley were concerned with the organization of knowledge; I believe that this is the principal subject matter of the philosopher — the area in which one hopes to get help from him. Their orientation was behavioral, and their procedures for the organization of knowledge were deliberately designed so as to correspond with those of science. Finally, they were interested in the status of systems and interrelations between systems. In this area they made some

14

distinctions which I believe provide just the kind of help needed.

Dewey and Bentley start off, as did Whitehead, with distress at the state of contemporary logic. Whitehead's complaint was that logic pretended to be exact though its methods led to no exact results. His solution was to let it be as vague as was consistent with its subject matter, and he invented a special language for the purpose. Dewey and Bentley took an opposite tack. They held that the vagueness of logic was something to be overcome. It resulted, they believed, from the uncertain and changeable status of the words used by logicians. This flaw they traced to the influence of modes of thought inherited from the past which are incompatible with each other and inconsistent with current knowledge. The arguments they advanced to make this point cover much the same ground as Whitehead's exposition but exhibit none of his patience and appreciation for the past. Their proposed solution was not to invent a special language but to review the list of common words in use, throwing out those that were impossibly and irretrievably vague and overhauling those they decided to keep. The model for the retooling of terms was that of scientific specification. Just as the common words "heat," "force," and "energy" had acquired increasingly specific and definite meanings in the realm of physics, so the words "fact," "action," "event," "object," and other stock-in-trade terms in logical inquiry should be pinned down to precise designations, while others, such as "concept," "real," "subjective," "objective," and "metaphysical," should be discarded as irremediably vague. They regarded the process of selecting and firming-up these words as itself tentative and exploratory and proposed a list of twenty-two reasonably firm terms which they called "Suggested Experimental Naming." Using this list of terms, they then developed a framework within which they proceeded to develop a program for the reorganization of knowledge.

I do not propose here to review this list of terms or to present their program in its extended form. Rather I wish to select a few of their key terms which will become essential to our concerns here. The terms which we will consider are "fact," "event," "name," "object," and "action." Such selectivity perhaps does Dewey and Bentley an injustice. No one who goes to the trouble of setting up a system of interlocked terms for dealing with an important and extensive subject matter likes to have a small portion of the whole pulled out of its context. The risk of distortion and misunderstanding in such a procedure is high. To mitigate the risk, however, I would like to present the general outlines of their approach. I also want to make some points about it that they do not specifically make.

The approach stems from Dewey's essentially pragmatic point of view. In the background are William James and Charles Pierce with their plain, matter-of-fact, no-nonsense approach to what men do in the pursuit of truth and knowledge. The examination of men's actions in behalf of knowledge and of the action of what is being examined are the heart of the matter. The focus on action corresponds to Whitehead's emphasis on process — but with a difference. Whereas Whitehead attempted to get rid of archaic modes of thought by inventing a new language, he ended by reintroducing much of what he had hoped to expel. Dewey, using a conventional language and a down-to-earth approach, succeeded in introducing a more consistently novel point of view. How did this apparent paradox come about?

If one inspects the imagery which has been traditionally embedded in the language of logic and epistemology, one is struck with the degree to which it seems to have been modeled on the technical operations of architecture and manufacturing. The implicit metaphor is predominantly concerned with constructing, building, or forming something. Thus arguments have to rest on a solid foundation or be supported by adequate premises. Then they have to be well constructed. Much of the imagery is concerned with position in a uni-dimensional space-time continuum, referring to what is put where and in what sequence. Premises and propositions refer to what has to be put into place first and properly, lest the whole construction become shaky and fall down. In other words, the uni-dimensional image is usually vertical, like a tall building which is meant to be impressive and to last for a long time. Therefore the firmness of its base requires careful attention, and the contrast between what is more basic or more superficial becomes important. Much of the imagery is specifically directed at what is placed underneath what. The word "hypothesis" is something which is placed under everything else, both in its everyday use and in its etymological derivation from the Greek verb *hypotithenai* (to put under). The word "supposition," of Latin derivation, has the same origin and meaning.

The Latinate word "substance" is similar in origin, but its meaning veers off into the imagery of small craft manufacturing, as of a boat, a vessel, or vase. Substance is something out of which something else is formed or made. It is akin to matter or material which is from the Latin noun *materia*. The Latin word may be

16

derived from *mater*, which would signify the mother-stuff out of which everything else is formed, but in its ordinary sense it referred to various kinds of wood used in manufacture. The objects of manufacture had to be formed out of their mother-stuff or substance in accordance with a pre-existing plan or design. From this technical operation there flow such words and meanings as form, formulate, and formulation. Also, that most difficult and troublesome of all words, "idea."

The word "idea" originally meant "to see," but in the writings of Plato and Aristotle it came to mean what was seen in the mind's eye, the mental pattern, the pre-existing plan or design. In this fashion, because a pre-existing design was important for the manufacture of a vase out of clay, what was thought to pre-exist in general, idea and substance, became important to the whole fabric of logic and philosophy as it was handed down to us from classical Greek times. The assumption that there is something absolute which pre-exists all formed things became firmly embedded in logical discourse.[10]

The preceding discussion would seem to bear witness to the possibility that a philosophy is composed out of the technical and scientific resources of a particular age. But once firmly embedded in the typical statements of a philosophical tradition, the imagery of its derivation becomes fixed and can be modified only with difficulty by appeals to the new scientific or technological procedures of later times. The latter have to fight their way in, so to speak, and struggle to secure accreditation. They then live uneasily, side by side, with the older images, conducting unofficial warfare and making the language of philosophy more and more difficult to understand.

It was this unphilosophical tumult that Dewey and Bentley wished to correct. To do so, they made use of three images which had always lain alongside the images drawn from manufacturing and building techniques in classical logical discourse and which had done so without causing much trouble. These three had simply been overshadowed by the architectural and handicraft images. The auxiliary images were associated with seeing and traveling. Seeing, looking, or inspecting as a model for philosophical statement were embedded in such words as "idea" and "observe,"

---

[10] We are not here considering the tremendous reinforcement of this sort of assumption from the classical background of religious belief in a deity as "Creator," "Prime Mover," or "Maker" — that is, God as manufacturer of man and universe.

though the original meaning of these words was much altered as logic hardened into a fixed procedure.

The original connection between seeing and truth is exhibited in the preclassical figure of the Seer — old, blind Tiresias, indifferent to whatever sex or age or other human limitations he might have, dispassionately "looking" at what is. Seeing, now in the guise of scientific observation, was selected by Dewey and Bentley, as one of the three images they were willing to introduce into their list of *mots justes*. Knowing and the known become what is discerned and discernible through scientific observation. Tiresias, equipped with technology, becomes the scientific observer.

The second image in classical logic which was retained by Dewey and Bentley is associated with movement and action in unfamiliar territory. It is concerned with getting into or being led out of, with points of origin and endings, goals, and with ways of getting there. Out of this travelogue imagery we get such phrases as "ends and means," "induction and deduction," and the "leading idea."[11] The terms "education" and "training" similarly refer, etymologically, to the situation of being drawn or dragged, pushed or pulled out of ignorance into knowledge. The word "axiom," in like fashion, is from a Greek verb (*agein*) meaning to lead or to drive, by way of an adverb (*axios*) meaning worthy, and could thus be roughly understood as "a good lead" or one generally agreed upon. Such words as principle and general are more ambiguously drawn into the languages of logic since they have one foot in the domain of founding and making. In their more important sense, however, they are related to the image of the chief or leader of a group. The guiding principle and the major generalization top all other modes of explanation. "Explanation" itself refers to making something plain or level, the better to get to where one wants to go.

Dewey and Bentley introduced these travel images into their

---

[11] For the thoroughgoing behaviorist, the word "imagery" as used here is an explanatory fiction. I agree. In company with many similar devices, however, it serves as a convenient shorthand. A more objective behaviorist phrasing would state: (a) that the set of stimulus and reinforcement contingencies specific to the situation of traveling had produced, through operant conditioning, such verbal responses as "means and ends" and "goals"; (b) that such verbal responses had been generalized and, through stimulus induction, were now emitted for a wider set of contingencies associated with interverbal stimuli. A completely objective description of this nature is too laborious and specialized for our purposes. No harm is done, however, if the reader takes it for granted that our procedure is necessarily incomplete.

version of a contemporary epistemology. Knowing is defined as the product of inquiry or exploration, always tentative and subject to revision because of subsequent inquiry. Logic is one method of observational inquiry into complex subject matter, taking its place alongside other methods more associated with instrumentation and manipulation. The word "method" is also connected with a Greek travel image (*hodos,* meaning way or path) and refers to orderly comportment during one's journey, constituting a repeatable procedure. The word "approach," for which I have a certain predilection, similarly refers to orderly observation during one's travels into the unknown. If travel is a labor (cf. "travail"), then our work is eased when we all do it together and in the same way. Thus for the method of logical inquiry Dewey and Bentley specified a series of "postulations."[12] These represent not fixed truths, principles, or given-in-advance axioms but simply provisional conditions or statements for beginning a search or inquiry. They vary from subject matter to subject matter, and no one set of postulations is considered to be more true, more real, or more basic than another. For expressly epistemological inquiry, they specified a set of postulations, the substance of which is that knowing and the known represent natural, observable, human events, just as much the product and the subject matter of research as any other natural event.[13] Knowledge is of both knowing and the known, resulting from inquiry. But it is an important part of their postulations that the process of inquiry or observation be seen as circular, proceeding from knowing to known and back. To understand this view of the observational process, it is now necessary to pick up the third image which they resurrected from classical logic. This has to do with the function of words themselves and comes close to the Biblical "In the beginning was the Word." "Logic" as a word is derived from the Greek morpheme *logos,* which itself means word. All our "ologies" — our psychologies

---

[12] They always preferred to use, if possible, a participle or gerund rather than a substantive noun. Accordingly, "postulation" is preferred over "postulate." The advantage is the emphasis on the continuous behavior of man—his actions—over the static product of his action, which always entices us to imagine a concrete, manufactured thing or entity.

[13] The origin of their chosen word is to the point. It comes from the Latin word *postulatum,* meaning a thing granted in response to a demand. The ultimate derivation is from the verb *poscere* (through *postulare*), which means to ask, seek, or search. Apparently, if something is demanded or asked for during a search, something is likely to be found or granted. What is granted then becomes the condition for further searching, the "postulation." The process is circular.

and physiologies — are heavy with words. The point is too obvious for extended discussion: to be fixed at all for human attention, our knowledge must be put into words. There it undergoes the dangers of over-fixation, on the one hand, and of lack of clarity, on the other. The whole thrust of classical logic was to increase clarity, introduce optimum fixation, and appropriate order into our use of words in order to build truth. The result was a beautiful construction, like the Parthenon.

But a temple is not much like a process of behavior. To get at the verbal component in the behavior process, Dewey and Bentley cut through the contemporary complexities of logical positivism and symbolic logic and designated knowing in large part as a process of naming. Naming, then, is one aspect of the behavior included in scientific observation, the one which is perhaps of most importance for logic and epistemology — in other words, for the organization of knowledge.[14] There are two aspects of naming as a process of knowledge which Dewey and Bentley stressed. One is that it is a behavior process. It can be treated like any other example of behavior for purposes of investigation. Knowing, as naming, has no properties of exactness, reality, or truth beyond the observational procedures and their limitations involved in the naming process. The second aspect is that the naming process, the name (word), and what is named are to be regarded as one process of observation to which Dewey and Bentley applied the title "transaction." Naming cannot take place without the simultaneous operations of the observer, the event observed, and the name attached to the event-as-observed. The transaction, in other words, is so mutually organized a process that to impute a separate "reality" to either the name, the event, or the observer-in-process-of-naming would be to fragment beyond justification the unitary character of the process. The name is thus "double-faced," participating simultaneously in the behavior of the named object or event and in the namer and his behavior.[15]

---

[14] For example, under postulation for Knowings and Knowns, they state: "(1) Namings may be segregated for special investigation within knowings much as any special region within scientific subject-matter may be segregated for special consideration. (2) The namings thus segregated are taken as themselves the knowings to be investigated. (3) The namings are directly observable in full behavioral duration and extensions." *(Dewey and Bentley 1949, p. 88)* The last point, of course, refers to the examination of the historical process, the history of ideas, of science, and the like.

[15] The manner of description here is very close to that employed by

Dewey and Bentley maintained that, for certain purposes, the naming process, the transaction, could be divided into parts. It is possible and necessary, for stated objectives, to consider only the event named, or only the behavior of the observer apart from the event, or only the name itself and the verbal system in which it occurs. When this is done, however, it is to be carried out within the framework of the overall transactional procedure for describing an observation. These separate, analytical procedures were given separate names by Dewey and Bentley. Since these separate names are of considerable importance to our own procedures, they must be considered in some detail.

Like Whitehead, Dewey and Bentley were observant of the new views of the nature of the universe arising from developments in modern physics. In particular, they were aware of Einstein's field concepts and of Maxwell's theory of electro-magnetic radiation. The effect of these developments had been, as previously noted, to destroy the concept of the permanence of particles and entities and even of matter in the physical universe. Attention was now to be focused on the operations of physical *systems,* as inclusive of entities or things. With respect to the description of such systems, Dewey and Bentley paid special attention to the language used by the physicist when he employed words instead of mathematical forms of description. For the pedigree of the word "transaction," for example, they quote from Maxwell's book *Matter and Motion.*

Because of our concern with the significance of the images used in logic and epistemology, I will quote somewhat more extensively from Maxwell's book than did Dewey and Bentley, so that the reader can follow the imagery more readily. The book consists of short, remarkably concise and clear paragraphs, under topical headings, describing and defining the field of physics as it had assumed form in Maxwell's thinking around 1877:

Definition of a Material System
    In all scientific procedure *we begin by marking out a certain region or subject as the field* of our investigations. To this we must confine our attention, leaving the rest of the universe out of account till we have completed the investiga-

---

B. F. Skinner in his attempt to give objective description of naming behavior. He called the naming "a tact," meaning that it functions as a contact between the event and at least two observers, who reinforce the naming response between themselves, in accordance with the rules of a linguistic community. (*See Skinner 1957, ch. 3.*)

tions in which we are engaged. In physical science, therefore, the first step is to define clearly the material *system which we make the subject of our statements.* This system may be of any degree of complexity. It may be a single material particle, a body of finite size, or any number of such bodies, and it may even be extended so as to include the whole material universe. *(p. 11)*

Mutual Action Between Two Bodies — Stress

The mutual action between two portions of matter *receives different names according to the aspect under which it is studied,* and this aspect depends on the extent of the material system which forms the subject of our attention.

If we *take into account the whole phenomenon* of the action between the two portions of matter, we call it Stress. This stress, according to the mode in which it acts, may be described as Attraction, Repulsion, Tension, Pressure, Shearing stress, Torsion, etc.

External Force

But if, as in "Definition of a Material System," we confine our attention to one of the portions of matter, *we see, as it were, only one side of the transaction* — namely, that which affects the portion of matter under our consideration — and we call this aspect of the phenomenon, with reference to its effect, an External Force acting on that portion of matter; and, with reference to its cause, we call it the Action of the other portion of matter. The opposite aspect of the stress is called the Reaction on the other portion of matter, *(p. 53)*

Different Aspects of the Same Phenomenon

In commercial affairs *the same transaction between two parties* is called Buying when we consider one party, Selling when we consider the other, and Trade when we take both parties into consideration.

The accountant who examines the records of the transaction finds that the two parties have entered it on opposite sides of their respective ledgers, and in comparing the books he must in every case bear in mind in whose interest each book is made up.

For similar reasons in dynamical investigations we must always remember which of two bodies we are dealing with, so that we may state the forces in the interest of that body, and not set down any of the forces on the wrong side of the ledger. *(Maxwell 1877, p. 54)*

What is clear in this imagery is the emphasis on seeing and naming whole systems or parts (aspects) of systems of behavior. The name given to the whole, the process, is, on the analogy to trade, "a transaction." We can look at (study) one side (aspect) of the transaction and name it "action" or "cause," or we can look at the other side and call it "reaction" or "effect"; but it is a unitary process. The system is a part of a field which we have marked off from the rest of the universe for observation through scientific procedure.

Maxwell was talking exclusively about material or physical systems. What Dewey and Bentley did was to generalize his description so that it would apply to the observation of any type of behavior. They also generalized the ways of describing physical events which antedated Maxwell's viewpoint — in other words, the description characteristic of classical Newtonian mechanics and the description utilized by pre-Galilean physics. Their summary statement in part reads:

> With this much introductory display let us now set down in broad outlines three levels of the organization and presentation of inquiry in the order of their historical importance, understanding, however, as is the way with evolutions generally, that something of the old, and often much of it, survives within or alongside the new. We name these three levels those of Self-Action, Interaction, and Transaction. These levels are all human behaviors in and with respect to the world, and they are all presentations of the world itself as men report it. *(Dewey and Bentley 1949, p. 107)*

They then go on to give a preliminary definition of these namings; using hyphens to stress the significance of the verbal elements in the names:

> *Self-action:* where things are viewed as acting under their own powers.
> *Inter-action:* where thing is balanced against thing in causal interconnection.
> *Trans-action:* where systems of description and naming

are employed to deal with aspects and phases of action, without final attribution to "elements," "essences," or "realities," and without isolation of presumptively detachable "relations" from such detachable "elements." *(Dewey and Bentley 1949, p. 108)*

In demonstrating how they further specify the range of application of these terms, I will skip around a bit in quoting from their book. Self-action is first given a summary dismissal which probably goes too far:

The character of the primitive stage of Self-action can be established easily and clearly by a thousand illustrations, past and present — all confident in themselves as factual report in their times, without suspicion of the way in which later generations would reduce them to the status of naive and simpleminded guesswork. *(Dewey and Bentley 1949, p. 108)*

Dewey and Bentley here violate their own views of descriptions as human behavior since an "illustration" cannot be said to have confidence or suspicion apart from its author. Furthermore, there is room in contemporary science for a view of systems as self-acting, provided that the limitations of the view are also stipulated. For example, the growth and maturation of organisms, insofar as the observer emphasizes only the statistical or normative regularities of growth in terms of stages and phases, may be seen as self-actional. The fact that the organism, as a system in transaction with its environment, cannot grow all by itself is not of importance so long as one is looking only at the intrasystemic regularities. To this limited extent, the organism is acting under its own powers, or internal controls. However, to push this point further would be to quibble, since Dewey and Bentley were referring mainly to a view that a system can act *exclusively* under its own powers. This point will become important later when we consider the place of structural and functional imagery in a philosophy of science.

As for the distinction between interaction and transaction, I can do no better than to quote, at some length, the series of contrasts developed by Dewey and Bentley:

Consider the distinction of the two as drawn in terms of description. If *Inter-action* is inquiry of a type into which events enter under the presumption that they have been adequately described prior to the formulation of inquiry into their connections, then —

Transaction is inquiry of a type in which existing descriptions of events are accepted only as tentative and preliminary, so that new descriptions of the aspects and phases of events, whether in widened or narrow form, may be freely made at any and all stages of inquiry.

Or consider the distinction in terms of names and naming. If *Inter-action* is found where the various objects inquired into enter as if adequately named and known prior to the start of inquiry, so that further procedure concerns what results from the action and reaction of the given objects upon one another, rather than from the reorganization of the status of the presumptive objects themselves, then —

Transaction is inquiry which ranges under primary observation across all subject matters that present themselves and proceeds with freedom toward the redetermination and renaming of the objects comprised in the system.

Or in terms of Fact. If inter-action is procedure such that its inter-acting constituents are set up in inquiry as separate "facts," each in independence of the presence of others, then —

Transaction is Fact such that no one of its constituents can be *adequately* specified as fact apart from the specification of other constituents of the full subject matter.

Or in terms of Activity. If inter-action views things as primarily static, and studies the phenomena under their attribution to such static "things" taken as bases underlying them, then —

Transaction regards extension in time to be as indispensable as extension in space (if observation is to be properly made), so that "thing" is in action, and "action" is observable as thing, while all the distinctions between things and actions are taken as marking provisional stages of subject matter to be established through further inquiry.

Or, with special attention to the case of organism and environment. If inter-action assumes the organism and its environmental objects to be present as substantially separate existences or forms of existence, prior to their entry into joint investigation, then —

Transaction assumes no pre-knowledge of either organism or environment alone as adequate, not even as respects the basic nature of the current conventional distinctions between them, but requires their primary acceptance in common system, with full freedom reserved for their developing examination. *(Dewey and Bentley 1949, pp. 122-23)*

We are now in possession of the full imagery of description for a philosophy of science as proposed by Dewey and Bentley. A description is a viewing or seeing, of events in wider or narrower perspective, arising out of a transacting between viewer and viewed. The imagery of travel comes through the demarcation of what subject matter is to be viewed and through the procedures set up for separating or combining observations over space-time. What is observed in the subject matter being studied is system or "action." What is called "fact" is the description of the transaction. What is called "truth" is the degree to which the description is warranted by the checking and rechecking procedures of observation, which essentially means visiting and revisiting the site of the observations. If a part of a system is to be viewed as separate from the whole, for the purpose of interactional observation, then under transactional observation it appears as an "aspect" of the whole system. Since no separation between knower and known is assumed *a priori,* what exists in the knower — his ideas or concepts — are essentially inseparable from the events he knows, though for interactional purposes they may be treated as if separable. Naming is a transactional process, indispensable for observation and separable for interactional purposes, as a system of names or ideas. What are named are "events" involved in transaction, and these events have spatial and temporal extension, of wider or narrower delimitation.

It can be seen that we have come full circle from the beginning to the end of the above paragraph. This circular description illustrates another aspect of Dewey and Bentley's procedure, which we have not discussed so far. They view a transactional description as essentially circular, proceeding from knowing to known and back, from one aspect of a system to another and then back to the first aspect. This circularity has often been decried in logic as an inadmissible procedure. According to tradition, deduction should proceed in a straight line from assumption; ditto for induction or generalization from observed fact. The position taken by Dewey and Bentley is that these linear logical procedures are fitted to interactional observation but not to transactional inquiry. Circularity is raised to the level of a principle of natural description. *(Dewey and Bentley 1949, p. 85)* This circularity is much like the "negative feedback" in communications theory.

26

Having reviewed the explanatory images retained by Dewey and Bentley in their transactional breviary, we will now consider the status of some images which they do not employ. Remember that our purpose is to enlist the aid of a philosophy of science and of a theory of knowledge in helping us to deal with the problem of the relations between systems of behavior — a matter that scientists, left to their own devices, have not been able to handle successfully. But even where philosophers are concerned, we cannot simply accept their say-so as the last word. We have to be reasonably certain that we have in hand all the materials necessary to construct an adequate description of intersystemic relations. We have seen that Whitehead's sense of the universe as an organism was over-unified, though we derived much help from his emphasis on process and on the relative nature of the distinction between the concrete and the abstract. However, we were dissatisfied with his presentation of the nature of process in that he tended to set the unifications of idea and thing — the "prehensions" — adrift in an expanding universe. Dewey and Bentley have anchored the unitary nature of process more securely in the behavior of men, as a transaction between man and nature. Their presentation is more operational than Whitehead's and more easily applied to a description of systems of human behavior. But we still have to ask whether anything of importance has been omitted from their formulations. This is of special significance in view of the extensive use we intend to make of the transactional mode of description.

In this connection, we can start by considering the status of the logical procedures based on building and manufacturing techniques in Dewey and Bentley's approach. As we have seen, they officially excluded almost all logical and naming procedures related to such images. Some words of building ancestry, such as "construction" and "formulation" appear "unofficially" in their texts, but are not mentioned in the explicit lists of permitted terms. One reason for the exclusion was the intimate historical connection of these images with such troublesome words as "matter," "substance," "essence," and "entity." All these words were, for them, of dubious or fictional status because of their connection with self-actional, archaic descriptive procedures.

Yet, as stated above, their opposition to self-action as a permitted form of description went too far. In throwing out all words associated with it, they also disallowed all procedures based upon forming, sorting, arranging, and patterning. These are procedures drawn from the crafts, architecture, and manufacturing which were of such germinal significance in classical Greek writings. Their ancestry, however, should not be held against them any more than it should be considered a point in their favor. The decision should rest on their utility.

It is difficult to see how an adequate mode of description of phenomena can exclude all considerations of the formal properties of entities. The behavior of men — their transactions — includes such matters as having to make decisions based upon form and pattern in things encountered in everyday contexts. Provided that one does not talk about formal properties as eternally fixed in some celestial factory or spiritual laboratory, provided that one sees them occurring or arising from transactional processes, to propose them for temporary use does no harm. Dewey and Bentley seemed satisfied to discuss "system" in an abstract fashion. This made it unnecessary for them to get into the details of the morphology and structure of systems in the concrete. Their "subject matters" were texts — what others wrote about scientific and logical procedures. Therefore they did not need to get their hands dirty, so to speak, with the opaque structural problems of actual systems, whether organisms or societies.

Let it be agreed, then, that the formal structures of concrete systems arise through transactional processes within and between systems. Let it also be agreed that, transactionally considered, structures are merely aspects of systems. Nevertheless, let us understand that within these agreements there is room for such procedures as preliminary classifying, sorting, or categorizing objects and events on the basis of their formal characteristics — to be changed as needed. There is also room for considering the state of an object or event as a structural matter. How solid, how put-together, how crumbly, or how diseased things are can be called states or conditions within systems considered, for the moment, self-actionally. Unless we make room for such descriptions, we have no way of handling diagnostic and nosological issues within medical affairs generally and in mental illness specifically.

We are not hereby setting up a formula for over-rating self-actional description. We are *not* recommending that a diagnosis of schizophrenia be understood as referring to a little detachable schizophrenic actor in the brain or mechanism in the psyche which is running the whole show. We are referring, rather, to a pattern within a system of behavior whose structure is sufficiently stable and unique to be discriminated from other behavior patterns and to be maintained relatively unaltered in the average environmental contexts in which it is observed. Thus we are talking about a condition of a behavior system — a condition which must be specified so that its function in relation to other systems, internal to or external to the organism, can be examined.

One other omission in Dewey and Bentley's compendium of logical discourse calls for comment. They omit any consideration of the topic of conflict and integration within systems. The reason for the omission is not clear. Perhaps they considered these issues perfectly plain problems of systems which had not caused any particular difficulty for logical inquiry. Perhaps they were so involved in professional controversies with other logicians that the issue of conflict was too elementary to bring up.[16] Perhaps philosophical problems of conflict as interpreted in the 19th century by Hegel and Marx had receded so far into the historical background that they were no longer visible to contemporary philosophers. At any rate, there is no mention of dialectics, whether of the classical or Hegelian order, though there is plenty of disputation in the text.

There is one further possible reason for the omission, and that is the close connection between interaction and conflict. In a conflict involving human beings, either as individuals or as groups, the issues at conflict rapidly become polarized, and a disagreement is likely to develop as to what is going on. The conflict can be described in transactional terms, as a mutual, reverberating process occurring in a system of relations. This is where the description should logically begin. However, as polarization develops and involves wider circles of friends and allies in the hostilities, each party to the conflict is likely to focus observation around his own interests. The conflict then becomes viewed as action and reaction and can be followed best by looking first at one party's behavior and then at the second party's response, like watching a tennis match. This is interactional description. It is impossible to give an adequate account of either conflict or integration except in both transactional and interactional terms.

Dewey and Bentley were so eager to dethrone interactional description that they may have suppressed a discussion of conflict and integration in order to avoid facing its interactional aspects. This is unfortunate for an adequate philosophy of science. We do not need to revive Hegel's schema of thesis, antithesis, and synthesis

---

[16] Bentley's style was polemical, and Dewey, while somewhat more tactful, managed to rough up quite a few philosophical writings and writers. Their book is full of scathing comments on those who commit self-actional sins or are addicted to entities.

in order to see that a ratio between strain and harmony is a feature of all living systems. The whole process of stability, instability, and change in living systems is associated with the relationship between partial states of conflict and integration. Whether one deals with physiological, psychological, social, or philosophical systems, some attention must be paid to these matters.

There are two reasons why it seemed worthwhile to go into so much detail in discussing the formulations of Dewey and Bentley. One is to make certain that we have covered all the issues necessary to a consideration of a *transactional field,* a subject to be taken up shortly. The second is that transactional concepts based on the Dewey-Bentley thesis have been making a slow but steady progress in certain areas of the behavioral sciences. "Transactionism" is likely to become a program of some importance to the future, and a critical review is desirable before it wins a wider audience.

Since the publication of *Knowing and the Known* in 1949, the development of transactionism has been in the hands of psychologists, psychiatrists, and sociologists rather than philosophers.[17] The two main lines of development have been in the fields of perceptual psychology and social psychology. Both lines of development have been extensively associated with the name of Hadley Cantril.

In 1950 Cantril published *The "Why" of Man's Experience,* and in the next few years he followed this up with a series of publications based on a transactional description of the social behavior of the individual. *(See Cantril 1950B, 1954B, 1955A, 1955B, 1958, 1962.)* In these publications, Cantril demonstrated that in a variety of occupational, recreational, and political situations the individual encounters problems ("hitches") the solution of which can be described as a process of transactional inquiry. In any one problem the choice of solution for the individual is related to previous solutions in such a fashion as to preserve constancy and consistency in his phenomenal world. The constancy of objects in terms of their physical properties is ascertained through such transactional inquiry, and this is the connection with psychological studies of perception. The constancy of social situations is also experienced through the life-long transactional inquiry conducted by the individual. Here, an important anchoring property of the event is its value pattern. Social choices are made within a pattern of

---

[17] Bentley made one additional summary statement of the formulations he had finally arrived at, changing some terms, but these novelties have not been adopted by others. *(See Bentley 1950.)*

value standards which have grown out of the process of value inquiry conducted by the individual. Such value inquiries are, of course, partly limited by the cultural environment in which the individual has existed. However, it is important to Cantril's humanistic position that culturally given values plus those acquired individually through inquiry can be rearranged or surmounted so that novelty or creativity can be one outcome of the encounter with a problem.

The perceptual line of transactional studies was brought to public attention by Cantril and his co-authors in 1949. *(Cantril et al. 1949. See also Cantril 1950A, 1954A, 1954C; Kilpatrick 1961.)* This approach combines transactional theory and interpretation with experimentation based upon the Ames demonstrations conducted originally in Hanover, N.H. *(Ittleson 1952)* The theory states that what is perceived in any actual situation is closely related to the set of assumptions based on past transactions with which the perceiver approaches the situation. The Ames demonstrations provide the perceiver with an ambiguous set of cues. The cues, cleverly arranged on the basis of visual perspective, make a room that is actually distorted, for example, look normal to the eye. Starting with his original assumptions about normal rectangular rooms, the perceiver, if he is misled, can correct his perceptions (interpretations of visual stimuli) only by transacting with the room, finding out how floors behave, bumping into walls, till gradually he forms a correct perception of the actual structure of the room.

This phenomenon corresponds to the transactional description of experience in which it is held that man and room are in a system of relations with each other, the exact nature of which must be explored through transactional inquiry. The experimental demonstrations bring out with exceptional clarity the unconscious nature and the tenacity of the system of assumptions with which the perceiver starts. The experiments have considerable relevance to that part of the theory of psychoanalytic therapy which is concerned with the process of "working through" previously unconscious assumptions (fantasies) about the self and others. They are also pertinent to the tenacity of the value assumptions which people exhibit in the definition of their normal existential habitat.

However, there is a hitch in the transactional descriptions offered by these writers in both the social and perceptual area. This flaw has been minutely examined by Floyd Allport in his review of theories of perception. *(Allport 1957, pp. 257-88)* The transactional description of man and room breaks down if we ask the question:

where is the percept of the room or where is the set of assumptions before the encounter takes place? It must be in the perceiver and not yet in system with the room. Where is the percept when the encounter takes place? Presumably, at that time it can be said either to exist between perceiver and room or to be "projected" on to the room. In any event, something in the perceiver, resulting from neurophysiological processes has been transferred out. This brings up, according to Allport, the inside-outside problem — a problem that transactional theory seems to skim over.

Though it can be said that the present percept is a function of past experience and present transaction, nevertheless, insofar as it is a function of something in the organism, what is this "something" resulting from past experience that it is a function of? The answer to this question can only be obtained from the observation that, from the standpoint of the man-room system, it is interactional and even self-actional. This is to say that, from independent observations, the actual configuration of the room must be ascertained by the scientific experimenter prior to the subject's encounter with it. Similarly, independent observations of processes within the subject — his visual acuity, his retinal sensory functioning, and the visual projection tracts in his brain — must be made in order to determine his visual capacity before the encounter. All this information must then be put together in various combinations by the scientific experimenter and fitted into the subject as a self-acting entity, into the room as a self-consistent structure, into the responses exhibited by the subject in the room as "tennis-game" interactions. Then at long last it can be assembled into a transactional description of the event as the function of many different structures brought into systematic connection within the event.

If this represents a fair account of what the scientist does in arriving at an explanation of the event, then it is evident that a transactional description is not enough for a complete account of the perceptual process. In all fairness, it must be said that Cantril and his associates never claimed that it was enough. They presented the transactional theory and associated experiments for what it could add to current knowledge. But in neglecting interactional descriptions they may have given the impression that transactional procedures were of overriding importance. There is some evidence that this impression is gaining currency. At any rate, a more balanced view might well recognize that objective description of the interrelation between systems requires all three modes of specifying the results of observation: self-action, interaction, and transaction.

However, it must also be expected that for all those who become interested in transactionism the transactional descriptions will receive a disproportionate amount of attention. This is likely to occur because the very endeavor to invent methods of transactional observation and description requires a concentration of effort which is likely to push the other two modes of specification into the background.

In 1952, participation in a multidisciplinary conference devoted to the prospects of formulating a unified theory of human behavior stimulated me to use the Dewey and Bentley formulations to create a model for relationships between systems of behavior.[18] Some aspects of this initial attempt were presented to the conference and were later published in the summary of the proceedings of the conference. *(Spiegel 1956B)* Parts of my presentation were quoted at some length in Roy Grinker's review of psychosomatic research and formed part of the strategy which he advocated for research procedures and theoretical generalizations. *(Grinker 1953, pp. 158-65)* Later, the concept of foci within a transactional field was used by Florence Kluckhohn and myself in a report (See Chapter Five) formulated by the Committee on the Family of the Group for the Advancement of Psychiatry. *(Spiegel 1954A)* In that report, the various systems of behavior which can be isolated within a transactional field were employed as point of reference for the analysis of family process.

Meanwhile, in various publications, I experimented with the concept of social role as a technical device for describing transactions in interpersonal systems such as appear in psychotherapy and in family systems. *(Spiegel 1954b, 1956a, 1957)* Somewhat later Grinker and his colleagues, continuing a study of the procedures of the psychiatric social worker, a study I had initiated at Michael Reese Hospital, used social role analysis to provide a transactional description of stages in the casework process. *(Grinker et al. 1961)* These stages were viewed as a continuum within a field of transactions, varying from the initial exploration process, through information exchange, giving of recommendations, experi-

---

[18] The conference was organized by Roy R. Grinker and Jurgen Ruesch, with the cooperation of Lawrence K. Frank, John Spiegel, and David Shakow. It met twice yearly between 1951 and 1957 at the Institute for Psychosomatic and Psychiatric Research and Training, Michael Reese Hospital, Chicago, and was financed principally by a grant-in-aid from the Carnegie Corporation. The composition of the members of the conference varied considerably over the years but was always multidisciplinary.

encing complementary relationships (supportive psychotherapy), to the final stage of modifying complementary relationships (intensive or insight psychotherapy). In this published study and in another publication detailed clinical illustrations were provided to demonstrate how transactional description serves to provide a larger field for the specification and discrimination of the processes of therapy than does the more usual interactional and self-actional modes of description employed in formal psychoanalytic writings. *(Grinker 1961)*

We will not here examine the details of the use of social role as a method of transactional description, since this is discussed in a later chapter.[19]

But there is a point about the use of role analysis and the transactional approach, as developed by Grinker and his colleagues, that bears discussion here. Grinker has presented these innovations not only as a method of research but also as a method for the conduct of psychotherapy. He contrasts the *transactional* inspection of the therapist-patient relationship — looked at in terms of the roles assumed by both parties to the transaction — with the *interactional* descriptions of the standard psychoanalytic technique. The latter are designated as both inadequate and misleading because of the interactionally isolated nature of the internal psychodynamics imputed to the patient, upon which the therapist's interpretations are presumed to have an effect. In all probability this criticism of psychoanalysis is mistaken, and the presentation of transactionism as a method of therapy is premature, if indeed not basically in error.

The differences between the approach favored here and Grinker's formulation are complex and difficult to describe before we have considered the nature of the transactional field. One difference has to do with a matter already commented on in discussing the work of Cantril and his associates. It is the assumption that transactional description alone gives a complete account of the interrelation between systems. It is probable that, properly specified, a transactional description will give a good account of variations in the system of relations which comes to be established between the

---

[19] The technique of social role analysis as a method for transactional description has also been applied to the subject matter of sociology, but transactional methods in general have made very little headway in sociological circles. For a direct transactional application, see *Goode 1960*. For what might appear to be transactionism, because it uses economic exchange as a model, but which is actually an interactional approach to sociological theory, see *Homans 1961*.

therapist and the patient. Within this focus, however, it will give only a superficial account of what processes occur within the patient or within the therapist.

To describe the process within the individual, regarded separately, the investigator must use another vocabulary which refers to the personality as a system in its own right. My own preference is for the vocabulary and the concepts of psychoanalysis, but this choice of theory and concepts should obviously be left open to the particular investigator. What is not an open question, it seems to me, is that, with respect to the therapist-patient system transactionally considered, what goes on within the patient or within the therapist must still be interactionally and self-actionally considered. Interaction will come in because the patient will say or do something which has an effect on the therapist, and the latter will respond in some way as a result of this effect. He will be enlightened or confused or have some alteration of his state and will exhibit some behavior as a function of his altered state. Whatever behavior the therapist exhibits will then elicit some responses — some change of state — within the patient. This is the tennis-game aspect of the interaction.

But self-action as description of the event will also be required, because a complete account will necessitate the assembly of information about the patient's past history and current psychodynamic situation. The grouping of such information involves seeing the personality as a reasonably self-consistent and self-perpetuating structure, no matter what its fractures and conflicts may be. Here we should recall the lesson from Whitehead: what is at issue is how the phenomena of nature are to be viewed, what aspects are taken into consideration as we abstract from the data of observation. The three different modes of abstraction — self-action, interaction, and transaction — are to be regarded as complementary ways of specifying the data which are needed for a full description of the event, depending upon what focus the observation is centered upon. How to pass from one mode of description to the other, this is the ticklish question which we will attempt to deal with in the next chapter. But almost certainly it cannot be dealt with satisfactorily by abolishing everything but transactional description.

Another difference between Grinker's approach and the one favored here is that he regards social role theory and analysis as already sufficiently developed for transactional description. This is a chancy proposition. As one who has been working with role concepts for a long time (and perhaps because of this) I believe that they are still in an unfinished and incomplete stage of development. Reliable methods for assessing the content of roles are just being developed. They hold much promise for the future, but they need to be more securely anchored in our understanding of the various systems of behavior than they are at present. As bridging concepts, passing from one system of behavior to another, they are too shaky and insubstantial to carry much freight at this time. If they barely pass muster for descriptive purposes, it is probably unwarranted to base a method of therapy upon them. They can certainly help the therapist to sharpen his understanding of what is taking place in the therapeutic situation, and they can broaden his range of observations. But until we can obtain a better purchase on all the factors which have to be considered in relation to a transactional field, no method for producing a change in behavior can easily be based exclusively on the transactional approach.

These considerations lead us to the threshold of a discussion of the transactional field. We are now in possession of all the background information which we require for this purpose. We have seen how transactional inquiry arose from problems in the theory of knowledge and of logic and how it has been adapted for perceptual and social psychology and for psychiatry and social casework. It is now our task to see how transactional inquiry can be used in order to obtain a more definite picture of the relation between systems. Throughout this chapter I have been rather abstract and indefinite in discussing systems. The appearance of vagueness stems from the fact that we were interested in finding a consistent language for the description of behavioral systems in general and a logic for discriminating their behavior from that of objects or entities. But we have said very little about actual systems of behavior and nothing about the formal aspects of their relations with each other. It is to this prospect that we now turn our attention.

TWO

The Transactional Field

The anatomy of the world is logical, and its logic is that of a university professor—it was thought. Up to about 1850 almost everyone believed that sciences expressed truths that were exact copies of a definite code of non-human realities. But the enormously rapid multiplication of theories in these latter days has well-nigh upset the notion of any one of them being a more literally objective kind of thing than another. There are so many geometries, so many logics, so many physical and chemical hypotheses, so many classifications, each one of them good for so much and yet not good for everything, that the notion that even the truest formula may be a human device and not a literal transcript has dawned upon us.

The serious meaning of a concept, says Mr. Pierce, lies in the concrete difference to some one which its being true will make.

—*William James*, The Meaning of Truth

Considering the number of geometries, logics, hypotheses, and classifications mentioned by William James in the above quotation, one has certain qualms about proposing anything which adds to the list. Yet the "multiplication of theories" is just the problem which we have to cope with in this chapter. And there does not seem to be any way of coping except by proposing a new concept for bringing

37

the assortment of sciences into some relation with each other. Especially in the behavioral science area, we have too many unrelated facts and theories. "A pluralistic universe" is a comforting idea, but it is no antidote for conceptual confusion and disorder. Some way must be found for bringing the subject matter of the various sciences into provisional order.

If the universe, as Whitehead said, is really one huge process and only appears to be fragmented because of man's method of abstracting, or if, as Dewey and Bentley said, it is actually a system of transaction which has been pulverized by man's predelection for self-acting and interacting entities, then the solution to the pluralistic disorder would involve constructing a concept of this overall system or process. The ancient and honorable problem of the relation of the one to the many can be solved only by finding a pattern in which the many appear as parts of the one. However, as soon as we reach this point in what seems to be a logical argument, we encounter a hitch. What are the parts that are to be assembled within the overall system? There is a long list of sciences and subject matters. How do we fit them together?

Here we can bring to our aid an assumption discussed in the previous chapter. The parts are not out "there," in a prefabricated universe, waiting for us to find them and unwrap them as they come, fresh from some supernatural factory. They are made at home, so to speak, by man's own processes of inquiry. On the other hand, they are not made up out of whole cloth but arise out of his transactions with and within the universe. An important dimension of the inquiry is the choice of a focus of observation. As Maxwell so concisely put it in the excerpt from his book *Matter and Motion*, quoted in the last chapter, "In all scientific procedure we begin by marking out a certain region or subject as the field of our investigations. To this we must confine our attention, leaving the rest of the universe out of account till we have completed the investigations in which we are engaged."

There is one exception which we must make to Maxwell's statement. We can no longer afford, in any science, to focus exclusively on one region and to leave the rest of the universe out of account until we complete our investigations. We never actually "complete" our investigations, the nature of science being a continuous process of inquiry. Completeness is an illusion; and if, in any one science, we forever keep the rest of the universe out of account, we will never be in a position to consider the whole. It is just because of the strategy based on illusory completeness that we are in our current difficulties.[1]

To return to the first part of Maxwell's statement, it will help to note that, as he says, we begin by marking out a certain region for our investigations. If we begin by segregating a certain region, then that region, which we create by our own focusing and demarcating, must be part of a larger field, composed of other regions which we can similarly mark out by focusing our observations on them. What we have to search for, then, are regions or foci, related to each other in a total field. But how are we to determine what these regions may be?

It is best to put this question off for a moment in order to ask, "What do we mean by a field?" "Field" is a vague, all-purposed word. Unless we can give it some firm meaning, our whole subsequent discussion will be unanchored and unsatisfactory. If we are to search for foci or regions in a field, we have to depend on a specification of the nature of a field. We have to know in which field we are looking.

Maxwell says, in effect, that a field is a portion of the universe that we make the subject of our investigations. This definition clearly includes in one perspective both the part of the universe being marked off and the process of investigating it — in other

---

[1] "Completeness" is one of our troublesome, vague words. We cannot give it any exact meaning, although the theory of sets in mathematics may ultimately represent a solution to the difficulties for a theory of knowledge currently created by the vagueness of this word. For the present, it may help to distinguish two different sorts of events or occasions which the word roughly characterizes with respect to inquiry. In the first set of events, the word refers to the completeness of a description, given the status of current knowledge—that is, all the variables which we know about have been considered and placed in a series of mutually contingent systems. Under this characterization, some variables may be ruled out for the purposes of the inquiry, but their potential effects have been considered. For example, their effects under the terms of inquiry are considered to be constant. The second sense of the word admits that as yet unassessed or undetected variables may exist, but assumes that complete knowledge of a given set of events is theoretically possible. Under the first meaning of the word, we make many errors during the course of inquiries by not taking into account a sufficiently wide and precisely defined range of variables. Under the second, we make many errors, by not allowing for the unavoidable incompleteness of knowledge. We assume more potential knowledge and more potential certainly than are warranted. This is the strategy of illusory completeness. There will always be an unmeasurable but large residuum of unknowns which prevent any inquiry from being completed. The inquiry will ultimately be transformed into new terms rather than completed.

39

words, it is a transactional statement. To put it somewhat differently, a field is an extent of the universe covered by our investigations. More simply, it is the extent of our investigations.

The advantage of this simplified definition is that it does not impute any special *a priori* reality to the field. For example, the field we are discussing is not to be confused with the field concept in physics. That concept refers to the structure of the space-time continuum, which can be described mathematically through the equations of Maxwell and of Einstein. The physical field concept is a part of the "field" which we are defining because it is a part of "the extent of our investigations." But the two notions must be firmly differentiated from each other. In the same way, our "field" is not to be confused with other postulated existential fields in psychology, such as occur in Lewinian fields of theory.

Even though no special, *a priori* reality is granted to our field, it does refer to the extent of our investigations, and therefore its extension in space-time can be roughly characterized. What is real about our transactional field is that it *is* what is being investigated (also what has been investigated and what is about to be investigated).[2] At the time the United States began planning to send a manned space vehicle to the moon, reaching for the moon had always been characterized in the past as a symbol of unrealistic ambition. Thereupon the subject became part of the transactional field extending into the future through current investigations and planning. Other parts of the field reach far into the past. Investigations also reach into the interior of the earth and the depths of the sea, into the interior of the atom and the depths of the personality. But we cannot give anything but these rough and ready characterizations of the extent of the transactional field since we do not know its boundaries or limits. Today's research may extend tomorrow's . boundaries in unpredictable ways.[3]

---

[2] On this view, Descartes was not so wrong as he is pictured in some quarters. He was merely lonely. *Cogito; ergo sum* is the formula for reality of a lonely man. If we understand him to mean by *cogito* isolated (and agitated) inquiry into the facts of existence, including his own existence, then he is close to our view that what is real is the fact of inquiry, currently much reinforced through being a collective enterprise. Descartes had few scientific or intellectual colleagues and no psychotherapist to help him through his agonies of doubt.

[3] It is probably this indeterminate aspect of the field of knowledge and the instability of its boundaries that caused Whitehead repeatedly to implore scientists and logicians to stop pretending to an exactness which new discoveries were constantly refuting. The problem of unsupportable exact-

Our inability to give any exact specification for the extension of the field, however, is not nearly so important as our ability to characterize its formal qualities. Having defined its general attributes, we can return to the question of how we are to determine the specifications for the regions in the field. We are looking for a pattern which will relate parts to whole. Because of my confidence that the field has a pattern — a structure — I have called it a transactional field instead of the even simpler field of investigations. Fields of investigation (or knowledge) would simply be a list, with no formal or patterned specifications. But if we talked about a field of transaction, then we must take account not only of what is being investigated but also of the methods and products of investigation and their relations to each other. We will be concerned with the functional relationships between the regions in the field. This is different from a list or classification. Lists are reminders not to forget topics which may be only randomly related, and classifications exhibit a static order. What we are looking for is an arrangement of regions which will exhibit dynamic relationships.

There is one other formal aspect of the transactional field (as opposed to a list or classification) that we ought to discuss before taking up the specification of its regions. If the field is transactional, then all its parts are interdependent. No one of its parts could be omitted without destroying the whole field, for all are conceived as being in functional relation with all others in an inclusive system of relationships.[4] It is not that the whole is greater than the sum of its parts. Rather, the whole is a way of exhibiting the functional relation between parts. Whole and parts are complementary and indispensable to each other. If this is so, then we have to consider a pattern which will be consonant with this stipulation.

The solution to the formal problem of the regions to be selected and of their arrangement in the field is illustrated in Figure 1. Because of the principle of the interdependence of the regions, the justification of the particular regions selected (and named) and

---

ness attaches also to the words "fact" and "reality." These words imply an all-or-none quality. A statement is either factual, or it is not; it refers to something real or unreal. My position, following Dewey, is that what is said to be factual or real occurs on a continuum of more or less warranted statements and is always subject to revision based on further inquiry.

[4] The word "system" is from a Greek combination of roots which means, literally, what stands (or falls) together.

FIGURE 1

Foci within the Transactional Field

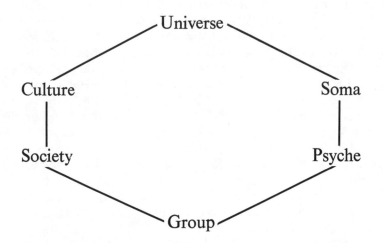

of their formal arrangement in the diagram have to be considered together. They are mutually contingent aspects of the pattern.

The regions are called "foci" because of the large element of focusing, inspecting, or attention-directing that is involved in the demarcating of the subject matters of knowledge. The foci are knowings that we look at or study and arrange together because, as a result of our operations, they appear to be systems composed of essentially the same kinds of processes. They are definitely not entities, and nothing presumed to be an entity on the basis of self-actional or interactional description can be fitted into a particular focus. Or, to put the matter differently, anything said to be an entity, whether sticks or stones, selves or personalities, nations or states, has to be spread around or divided up between various foci in the field.

To illustrate just this particular point, the personality of John Doe appears as an entity when it is contrasted in interactional inquiry with the personality of John Smith. Their personality patterns appear sufficiently persistent and discriminate so that they can be recognized as unique and existing things by the friends and enemies of both. But if we shift from interactional inquiry to transactional inquiry, then we ask a different sort of question and propose a different set of prescriptions. Suppose John Doe is a fat man with the peculiar grace and bouncy gait that some extremely heavy people can exhibit. If we are to study this somatic paradox in his "personality," then we must investigate his somatic processes, anatomically and physiologically, and see how they correlate with his psychological processes, since, like anyone else, he will probably not be bouncy if he gets depressed or if he knows that we are studying his bounciness. Similarly, we have to find out how his graceful carriage is related to the terrain he traverses, since it may turn out that his elegant equilibrium is dependent upon his remaining on perfectly flat ground, with no inconvenient heights to surmount. Finally, it can be assumed that this physical aspect of his "personality" will vary depending upon what group he is associating with at the time and what is going on within the group.

If we took any other aspect of his "personality" — say his intelligence, or his sense of humor, or his self-esteem — we would, in like fashion, have to discover the varying circumstances of which the behavior in question was a function. Under such scrutiny, the self as personality tends to disappear and to be replaced by discrete behaviors and the systems of which they are a function. In these circumstances, to recover the personality as a coherent structure requires a different sort of operation, to be discussed later. But the case would be no different if we were to take stones, sticks, stars, or states. Their status as entities would tend to dissolve under transactional inquiry. We would be left considering the physical, biological, and social systems involved equally in their behavior and in the way we make our observations of their behavior.

The foci which we have placed in the diagram, then, represent regions of knowledge about systems of similar processes within the field. Whether we have named them appropriately, grouped them together efficiently, or arranged them usefully is now in need of demonstration. The easiest way to proceed with the demonstration is through a specification of what processes are to be included within each focus and of how the foci are interrelated.

Let us begin with the focus labeled Universe. It embraces our knowledge of all process which can be designated as non-living or inanimate, in the ordinary sense of these words. It includes the subject matters of physics, chemistry, astronomy, and geology and their assorted operations and instrumentations. However, since we are referring not to a list of sciences but to the systematic involvement of physical processes in a wider field of knowledge, this focus refers to the anticipated functions of the non-living world in any type of inquiry. It speaks for the implications of such varied matters as climate, physical layout or terrain, habitat, atmospheric pressure, and speed of movement for human and animal behavior. It represents the setting, in a space-time framework, in which any inquiry takes place. For any particular inquiry, of course, the space-time setting can be enormously expanded or minutely contracted, but it is always a part of the field of investigation. A description of the Universe, then, is a permanent part of an inquiry. At the same time, whatever is said to be known in advance about the Universe as a contingent aspect of the inquiry is drawn from parts of the field other than the Universe itself.

Next, let us consider the focus called Soma. This is an awkward word, but it avoids some difficulties posed by alternative candidates. The focus designates our knowledge about all life processes characterized by physical exchanges with the Universe. All matters covered by the anatomy, physiology, and pathology of organisms, large and small, are included within it. The boundaries of living systems and energy transportations across boundaries and within boundaries as referred to the Universe are embraced by it. Somatic changes in single organisms or in populations of organisms relative to the space-time setting of the Universe occur within it. Thus simple adaptations to changes in the Universe — whether in greatly extended space-time settings (evolutionary adaptations) or in contracted space-time settings (instinctive or unlearned adaptations) — are specified for this focus. With respect to both types of adaptations, insofar as knowledge is related to sensory inputs and insofar as any inquiry is dependent upon energy exchanges (transactions) between the human organism and the Universe, this focus is essential to the field of knowledge.

Moving along to the next adjacent focus, we propose the term Psyche in spite of the possibility that it will be confusing to some readers. It evokes images of detachable souls and has other undesirable connotations. Nevertheless, we consider it useful precisely because of the symbolic meaning adhering to it. As a focus, it refers to knowledge about energy transformations that are involved in complex processes of adaptation. For simpler organisms, learning to respond to complex environmental stimuli is within this focus. For higher organisms learning to elaborate and respond to symbolic transformations, both verbal and non-verbal, of complex events is specific to this focus. All psychological processes involving cognition, perception, problem solving, conflict elaboration and reduction are

44

included in it, as are all behaviors specific to situational contexts, whether in restaurants, air raids, parliaments, or bedrooms.

Speaking of behavior specific to situations moves us to the edge of the focus labeled Group. Here we encounter transactions which occur in small face-to-face groups, and it is in such groups that behavior receives situational definitions. Most human affairs take place in this setting, solitary and mass behavior being the exception rather than the rule. Thus within this focus is included all knowledge of the behavior of group members as organized into group processes. Group problem solving and decision making, conflict-stimulation and conflict-resolution, ways of communicating within and between groups, allocations of responsibilities and divisions of labor, group cohesion, leadership and task fulfillment — all such processes are under inquiry within this focus. And, looking at the process of inquiry itself, that process is inconceivable without some group to support it, challenge it, block it, or overcome the blocks to it.

Strong as they may be in courses of action and sheer persistence, small groups do not exist in isolation from each other. They are interwoven in larger systems of extended groups characteristic of social systems. This focus we label Society. It is concerned with our knowledge of processes within and between large-scale social systems in terms of social class and other prestige or power systems, the processes within the occupational and economic systems, the family systems, the educational, religious, and recreational systems, and the norms of behavior in each system. Changes in social systems or their parts over broader or narrower space-time segments, as well as processes of social control incident to change, are specific for this focus, insofar as these changes and control processes represent patterned, overt behavior.

However, insofar as our knowledge of social control and change is concerned with *the meaning* of social behavior to members of social systems, we have moved into that part of the transactional field which we call Culture. This focus covers knowledge of the meaning and function of concrete and abstract social forms for the maintenance of the social system. Thus it is concerned not only with the material culture (the artifacts) of past and present social systems; it is also concerned with linguistic systems and with systems of belief and of values. In the past, in parts of Western culture the production and appreciation of artifacts has been considered a value in and of itself. Art for art's sake! Similarly, belief systems and value systems have been considered *sui generis* — an absolute, self-contained or God-given. These positions are taken within self-actional views. From the point of view of the transactional field of knowledge, artifacts, values, and belief systems are tied into the whole network of interdependent processes, to be inquired into with respect to their functions for other parts of the field and with respect to changes in them stemming from changes in other parts of the field.

These brief sketches of what is to be included within the range of coverage of the various foci are not intended to be anything but suggestive. A full description would require a treatise; all that can be attempted here is the presentation of some aspects of the problems raised by the transactional field concept. For example, we cannot take up here the question of why there should be just these six, rather than five or seven foci in the field. Nor can we deal with the question of whether the processes included within one or the other focus are actually similar enough to justify their being grouped together.[5] There are, however, a few properties which can be ascribed to the transactional field, once it is viewed in the above fashion, which we wish to discuss (again, all too briefly) because of their bearing on research.

Once the field is set up with the formal pattern of interdependence of foci, then several questions arise with respect to changes occurring in the field. Changes in the field can occur both because of the way in which events focus inquiry and because of the way in which inquiry seeks out events. It is worthwhile to differentiate these two determinants of change and to look at them separately, even though they belong together in the transactional process.

Events which occur in such a way as to focus inquiry upon them may precipitate change wholly within one focus, within two or more adjacent foci, or simultaneously within all foci — that is, within the total field. Changes which are produced within one or two

---

[5] For example, it might be argued that the distance from the Group focus to the Social focus covers too much ground and that there should be an intermediate focus between them labeled Community. Certainly there are many community studies which do not take into account the whole social system of a political state. In all likelihood, however, the processes within a community are sufficiently similar to those in the larger overall social system so as to merit the community's being considered as a subsystem of the Social focus. Similar arguments could be made for the insertion of other intermediate foci in the field, but all such matters will have to wait for a more extended consideration of the transactional field than can be provided here.

foci we call "small alterations of the field"; those that involve three to five foci we call "large alterations of the field"; while changes in all foci are "total alterations." Small alterations, involving one or two adjacent foci, are the ones most commonly investigated in the usual procedures of science. Changes in Universe, Soma, Psyche, and in other foci are commonly studied independently of changes in other foci. Because only a relatively small number of variables needs to be controlled in order to carry out such studies, they are more adapted to scientific method, and events which can be handled by such methods will tend to be investigated. Similarly, events producing change simultaneously in two adjacent variables — such as between Psyche and Soma, Culture and Society, or Group and Psyche — can be studied, though with much more difficulty, through the canons of scientific inquiry. As soon as changes in one focus are to be investigated transactionally in connection with the mutual influences of another focus, severe problems arise, which we are becoming more experienced in solving.

The problems which arise when we pass over to the investigation of changes between two foci are of three sorts. The first is concerned with differences in rates of change between the processes in one focus as compared with those in the second. For example, as between Psyche and Soma, in general somatic processes occur much more rapidly than the corresponding psychological changes, which makes the procedures for the assessment of reciprocal change difficult to establish. As between Psyche and Group, psychological changes tend to occur more rapidly than group changes. Generally, as one goes clockwise around the transactional field, starting with Soma, changes tend to become slower, though there are important exceptions to this rule. When one gets to changes in Culture, the rates of change are comparatively sluggish. There are, of course, good reasons for these comparative differences in rates of change, but they make for considerable difficulty in setting up adequate research designs.[6]

---

[6] The reasons are: (1) the increasingly larger space-time segments involved as one moves around the field and (2) the increasing complexity of long-circuiting, or delaying processes as the space-time segments broaden. As with everything in the transactional field, there are counter-processes working in the opposite direction. For example, the increased efficiency of modern space-time communication networks tends to cut down delaying processes within Culture, and there is no doubt that cultural change is taking place at an accelerated rate as compared with previous times. Nevertheless, as a study of value orientation changes in Italian-Americans and Irish-

The second difficulty in setting up an adequate inquiry covering two foci is concerned with the problem of the transformation of processes as between two foci. Somatic processes are transformed, somehow, into psychological processes, and these somehow into group processes and so on around the field. Cultural processes are constantly transforming the universe. Yet this is the weakest element in the interconnected chain we have called the transactional field. We lack adequate transformation hypotheses. Nevertheless, we do have some tentative transformation concepts at hand, and the investigations reported later in this book are designed to test the utility of one of them. This is the concept of social role as a way of handling the transformation of psychological processes into group processes, and thus into social and cultural processes. Many obscure problems in the transactional field would become much clearer if we were provided with a greater number of transformation concepts to try out in various research designs.

It should be clear that transformation processes cannot be uni-directional. In order to be adequate, the concept should be so formulated that it provides for reciprocal and opposite transformations. To take transactions between Psyche and Group as an example, the transformation concept should stipulate both how psychological processes are translated into group processes and (the reverse) how group processes are turned into psychological processes. The social role concept is a model of this sort. We can stipulate that personal motives can be satisfied only through their being organized for action, under psychological controls, through the patterning of social roles. Action becomes transaction, as between these two foci, then, through organization into reciprocal role behavior, and this can occur only within small groups. To shorten the formula, we can say that psychological motives are registered as conditions for taking social roles. In the reverse direction, when the group process disorganizes or frustrates the roles into which the person's actions have been transformed, then the actions involved must be reorganized and reformulated within the person by his psychological processes. Since the group process consists of the distribution and assignment of roles between members, the transformational process is a delicate and continuous operation, always subject to possible disturbances which have consequences both for the group and for the individual.

Americans shows (see Chapter Six) the rates of change over generations for these groups in value orientations is much slower than changes in their somatic status.

The topic of consequences accruing simultaneously for both group process and psychological process points to the third problem in dealing with two foci. This is the problem of the fit between the systems of the two adjacent foci. I have selected the expressions "fit" and "fitness" in place of other descriptive terms, such as "integration" or "stress," because I would like to save these latter words for the description of process within a single focus. As between two foci, fitness refers to certain characteristics of the process of transformation. The function of transformation processes is to fit together the systems of adjacent foci so that they attain an equilibrium in which each facilitates the operations of the other. But, as stated above, this is a delicate matter, subject to many kinds of disturbance. Whatever the origin of the disturbance, I will call its presence a sign of "strain." Fitness and strain, then, are opposite ends of a continuum of relations between adjacent foci.

We know so little about processes of transformation that we can give only rough characterizations rather than specifications of how the process takes place between the various foci. However, we are provided with plenty of signs of fitness and strain between the foci. These can be illustrated by simple examples occurring at each juncture of a pair of foci. As between Universe and Soma, transformation processes center upon life and death and the transition between living and inanimate processes. In contracted space-time segments, the viruses are good examples of transitional forms. They can be regarded as animate or inanimate depending upon which focus, Soma or Universe, they are referred to. They can either facilitate interchanges between the two foci or interfere, causing disease or death. In more expanded space-time segments, ecological relations between organic systems and geological formations on the surface of the earth may function so that there is a continuous maintenance of configuration between the two or in such a fashion as to disrupt the relationships with abrupt, irreversible changes accruing to both. However, this is an extreme version of the effects of strain between Universe and Soma. In the more usual version, the strain is registered in periodic or cyclical shifts of equilibrium between the two foci. It seems likely, in fact, that periodic or oscillating shifts in equilibrium are more characteristic of strain between any two foci than total disruption.

Signs of strain or fit between Soma and Psyche are the principal subject matters of psychoanalytic and psychosomatic studies. Psychoanalysis has attempted to frame a transformation concept around the topic of instinct or drive as the psychic representative of a somatic process. However, there is a fairly general consensus that this is a crude characterization which has been useful in the absence of a more adequate specification of how somatic processes are converted into psychological processes. Instead of explaining, it states what needs explaining. Nevertheless, in spite of its crude and preliminary character, it has been useful for the investigation of the relations between Soma and Psyche. The signs of strain between Soma and Psyche are registered in what is usually called the "subjective" or "phenomenological" aspect of mental and psychosomatic illness. The stated symptoms of illness, insofar as they are concerned with what the person complains about or can report on the basis of self-inquiry, are useful data referring to the ratio of fit to strain between Soma and Psyche.[7] But these data must be translated into a language capable of describing the strain of which the symptoms are evidence. In psychoanalytic theory, this is accomplished by means of the concepts of the mental representative of the somatic system and the psychological systems which are set up to control or modify it. Strain itself is experienced, in subjective report, as anxiety, somatic pain, depression, and their derivatives. Fitness is reported as happiness, confidence, or mastery of self.

In investigating the relation between Psyche and Group, we can make use of the transformation concept previously mentioned: the social role structure of the interpersonal relationship. So far as the data of inquiry are concerned, observations must be made both on the basis of self-report *and* on the basis of the study of overt actual behavior between group members. From reports of self-inquiry, one learns how the person experiences his relations with other group members — to the degree that he knows about it — and why he has chosen one rather than another role to satisfy his

---

[7] Self-report has a controversial status in the sciences of behavior. Under the word "introspection" it has been regarded as generating data that are useless because they are not subject to verification. In psychoanalysis, self-report is the essence of the method of inquiry called "free association." If we subsume all such procedures under the term "self-inquiry," then they fall in a continuum of methods of inquiry none of which have the status of being "better" or "worse" than others but merely that of being useful for carefully delimited areas of inquiry. Data based on self-inquiry and subsequently reported to other observers are, on this view, indispensable to inquiry on the relations between Soma and Psyche in the human subject. The assessment of the reliability and consistency of such data depends upon operations similar to the assessment of data derived from other parts of the transactional field.

psychological motivations. From observation of overt behavior one learns how the group controls the allocation or withholding of roles between group members on the basis of its own principles of organization. Within this transformational structure one can then examine the signs of fit and strain between Psyche and Group. Signs of strain will appear persistent as conflicts in personal relations within the group and/or as excessive hostile, protective, anxious, or depressed responses in group members. Good fit will be manifested by conflict-free relations within the group and individual feelings of satisfaction about belonging to the group.

When we move to the description of the relations between Society and Group, we are hampered by the absence of formulated transformation concepts. What we are provided with are structural and functional concepts which could form the nucleus of such a concept. Structurally, most small groups are described as fitting into a network which constitutes an extended system or organization. Nuclear family groups belong to extended chains of relatives; baseball teams belong to leagues; work groups are parts of industrial, commercial, or service organizations. All such organizations and extended systems are themselves fitted into even more extensively structured systems — the family system, the occupational system, the political system, etc. — of the overall society. Functionally, small groups are described as performing services for the maintenance of the larger systems to which they belong; in turn, these more extended systems perform essential services for their small groups in a reciprocal process.

Even in the absence of an adequate transformation concept, we can look at the relations between Society and Group in transactional forms if we consider the relation between social roles and social norms. Small groups are organized for carrying out specialized social functions. These functions can be described in role terms. Family groups perpetuate domestic roles; baseball teams carry out recreational roles; work groups are organized about occupational roles. All these roles represent activities essential to the survival of the overall social system. Thus it is on the basis of their essential role functions that groups are accepted into the extended systems and that the extended systems are attractive to individual groups. Because of this reciprocal process it is important that the role functions of groups be carried out in accordance with the norms of the overall social system or of its various parts. By the same token, it is important that the norms of the social systems be acceptable to the small group and its members. We can define social norms as standards of appropriateness governing the patterning of the different social roles performed within groups. These standards, then, control the degree of fit between the group and the extended social system.

Given this definition of the function of social norms, we can infer that good fit will be a product of the correspondence of the norms of the small group with those of the extended system, while strain will result from an increasing discrepancy between the two. Signs of strain will be recognized in the conflict of relations between dissident groups and the extended systems to which they are connected. Since a small group may be connected simultaneously with different chains of extended systems, the signs of strain may not be everywhere apparent. For example, a nuclear family may be embroiled in controversy with a school — say, over the propriety of a child praying or not praying in school — while, at the same time, it receives support from the extended family system to which it belongs and perhaps from other neighborhood systems with which it is connected. The support indicates the equivalence of norms controlling the role of the student between the family and its supporters.

The divergence of norms between different subsystems of society over the patterning of the same social role leads us to a consideration of the relations between Culture and Society. The existence of the different subsystems of society points to the process of differentiation discussed in Chapter 1. Different subsystems may hold divergent standards of appropriateness for the *same* role behavior. It is in that part of the transactional field which we have labeled Culture that variations in social forms and standards are processed. Cultural inquiry is concerned with the search for synthesis and appropriateness between a society and the universe which it inhabits. The inquiry within Culture leads to the production of systems of belief, which are called religion, philosophy, mythology, or science, depending upon the orientation of the observer vis-à-vis his belief system. Whatever the belief system may be, it will have something to say about the nature of the universe, of the society, and of the standards of behavior appropriate to subsystems of that society in view of the nature of the universe.

There have been many names given to the process which controls or sets norms for behavior between Society and Culture. Ideals, ethics, morals, commandments, taboos, mores, customs, and cultural orientations all name one or another aspect of this process. The expression preferred here, because of its suitability as a transformation concept, is "value orientation." The definition of value orientation and the theoretical assumptions governing the variations in a system of values are discussed in Chapter Five. Here it is sufficient merely to mention the most general features of a system of value orientations as mediating between Culture and Society.

In the course of cultural inquiry, every society faces issues of choice between alternative modes of action arising as possible responses to concrete situations. Generalized solutions to the common human problems posed by these concrete situations are variously elaborated, but the variations in solutions are neither infinite nor random. They consist, rather, of a limited range of possible choices, and, if one looks at the range of solutions developed in cultures throughout the world, there is consistency and similarity with regard to these products of inquiry from culture to culture. What is varied is the pattern of evaluation which rates one solution as preferable to another. This is one of the specifications — perhaps the principal one — of the word "value": the ranking of an ordered set of choices from most to least preferable. Because cultural inquiry must deal with matters of such great complexity, and adjust them to the requirements of the various subsystems composing even the simplest of societies, the rank order of value orientations is not uniform within any actual culture. There is variation in pattern of rank orders for the different subsystems of the society.

It can be seen, then, that the transition from norms governing social roles to the meanings given those role activities within the culture occurs through the rank-ordering of value orientations. It is in this sense that the pattern of value orientations functions as a transformation process. The norms of role behavior must be consonant with the cultural value orientations which sanction them and with the cultural meanings which make them worth preserving. Strain between Culture and Society occurs when the pattern of value orientations held within the different subsystems — and, at the worst, for the overall society — are inconsistent with each other or with the directions in which the cultural belief systems are changing. Value orientations fit well when they consistently relate concrete norms to each other, to the organization of subsystems, and to the beliefs held within the culture. The signs of strain appear when patterns of role behavior within subsystems are incongruent with each other. Different and inconsistent cultural sanctions are appealed to for the justification of the incompatible norms: e.g., means rather than ends versus ends rather than means, an eye for

53

an eye versus charity and compassion, appeal to the future versus appeal to the past, long-term views versus short-term considerations, the importance of controlled performance for others' sake versus the value of self-expression, and so on.

Such dichotomized choices appear only when strain is severe and the conflict of values is polarized. Under these circumstances, the strain may manifest itself widely in social conflicts and in struggles for dominance between competing cultural beliefs. When ordered variation in value orientations comfortably fits the norms for institutional behavior into the belief systems, dichotomized and hardened choices subside. Instead, one sees a ranking of behavior choices, each fitted to its proper occasion. Social harmony and cultural consistency, the signs of good fit between Society and Culture, are evidenced in the possibilities of the application of "wisdom." What is called wisdom varies concretely for each culture. But what is common to wisdom in all parts of the world is the opportunity to review the possible alternatives of choice through a calm, wide-ranging inquiry into the consequences of each choice, both for the culture and for the society.

Proceeding to the last juncture of foci, between Culture and Universe, we encounter the functions of the belief systems of culture as they translate the visible world into forms suitable to the structure and function of society. Here, again, the reciprocal transformations are never quite smooth. The universe is discovered in unexpected or unfathomable forms. Culture must deal with the great, relentless conditions which the universe has imposed upon mankind — the inevitabilities and inequities of birth, sexuality, death, conflict, catastrophe, and change. The old order passes. The new order requires, to some degree, a reassessment of beliefs and a reassortment of values. The belief systems, so difficult to elaborate and assemble in ways that tie together all loose ends, can change only at a relatively slow pace lest they collapse, disrupting the delicate balance between the world and the society of men.

Signs of strain between Culture and Universe are seen in the shakiness of the traditional belief systems. Collapse of belief in what the culture has to say about the universe can lead to the disappearance of the culture itself as an integrated system. Lesser degrees of strain are registered as anomie — the perception of life as meaningless, the frantic search for new meanings, the revival of outmoded forms of belief, or cynical justifications of nonbelief. Good fit is manifested as firmness in the going belief systems and in the possibility of productive inquiry within the terms of belief.

54

We have now completed boxing the compass at each juncture of foci. The tour of inspection was undertaken for the sake of acquainting ourselves with some of the problems which must be dealt with if we are to study the interrelations between two foci. Brevity, clarity, and a tone of confidence were appropriate for such a general review. But it should be evident that we are far from being able to define the terms of adequate description and analysis for the transformation of process between any two foci, to measure differences between rates of change between them, or to specify the conditions making for fit and strain.

A transactional inquiry confined to any one of the foci in isolation from the others is of course more manageable. Within each focus there will still be many obstacles to adequate description, and some of the foci are much better developed than others. Some of the obstacles have been created by a certain tendency to disorder in the process of inquiry — a failure to keep the foci adequately differentiated from each other. Others result from lags in method development and conceptualization. But on the whole, in comparison with the study of relations between foci, the single-focus investigations have succeeded in producing useful findings through the ordinary operations of scientific procedure.

Given the difficulties of inquiry into the relations between two foci, which I have termed a small alteration of the field, it can be predicted that inquiry into large alterations or total alterations of the field will be troubled by greatly compounded difficulties. Experience in fact has shown that the problems arising in the course of an inquiry into large alterations of the field are of such magnitude as to seriously impair the ability of the investigator to adhere to the canons of scientific procedure. Accurate observation, careful recording of data, measurement, analysis, and hypothesis testing tend to be replaced by speculative reconstructions of cause-and-effect relationships, by all-embracing theories, or by journalistic accounts in which the relation between observed fact and theoretical explanation is not made explicit and thus works in unseen ways. Another and quite usual departure occurs when theoretical constructions are hypostasized and dealt with as if they were matters of fact or as if proof that they are descriptions of empirical events were no longer required.

Such inadequate responses to inquiry into large alterations in the field could be written off as part of an expected pathology in any field of knowledge. Not all scientists are good scientists, and not all fields of knowledge are soundly based. One can expect to find an admixture of speculative nonsense and strange-sounding truth throughout the realms of science and scholarship. It may not be easy, in the first instance, to distinguish one from the other. One must be patient and let history decide what is enduring and what ephemeral in the course of science-making. It appears, however, that the inadequacies, whatever their nature, are not haphazard or accidental in origin. On the contrary, they occur as a result of the kinds of problems which can be expected to arise within the transactional field whenever large or total alterations within it are under consideration. Furthermore, the types of errors which can be expected to result from the investigation of large or total alterations are systematic and (within limits) predictable.

Before taking up the typical errors, let us review the occasions which lead to the investigation of large or total alterations in the field. As we stated previously, they can, rather artificially, be divided into two different kinds: those which are determined by events and those which are determined by the scientific interests of the investigator. In the first case, the events which (seem to) demand investigation are of such a nature that they are of necessity spread out over a number of contiguous foci. The events of war, of catastrophe, and of all widespread and rapid social change are of this type. The events of combat in wartime, for example, produce functional change among troops which impair their ability to be effective and which require investigation and treatment if the armed services themselves are to be maintained at optimum levels of efficiency. Because of the nature of the combat situation, such an inquiry must include a study of the physical environment, of somatic responses to the physical hardships and deprivations, of psychological alterations in adaptive functions, of the structure and function or malfunction of the combat unit, of the organization of role systems in the armed services and, indeed, of the nation involved in war. Changes occur in all the foci, reverberating synchronously, playing upon each other in such a fashion as to make it exceedingly difficult to keep track of all the processes clamoring for attention. It is a struggle to record the changes faithfully and to correlate them for purposes of analysis. This is an example of the state of affairs which we describe as a total alteration of the field.

A similar totality of changes in the field is associated with such events as a migration of peoples — for instance, the transplantation of North African and Oriental Jews to Israel — and with extensive catastrophe from hurricane or other sources affecting an entire population. Lesser but still extensive changes in the field are evident in connection with such events as juvenile delinquency, racial discrimination, and political movements headed up by emotionally disturbed leaders. The list could be much extended, but all the examples would be characterized by the prominence and far-reaching effects of the turbulence in the field caused by their existence — a characteristic which has led to their being labeled "social problems."

In contrast to the large alterations in the field which present themselves for inquiry because of their socially troublesome characteristics are those that have inquiry focused upon them because of the scientific outlook of the investigator. By the expression, "scientific outlook" we refer to a vague characterization of the behavior of scientists in terms of narrowness or broadness of interest. Some scientists confine their investigations to narrow specializations or subspecializations in their own field. Others not only inform themselves of developments in fields other than their own but also prepare themselves for interdisciplinary inquiry with respect to problems demanding observations of several contiguous foci in the field. The words "broad" or "interdisciplinary" are not satisfactory designations of either the motivations or the behaviors of such investigators. Nor is it satisfactory to describe their behavior in terms of communication or information processes, exclusively, though these matters are involved in their transactions. The whole subject of how scientists communicate and behave with respect to their colleagues, their subject matter, and their public needs more inquiry. Indeed, this chapter is an effort to contribute an element of order to this particular topic.

However we eventually come to characterize the "broad" scientist, the fact remains that investigators of this persuasion seek out research problems which involve large alterations in the field. They "see," sometimes dimly, at other times acutely, the interdependence of foci in the field. Out of their sometimes painful awareness that the phenomena which interest them cannot be confined to their own specialized field of knowledge, they make attempts to ally themselves with investigators in neighboring fields, or, lacking this opportunity, they attempt to absorb the needed information and techniques of inquiry and thus to carry out a broad investigation by means of their own resources.

An example of such a choice of research problems is the investigation of the relation between the structure of an organization and the behavior of its personnel. Studies in mental hospitals of the relationship between the disturbed patient and the structure

57

and function of the ward, of the roles of patients, of ward personnel, and of administrative personnel, and of the complex transactions within the entire setting as they relate to the prospect of behavior change in the patient feature precisely the seeking out of inter-dependencies. Another example is the comparative study of mental health and illness in different cultures, since such investigations require that the observer define the culture, the social system, the family groups, and the individual behavior being compared. The most apposite example of all is found in the study of the family. This subject matter lends itself equally to confinement to one focus or to simultaneous study from the point of view of several foci. The family can be studied exclusively as a small group system. It can just as well be looked at as a subsystem of the larger social system. It can be viewed as a process of transaction involving two foci, such as between the psychological systems of the family members and their group interrelations. Or it can be regarded as a process of transaction involving all the foci. The choice of foci is up to the investigator.

No matter by which of the two methods — the demand of the event or the interest of the investigator — a large alteration of the field is brought under consideration, the observational task of the investigator is more troublesome than it is in the case of small alterations. We have discussed the nature of the pitfalls which will be encountered. It is now opportune to discuss some errors which typically appear as a result of wrestling with these problems. The discussion of errors will not be exhaustive; on the contrary, we are now considering only those errors which become manifest as a result of viewing interdisciplinary research from the standpoint of the transactional field, leaving out of consideration the host of possible mistakes that are the constant companions of any investigator.

There are four types of error which arise as responses to large alterations in the field: (1) the over-estimation of one focus; (2) the skipping of foci; (3) the fading of foci; and (4) the collapsing of foci. All can be considered as inappropriate responses to com-plexity, but their origins, consequences, and possible correction vary sufficiently to make them worth considering separately.

Over-estimation of one focus is probably the most common of the four. Typically, proponents of the focus in question push it forward as the most valuable area of knowledge and rate other areas as secondary or of no importance. The terms of devaluation of the other foci may vary. They may be called unscientific; or, if allowed to be known as scientific, their yield of knowledge may still be judged trivial. When not labeled trivial or unscientific, they are likely to be condemned as mechanical and dehumanized. Obviously, the way other foci are ruled out of court depends upon which focus is being aggrandized. If Universe is being touted — usually by the so-called "hard" scientist — then the other foci are apt to be dismissed as "soft," which is to say that their methods are not considered reliable. For the scientist involved in an over-evaluation of Universe, Soma may come out a poor second, biology being viewed as having at least some practical value even though rather short on "laws of nature" and elegance of theory. The remaining foci are deemed hardly worth considering as areas of firm knowledge.

One might suppose that the "hard" scientist earned his lofty attitude through the manifest benefits of physics, chemistry, and engineering for an industrial society. But over-estimation of a focus is not, apparently, conditioned by pride in practical results. Rather, it is more likely to be, as suggested before, a response to complexity. This, at any rate, seems a more plausible explanation for the over-estimation of Psyche — a focus which has not yielded practical benefits in such proportions as to silence all doubters. Some proponents of this focus, nevertheless, regard its core of knowledge as of such brilliance as to put all else in the shade. Such an attitude is common among a certain stratum of psychoanalysts, though it diminishes for the group as a whole. It is also found in psychologists of other persuasions, though less forcibly expressed. Psychoanalysts in the past have tended to be more vocal, even strident, in making the claim that psychoanalysis is unique and takes precedence over other modes of knowledge or of inquiry — an attitude that reduces history, philosophy, and sociology, for example, to fields of "applied psychoanalysis."

Reductionism, in fact, is the sign that aggrandizement of a particular focus is in operation. It can occur with respect to any focus; and when it does occur, its advocates universally believe that it couldn't have happened to a nicer discipline. The sociologist takes pride in the invention of the sociology of knowledge, to say nothing of the sociology of religion, of science, of the family, of education, and of practically anything. In the end, what is *not* socially determined? To such occupational narcissism, the anthropologist can respond with his own variety of superior outlook. *Culture* is *not* socially determined, says he, haughtily, like Sam, the serious Rover boy. Or with amusement, like Tom, the fun-loving Rover. For he has traveled, and he has been to the night schools of the primitive world. He has seen cultures all over the globe. He knows their infinite variety, the power of their myths, the magnetic force of their languages and beliefs. He knows that it is the culture which determines the forms of society, subsidiary structures like religion, science, the family, education, and practically everything else.

The consequences of these professional love affairs are harmful in other than interdisciplinary contexts. Quarrels over priority, precedence, and status are not calculated to build confidence in the sciences — nor in any of the intellectual disciplines — among members of the lay public, no matter how often they are told that the security and welfare of the nation rests upon them. But it is in respect to the possibility of breaking down barriers between disciplines and of advancing knowledge in areas where progress is most needed that over-estimation of a focus works a particular hardship. One can sympathize with the basic motive: to reduce complexity. We all struggle enough with the problem of facing too many irregular phenomena in our own areas without having to worry about what is going on in someone else's province. If we must worry, however — and in truth we must — then it is not an appropriate solution to dismiss the other fellow's area as worthless; nor is it appropriate to reduce everything to one's own area in order to make it familiar territory. All regions must be understood in their own right.

The reason that we must worry about the other fellow's area is because of the interdependence of the foci in the field. The isolation of the foci and the development of specialized disciplines for their investigation is a necessary step in the process of inquiry. Without this step there could be no orderliness of inquiry and no possibility of scientific acquisition of data. But its usefulness is limited. The isolation of systems of behavior in any of the foci should logically lead to the next step: the study of the transactions between systems in different foci. As science grows, a multidisciplinary investigation of behavior is logically inevitable. Over-estimation of a focus merely holds back for a time but cannot prevent the investigation of large alterations in the field.

The second type of error — *skipping of foci* — is more serious because it appears to be less irrational than the first. For this reason, it seems to be a more acceptable method for reducing complexity. In this type of error, the interdependence of systems is officially recognized, but the investigator adopts the attitude that any system within any of the foci may be observed any time and correlated with any other. The order of the interrelations of foci in the field is disregarded. The research strategy which the investigator adopts is based on the assumption that if all systems are interdependent, any two or three or four of them can be correlated with each other for the sake of a particular investigation; the choice of systems is assumed to be utterly free.

This assumption is not consonant with the formal characteristics of the transactional field as described. I have suggested that the foci in the field are related to each other through transformation processes in such a fashion that their configuration is not random. Each focus can appear only in relation to the two foci on either side of it. To put it baldly, each focus is a *creation,* generally of the field as a whole but specifically of the two foci between which it occurs. There would, for example, be no knowledge of the Universe did it not impinge itself between the Culture's ways for dealing with it and the Soma — that is, the possibility of physical or biological survival of the human organism in a world shaped by the culture's stock of beliefs and repertoire of tools for the acquisition of food and shelter. Were it not squeezed between Culture and Soma in the context of survival, we could forget about the actual Universe and substitute for it our utopian or apocalyptic fantasies or abolish it altogether in favor of a Nirvana. It is somatic pain or hunger that brings us to our senses and initiates fresh inquiries into the nature of Universe.

We could make a similar case for the logical necessity of each focus of knowledge appearing exactly where it does in the configuration of the field. What is more important to the present discussion, however, is that if the assumption of the logically fixed configuration of the field is correct, then the choice of systems for investigation is not altogether free. If the order of succession of foci in the field is disregarded, then any focus can be related to any other, and the choice of systems is free. On the grounds of field logic, this could not occur without destroying the significance of a focus. It would be tantamount to saying any phenomenon of behavior will have some social, some cultural, and some biological aspects and it doesn't matter how one goes about putting them into the investigation or leaving them out. If we happen to have a sociologist at hand, why not put him on the research team and see what he can find out? A research strategy based on such haphazard views of field phenomena would be illogical and would lead to results which would be difficult to comprehend. The nature of a field requires that the foci to be included in an investigation be taken up in their order of succession and that no focus be passed over. In other words, if an investigator wishes to relate somatic phenomena (any genetic factors) to social phenomena (any social class variables), then he must take account, in *some systematic fashion,* of the intervening psychological and group factors.

The scrambling of foci does not always take place because of haphazard or random views of field processes. Quite frequently it occurs by deliberate design; the investigator is fully aware of what intervening factors have been omitted. There is no objection to this procedure if the aim is to establish an empirical correlation. Suppose an investigator wishes to find out whether cardiovascular disease is more prevalent in a lower-class population than in an upper-class one. Such a correlation of somatic with social phenomena overlooks Psyche and Group. This skipping of foci, however, does not produce any difficulties so long as it is confined to a pure correlation. Should the investigator wish to go further and establish a cause-and-effect relationship in regard to his finding, then he could ill afford to omit Psyche and Group. He would then be dealing with a process through which somatic systems were subjected to differential strain. He would, therefore, have to look for the sources of somatic strain as they occurred with respect to psychological systems as these, in turn, are influenced in family and other small groups within the classes.

We are now face to face with the full range of complexity occasioned by large alterations in the field. It is not easy to design research taking into account all these interrelated systems. The temptation to leave something out is strong and practical considerations may, indeed, require a drastic elimination of many interrelationships which, on logical grounds, should be included. But these practical difficulties can be got around without totally excluding or ignoring the intervening foci. The number of systems in each focus to be observed can be reduced. Or the research can be broken down into parts, each part examining the relation between two foci at a time. Or the research can be set up in such a fashion as to hold one of the foci constant while variations in the others are observed. As stated above, what is important is that the investigation take account of the intervening foci *in some systematic fashion,* even if this means only that the inquiry into their influence must be postponed for a future study.

This may seem to be only a small or even insignificant requirement. But it looms large if we consider some of the results of past errors attributable to the indiscriminate skipping of foci. The most notable example is found in the interdisciplinary approach which has been called "Culture and Personality." Proponents of this approach have attempted to establish a direct link between Psyche and Culture, either skipping over Society and Group or treating them in a helter-skelter fashion. The linkage is supposedly established through the concept of "a model personality" which is characteristic of most people in a particular society. The concept of "national character" is an example of a model personality construct.

What this concept does is to collapse culture into personality and personality into culture in such a fashion that the distinctions between them become lost. Culture is interpreted as personality at large, so to speak, because it is behavior representative of most of the people in a society; personality, by the same token, is seen as a miniature culture assemblage operating in the isolated individual. Psychological systems are invoked unsystematically, and mainly for the purpose of propounding that culture becomes intertwined with personality first by internalization and subsequently by externalization through projection. Small-group systems, such as the family and its child-rearing customs, may or may not be thrown into the hopper in order to broaden the explanation of how the culture gets into the personality (and out again) in the process of culture transmission or "enculturation."

One may sympathize, again, with this undertaking as an attempt to reduce complexity. It cuts across many disciplines with remarkable dispatch. It makes the study of large alterations in the field seem simple. Indeed, in historical perspective one must give credit to the initiators of this approach for the boldness and vision with which they tackled the mounds of cross-cultural data and the web of psychoanalytic theory in order to construct a coherent picture of the relations between cultural and psychological processes. The interdisciplinary enterprise is much advanced because of their pioneering efforts, even though we are now aware of the over-simplifications in their initial formulations. Without simplifying, they would not have been able to demonstrate the connections at all. Anthropologists would have continued constructing ethnographies and worrying about the origins and functions of cultural practices, while psychiatrists would have gone on investigating personality traits and disturbances in citizens of their communities, believing that what they observed as mental health or illness was representative of all of mankind.

Yet the correlation of culture with personality was obtained at a price of reduction in complexity which today we are no longer willing to pay. The omission of Society and Group from the cross-correlations has meant the omission of cultural variation within and between societies. The culture-and-personality school postulated one cultural configuration and one "modal" personality type for each "culture." In any society, however, the culture does not present itself as a unified, monolithic whole. It appears as a system of beliefs and value orientations which are patterned variably for the different parts of the social system and which are constantly subject to change. Nor is the individual directly related to the society's stock of cultural beliefs and orientations. The relationship is obtained systematically through his participation in the family and in other small groups in shared activities. It is these activities which are patterned in accordance with variation in cultural orientations for the part of the social system in which they occur. This orderly variation makes room for the inevitable variation in personality types — a variation which receives contributions from both the somatic and the psychological systems of the individual.

These remarks illustrate what is to be gained from keeping to the built-in complexities of the transactional field where inter-disciplinary research and theory are concerned. By tracing the connection from Psyche through Group and Society to Culture, we make a place for ordered variation within each focus and thus take account of the intricate variability of behavior phenomena. At the same time, instead of viewing the variability as random we comprehend it as occurring in accordance with the relationship between the foci. Thus, for the single cultural configuration and the single "modal" personality of the culture-and-personality formulations we would substitute (as shown in Chapter Six) a rank ordering of dominant and variant cultural orientations within each society. Granted, the dominant pattern of cultural orientations characterizes a culture as a whole insofar as it is possible to make such a characterization, given the variant patterns which are inevitably present. Where personality is concerned, however, such a simple concept as "modal" personality is untenable. To characterize "the personality," transactionally, would require a more complicated operation because one would have to specify, for each isolated individual, the pattern of cultural values, of social activities, or psychological adaptations and defenses, and of somatic processes of which he gives evidence. Personality, in other words, is the name for a cumbersome patchwork concept derived from all parts of the transactional field.

To pursue the problems of personality description further

would take us into a discussion of the differences between transactional, interactional, and self-actional description — a matter best considered later. For the present it is sufficient to complete the discussion of the skipping of foci by pointing out that this error is not confined to the culture-and-personality approach. It occurs in several other approaches to behavior study. Another familiar example of this type of error is found in the narrow "behaviorism" based on either classical or operational conditioning and in the "learning theory" formulations derived from them. Here, Psyche is directly linked to Universe; Soma is passed over or given minimal attention. A behavior response is associated directly with the physical contingencies in the environment — the stimuli — which precede it. A somatic "drive state" related to the response may or may not be specified. It is usually assumed that some somatic state is related to the response, but the somatic processes themselves are not a subject of inquiry. The conditioned responses, which are built up into behavior systems, are dependent purely upon schedules of reinforcement, which means reduction of the drive state whatever its origin.

As is always the case when foci are skipped, the reduction in complexity is extensive. The range of process under inquiry is so narrowed down that the regularities peculiar to the stimulus configuration and the behavioral response are easily determined. This is a gain on the side of the possibility of demonstrating invariant or "lawful" relationships in behavior processes, and this gain cannot be dismissed. Furthermore, the demonstrated relationships can be put to practical applications in the area of teaching and learning. The contribution to the field of knowledge stemming from this approach is, therefore, solid. But the contribution is limited, and its limitations become specially evident where interdisciplinary research is concerned. The omission of Soma as a focus of inquiry means that variation due to physiological processes are excluded from study. Somatic systems governing the acquisition of responses during growth and development and during states of pathology or disordered function are not, in the usual case, made a part of the investigations of the "conditioning" school. Furthermore, so few psychological systems are included in the inquiry that the relation of the response to delaying and inhibiting processes such as occur in fantasy and defense are not brought under study.

There could be no objection to this extensive omission of systems if conditioning and learning theory included a program for the inclusion later of what was initially excluded. As a matter of fact, some members of this school of thought are currently attempting to broaden their range of investigations to include neurophysiological processes. What is objectionable is the doctrinal assertion, so often put forth, of the necessity of rigorous exclusion of intervening systems in order to preserve scientific "purity" and methodological precision. For if the acquisition of responses cannot be related to central nervous system regulatory processes, as well as to the environmental configuration of stimuli, then we will never have knowledge of the origin of variations in behavior apart from those under the exclusive control of the environment.

So much for planned skipping of systems and foci. In turning our attention, now, to a related type of error — *fading of foci* — we approach a phenomena which is more difficult to describe because it is unplanned and not under full conscious control. Fading of foci is a little noted and somewhat mysterious event which occurs when three adjacent foci (or systems of any kind) are lined up for simultaneous investigation. The system in the middle tends to fade from awareness, to be difficult to keep in focus, almost as if some perceptual inhibiting process were at work. It cannot be said with any assurance, however, that an innate tendency is at work. The only certainty is that what assumes prominence in awareness is the operation of the two outer systems. They become so prominent that the middle focus seems dim or keeps being overlooked. The three-term proposition dissolves and becomes polarized in the form of a two-term process: a dichotomy.

These observations will probably seem empty to those who have not undergone the experience. Accordingly, some brief illustrations are in order.

Suppose an investigation starts out with the intention of studying the relations between Group, Psyche, and Soma. In the research design, Group is represented by a nuclear family containing a schizophrenic child, Psyche by the inner psychodynamics of the schizophrenic child as well as by the internal psychological processes in the presumably normal family members, and Soma by the somatic needs (for nutrition, sleep, and orderly bowel and bladder function) within the family members. Let us say that the seven-year-old schizophrenic male child in this family hoards food, wets his bed, and soils his pants, is periodically violent and abusive toward his parents, and cannot be maintained in school because of his antagonistic attitude toward his teachers. The object of the inquiry is to determine whether the child and his parents can be helped through family group psychotherapy and whether the causes of the child's bizarre behavior can be determined.

Now, at the outset of this study, the investigators have every intention of acquiring data on the psychological processes within the disturbed child and other family members on the basis of psychodynamic formulations (that is, generalized psychoanalytic theory). Attempts are made to gather information on the child through psychological tests but are frustrated because the child will not cooperate with the tester. Observation of the child's behavior reveals his excessive fear of physical contact with others, based on the expectation that he will be overpowered and will have to endure a physical assault, either for the purpose of forcing food into him or for the purpose of giving him an enema or some medication to control his bowel function. Observation of the parents gradually uncovers, in the context of considerable initial denial, that episodes of violent physical struggle between the mother and the child actually do take place. Under extreme anxiety about the possibility of the child's starving, she literally pinions him and forces food upon him. At other times, in anger because of his soiling the bed and his clothes, she holds him down and administers enemas or cathartics. Further, it is discovered that the husband has episodes of alcoholism, during which he not only drinks continuously but also physically assaults his wife and, though much less frequently, the child. During these times, the mother is so preoccupied with her husband's behavior and with her need to protect herself and her child, that her usual concern about the child's eating and elimination are not in evidence. In addition, she is brought closer to her son through her husband's antagonism toward him and his accusations that she favors him and babies him. When the husband's drinking subsides, she then becomes alarmed that she has neglected her child, and believing that he has lost weight and become more "dirty" in his habits as a result of neglect, she resumes with full force her disciplinary devotions to the boy.

With these transactions in full view, the attention of the investigators becomes focused on the cycles of disturbed interpersonal relations in the family as connected with the child's symptoms, both of which more and more appear together as a one-to-one affair. The child's fear of attack from others and his eagerness to control his food intake for himself, through hoarding, and of determining his own rhythms of bowel and bladder function, through defiance, appear to be the function of a relation between his own somatic processes, including fear and anger, and the behavior occurring in the environment. On the side of parental deficiencies, the currents of pathological behavior between all three family members, running their courses in cycles of increased or decreased tension, appear largely as a function of group regulatory processes related to the inability of each to satisfy the basic needs within the others. As this picture of the relationship between somatic needs and interpersonal process becomes more and more prominent, interest in specifying the nature of the psychic structures and functions within the family members drops. It does not disappear altogether, but in comparison with environmental events it fades in importance. The functions of gross psychological systems such as anxiety, identification, and projective mechanisms will probably continue to be included within the inquiry, but specificity of detail will be lost. Observational data which would, on other counts, be held steadily within the psychological focus — especially psychogenetic data — will be redistributed so that they appear as aspects either of somatic events or of interpersonal events.

The disappearance of the middle term (the excluded middle?) can easily be observed in other focal groupings. The disappearance of Group from a Psyche-Group-Society combination often occurs in studies of the structure and function of hospital wards. Ward structure is the product both of a small-group process and of the institutional structure of the hospital. When the investigation centers on the ward with the intention of investigating both psychological process in ward and patient personnel and the structure of the hospital as a social system, the group process in the ward is likely to be sacrificed to the observation of the other two foci. The investigation will produce much data on the social psychological characteristics of ward personnel and on administrative practice in the hospital, personnel-patient ratios, prestige systems, communication systems, and the like, but the day-to-day or week-to-week variations in interpersonal relations on the ward will be overlooked. They will not vanish altogether, but the tendency will be to attribute them either to differences in occupational status and communication systems among ward personnel or to the attitudes and defenses of the personnel.

The fading of a middle focus may turn out to be merely a special case of the fourth and final method for reducing complexity: *collapsing of foci*. In this error, foci which should be maintained in careful differentiation from each other are fused, usually under some conceptual tag which obliterates the boundaries between them. A typical example is the use of the word "milieu" in studies of mental hospitals. This word has achieved a certain popularity in the literature of social psychiatry. Its use frequently makes it unnecessary for the investigator to specify what aspect of the hospital is under observation. It may refer to the physical aspects — color scheme of rooms, layout of buildings, presence of locked or open doors — which I would assign to Universe. It may refer to the value orientations and belief systems of hospital personnel and of the community in which the hospital exists. Or it may mean the decision as to what therapeutic technique will be practiced in the hospital. (Transactionists would place beliefs and preferences within Culture.) It may refer to the parts of the wider social system with which the hospital is in contact, such as the upper or middle class which a private mental hospital serves versus the working class serviced by public facilities; or it may refer to the internal organization of the hospital — both of which deserve to be placed in Society. Or it may refer to the interpersonal relations which obtain in various wards of the hospital, which belongs within the Group focus. Often it refers simultaneously to a bit of all of these operating together.

This compounding and confounding of foci — each of which has a separate effect upon observable phenomena — causes inestimable confusion in studies of the effects of various therapeutic regimes. For example, since the early 1950's there has been considerable disagreement in the literature of hospital studies concerning the effect of three different therapeutic practices: drug therapy, psychotherapy, and milieu therapy. Each method of treatment has had its sometimes intemperate advocates. With the introduction of the phenothiazines, the so-called "tranquilizers," psychopharmacology became a slogan, and many claims were made about the effectiveness of drug therapy in reducing symptoms and facilitating discharge of patients from the hospital. Counter-claims, however, were made by the proponents of the two other methods. The advocates of psychotherapy claimed that where sufficient numbers of psychotherapists were available in the hospital, drug therapy was unnecessary. In addition, they argued, the effects of drug therapy were only temporary, and some of the undesirable side effects of the tranquilizers could be avoided by the more rational psychotherapeutic regime. To both of these partisan viewpoints, the enthusiasts of milieu therapy maintained that whatever benefits accrued for the patient from either drug therapy or psychotherapy was a result of the altered interpersonal environment within the hospital, an improvement brought about by the more hopeful and supportive attitudes of doctors, nurses, and attendants who administered a method of treatment in which they believed intensely.

More disinterested observers of this controversy have attempted to design studies capable of determining which of the three procedures is the most effective and whether a particular combination of the three is more effective than any one alone. The studies along this line, however, have not produced any clarification of the issues. Ingenious though they have been in the use of control groups and "double-blind" procedures, the controversy remains unsettled. If one views this scene from the standpoint of the transactional field, one would not expect any enlightenment to flow from the research designs ordinarily employed. For they uniformly take for granted the terms of the dispute: that drug therapy, psychotherapy, and milieu therapy can be distinguished in respect to their effects on the patient.

According to the logic of the transactional field, such a distinction would be impossible to establish. The usual research designs ignore transactional effects — that is, the interdependence and mutual influences between systems operative in the field. They assume that such effects can be avoided through the use of control groups and double-blind procedures. The usual research design calls for the following procedure: in the hospital in which the investigation is being conducted, a sample of patients is selected such that all the variables related to the patients are similar. The diagnosis, severity of the disability, age, sex, duration of illness, length of stay in hospital, etc., are either similar or are stratified so that the groups of patients subjected to the procedure under study will have the same composition. The sample is then divided into three equal groups, one of which receives only drug therapy, one only psychotherapy, and one only milieu therapy. Since all the patients are in the same milieu insofar as they are in the same hospital, isolating the effects of the milieu from the other therapeutic procedures constitutes a difficulty. But, let us say, this problem can be resolved in two ways. If the milieu is the decisive factor, then the patients who receive no psychotherapy and no drug therapy should show the same rates of recovery or improvement as those who also receive psychotherapy and drug therapy. In this set-up, patients receiving drug therapy and psychotherapy are scattered in various wards throughout the hospital. On the other hand, if it is desired to study the separate effects of the milieu, then the patients in the third group are placed on a special ward where the ratio of nurses and attendants to patients is increased and where the patients receive more individualized attention in relation to their illness but receive no psychotherapy and no drug therapy. Meanwhile, those professional persons who are responsible for assessing the response to each of the three modes of therapy through psychological test procedures, individual interviews, and observations of general behavior of the patients in the hospital have no knowledge of which patient is receiving which type of therapy. Thus their judgments are not biased by their existing expectations with respect to the superior effects of one versus another mode of treatment. To make doubly sure that the treatment effects are not under the influence of suggestion, the hospital attendants who administer drugs to the patients included in this sample do not know whether they are administering the drug in question or some innocuous or ineffective placebo. Similarly, with respect to patients receiving psychotherapy, the ward attendants do not know whether patients are leaving the ward for the purpose of receiving psychotherapeutic interviews or for some other purpose. Both the group of patients receiving placebo medications and those leaving the ward for non-therapeutic contacts with hospital staff are included in the assessment procedures.

Now, let us suppose that this research design can be established and carried through without "leaks" which subvert the double-blind procedure. Can it actually be anticipated that the effects of the different treatment regimes will be distinguishable? According to the assumptions of transactional field logic, we would have to say no. Our negative answer would be based on two objections: that the research design collapses significant foci in the field, ignoring their variable effects, and that the design is based on interactional description. Let us postpone a consideration of the objection pertaining to the interactional approach, for the moment, and look only at the results of collapsing the foci.

Let us suppose that the procedure described above is instituted in a large state mental hospital which emphasizes custodial care for its inmates and is able to supply, on the basis of volunteer psychiatrists drawn from the community, a modicum of psychotherapy. The results of the investigation show that drug therapy produces greater rates of improvement in patients than either psychotherapy or milieu therapy. One can expect that advocates of both psychotherapy and milieu therapy will protest this outcome. The advocates of psychotherapy will state that the low-income, working-class patients in this hospital are not suitable for the type of psychotherapy which the volunteer therapists are trained to administer. The psychotherapy which is good for upper-class and middle-class patients, they hold, needs to be modified for this group of patients. For example, it should be combined with group therapy and family therapy. At any rate, in one way or another, they claim that psychotherapy has not had a fair test. The advocates of milieu therapy, on the other hand, protest the findings on the basis that the level of milieu therapy, in such a large state facility, is below par. They describe patient care in this hospital as medieval, punitive, and anti-therapeutic. Thus milieu therapy has not had a fair test. The good outcome for drug therapy, both groups maintain, is merely a sign that when patients are made more tranquil through medication, ward attendants find them easier to manage and are less punitive to them. As a result, the patients do better. Finally, the advocates of drug therapy triumphantly proclaim that the investigation demonstrates exactly what they predicted: that psychopharmacology is the best method for treating mental illness because the illness itself represents the outcome of a disturbed biological process.

For the disaffected reader, and for all the skeptically minded, this situation may illustrate a conclusion to which they had long ago come without its help: that psychiatrists are adept at explaining any outcome whatever in line with their presuppositions. What about the friends of psychiatry? What aid and comfort can they bring to this scene of controversy? They can recommend that the investigation be repeated in a community mental health facility which is characterized by a better milieu, one which is more tailored to the needs of the individual patient, while still maintaining the same socio-economic class levels for patients admitted to the hospital. In addition, so goes the recommendation, the investigation could be carried out in a third type of facility — a private mental hospital catering to middle-class and upper-class patients and featuring extensive and expensive psychotherapy. When the results of the research in all three facilities are compared with each other, conclusions no longer open to question should result.

Alas for the friends of psychiatry, and alack for all the statistically sophisticated consultants it employs. The comparison of results obtained satisfies no one. The new findings are that in the community mental health facility drug therapy and psychotherapy show no better results than milieu therapy alone, while in the private mental hospital psychotherapy shows results slightly better than milieu therapy alone, and both prove superior to drug therapy. According to some, the new results demonstrate merely that the type of hospital has something to do with the efficacy of the various treatments employed in it. According to others, the new findings are still open to many criticisms, and nothing in the controversy is settled. Drug therapy advocates claim that in the community mental health facility and in the private mental hospital the doses of drugs

72

prescribed were so low and the length of time over which they were used was so short that a fair test of drug therapy was not made. Other drug therapy proponents complain that the patients in the community mental health facility and in the private mental hospital are too different from the chronic, excessively regressed patients found in the large state mental hospital where drugs proved superior to other methods. The results, therefore, are not comparable. Milieu therapy enthusiasts, though pleased with the results in the community mental health facility, maintain that the slightly superior effect for psychotherapy in the private mental hospital is attributable to the fact that in this hospital psychotherapy has a high standing with both staff and patients. Patients not receiving psychotherapy are regarded as somehow not quite making the grade, and this point of view naturally affects the patients' views of their own progress and feeds back subtly into the assessment process.

What is interesting about this melange of critical reactions is that it is so close to coming to grips with the collapse of foci involved in the original research design and in the basic thinking about the three types of treatment. It is seen that something in the hospital system makes one method of treatment preferable to another, that this has something to do with the type of patient in the hospital, with the attitudes of staff, and with the organization of the hospital. But as long as the relevant distinctions are tied to terms which disregard or collapse the foci which need to be examined, the situation remains obscure. In order to clear it up, the designers of the research would have to abandon their interactional thinking and their reliance on double-blind techniques. They would, of necessity, be required to post observers in the hospitals who, far from being "blinded," were instructed to talk to everyone concerned with each method of treatment in full, open knowledge of who was receiving what therapy. Instead of information withholding, maximum information giving would be relied upon. The observers, in other words, would be placed in a position to study the experiences of patients in the three groups — their feelings, thoughts, fantasies, and value orientations — and, in the same way, the experiences of the staff with reference to the use of drugs, the use of psychotherapy, and the use of hospital facilities per se. In this fashion they could discover what difference to the successful employment of drugs or psychotherapy the value orientations and beliefs of key groups in the hospital might make, what conflicts among personnel or among patients or between personnel and patients got in the way of the effective use of one or another treatment method. The story would unfold. The mutual influences between values, beliefs, status, social class and ethnic status, the organizational hierarchy, treatment procedure, response to treatment, psychological functions, and somatic processes would come out of hiding. The situation would be revealed in all its complexity and with a good deal of its disorder showing. For we are here dealing with that most difficult of all situations of inquiry: a total alteration of the field. Considering the inevitable problems of sorting and separating the influences emanating from the different foci in so broad-gauged an inquiry, nothing will avail except a full recognition of the complexities involved. Concern for the reliability of judgments — of which the double-blind technique is a reflection — can wait for a later time, after the complexities have been at least partially unraveled.

This is a good point at which to return to the effects of interactional description on the research design just discussed. As stated above, confusion and lack of clarity in investigations of the various types of therapy occur in part because of the use of interactional description for events better envisioned in transactional terms. Interactional description assumes that A, an entity of some sort, does something, B, to C, an entity of another sort, producing D, an outcome of some sort. In the above investigation the A's are mental hospitals of various sorts, the B's are the various modes of treatment, the C's are the patients, and the D's are changes in the symptoms and behavior of the patients. The linear cause-and-effect chain of interactions is traditional scientific description. As stated in the previous chapter, interactional description — as well as self-actional description — has its place. Interaction should not be thrown out of court simply because of the salience and importance of transactional description for certain purposes. But it must be reserved for suitable occasions. It is not suitable to think of therapy as something done to a patient, similar to greasing a car or broiling a steak. Nor is it suitable to think of a mental hospital as doing something — as the agent. True, the word "patient" means recipient of an action initiated by the "agent," and our scientific training — and, even more so, our medical training — has been heavily spiced with interactional thinking. But if one looks at the situation objectively, is it not evident that the patient influences the therapist's behavior; he acts upon the therapist. Similarly, the therapists within the hospital act upon the administrators, who act upon the Boards of Health and public or political agencies responsible for them. Wherever one looks, one sees two-way, reciprocal processes rather than uni-directional linear chains of cause and effect. If therapy is no more something done by the therapist to the patient than it is something done by the patient to the therapist, and if this process is no more something instigated by hospital administrators among their staff than it is something begun by the staff and urged upon the hospital administration, and if staff-administrator relationships represent a process which influences community agencies as much as it is influenced by them, then we are faced with a field of to-and-fro processes which cannot be made to look like a set of one-way streets. In brief we must reckon with transactions, not with interactions.

In transactional inquiry, we are faced with the need for comparing the effects of one type of system of transactions with another. We ask: if a change is introduced in one system, what effects are subsequently noted in neighboring systems, and how do these effects circulate back to the system in which we first noticed the change? In interactional inquiry, we are faced with the need for comparing the effect of an external change on an entity — on its internal structure and on its external behavior — with the effect of some other change on the same entity, or with the effect of the same change on a different entity. Interactional inquiry can safely take place within the framework of transactional inquiry. For example, let us say that we regard the therapist-patient system as a transaction to be subjected to transactional inquiry. Specifically, we wish to know what its effects as a system are in transaction with the systems of nurse-patient relationships, on the one hand, and with the system of family-patient relationships, on the other. Planned change is to be introduced only in the therapist-patient system. The observers are to keep track of changes reverberating from this system into the nurse-patient system and the family-patient system and back to the therapist-patient system. In this general transactional context, the observer of the patient-therapist system will be conducting interactional observations with respect to the patient and the therapist separately. He will investigate the effect of the therapist's interpretations and behavior on the concepts and fantasies that the patient has of himself, of the nurses, and of his family. In this kind of interactional description, the acts of the therapist are grouped into classes and the effects of these classes of action on the patient — of inputs into the system — are compared with each other. A certain class of actions, for example, produces resistance, while another produces acceptance, and a third releases fantasy: the release of fantasy is followed by more acceptance of the nurses. Similarly, the observer will be investigating the effects of the patient's behavior on the therapist as interaction. Certain behavior by the patient lead to the therapist's instructing the nurses to give the patient greater freedom; other behavior by the patient may have an opposite effect on the therapist. These are interactional cause-and-effect chains. In actual observation, the transactional effects are reconstructed from such interactional descriptions; or, as we noted above, interaction is placed within the context of the systems in transaction. But no transaction is ever observed except through the medium of sets of interactions.

We can now see that the transactional approach has to do with envisionment: with how one looks at and interprets data as contributions to knowledge, thus with how one sets up a research design looking forward to the interpretation. The details of observations are usually seen as interactional: something is done, or something happens, and the results are observed. A question is asked, a drug is administered, an answer is given, an effect is witnessed. But the understanding of what takes place, the description of the events witnessed, *can* be held within the interactional framework, can be ascribed to wider transacting systems, or can be traced to narrower self-acting entities or objects.

Perhaps special mention of self-action should be made here. Volumes of information and of data have been put together in which the self-acting person is at the center of inquiry. What is the place of such inquiries in a field of knowledge based on transacting foci — that is, systems of processes — and not on objects or entities acting under their own powers?

As stated in the previous chapter, Dewey and Bentley went too far in ruling all self-actional description out of bounds. They declared that self-actional concepts were archaic and unsuited to our transactional times. Only the persistence of bad intellectual habits, according to Dewey and Bentley, could account for the constant eruption and intrusion of such an unreasonable, old-fashioned approach to scientific description. But their point of view was probably itself unreasonable and inflexible. Self-actional description is necessary and valid for certain types of events; to abandon it would be either to falsify or to distort the event beyond recognition for the sake of maintaining logical consistency or for the sake of reducing complexity. As argued all along, the chief source of error in interdisciplinary endeavors comes from the premature effort to reduce complexity and to maintain consistency. Furthermore, self-actional description is not merely archaic. It is true that in the past self-actional concepts were over-generalized. Take stones, for example.

Today we know that a carved stone object — an idol — cannot cause good or evil events to occur through its own power: it operates only through its involvement in a system of religious meanings and practices. We also know that if an idol falls to the ground, this event does not occur through its self-determining wish to reach the earth, its natural resting place, but happens because of the object's involvement in a system of physical relationships which we call gravity. We nevertheless continue today to recognize that carved stone objects can be beautiful and moving to the observer, while falling stones can be dangerous. We know these things from our interaction with stones, in accordance with the previously stated formula that all observation begins as interaction. However, we can use this interactional derived information in different ways. We could consider the beautiful statue as an example of an aesthetic style, as aspect of the culture of a particular society, and so place the information within a transactional description. However, we could regard it as an object in its own right, producing an effect on the observer because of its shape, color, texture, and because of its history: who made it, where it has been located, and how used and enjoyed in the past and present. All this information, allocated to that statue, makes it a unique entity — an object which has some of its effects upon observers because it is its very own self and not anything else in the world. To this extent, its effects must be described in self-actional terms; they are specific to the selfhood — the "one-and-only" aspect — of the object.

If this can be said of stones, then certainly claims for the validity of self-actional description where persons are concerned are all the more secure. It would seem that the sense of the argument which confronts us is not whether self-actional concepts are ever valid. Rather, we need to judge when are they valid and how are they to be fitted into the transactional framework. Can we specify the conditions within which it is meaningful to use self-actional description, in the context of the transactional field? If we can specify the conditions within which self-actional descriptions are valid, will these conditions automatically apply to events, or will a decision for or against self-actional description have to be made in each case?

These questions are not easy to answer. They are worth raising for several reasons. One reason is that investigators in so many disciplines face such questions in dealing with possible modes of analysis of their data. Another reason is in order, hopefully, to initiate a debate or dialogue in this area. Up to the present, scientists and scholars have been rather silent on such matters. Those who are interested in general systems theory try to convert all phenomena into systems and processes, leaving nothing for the apperception of entities and objects. Is this correct? I think not. A good friend and colleague, Roy R. Grinker, who more than most others has attempted to solve problems of transactional description in the subject matter of psychiatry, tends to deprecate psychoanalytic theory and practice on the grounds that psychoanalysis is derived from self-actional description. Yet there is good reason for holding that psychoanalysis is, like most other descriptive enterprises, derived from all three modes of codification: self-action, interaction, and transaction. The question for psychoanalysis, as for the other sciences of behavior, is the one we are posing: where are the cut-off points between self-actional, interactional, and transactional descriptions?

In what has been said generally about describing self-acting entities up to this point, there would appear to be two implicit conditions which ought to be spelled out. (1) Self-action is used in the description of an entity or a system when the entity (or system) is treated as a unique item rather than as one of a number of items in a set or series (class), any one of which can substitute for the others in a transaction. (2) Self-action is used in the description of an entity or system when that entity (or system) is able to perpetuate itself despite greatly changed internal and external transactions. For the sake of simplicity, call the first condition that of uniqueness and the second that of autonomy. We should now ask, what are the subsidiary conditions associated with uniqueness and autonomy?

Uniqueness is a composite attribute. The test of its presence is, as suggested above, whether or not some other member of the class or series will do just as well in the transactions at issue. If no identical substitute is found, then we can say that uniqueness is present. When present, it derives from two main sources. The first is the configuration of the entity or system — its formal characteristics or properties. The second is its history — the record of change or endurance in its formal characteristics. Whether we examine the uniqueness of a ship, a person, or a nation, these aspects — formal characteristics and history — will always be at issue. If the ship is "Old Ironsides," a frigate, its uniqueness does not attach to the fact that it is a frigate. This connection makes it merely a member or representative of a class of ships. Its uniqueness consists of its exact size, shape, and weight, as a frigate, and to its history — the actual facts of its persistence over time, its construction, the reasons for its being built, its uses in the naval engagements of the nation, its periodic decommissioning and recommissioning, the men who were in charge of it, and the symbolic meanings it has assumed over time and into the present. No other ship can have exactly this same combination attached to it.

If we were to inquire into the uniqueness and autonomy of a nation, we would encounter the same matters: the formal characteristics and history of the nation — how and why it came into being, its growth and development, its near demise and lucky escapes, its rejuvenations, or its actual disappearance and conversion into some other type of political entity. All these matters of survival would be fit for self-actional descriptions: the struggles undertaken by the entity, or on its behalf, for opportunities to persist and maintain intactness. It is these struggles which endow the political entity with its thing-like qualities, even though, from the transactional viewpoint, we would have to describe a nation not as a thing but as a complex social system.

So it is where the much more troublesome matter of the human being as an individual is concerned. We know how to assemble the data of inquiry about him into the various foci of the transactional field. We know how to ask the transactional questions about the relationships between foci where his behavior is concerned. We also know that, when we make observations about his behavior, we acquire our data through interaction with him and that we can carry such interactional inquiry into many different cause-and-effect chains. But what shall we do about the self-actional description of his behavior? How can we go about making such descriptions without getting carried away in the swift and engulfing current of such concepts as "free will," "ego," "self," "superego," "mind," and other words suggestive of little entities pulling strings and carrying out secret operations somewhere within the cranium? Can we describe the person as self-determining and autonomous without invoking intra-cerebral automatons?

One answer to this question is that we can find the dividing point between self-actional description, interaction, and transaction in individual human behavior on the basis of the principles already set forth. Whatever has to do with the history of the isolated individual is treated as self-actional whenever his unique, individualized behavior is under consideration. For example, where psychoanalytic theory is concerned, the relation between symptoms, defenses, and psychogenetic background are to be described in self-actional terms for the defined, isolated patient. They constitute a unique configuration, a structure, and can be expected to persist unless some process is brought to bear upon them. If the process is psychotherapy, it can be viewed in interactional terms: the acts of the therapist having certain effects upon the psychological (self-actional) structure within the patient; conversely, the persistent, repetitive acts of the patient having certain effects upon the psychological structures within the therapist. These interactional effects can be described in terms of the theory of transference and counter-transference as it has been developed within the psychoanalytic literature. Finally, insofar as the subject matter being dealt with by both patient and therapist is concerned with persistent, unconscious fantasies, the description can be posed in any of the three modes. They can be talked of as uniquely characteristic and persistent behavior of the patient — as self-actional description. They can be discussed through interpretation designed to clarify or modify them or to bring them into conscious awareness — an interactional description. They can be considered from the point of view of the systems of behavior involved in them: the somatic satisfactions sought for, the role partners conceived as supplying the satisfactions, and the actual roles and social settings in which the satisfactions are expected to occur. This approach to fantasy formation is transactional.

In this illustration, psychoanalysis serves as a representative of a large number of methods for codifying the behavior of the isolated human person acting as an individual. The point is that any of these methods incorporate self-actional, interactional, and transactional descriptions. Which mode of description is used will depend largely upon the purposes of the inquiry. The reason that it is important for us to determine the relation of self-actional to transactional description is because transactional description is here advocated as not only possible but preferable for interdisciplinary inquiries. Our starting point was the question of how to relate all the various methods and theories extant in the various branches of knowledge to each other so that interdisciplinary investigations could reasonably proceed without being overwhelmed by the complexity of the issues, on the one hand, or oversimplification, on the other. The response was to propose the notion of the transactional field, with the various foci representing areas of knowledge and with the interdependencies of foci representing criteria for pursuing more knowledge. Within this transactional setting, then, some principle is required for deciding when, how, and for what purpose to use information which has been assembled for self-actional description. The principle established is this: self-actional description — that is, making reference to an entity and its unique history and configuration — is required whenever the information of the transactional field is to be assembled within a past time perspective. In other words, it is history that forces us to abandon transactional description in favor of self-actional ascriptions.

This may seem a tautological argument. We define self-actional description as assembling information about the unique history and configuration of an object, entity, or system. We ask when such description is to be used. We answer: when an interest in the past of the object, entity, or system requires a historical perspective. Perhaps we have reasoned in a circle, but in running the course we have come upon an important distinction and a dilemma. If we wish to adhere rigorously to transactional description and inquiry, then we must confine our observations to current events — to systems and processes occurring before our eyes, so to speak. But in the sciences of human behavior we are required to interest ourselves in the past. We need to inquire into the history and development of persons, families, communities, industries, and cultures in order to understand the present situation. If, whenever we inquire into the past and assemble this information in some coherent manner, we must, concurrently, put aside transactional description in favor of self-actional description, then we should at least know why this is necessary and how to assess its consequences.

A full discussion of this topic would take us too far afield. In brief, the problem is again a product of complexity, now compounded by the voluminous nature of data accumulated over time. Even if these data are gathered through observational techniques which give careful attention to the transactional nature of inquiry, when the historical materials are assembled, their transactional description is lost and their interactional base obscured. This effect comes about because one cannot tell or write or compound or fabricate the story of a relationship per se. One tells of a subject — a person, family, or state — which undergoes multiple relationships in the course of time. Even if we treat the subject of our tale as a system in transaction with other systems, the other systems will pale and fade into the background while *the* system becomes *our* system, increasingly the hero (or villain) of the story, steadily looming in the foreground and overshadowing all the systems or entities — all the other persons, families, or states — with which it has been in transaction. The reader as well as the narrator of the history appropriates the subject, makes it his own, identifies with it, while those others are subjected to counter-identification: they remain those somewhat alien persons, families, or states with which our own person, family, or state has had relations in the course of a few years, decades, or centuries.

As information concerning the past is more and more assembled around a subject, shaping it over time, the self-actional description is further compounded by the issue of selectivity. In the writing of a history, or in its telling, what is required is a mass of concrete detail. But not all the detail can be used in the telling or writing. A selection must be made, decisions taken about what to use and what to discard. The decisions, unfortunately, are themselves under the conscious or unconscious influence of the theories held by the writer of the history about the causes of changes over time in the subject. If the writer informs the reader as to the nature of his theories or if the histories are written for the express purpose of illustrating the theories of the authors, then the reader is in a fairly good position to assess the reliability of the stated relation between concrete detail and the abstract principles they are meant to illustrate. "Fairly good" should not be construed optimistically, however, for the reader is usually not able to check up on all the concrete data which the author has decided to exclude and which might, conceivably, contradict the abstract theoretical principles for which the author wishes to claim credibility.

The necessity of selection in the writing of a history means that no two writers will construct a history in exactly the same fashion. If the history is long and full of detail, it is likely that no two readers will understand it in exactly the same way. Let us call this source of variability the *Rashomon effect*, after the well-known Japanese tale of the differences between three accounts of the same set of events. The Rashomon effect increases the force of the self-actional description. This tendency arises from the fact that in any public or private discussion of history, as transmitted from author to reader or narrator to listener, claims are made for the correctness of the interpretation by some and are contested by others. Or the same process may occur wholly as inner debate within one of the listeners. At any rate, as a result of the Rashomon effect and the subsequent tendentious struggles over which version of the historical account to believe in, the interpretation which is finally arrived at is projected backward in time. It assumes a notable increase in firmness as it is steadily reinforced through the effects of hindsight. It now seems quite evident that the whole outcome of the story is already contained in its beginnings. Considering the starting point, it almost had to come out the way it did. This is post-diction: the conviction that, if one had only been daring enough, one could have foretold the end from the beginning.

We are now confronted with the full effect of self-actional description. The entity is regarded as pre-set, like a clock, ready to unwind, to roll outward and onward in its inevitable and majestic course of action. It matters not at all which system in the trans-actional field has become wrapped in self-actional glory. It could be any one of a number of systems within the somatic focus whose history, having been exposed and laid out, now predicts the shape of things to come. The genetic endowment of the organism or of the species — the specificity of genes on their chromosomes — is commonly pictured in self-actional terms. The statement that ontogeny repeats phylogeny is typical of the scriptural quality adhering to fully self-actional pronouncements. So it is written; so the texts say. In psychoanalytic theory, the psychosexual time-table — phallic following anal following oral phases of development — has the aura of the predetermined, inevitably unfolding, self-explaining, built-in generator. And, again within the psychological focus, the history of the individual, once it has been set within its ontogenetic frame, functions as a self-starter, a destiny which the person can do little to avert. When people reflect on the history of their political state, they are likely to conjure up manifest or latent destinies and other historical principles which supposedly steer events toward present ends.

The difficulty with self-actional description is its hypnotic, self-reinforcing tendency to dominate and sway judgments in its favor and to suppress evidence not in its favor. Its powers of persuasion are not based on rational weighing of pros and cons but stem from the magical belief, left over from childhood, in the invisible agent, the power behind the throne, the real director and guide of future events. Any scientific, hypothetical construct can fall heir to this uncontrolled, self-actional point of view and be regarded as a behind-the-scenes operator rather than a process. The ego, gravitation, evolution — all such patterned processes may be regarded as agencies ready to supervise behavior and make it conform to their bidding.

On the basis of this brief exposition, it is evident that self-actional description is bound to creep into any historical approach to data. It will have the effect of prejudicing the data and of shaping it into the forms pre-selected by the observer. At the present time, we cannot propose any viable safeguards against the many possible sources of error in such a procedure. Histories, whether of persons, families, or cultures, are reconstructions of the past necessary for the provisional understanding of the present and future. It may well be that in the years ahead more adequate methods of coding, correlating, and analyzing data referring to past events will, particularly with the help of computer technology, reduce the degree of error and handle the degree of complexity in the data with more effciency than has been possible so far. Apart from this possibility, protection is dependent upon a steady effort to translate the historical or self-actional type of description into the complex patterning of systems-in-process-with-systems characteristic of transactional description.

Part II

Social Roles

Spiegel's development of the social role concept was guided by transactional considerations. A conceptual bridge between the social and cultural dimensions of the transactional fields became imperative.

His social role classification system provides for a high degree of specificity in the description of interpersonal relationships. This accuracy in role designation makes it possible to relate the broad variation in cultural values to the differential patterning of interpersonal relationships in a wide range of sub-systems within the society.

The richness which this classification brings to the understanding of interpersonal relationships becomes evident in Chapter Four, The Function of Social Roles. Here Spiegel examines the interpersonal process within various sub-groups of society viewed as homeostatic systems. The inevitable disequilibrium that characterizes these sub-systems in the form of interpersonal conflict, and the efforts at reequilibrium (conflict resolution) are examined. He relates the structural aspects of social roles in different groups to the processes by which they attempt to effect a resolution of conflict when it arises. The various strategies that are employed in these efforts at interpersonal conflict resolution within various sub-systems of society are elaborated.

THREE

Structure of Social Roles

Although social factors have always been vaguely and peripherally recognized in medicine, it has only been in recent years that a flurry of research in the social sciences has pointed up the causal relations between disease and the social environment in which it develops. Even so, these advances have taken place in a general atmosphere of indifference. It is to be hoped that attitudes will change.

My hope that the social sciences will receive a warmer welcome in medical and psychiatric circles is somewhat tinged with anxiety. I am concerned that the collaboration between social science and psychiatry has not advanced far enough to be in the position of having a substantial and marketable product. Americans are prone to oversell and overbuy — to their subsequent regret. I am certain that interesting ideas and some interesting findings have been turned out in the name of social psychiatry. But I doubt that it has accumulated and is ready to deliver a solid body of research, theory, and method — especially therapeutic method. For this reason, I am not at all sure that we are ready to claim attention for so substantial and respectable sounding a field as would be denoted by the expression "social psychiatry." This name has been used in a somewhat desultory fashion for the last thirty years. There are a number of arguments for taking the position that it includes too much and claims too much and that we would be wiser to settle upon a more modest expression such as the "social aspects of psychiatry." In order to demonstrate the merits of this position, I would like to undertake a very brief review of what can be said about this field.

The activities characteristic of social psychiatry can be roughly grouped in four principal classes. The first contains the well-known ecological studies initiated by Faris and Dunham. Starting in the era when enthusiasm for the sociological study of the city was at its height, these investigations attempted to discover causal relations between population movements within the urban community, the disorganized social life of slum areas, and the high incidence of mental illness in those areas. They attracted a good deal of attention at first but later bogged down in an unresolved controversy over whether the social disorganization of slum areas gave rise to a higher incidence of phychosis or whether disturbed people tended to migrate to these areas in a spiral of downward mobility. *(Faris and Dunham 1939)*

Investigations of a second type have attempted to correlate the incidence of various mental disorders with an assortment of more or less static membership variables ranging from socio-economic through particular ethnic groups and religious sects to whole cultures and national groups. Considerably influenced by anthropological as well as sociological thinking, these correlational studies have proved to be sturdier, more sophisticated, and more fruitful than the ecological investigations. They have presented convincing evidence that the various social factors have *some* influence both on the type and incidence of different mental illnesses and on the way they are identified and treated within the group. They have not been able to show how this influence is exerted, but the provocative epidemiological questions raised in the course of such studies have led to a small number of excellent publications, of which an example is *Social Class and Mental Illness* by Hollingshead and Redlich.

The third class of writings that can be vaguely included in the area of social psychiatry are the contributions of the Neo-Freudian, sociologically oriented psychoanalysts such as *Sullivan 1953 and 1965, Horney 1937, Linton and Kardiner 1939,* and *Fromm 1941.* These authors have presented no systematic empirical studies of the relation between social factors and mental illness. Their significance lies rather in their point of view. The majority of psychoanalysts had previously emphasized the purely intra-psychic factors in the etiology of mental disorders, dismissing environmental factors as "accidental" or, at best, secondary detriments. The Neo-Freudians, in contrast, perceived the importance of the environment to the function of the individual and called vigorously for more detailed attention to the social and cultural aspects of mental illness. With the exception of Erik Erikson, these writers have taken an impressionistic or quasi-theoretical stance, but their point of view has been quite influential, especially among those in related professional fields. Erikson (1950) has distinguished himself in this group by his pioneering efforts to tackle the thorny theoretical problems embedded in the field, through the development of new concepts designed to bridge the gap between the individual and the society.

The fourth class of investigations expressive of the aims of social psychiatry embraces interdisciplinary study of the relation between mental illness and specialized social settings. Among the settings studied here are the mental hospital, the military services and military combat, Chinese Communist thought reform camps, civilian disasters, and, last but not least, the emotional and interpersonal environment of the family.[1] In contrast to investigations of the second type discussed above, where large-scale but static social variables such as social class or religion are correlated with type and incidence of mental illness, these investigations of specialized social settings have emphasized process rather than structure. For example, the investigators have tried to find out what type of staff relations within a mental hospital foster recovery in the patient in contrast to those ideologies and institutional arrangements which maintain illness or even intensify it. Because these studies of specialized environments attempt to demonstrate how a particular social variable exerts its effect upon the adjustment of the individual, they have aroused a good deal of hope that the insights thus gained can be used to improve the care of patients and ultimately to prevent the development of mental illness in large segments of the population.

Finally, to round out this brief review of the field, the contributions of the many social scientists whose work has not been

---

[1] On mental hospitals see *Stanton and Schwartz 1954*; *Greenblatt* et al. *1957*. On military pressures: *Grinker and Spiegel 1945; Kardiner and Spiegel 1947*. Chinese camps: *Lifton 1961*. Natural disasters: *Clifford 1955; Spiegel* et al. *1955*. Family environment: *Ackerman 1958; Bott 1957; Jackson 1957; Lidz* et al., *1957*.

centrally connected with social psychiatry but who have made indirect contributions to it should be mentioned. For example, Talcott Parsons, a sociologist whose principal interest has been in the theory of social systems, has illuminated certain aspects of the doctor-patient relationship through his analysis of the sociology of medical practice. *(Parsons and Fox 1950, Parsons 1951, pp. 425-79)* Parsons has also written extensively on the relation between social structure and personality development. *(Parsons and Shils 1951, Parsons et al., 1954, and Parsons 1958)* The comparative studies of the socialization of children in various preliterate societies made by Margaret Mead, a cultural anthropologist, have greatly increased our understanding of the relationship between culture and personality both in sickness and in health. *(Mead 1949, Mead and Metraux 1953)* Clyde Kluckhohn's clarification of the mutual influences between anthropology and psychoanalysis *(Kluckhohn and Murray 1953)*, and Florence Kluckhohn's theory of cultural value orientations *(F. Kluckhohn 1950, 1953, and 1958)* have helped to bring order into the confusing interpenetration of personality systems and cultural systems. Many others deserve to be mentioned from this point of view, but these are the social scientists that have most influenced my own thinking. *(For good reviews of past contributions to social psychiatry see Eliot 1955 and Dunham 1955. For reports of more recent collaboration between social scientists and psychiatrists, see Pollak 1956, Stanton and Schwartz 1954, and Leighton et al., 1957.)*

I must emphasize that this sketch of the field of social psychiatry is a purely personal one. The area is presently so loosely organized that it would be difficult to obtain consensus regarding what activities should be included within it. For example, I don't know anyone who calls himself a social psychiatrist — at least in public. It is a field without any active practitioners. It seems rather to be an avocation or research interest of people whose central professional concerns lie elsewhere.

The difficulties lying in the way of establishing social psychiatry as a separate field either of research or of therapy are considerable. As an area of research, social psychiatry is problematical because its lines of demarcation violate the inherently field-structured or transactional nature of human behavior. Whether in sickness or in health, human behavior is always simultaneously determined by biological, psychological, and social factors. *(Spiegel 1956b)* It is true that for research purposes this complexity must be resolved by emphasizing one set of determinants while trying to hold the others constant. But the sophisticated investigator is always aware of the potential influence of those variables which he is attempting to hold constant as best he can. I see no very good reason for calling research in this area social psychiatry. If this terminology were to be consistently followed, we would have to divide all mental health research into three parts: biological psychiatry, psychological psychiatry, and social psychiatry. While a case might possibly be made for this tripartite division on purely heuristic grounds, it would serve merely as a temporary expedient made necessary by our basic ignorance of the interrelations between these three sets of variables. Even so, I prefer the generic term, psychiatry, and would rather talk about the biological, psychological, and social *aspects* of disturbed behavior. The word "aspect" is a timely reminder that the research activity in any of these three subdivisions is determined by what the observer has chosen to look at, not by what exists independent of the observer in nature.

We stand on even shakier ground if we attempt to defend social psychiatry as a field of practice. It is true that adequate care of the mental patient requires that attention be paid to the environmental factors contributing to his illness. But the question then arises whether the treatment of the environmental factors should be turned over to one type of practitioner — the social psychiatrist — while the psychological factors are in the hands of a second, presumably the ordinary or psychological psychiatrist. Again it is possible to make some sort of case for this arrangement on practical grounds. It might be said, for example, that this is very like what happens in the usual outpatient clinic. There the psychiatrist conducts psychotherapy with the patient while the psychiatric social worker attempts to correct the behavior of significant people in the patient's environment. Doesn't this make the psychiatric social worker's function equivalent to that of a social psychiatrist?

The answer to this question, however, is a decided no. For the psychiatric social worker merely conducts a form of psychotherapy — now called "casework" — with the patient's relatives, employers, and so forth. Calling this practice casework obscures the fact that it is based on the same theory of disturbed behavior as is psychotherapy. The crucial point is that casework is not based on a *social* theory of disturbed behavior, and there is a very good reason why it is not. Such a theory does not exist. Social work and social psychiatry are thus in the same difficult straits: they represent applied sciences in search of a basic science which has not yet been developed. The difference between the two is that social work has had to meet the practical demands of its clients by elaborating methods based on ad hoc or borrowed concepts, piecing them together into the best possible working philosophy, while social psychiatry has existed in name only and thus has not had to face its impasse. To repeat, there are no practicing social psychiatrists.

The absence of a social theory of disturbed behavior is a painful and frustrating thing for all of us who are interested in this aspect of our patients. We lack the basic concepts which would enable us to perceive and describe the social dynamics influencing their behavior. We don't know how to detect the basic units of social behavior, much less the mechanisms and processes, the structures and functions characteristic of the social determinents. In their own disciplines the social scientists have not reached any consensus about these matters. There is no generally accepted systematic theory in sociology or anthropology, only a number of rival theoretical or anti-theoretical positions. They are still largely empirical sciences. This is not said in a captious spirit, since no field can be criticized for the slowness of its development, especially one so young as social science. Furthermore, psychiatry is itself not so strong in well-tested theory as to justify a raised eyebrow. Despite the many contributions which psychoanalysis has made to a theory of psychodynamics, the concepts which it has provided are vague and difficult to relate precisely to their behavioral equivalents. For this reason psychoanalysts tend to make empirical decisions in their practice but clothe them in theoretical-sounding language, so that the raw empiricism is not so evident. As a result of the present situation in both social science and in psychiatry, the outlook for constructing a social theory of disturbed behavior is fairly gloomy. The problem to be solved at the outset is this: how can the empirically derived concepts of social science be articulated with or translated into the concepts of psychoanalysis? For example, how can an empirically measurable concept like "group norms" in sociology or "cultural values" in anthropology be linked to a theoretical construct like the "super-ego" in psychoanalysis? According to psychoanalysis these group norms and cultural values are supposed to reside in the super-ego, but no one knows how to test this assumption.

Diffcult as it may sound, there is no reason to think that this problem is insoluble. For one thing, it has to be solved for the sake of the future development both of social science and of psychiatry. The need, however, is not enough. The particular obstacles lying in the path of progress must be correctly identified. In my opinion, one of the major obstacles is the problem of scale. Psychoanalysis and psychiatry deal with small-scale processes within the individual. Apart from what is called "small-group research," social science deals with large-scale processes in parts or the whole of the social system. I don't see how it is possible to bring empirical processes so different in the scale of the observational field into congruence with each other. It would be more sensible. I should think, to choose some middling process, one which intervenes between the individual and the larger systems. For this purpose I have chosen, as the empirical ground upon which to develop a social theory of disturbed behavior, the structure and function of interpersonal relations within small social systems such as the family and the doctor-patient relationship. The scale of the process in these settings is small enough so that it can be observed in terms of defined persons and their personality processes, yet large enough so that it can be related to the group and its social dynamics.

In addition to the appropriately scaled empirical setting, the solution of the theoretical problem demands the selection or invention of an empirical construct which is capable of mediating between the personality and the group systems, embracing both of them. Furthermore, it must be so intricately designed as to be able to catch the complexity, subtlety, and variety of interpersonal relations. I realize that the criterion of intricacy violates the usual prescription for the advancement of science by means of parsimony and simplicity of basic postulates. I would agree to these desiderata and to the search for simple and universal propositions (the laws of nature) which has been so effective in the natural sciences. I believe, however, that it is premature to conduct such a search in the behavioral sciences, for we do not yet possess the type of invariant unit one finds in the natural sciences. We have to wait for the discovery of such constancies before we can frame simple laws. Our problem now is to design concepts whose complexity and ambiguity is appropriate for the kind of observation and measurement which are within our technical means. It took, for example, many years for physics to reduce the ambiguous concepts of "force" and "space" to simple and measurable propositions. *(Jammer 1957a)*

None of the behavioral sciences has yet succeeded in systematically describing the things that people do, the actions they take in their everyday, intimate affairs. This arena has been left to the novelists and playwrights, as if science were forbidden to touch the materials of the arts. Many humanists actually dread the approach of science to what has been the stronghold of literature because they are afraid that scientific order can produce only sterility and disenchantment. That science may lead to deepening insight and a release of creative imagination is not as well understood as it should be. Psychoanalysis has illuminated the depths of the personality, and its inner motivations. The social sciences have revealed the grand design of social systems and have cast some light on the forces and conflicts which lead to change. And art has profited from both these advances.

It seems to me that the construct of *the social role* has all the attributes needed for this task. It has already been considerably developed in social science theory and has been used by a few psychiatrists to describe selected aspects of disturbed behavior. But the concept needs a great deal of elaboration in order to serve as a basic unit for the observation of interpersonal behavior. What I describe about the structure and function of social roles has grown out of the work I have done at Harvard with Florence Kluckhohn and a number of other colleagues in studying the impact of variation in cultural value orientations on the interpersonal relations within the family and on the psychological adjustment of the individual family member.

SOCIAL ROLE AS THE OPTIMUM UNIT OF INTERPERSONAL BEHAVIOR

At the outset, the social role concept, or any construct used for the description of interpersonal relations, must need four scientific criteria with respect to units of observations. First, it must represent a sufficiently discrete and observable unit so that it can be determined by operational procedures rather than by intuition. Second, it must be sufficiently broad and inclusive so that it can apprehend all behavior known to occur in intimate relations. Third, it must be sufficiently novel in its approach to raw behavior so that it can penetrate the stereotypes of common-sense observation and permit us to perceive forms of behavior not previously described or named. Fourth, it must be so oriented to the basic process of behavior as to yield a useful classification in terms of larger units or classes.

The psychological sciences such as behavioral experimentation, psychoanalysis, and psychiatry have, on the whole, proceeded in their work on the assumption that, though we know *what* we do, we don't know *why* we do it. The social sciences, on the other hand, have assumed implicitly that we don't know *what* we do; the actual forms of social behavior must therefore be investigated, described, and compared with each other, so that we can be certain that they occur, with such and such frequencies in such and such groups. The reason for this difference is that it is apparently much easier to collect data about the behavior of one person than about the behavior of large groups, and, in the end, we are all perfectly familiar with our own behavior as individuals interacting with other individuals. But I believe this is a fallacy. We are certainly familiar with our interpersonal behavior, but we have very little knowledge about it. We don't have sufficient knowledge to permit a classification of the forms and varieties of actions which occur in intimate relations. It is the kind of familiarity which breeds indifference. Most of us feel that we are so well acquainted with the possible combinations of events in social relations that we don't want to be hammered over the head with a classification of the obvious or trivial. But this would not be the first time that science has found it necessary to proceed with what is obvious, in fact staring us in the face, and yet strangely neglected. I would regard it as a sign that our knowledge, in contrast with mere familiarity, is increasing should we discover how to order the elusive and variegated events of interpersonal relations.

I am not sure that the social role concept can be constructed so as to meet all these criteria, but it does seem sufficiently promising to merit testing in order to find out what its limits of use may be. Similarly, I do not think that the collection of concepts I am about to describe under the general heading of role analysis constitutes the much-needed social theory of disturbed behavior. Rather, I look upon these concepts as useful steps in the development of that theory.

Although the words "social role" seem almost self-explanatory, they have actually been used in many different ways in social science. I have found the following definition useful. *A social role is a goal-directed configuration of transactions patterned within a culture or subculture for the functions people carry out with respect to each other in a social group or situation.*

The definition is designed merely to be as explicit as possible about the various assumptions built into the role concept. It is assumed that any role is directed toward some end and that this goal may be defined, simultaneously, from the point of view of the individual or from that of the social system. When we talk about the goal from the standpoint of the individual, we usually refer to this as his "motivation." Looking at the same behavior through

95

the eyes of the social system, we talk about its "function" for the social system or group. In other words, we assume that an individual would not undertake action in a social situation unless he was oriented toward some goal, either of gratification or of defense. At the same time, we assume that whatever he does is going to have some consequences, functional or dysfunctional, for the group.

The word "transaction" in the definition covers two major features of the social role. The first is that a role is an assembly or arrangement of actions. It is important to keep in mind the distinction between an act and a role. The distinction is analogous to the relations between atoms and molecules. An act, such as striking a match or sitting down in a chair, is not a role. Such single acts can appear in many different roles. There are literally thousands of different acts, and at the present time there is no way of classifying them except in terms of roles. The definition of the specific role, therefore, is always made through a description of the acts of which it is composed.

The second meaning of the word "transaction" covers the meshing or gear-like process of interpersonal relations. Any act of a person in his role must fit into the reciprocal and complementary actions of his role partners. No single person can hold a role apart from the complementary acts of his associates. Even if he wishes to take a solitary role, he must first get their permission to leave him alone (or else get lost). Reciprocal actions move people through their roles from the cradle to the grave and thus constitute the functional aspects of role systems. To get at function, one asks what fosters or interferes with the maintenance of complementarity in role systems. The role is thus the regulator and stabilizer of human behavior.

Finally, although social roles occur in all societies, there is wide variation between social groups concerning the way the same roles are to be enacted. The actual patterning of the role is adjusted to the value orientations of a total culture or subculture. The values of a culture determine not only what acts may or may not be included within a role but also who gets to have what role. All societies establish rules governing the distribution of roles among their members, since perfectly free allocation would result in chaos. For example, families emigrating from rural Italy to this country believe that children should be under the control of the family until their marriage and to a large extent even after marriage. Furthermore, they have a lively sense of the possibilities of evil outcome in human relations, particularly around the issue of sexual

96

behavior. On the other hand, middle-class American families believe that their children should become independent of the parents as soon as possible, and, if there is anything evil about sex, the child should be taught how to control himself. As a result of these differences in cultural values, the unmarried daughter of an Italian family is not allowed to have dates with a boy unless he has announced that he intends to marry her. And this marriage is usually arranged by the parents. If the parents suspect that casual dating is taking place, they become terribly upset. American middle-class parents, on the contrary, worry if she fails to get enough dates to be defined as popular and attractive. It is her job to get herself a husband, not theirs, and she might be failing this assignment.

Such examples show how the value orientations of a culture define the specific patterning of roles and govern the rules for the allocation of roles to various classes of persons. Roles form the structure or scaffolding of interpersonal events, but, as the above examples show, there are a number of different aspects to these structural elements. In order to see how the structure is put together, we have to be certain that we have isolated the various structural elements — the nuts, bolts, and beams, so to speak — as precisely as possible. If we can get these matters sorted out in a correct fashion, then we will be able to determine how all the various roles are related to each other in a general scheme of classification.

It is possible to distinguish six structural elements involved in the general classification of roles. The first element is the Goal Structure of the role. The Goal Structure is defined by the answer to the question: what general or specific function, for the individual or for the society, does the particular role fulfill? But since there are a great many particular roles, a classification scheme requires some abstract grouping of the varieties of functions which can be found in any social system. These groupings may be formulated in terms of three abstract categories: (1) the formal characteristics of goal structure, (2) the general or specific ordering of roles within the formal characteristics, and (3) the class of roles assigned to each of the orders (Table 1).

The second structural element is the Allocative Structure of the role. This category refers to the general rules governing the distribution of roles in the social system. The Allocative Structure varies with the order of roles within the Goal Structure. Again I would like to postpone discussing the correlation between Allocative and Goal Structures.

The third element is the Value Structure of the role. As I have

TABLE 1

General Classification of Social Roles

Goal Structure			Allocative Structure
Form	*Order*	*Class*	*Type*
FORMAL	Biological Roles	Age, Sex Body Management	Ascription Legitimation
	Semi-biological Roles	Ethnic, Class Domestic	Ascription Legitimation
	Institutional Roles	Educational, Esthetic, Occupational, Religious, Intellectual, Political-economic, Recreational	Achievement Validation
INFORMAL	Transitional Roles	Sick, Dead, Mourner, Criminal, Traveler, Visitor, Guest, Host, Stranger, Messenger, Friend, Enemy, Exile, Scapegoat, Leader, Follower, Informant, Interviewer, etc.	Adoption Assignment
	Character Roles	Hero, Villain, Fool, Weakling, Prankster, Sadist, Masochist, Exhibitionist, Liar, Seducer, Victim, Rescuer, etc.	Adoption Assignment
FICTIVE	Mythological Roles	Gods, Spirits, Ghosts, Witches, Dragons, Super-Men, Poltergeists, etc.	Assertion Affirmation
	Imaginary Roles	Any of the above roles	Assumption Recognition

already indicated, cultural values govern both the particular assembly of acts within the role and the variation in the rules for allocating roles to individuals within different societies. In some of my own research, I have been using Florence Kluckhohn's theory of variation in cultural value orientations *(F. Kluckhohn 1950, 1953)* to describe the interplay between Goal Structure, Allocative Structure, and Value Structure of the role. Because this scheme is quite complex and because it is described in Chapter 4, I will omit detailed discussion of it here but will refer to it from time to time when giving illustrations of the method of role analysis.

The fourth category of structural elements is the Technical Structure of the role. This is perhaps not the most apt way to refer to the degree of agreement between people about the way the role should be carried out, but I have been unable to think of a better one. The fact is, however, that some roles exist in a clear, definite, and unambiguous form, while others are quite hazy and badly grasped by the actors in a social situation. In the latter case, the difficulty in knowing how to perform the role may have several causes. (1) The role may have been newly elaborated within the social group, and there may not have been time for it to take a stable and definite form. (2) The role may be a traditional one subject to modification in the process of social change. Roles that are undergoing rapid change of form under the pressure of changing or conflicting cultural values are always technically ambiguous. This currently distinguishes parent-child roles in American middle-class society. The great number of how-to-do-it publications concerning parent-child relations is a sign that no one really knows how. (3) The role partners may have encountered a new version of a role they had previously learned under other circumstances. This occurs routinely in the course of horizontal or vertical mobility. Immigrants, for example, have to learn the American version of many of their formal roles, and this quite frequently produces technical confusion. When the roles they are trying to re-learn are themselves ambiguous, the resulting strain is intense. (4) The roles may be unfamiliar to the participants because they have not experienced them before in their life cycle, as in sickness or in the aging process. This is, of course, the general point: when new roles have to be learned for any reason, their Technical Structure is apt to be shaky at first.

In fifth position is the Biological Structure of the role. This category is concerned with the fact that roles are fashioned within the social system for the biological characteristics of its members.

Such organizations as G. K. Chesterton's League of Red-headed Men and various Fat Men's Clubs, Tall Girls' Clubs, and Alcoholics Anonymous — as well as the old wheeze that "Gentlemen Prefer Blondes" — are extreme examples demonstrating that the biological characteristics of the role partners may be the dominant structural element in a role. Usually, the Biological Structure plays a more subdued part in the organization of a role. While short boys will probably not compete for positions on their school's first-string basketball team, they can still play basketball.

Finally, every role is organized, in part, on the basis of its Instrumental Structure. This sixth category deals with the fact that, civilization being what it is, roles can't be carried on without the aid of a variety of artifacts — tools, equipment of all sorts, clothes, uniforms, eyeglasses, and other necessary facilities such as money!

THE CLASSIFICATION OF SOCIAL ROLES

I regard the isolation and detailed description of the various structural elements as a problem in the taxonomy of social roles. The implied reference to taxonomic systems in biology is more than an analogy. In biology, some method and system of classification had to be found in order to determine how the varieties of animal and vegetable life were related to each other. Before the invention of the binomial system by Linnaeus, there were many different ways of naming animal forms and of approaching the problem of morphology. None of them had succeeded in bringing order into the descriptive system. The biologists of the 17th and 18th centuries, however, had one strong advantage over the social scientists of the 20th century. This was the museum as an institution for preparing and inspecting animal and vegetable forms. In their anatomical museums, the biologists could mull over the dead specimens, even though somewhat distorted, comparing these with each other in order to discern the hidden design of organic forms. Contemporary social scientists have lacked both the museum and the specimens. There have been no systematic and scientific methods for preserving specimens of behavior. It is true that an enormous and unused collection of specimens of human behavior lies ready at hand in the body of world literature — preserved by the observing and recording activity of the novelists, poets, and dramatists. But social scientists feel uneasy about using this material, for they are uncertain of its relation to "real" behavior. In addition, motion pictures, tape recorders, and other devices are beginning to make another kind of recording and storing of actual behavior possible. But the problem of apprehending the specimen of behavior and of preserving it remains to be solved through technical development.

I believe that these six structural elements can be used for taxonomic purposes. But they are all quite complex categories, and it is therefore difficult to see how to use all of them in constructing the classification system. This problem can be simplified by breaking it into two parts. The first part consists in establishing a General Classification of Social Roles, using only the Goal and Allocative Structures. This produces a scheme which has general applicability in any social system but gives little detail about the variations between roles when one social system is compared with another. For comparative purposes, then, one would have to construct a Special Classification of Social Roles, using all six categories. Since this is a much more complicated and time-consuming task, I will confine my discussion here to the General Classification. It should be said, however, that role analysis in any concrete context requires use of the Special Classification which distinguishes that particular context.

FORMAL ROLE CLASSIFICATION

If we now turn our attention to the general classification of roles (Table 1), we see that the formal roles are divided into the Biological, Semi-biological, and Institutional Orders. Formal roles embrace the fundamental issues of any social system. They concern those matters of behavior which, because the organization of the total society is based upon them are never taken lightly. They are also the most general roles in the social system in that no single member of the society can escape their implications. We always occupy our formal roles; there is, so to speak, no exit except through death. In the Biological order, for example, we are always occupied with the details of our age, sex, and body management roles, whether or not we are conscious of this. Let there be any deviation from the standard way we are supposed to handle our bodily functions as middle-aged men or women, then this becomes immediately noticed and arouses strong feelings, usually negative. Of course, all roles involve the expectations for behavior in accordance with one's position in life, but in the case of biological roles the expectations are implacable. There is little or no leeway for variation or spontaneous exemption from the universally ascribed behavior. For this reason the type of Allocative Structure associated with the Biological order is ascription. This means that there is no question of individual decision in the way these roles are taken — at least not from the point of view of the social system. Some individuals may — and indeed, as we know from our psychiatric practice, often do — protest, consciously or unconsciously, about this ascription. They may not want to occupy the age role expected of them for their years, but, as in psychological regression, may long for a much younger one. But, if they try to take — or, as we would say in the language of psychodynamics, "act out" — the younger age role, they will encounter strong disapproval from their role partners.

It will be noticed that the Allocative types are set up in pairs. This formulation is established in order to take account of the reciprocal nature of role behavior. Whatever allocative basis Alpha acts upon involves some form of agreement from Beta and Gamma. For example, if Alpha decides to act out his wish for a regressed age role, Beta and Gamma have to decide what to do about it. As his partners in the role system, their own age roles are suddenly being impinged upon. Should they take the part of an older person to the infantile behavior of Alpha? Or should they indicate their reaction to Alpha's violation of the ascriptive structure by telling him to act his age? If they take the first line of action, or if they mask their inner feelings and do nothing, then they have *legitimized* Alpha's behavior. For we all continually legitimize (or illegitimize) each other's behavior in our Biological roles.

The Semi-biological order, like the previous one, is concerned with the biological underpinning of social behavior, but only in part. Kinship, ethnic, and class roles are also in part semi-institutional roles. For example, everyone is born into an ethnic or class group because of his family's location in these structures. This is his biological point of departure in life, but it is subject to considerable variation from society to society. For example, in American society it is not strictly accurate to say that class roles are universally allocated by ascription. A lower-class person may rise in the system, if he has the skill to climb up through his occupational roles. This example of an achieved role from American society demonstrates the danger of taking this general classification too literally, since only a special classification involving the value structure of American class roles could accurately describe the situation. However, even should the working-class person rise in the system, he might have difficulty bringing his Biological roles, such as body management, into accord with his new position. Changing one's class role is difficult enough, but not so hard as changing one's accent, facial expression, and manner of gesturing. These same considerations apply to ethnic roles and to most kinship roles.

Institutional roles need little comment here, since they are the best known and most widely studied of all the social roles, at least by American sociologists. They constitute the work-a-day world of performance and successful or unsuccessful activity. The principal point to be made here is in connection with their Allocative Structure. These roles are taken by achievement. There is no universal expectation that an individual must occupy an Institutional role, but if he wishes to, he must earn his right to it. He must obtain a license, a diploma, or some form of ceremonial recognition of achievement. Reciprocally, in taking their roles vis-à-vis this individual, his role partners validate his right to the role on an achieved basis. Invalidation results in the individual being dismissed or excluded from an Institutional role.

It will be seen that, as one goes down the list of Formal roles, the roles proceed from a more general to a more specific level. Because we always occupy Biological and Semi-biological roles, whereas we may or may not occupy Institutional roles, the latter exercise a controlling influence over the former. For example, women may be excluded from some parts of the occupational system on the basis of their sex role; and even when they are admitted, the patterning of roles between the sexes continues to structure the way people behave in their occupational roles. This point was made some years ago by Florence Kluckhohn, and she is responsible for most if not all of the issues I have discussed in relation to Formal roles, including the descending arrangement within the classification scheme. *(F. Kluckhohn 1961)*

Secondly, it should be stated that the distinction between ascribed and achieved roles was originally made by Ralph Linton. He did not develop the Allocative Structures in such detail as I have attempted for this classification scheme, but his formulation of the relation between roles, total societies, and individual behavior has greatly influenced my own thinking. *(Linton 1936)*

Lastly, I should like to make the perfectly obvious point that this scheme proceeds only to a certain level of abstraction in the classification of the Formal roles. For example, it would take a volume to report in detail on the large number of particular roles falling within the occupational and religious classes. However, such a breakdown can and should be worked out for the Special Classification within a concrete social context.

INFORMAL ROLE CLASSIFICATION

With certain exceptions, the Informal roles have not been so widely studied by social scientists, and I must take either the credit or the blame for the breakdown of the order into Transitional and Character roles *(Spiegel 1956a)* Whereas Formal roles are assembled within the social system into much larger units such as organizations and institutions of all sorts, the Informal roles are confined for the most part to small groups. Certain of the Transitional roles, in American society, it is true, have gained institutional status, such as those of the sick and of criminals. But this is because Western societies have undergone such tremendous internal differentiation. Guests, hosts, visitors, and strangers, on the other hand, have retained their informal status. Transitional roles are designed to transport the individual from one social situation to another. This is what is behind the saying "A friend in need is a friend indeed," since what are friends for if not to help when the individual is in trouble. It may sound strange to talk about the roles of the dead in the same context as friends and enemies, though not to those familiar with Freud's writings on the subject of death. *(Freud 1913)* But it is a fact that every culture has elaborated complex roles for the dead and has patterned the behavior of their role partners, the mourners.

Character roles are not usually treated as roles at all but are counted as traits of the individual. This is logical enough if it is realized that traits represent the static designation for behavior which the individual expresses in his relations with others. I think it preferable to talk about such types of behavior as roles, since this method of description requires designating the reciprocal responses of role partners. Being static, traits inevitably suggest that the behavior is somehow *in* the individual — a property or quality of the personality. The more dynamic description as role behavior reminds us that a trait is merely a way of responding to others which the individual may or may not manifest in action. Every sadist requires his masochist as a role partner. If he doesn't find one, his cruel behavior will be turned aside or neutralized in some way so that he will no longer be able to enjoy it. Every hero requires his admirer, every voyeurist his exhibitionist.

To put matters of character formation in this way has the advantage of calling attention to the fact that behavior must originally have been learned, through the usual processes of conditioning, in interpersonal relations. We all know that this is true, but we tend to forget or deny it — probably because we have been taught to organize our thinking around the concept of "personality" and all that it includes in the way of internal drives and defenses. This can easily make us think that the spectacular machinery of the personality somehow got assembled by itself under the magnetic play of internal forces. But if character traits are also roles, then they are subject to the usual rules of allocative structuring. The social system must exert some control over the issue of who has the right to what Character role. In the case of Informal roles generally, allocation is on the basis of adoption-assignment. This is to say that so far as the social system is concerned, anyone is free to adopt a character role if he can successfully assign the reciprocal role to a role partner. Let us take the case of the exhibitionist, not the overt sexual variety but the individual who always expects to be the center of attention. As he adopts this role, he assigns his associates the reciprocal role of voyeurist, since they are literally expected to keep their eye on him, not on others. However, things may not take place so smoothly for our exhibitionist, since his intended role partners have the right to accept or refuse this assignment. If they refuse to look, he is deprived of his role and has to search elsewhere. Now if we ask the question of his motivation — why should he want to adopt this role? — we can answer in terms of the purely intra-psychic situation. We can describe his partial sexual fixation at the phallic level and allow for the influence of his castration complex. I would not quarrel with this description, but it is not enough. For we would discover, if we looked into his childhood background within his family, that his mother or father, or perhaps both, enjoyed looking at his body, particularly his genitals, although they refused to admit this to anyone, even themselves. This would signify, in the language of role analysis, that they implicitly adopted the role of voyeurist and assigned their son that of the exhibitionist. Children are hard put to refuse such role assignments, not only because of the libidinal gratification they entail, but also because of their position with respect to the technical structuring of roles. So far as they are concerned, their parents are the arbiters of how they are to take their roles, at least until the age of disillusion sets in. A further difficulty for the child in this case arises from the refusal of the parent to admit his role behavior. If the child were to protest, the parents would deny their part in his behavior. Such masking of implicit roles is a functional aspect of role behavior, to be discussed subsequently. But I would like to point out here that it is intimately connected with the development of pathology in the child.

THE CLASSIFICATION OF FICTIVE ROLES

Finally we turn our attention to the Fictive roles. Here, again, I must take responsibility for their formulation in the classification scheme. On this point, I would like to say that I regard the arrangement of Informal and Fictive roles as highly tentative and subject to change without notice. I am dissatisfied with many of the features of the classification of these two forms and am proposing them mainly as a basis of discussion.

One of the unsettled questions about the classification scheme is that it seems quite likely that there is a causal or perhaps evolutionary relation between Formal, Informal, and Fictive roles. There is some likelihood that Informal roles grow out of strains in the Formal role systems, and that Fictive roles are generated by strains in the Informal roles. At any rate, it is clear that considerable strain exists in every society around the Informal roles and that every culture has elaborated ways of escaping from this difficult reality by the creation of a set of roles not known on earth or in this life or in the life of the particular individual. Such roles are created in fantasy because reality has proved too difficult. Freud provided us with some of his most illuminating insights in his writings in this area. (Freud 1900) Supernatural roles, the creatures of illusion, are provided to explain the unexplainable and to resolve the chief conflicts of a culture in some rough and ready way, no matter how distant from the testable world of reality. They are important to the issues of role analysis not only because of their illusory function as solutions for the problems of a society but also because they organize the behavior of individuals, insofar as they inspire belief.

The question of belief brings us to the issue of the Allocative Structure of Mythological roles. The question of how mythological figures such as gods, spirits, ghosts, and witches claim their right to their roles is a tricky one, inasmuch as they are inventions of the human mind rather than tangible, real beings. However, the human mind is infinitely resourceful, and it has thought of a way out of this impasse. For these figures are given the right to assert their claim to their roles. Gods thunder and shake the earth, spirits, such as Satan, intrigue and cajole, ghosts terrify, and witches work magic in order to convince the frequently resistant human being of their rights to their roles. Whether convinced or not, their human role partners are given — at least in some societies — permission to affirm or deny such rights.

Imaginary roles are the more important of the two fictive categories to the issues of psychotherapy and the doctor-patient relationship. So far as I know, they have scarcely been studied by sociologists and anthropologists, but they deserve to be, because they are definitely patterned by social interaction. By an Imaginary role, I refer not to a private and unexpressed fantasy but to the provision made by every culture that an individual may, under certain circumstances, take a role that is not his own or is not suitable to him in terms of the usual Allocative Structure of that role. Thus Imaginary roles occur in situations of legitimate pretense, as in play, in effects and performances produced for dramatic impact, or in any staged and artificial context. For example, a five-year-old child playing with her doll in the presence of her mother may pretend to be the mother of the doll. A "mother" falls into the kinship class of the Semi-biological roles, and it would be illegitimate for a five-year-old to take this role on the usual allocative basis of ascription. However, the child can get away with being a mother on the basis of pretense, by indicating to her elders that the role is merely taken by assumption. Assumed roles are always held at some reasonable distance from "reality"; they are half serious, half playful imaginative versions of a reality to which the individual can't lay claim at the moment, for one reason or another. In assuming a role, an individual has the right to take any role he may wish for. Therefore we can't list representative examples of Imaginary roles in the classification table.

When one person assumes an Imaginary role, his role partners have several choices of allocative response. For example, the mother of our five-year-old child may simply subscribe to the assumption of role that has taken place and comment from time to time on the way the playful activity is going, without entering into the play herself. This recognition on the part of the mother of the meaning and value of the child's playful actions is, of course, highly important to both child and mother. In a moment, I am going to comment on the analogous structuring of roles in the therapist-patient relationship. But right now, I want to point out that the mother has two other possible responses. First, she may assume a role herself and enter directly into the child's play. For example, if the child is assuming the role of "mother" to her "sick" doll, the actual mother may assume the role of "doctor" or "nurse" and carry out the game to some mutually satisfactory endpoint. On the other hand, she may not only refuse to enter into the play but may also become upset at the child's assuming a role in this fashion and may attempt to discourage or forbid it. This is not so likely to happen in the case of doll play, but we have noticed in our study of the families of emotionally disturbed children how often the parents can misunderstand the allocative basis of their child's roles. In some cases they fail to see that a child has assumed an imaginary role, and so they treat the playful behavior as if it belonged to an achieved or adopted role. In this event, the parents become indignant at the supposed infraction of proper and reality-oriented behavior. In other instances, the parents treat unacceptable achieved or adopted roles in the child as if they were assumed. This means that seriously disordered behavior is treated as if it were merely playful and not to be taken seriously. In either case, the child's orientation to his own inner identity is misdirected. We have seen children so confused about the difference between Formal, Informal, and Fictive roles that they either sat frozen in the therapeutic interviews, afraid to play at all, or else treated everything that happened as if it were a game or fantasy. In such cases the allocative roles have to be lived through and re-learned in the therapeutic situation.

I would like to emphasize that Imaginary roles are not to be confused with the inner fantasy life of the individual. They are a socially acceptable way of acting out an inner fantasy, but there the connection stops. It is important to keep in mind that role analysis in general has as its subject the things that people do in transaction with others — their external behavior — and thus is not directly pertinent to the inner fantasy life. It is true that the *content* of a fantasy may be analyzed in terms of its role structure. But the *dynamics* of a fantasy — its function for the psychic integrity of the individual — is a topic not for role analysis but for psychoanalysis.

ROLE STRUCTURE IN THE THERAPEUTIC SITUATION

As we all know, psychotherapy moves through a succession of stages, and it is this matter of the stage of relations between therapist and patient that I would like to translate into the language of role analysis.

The relationship begins with a complementary arrangement of Formal and Informal roles. The therapist's role is in the Institutional order (occupational class), taken on the basis of an achieved Allocative Structure. Diplomas and license on the wall, the therapist sits in his office in the midst of his occupational instruments: desk, telephone, chair, couch, writing pad, and tape recorder. He presses a button on his desk to signal his occupational role partner, the secretary, that he is ready for his next appointment. In walks someone he has never seen before; let us say a Mr. Antrobus. Who

108

is this Mr. Antrobus? Under what label does he gain admittance? Possibly he is a stranger, possibly a visitor, perhaps even a patient? These are all Transitional roles, indicating the impermanence of the approaching relationship — whatever it may turn out to be. If Mr. A. is a potential patient and someone whom the therapist has never seen before, then his actual status as a patient is something that has to be established and agreed upon between the two of them. However, that Mr. A. comes at all shows that he has adopted a sick role and is validating — for the time being at any rate — the competence of the therapist. For, after all, he might have been very ill for months while refusing to admit it — that is, refusing to adopt the sick role. Still, the confirmation of his right to the sick role is withheld until the therapist accepts the complementary role which Mr. Antrobus has assigned to him, by agreeing that Mr. Antrobus is sick and in need of treatment by him. This is the take-off point for therapy. The therapeutic contract is now in force.

Long before this point has been reached, however, other Transitional roles have slipped into the role structure. As an interviewer, the therapist has had to extract case history details from Mr. Antrobus, the informant. Mr. Antrobus has also found himself responding to some extent to the therapist's friendly interest — so perhaps he has found a friend. In addition, at times Mr. Antrobus has led the conversation, at others the therapist has changed the subject. So both the friendship and leader-follower roles have been characterized by an exchange of roles, between therapist and patient.

The mutual accommodation in all these Transitional roles may not be too uncomfortable for either partner, but once the therapy begins, something new enters the picture. Soon Mr. Antrobus discovers that he has told practically everything he knows about himself to the therapist, and now he doesn't know what he is supposed to be doing. He is having trouble with the technical structure of his role, and so he asks the therapist for guidance. The therapist finds himself assigned to two new Transitional roles: advisor and teacher. He may or may not be chary of accepting the advisor role — depending upon his view of the patient's psychological condition — but he can ill afford to refuse the teacher's role. For there is no reason to suppose that Mr. Antrobus knows how to respond in the role of a patient in psychotherapy, no matter how many books he has been reading about it. He needs to be instructed about how to proceed, either implicitly or explicitly. Realizing this, the therapist relieves, at least in part, the patient's discomfort by instructing him to talk about whatever comes into his head, to feel free, to recount a dream, or to supply a missing piece of information about his past life. Whatever instructions the therapist gives should, in addition, be appropriately oriented to Mr. Antrobus' value structuring of his Biological roles. Since age, sex, and body management roles are the most pervading aspects of the way the patient presents himself in the relationship, the cultural orientation according to which they are patterned must be given detailed attention at all times.

Once past the normative hurdle, the role system is off to a good start. Normative difficulties can be expected to crop up again, but now they will increasingly be revealed as substitutes for some other snag in the role structure. The role system, accordingly, moves on to enter a wobbly phase in which it oscillates between the initial Formal and Transitional roles with which it began and a new set of Character and Imaginary roles which have not yet been firmly established. In this process, the therapist plays a prominent part as teacher and leader. I realize that this statement is in contradiction to the so-called "passivity" of the therapist, but I have always considered his behavior as one of the most active forms of passivity imaginable. The fact is that the therapist shows the patient that it is possible to *assume* roles in his presence. By recognizing much of the behavior of Mr. Antrobus as a trying-on of various roles to see how they affect the relationship, the therapist gradually modifies Mr. Antrobus' awareness of his own activity. The name which we usually give to such recognition of the Allocative Structure of the roles in therapy is "interpretation." But there are many different kinds of interpretation. In my opinion, this word carries too much freight. To specify the Allocative nature of this sort of interpretation adds clarity and definition to the various kinds of behavior permitted to the therapist.

As the therapist gradually succeeds in transforming the patient's awareness of the Imaginary nature of his roles, Mr. Antrobus becomes more comfortable in displaying aspects of himself in behavior which had previously been reserved for fantasy. Since the therapist only rarely assumes an Imaginary role himself — that is, he seldom enters directly into the drama that is being enacted — Mr. Antrobus finds significance in the comments being made about the meaning and value of his Imaginary roles. At times, the comments the therapist makes arouse anxiety in him, at others he finds comfort in them. He may discover, for example, that if he wishes to take a regressed age role, he can; the therapist will neither scold him for putting on an act nor pretend that this is real behavior. Instead, he will comment on its possible meaning to him or to the patient. For this acting out in the Imaginary role structure is what we ordinarily call "the development of the transference neurosis."

Learning to assume Imaginary roles is a very difficult thing for the patient, and it is always accompanied by much resistance of a kind to be discussed in the next section. One structural aspect of the resistance, however, should be mentioned now. That is the patient's introduction of innumerable Character roles into the relationship. His ability to adopt and relinquish one Character role after another can mount in a kaleidoscopic and overwhelming fashion. He becomes, by turns, the victim, the hero, the fool, the rescuer, automatically assigning the reciprocals of these roles to the therapist. The therapist's job, during such interactions, is to dodge the assignments. He may occasionally accept one or two of the assignments if they happen to be true — that is, they represent roles which the therapist has previously adopted. Usually, he refuses the assignment, while patiently demonstrating the imaginary basis of these maneuvers. This is to say, in the ordinary descriptive language of psychotherapy, that the therapist admits his counter-transference activity when it is clearly affecting the patient, but this occurs infrequently, and for the most part the therapist interprets the patient's activity as a defense in the interests of the transference.

Imaginary roles dominate the relationship for a long period of therapy. Eventually, however, the role structure moves to a new, and terminal phase characterized by a return to the Transitional and Institutional roles with which it began. As the patient experiments with finding more appropriate roles outside the therapeutic situation, he is able to reduce the number of Imaginary and Character roles he takes in the therapy. The doctor becomes again just a doctor — friendly and hospitable, but not necessary to the role functions of the patient.

FOUR

Function of Social Roles

By way of preparation for contrasting the functional with the structural aspects of social roles, some general comments about the nature of structures, functions, and processes are in order. Such comments will be more cogent if we reflect upon the degree to which our insights reflect the linguistic patterns of everyday speech.

The English language is marvelously constructed for the purposes of art and literature in that it is so synthetic and symbolical. The same few words can signify a large number of different activities; the particular meaning of the linguistic assembly derives less from the words themselves than from their verbal or situational context. While this characteristic of our language gives great scope to the novelist, the poet, and even the advertising copywriter, it is, by the same token, not good for scientific purposes. Our English words do not stand sufficiently alone and still to yield stable analytical categories. This delinquency is all the more telling because, in the behavioral sciences, we have been unable to develop a special scientific vocabulary. We have shamelessly taken words from ordinary speech and have tried to give them a specialized meaning with our disciplines. I don't contend that this has not also happened in the physical sciences. The historian of sciences Max Jammer has beautifully described the scientific vicissitudes of such ordinary words as "force" and "space" in physics. *(Jammer 1957a, 1957b)* But I do contend that we are continuously being misguided in our efforts to develop improved observational techniques by failing to pay sufficient attention to the linguistic underpinning of the words and concepts we borrow so freely from our native language. We tend to rely too much on machine techniques and improved statistical methods to get us out of our observational difficulties. It seems to me that we would be well advised to pay more attention to the adequacy of our concepts, for machines and statistics can do only what man asks of them. They can't invent the categories they are asked to discriminate between.

We should be worse off with respect to the power of words to illumine or obscure were it not for the linguists such as Whorf and Sapir. They have shown how thought patterns based on unconscious linguistic patterns determine what we will be able to see — or "make out" — in nature. Our language is particularly given to making static, structural, or qualitative things out of processes. For example, we say "The weather is good" or "Tomorrow will be cloudy" as if "good" and "cloudy" were somehow qualities belonging to "weather" or "tomorrow." In French, one says "Il fait beau." "It makes good" at least indicates that something is going on, that weather is a process rather than a structural object with tangible properties. The perceptual bias is even more evident in our way of talking about events with longer time scales. For instance, we say "The table is red," indicating that for us red is a property of the table, a quality. It is almost impossible to shift this way of thinking out of gear unless we can learn to say something on the order of "The table is being red," "doing red," "making red" — or simply "reddening." In other words, "red" is as much an activity of the table as is "standing on the floor." In time the red may fade, and then we can say, at last, "It is fading," introducing process through the back door of the time scale.

Looking behind rather than through our linguistic screens, we see that structure and function are both aspects of process. When a process has a very long time scale compared to the span and tempo of human life, we are apt to notice it as a structure, because its form seems relatively constant and unchanging to us. Processes whose time scale is shorter and more condensed than ours appear less a matter of form than of flux and changing activity. From this point of view, structure appears as the static aspect whereas function is the dynamic aspect of the same basic process. Structure is a process whose time dimension has been cancelled, as when a motion picture film has been stopped at one point in its sequence. Form is action frozen in time.

These propositions seem quite plausible, but they do not adequately cover the relation of structure to function. For we all know that a structure exhibits a function. When the table is standing on the floor, its legs are holding it up. As structural elements, the legs maintain a supportive function. This activity on the part of the table's legs is something different from the functional activity within the legs which is simply another aspect of their inner process. How are we to bring these two types of relationship between structure and function into concordance?

The solution has to do with the relation between systems which are transacting with each other, within a field of activity. When we notice the relation between the activity of a subsystem and the larger system of which it is a part, then we call the activity of the subsystem a function. If we now shift our focus of observation to include the relation between this larger system and a yet larger segment of the total field, then the activity of the subsystem is described as a structure. For example, when we look just at the relation between the legs and the table-as-a-whole, we say the legs are supporting the table, that is their function, their contribution to the integrity of the system of activity we call "a table." If we now introduce into the field a human being sitting down at the table, then to the system of table-with-man-sitting-down, the legs become a structural item, which the man will do well to avoid hitting with his shins. At the same time, both the activity of the table as a whole and of the man in sitting down to it become functions of the field composed of table-with-man-sitting-down.

I have used the rather awkward illustration of man and table to make this roundabout point because, having got rid of animism in our thinking, we have gone too far in wiping all activity out of our awareness of objects. We have banished spirits, essences, and entelechies in a good cause, but we have gone overboard in making things appear to be merely passive objects of some external activity. In large part, this comes about because of the rigid and implacable subject-object form of the English sentence, and I often think that we ought to devote at least a half-hour a day in struggling against this major enemy of accurate observation. Students of semantics have long pointed out the dangers lurking within the friendly-seeming forms of our language *(See Korzybski 1958, Hayakawa et al. 1950, and Whorf 1941.)*

At any rate, the point is easier made in relation to less prosaic and more "scientific" subjects. Since Einstein's demonstration of the reciprocal relation between matter and energy, we have come to accept the proposition that behavior and substance are two faces of the same coin. We know that the functional activity of sub-atomic particles maintains the structure of the atom, that the physiological activity involving calcium, phosphorus, and protein transport mediated by the blood stream maintains the structure of bone, while the functional activity of the musculo-skeletal system maintains the structure of the body.

With this discussion as background we are now in a position to consider the relation between structure and function in role systems. The relationship is likely to be difficult to think through because of our habitual linguistic difficulties with thing-like objects. Just as our speech patterns rob so-called inanimate objects of goal-directed activity, so we don't know how to deal with pure activity except by making a thing of it. If we group interpersonal behavior into a role, then we begin to feel that it has become a thing — weighty, substantial, and wooden. The fear of teleology — connected, I suppose, with our not quite discarded animism — possesses us, and we tremble at the prospect of *reification,* the horrible suspicion that we have made something out of nature which is not really "there" and that we have imputed to it a set of functions which it doesn't really possess, except in our imaginations. This fear seems to me to be superfluous in that everything we know about nature has been manufactured, has been made up, and made out of our experience with it. Anxieties over the possibility of having constructed something out of our own heads apart from what exists in nature are futile. Rather, we ought to question whether or not we have manufactured something useful for ordering, predicting, and controlling the flow of events.

THE FUNCTIONS OF ACTS

Previously I described a role as being formed from an assembly of acts patterned according to cultural values so as to reach some goal in the social system. From this definition it would follow, in accordance with the foregoing discussion, that the function of the act was to maintain the structure of the role. Reciprocally, the effect of the role is to organize and maintain stability in the enormous repertoire of acts of which man is capable. These interrelations seem self-evident. For example, eating is a Biological role falling in the body management class. It consists of a repertoire of acts including such things as finding food, isolating what is edible,

115

manipulating the knives, forks, and other instruments required for these acts, chewing and swallowing, and finally cleaning the parts of the body involved in the process. Since it is a role and involves the complementary activity of role partners, all these acts must be timed to gear in with the acts of food preparers, food servers, and table partners. Now we are in a position to make a significant distinction. The occurrence of each of these acts represents a functional input which maintains the structure of the role. But the timing of the acts is not a function of the acts. It is a function of the role, and it serves to maintain the structure of the interpersonal system, or, as I would prefer to say, the role system. But timing is itself an act, involving a discrimination or judgment about the appropriate position of another act in a sequence of events. Thus we have to be prepared to encounter two different categories of acts: those which function in order to maintain the structure of the role and those which serve within and without the role to maintain the structure of the role system.

Before dealing with this complication in terms of role functions, let us return to a further consideration of acts themselves. If an act is to be considered a structure which functions to maintain the structure of the role, then it is fair to ask: of what functional system is the act a structure? What processes maintain its internal structure? But we have already established the existence of two different kinds of acts: those which serve to maintain the structure of a role and those which are in the service of the role system. The first category consists of concrete physical acts such as lifting, twisting, standing, chewing, or speaking — all of which come under the general formula "It's your move now!" Clearly, such acts are functions of the somatic process. The structures whose function maintains their integrity are neurophysiological and musculoskeletal. They fall under the purview of the biological sciences. On the other hand, the second category consists of judgments, di‹ criminations, thoughts, feelings, attitudes, impulses, and fantasi‹ about the place of a physical act in a role and the functions of a role in preserving the integrity of a role system. These acts seem properly to belong to the domain of mental function. They are topics in the disciplines of psychology and psychoanalysis. For acts which function to maintain the integrity of role systems also function to preserve the intactness of the personality. The two issues are only analytically separable. In behavior, they are intimately connected. From the point of view of role theory, however, the functions which maintain the structure of psychological acts are studied

116

by the methods and concepts of psychology and psychoanalysis. On the other hand, the way these acts function in the maintenance of role systems can be studied by the methods and concepts of role analysis. I hope that this formulation will help to make clear both the distinction and the connection between psychological and social systems.

COMPLEMENTARITY AND CONFLICT IN ROLE SYSTEMS

The role occupied by any one, isolated person has distinction and meaning only insofar as it functions in the maintenance of a role system. Role systems are somewhat fragile and unless properly maintained can easily come apart. When their structure disintegrates, we are more apt to notice the roles of which they were composed. Isolated roles are fragmented role systems. A role system which has broken down is usually replaced with another, so that the persistence of an individual in an isolated role is usually a sign of some disordered behavior. (Solitary roles are a special case, sanctioned by the social system.) Diagnosis of mental illness consists in large part of the specification of the isolated roles and role fragments, usually called "symptoms," displayed by an individual.

Because of the fragility of role systems, it is important to try to discern the functions which hold them together as ongoing processes. Unfortunately, this is extremely difficult because we don't yet possess the methods and concepts which are needed for a complete, detailed, and accurate observation of the functional aspects of social roles. However, certain preliminary statements concerning possible homeostatic mechanisms within the role system can be made. These mechanisms fall into three principal groups. First are those mechanisms based on the structure of the roles themselves. These will be discussed under the heading of complementarity and conflict in the role system. Secondly, there are a set of mechanisms which are brought into play when the complementarity of the role system is mildly threatened or reduced in the direction of conflict. These represent a set of normal adjustments within the role system which we will call role modifications. In the third group are two different sets of emergency measures which are triggered off when the conflict in the role system is high and it is threatened with complete disruption. These will be called role manipulations.

Before proceeding with the discussion of complementarity and conflict, it is necessary to define as precisely as possible what is meant by the expression "role system." As with the definition of a social role, the words seem self-explanatory, but precision is not so

117

easily arrived at. In the present state of our ignorance, a role system can be defined as the set of formal and informal roles occupied by two or more role partners in a group or social situation. Because of our ignorance, there are several vague aspects to this definition. For one thing, we don't yet know what are the limits to the number and classes of roles which can be included in a role set, although the sociologist Robert Merton is now beginning to determine these limits. Along the same line, we still don't know the upper limit of the number of persons who can be included as role partners within a single role system. It is obvious that above a certain number of partners the role system breaks apart and sub-group formation takes place. It is also clear that some role systems can contain more role partners than others, but we have little information on this source of variation.

Roles are fashioned within the social system so that the acts of the role partners form reciprocals of each other, somewhat on the model of the teeth of two meshing gears. To the degree that the acts of the role partners mesh with precision, the role system is well integrated and runs smoothly. Complementarity is a word that denotes the degree of meshing or integration in the role system, and it is a function of the degree of reciprocity between the roles of the two or more role partners. We don't as yet have a way of measuring either reciprocity or complementarity, but I hope that, as our methods of observation of role systems improve, we will discover techniques suitable for this purpose.

In a perfect world, all role systems would be characterized by the ineffable harmony that accompanies complete complementarity. Short of the millenium, however, the prospect seems dim. For there are too many sources of variation in the patterning of role structures. In order for absolute complementarity to be present, there must be exact reciprocity in all six of the structural elements of roles. The Goal, Allocative, Value, Normative, Biological, and Instrumental Structures must all fit together without bumps, grindings, or hitches. This would seem to be highly unlikely to occur, but something very close to it actually may take place in those situations which we call routines. In any highly trained team performance, whether on the stage, in the field of sports, or in the home, where the level of precision of reciprocal acts has been kept high through constant rehearsal, absolute complementarity may occur for varying periods of time. However, since this is a process which, to my knowledge, has not been systematically studied, I speak only on the basis of my impressions.

118

More directly pertinent to my own professional experience is the opposite situation. Because of gaps or discrepancies in one or the other of the structural elements of the roles, complementarity can't be maintained. As conflict increases, and the integration of the role system gives way to disequilibrium and potential disintegration, the behaviors which I have called role modification and role manipulation are evoked in order to avert the possibility of complete disintegration or rupture of the role system. The degree of conflict in the role system is a function of the amount of discrepancy between the roles in the system. Obviously, it is the inverse of complementarity. As with the latter, we have no way of measuring it at present but have to content ourselves with rough estimates.

In this connection, the more information we have about the role systems in any particular natural group gathered from systematic observation of the interactions of the role partners, the easier it is to form such estimates. I say this because I am not aware of any great amount of systematic observation of this kind. Small-group research in the fields of sociology and social psychology has contented itself, for the most part, with the study of artificial groups assembled for short periods in the "laboratory." Psychiatrists do not ordinarily study groups at all. Group psychotherapy is an exception which runs into the same difficulty that occurs in small-group research. The patients in group psychotherapy are artificially and arbitrarily assembled. The difficulty with all such artificial groups is that the participants have insufficient commitment to the role system. They have not chosen it spontaneously, and they know that the group will disintegrate shortly when its externally imposed goal has been reached. For these reasons, conflict in the role system may not evoke the full range of reintegrating mechanisms characteristic of the homeostatic process in naturally occurring groups.

The issue of the degree of commitment to a role system needs further elaboration. Up to this point, I have discussed the integrative mechanism in the role system only in relation to the reciprocity of the acts constituting the roles. But reciprocity is not the only cement holding the system together. It is a necessary but not a sufficient integrating principle. It is true, as stated before, that the goal structure of the role indicates the motivational element leading a person to enter a role. But the same goal could presumably be satisfied through the same role taken in a number of different role systems, composed of different role partners. In order to account for the tendency of an individual to persist in a given role system, and to undertake a variety of activities to prevent

119

its disintegration, we need the principle of the degree of commitment to a role system. This principle is another example of a point of articulation between role theory and psychoanalytic theory. In psychoanalysis, the same issue is dealt with under the concept of object cathexis. The degree and type of libidinal investment in the object accounts for the ego's resistance to separating from or relinquishing the object. In general, role analysis deals with the topic of object relations not in terms of the inner psychodynamics of the individual but in terms of its effect upon the processes within the external, interpersonal relationship. For this purpose, I prefer the transactional designation, role system, in place of the inter-actional description of the objects or persons or role partners involved in the relationship. The reason for this is that, as soon as the number of role partners involved in the relationship increases beyond two or three or more, the behavior of any one person becomes so intermingled with that of the others as to lose its independent force. It gives way to a field of behavior, and the descriptive problem can't well be handled by attempting to account, in turn, for the behavior of each member of the system. It has to be dealt with, descriptively, in terms of what is happening to the system of relations as a whole.

One further distinction must be made in regard to the issue of commitment. It is necessary to differentiate commitment to a role system from commitment to a role. In the latter case, the individual's attachment is not to his role partners in a given group but to the role activity itself. Here again, for the inner dynamics of this behavior we must go to psychoanalysis. Role commitment is an act which is pertinent to the issues of role analysis only insofar as it may lead to reciprocity or discrepancy between role partners and thus produce complementarity or conflict in the role system.

As with object relations, commitment to a role or to a role system is seldom a simple and uncomplicated process but is usually characterized by various degrees of ambivalence. From the point of view of role analysis, this ambivalence is significant because of its contribution to role conflict. In order to keep the inner, intra-psychic process differentiated from the external behavior which can be studied through role analysis, I think it is expedient to use a special and different terminology to describe the connection between unconscious ambivalence on the one hand, and, on the other, the unconscious conflict experienced by a person about what role to take in a role system. To this end, I have been in the habit of distinguishing the explicit role to which a person is committed

120

in the role system from the implicit role with which it is in conflict. An implicit role is one to which a role partner is actually committed but of which he is not aware. It is either opposite in character or incongruous with the explicit role that he is aware he is occupying. From intense study of role systems within the family, however, I have found that even this distinction between explicit and implicit roles doesn't cover the complexity of the way roles are delivered into the role system.

In attempting to construct operational definitions of the explicit or implicit status of any role in the role system, my colleagues and I have had to distinguish three different positions the roles may have in the awareness of the role partners. These are explicit, implicit, and equivocal roles. (1) Explicit roles are those which can be acknowledged by any of the role partners in each other's presence as occurring in the role system. (2) Implicit roles are those which the role partners can't acknowledge to each other or to themselves in any context. Nevertheless, they are present in the role system and clearly exert effects upon it. (3) Equivocal roles are those which the role partners can't acknowledge with agreement to each other when they are together but which they can admit as occurring when they are in another role system. For example, the wife in a certain Italian family was able to acknowledge to her therapist that she constantly criticized her husband, in most cases unjustly. In the presence of her husband, however, she denied playing the role of critic and substituted in its place the role of the victim of his supposed deficiencies. The husband, on the other hand, denied to his therapist that his wife ever criticized him, but he complained about her nagging, mildly, when with his wife. Thus both of these character roles were in equivocal status in the husband-wife role system.

Although both equivocal and implicit roles have complicated effects upon conflict formation and resolution, my purpose in discussing them at this point is to bring out one of their most prominent effects, one which any of the reintegrating mechanisms must deal with. This is the process of *polarization of the conflict. (See Spiegel 1956a.)* Because of the difficulty experienced by any individual in facing an inner conflict, and the temptation to get rid of it through the process of projection, as a discrepancy in the explicit role system increases, he may tend increasingly to impute his implicit role to his role partner. Now there will be two or more sources of conflict in the role system where previously there was only one. As polarization progresses, the role partner accepts the roles which have been imputed to him and projects his own implicit roles to the first person, who in turn accepts them. Thus the gap widens. This is the familiar process by means of which people or whole groups drive each other into increasingly exaggerated and untenable positions. What was formerly a predominantly shared, similar inner conflict has become a wide-open external rift, with each participant standing single-mindedly in opposition to the other.

While polarization of the conflict contributes to the apparent disequilibrium in the role system, it is not wholly harmful or dysfunctional. It dramatizes the wrong issues and calls attention away from the basic problem: the unresolved inner conflict of the role partners. Yet the postures it leads the participants to adopt are usually so preposterous and unrealistic that they are difficult to maintain and tend to break down of their own accord. At that point re-equilibrating mechanisms may assert themselves.

ROLE MODIFICATION

When the equilibrium in a role system is mildly disturbed by the presence of conflict, then the first group of homeostatic mechanisms — which I have previously described as role modifications — is likely to be brought into play. These acts can be considered as normal adjustments within the system. They consist of various approaches to the problem of discrepancy in roles which gives rise to the conflict, all which are characterized by maximum communication and exchange of information, in the sense of "Let's talk it over together." This spirit of "sweet reasonableness" appears in the context of role reversal — that is, the ability of the role partners consciously to identify with each other or at least to wish for such mutual identification. In plain English, in the face of a certain amount of disagreement, they try to understand each other's point of view. This is usually accompanied by a certain amount of joking with respect to their common predicament. The humor, however, is not defensive or designed to call attention away from the basic problem. To the contrary, it indicates that the role partners are not so heavily involved in conflict that they can't see its comical aspects. For role conflict always indicates an ineptness a lack of ability to resolve a snag in human relations. In the atmosphere of hope that the snag can be teased apart by the ordinary process of communication, the childlike but temporary difficulty appears laughable. The basic process behind the humor is probably that described by Freud (1905). The comedy arises from the quantum of psychic energy that is saved through the situation's being no worse than it is. For in the background lurks the possibility, experienced in previous situations, that the conflict might be insoluble, in which case it would be no laughing matter.

Talking over a disagreement can also be described as exploring the basis of the role discrepancy. For example, when a discrepancy occurs in the value structure of a role, it is likely to be obscure to the participants. There are several reasons for this difficulty in locating the actual site of disagreement. Cultural value orientations are themselves unconsciously built into the personality, and, without special training, we all have difficulty in becoming explicitly aware of them. They tend to masquerade as differences in personal taste, and appear to be unique aspects of the personality rather than widely shared attitudes. Second, one or several parties to the disagreement may have an inner conflict in value orientations, and this may make the admission of the difficulty, even if it could be accurately perceived, difficult. Third, cultural value orientations pattern the concrete act within the role, and it is much simpler to concentrate on the concrete problem while missing the rather abstract principles involved.

All these ramifications are condensed in the way such disagreements are often expressed: "Well, I don't agree with you." "People just don't do such things." "I never heard of anyone reacting like that." And so forth. This tone in the discussion frequently indicates that the speaker is trying to suppress an awareness of an equivocal role that in another role system he might very well take in just the same way. After a bout of flinging around such extravagant statements, in the course of polarizing the conflict, he may end up saying, "Well, to be perfectly honest, I guess I see what you mean; I suppose a person could react that way, but he shouldn't!" At this point the exploration conducted by the role partners has at last located the source of the discrepancy in their values. Further exploration may then permit them to pinpoint the value discrepancy through a discussion of the reasons each feels that the act in question should or should not be included in the role.

When the mutual exploring reveals that the discrepancy lies in the normative structure, and none of the role partners has sufficient information to decide whether or not an act is supposed to be included in the role or not, then they have to solve the problem by seeking some outside sources of help. Specification of the normative structure can be obtained either through consulting one of the many how-to-do-it publications or by bringing an expert consultant into the role system. Referral to a third party is, of course, the basis upon which any of the helping professions are able to intervene in an interpersonal problem. No expert services can be extended until the role partners have agreed among themselves, that, wherever the discrepancy lies, they don't possess the knowledge or technique needed for its solution. Just what expert will be consulted, however, depends upon the cultural values of the participants. He may very well not be a professional person but simply a friend or acquaintance whom the participants have confidence in.[1] However, if polarization of the conflict has taken place without being resolved, the expert may find himself serving not only as a consultant but also as a referee or judge of the merits of each position. Each party to the dispute appeals to him for support. Under these circumstances, it may be extremely difficult for him to avoid aligning himself with one or the other pole of the conflict. Of course, if this happens, the new role system will have turned into a coalition. This is a well-known problem facing all of us in the helping professions, particularly when we come into contact with families or some other group in which a patient is involved. Participating in a coalition may cause the conflict to subside in the sense that the polarization weakens, but it is likely to prevent the participants from examining the part that their inner conflicts have played in producing the external conflict. On the other hand, if polarization is allowed to subside of its own accord, then the role partners are more likely to find themselves facing the inconsistencies of their positions.

All these issues are found whenever a third party is called in or intervenes in a role system characterized by a polarized conflict. They are pertinent to the institutionalized forms of conflict resolution such as courts of law and arbitration and to the doctor-patient relationship in psychotherapy. In the latter case, the thera-

---

[1] In our family studies, my colleagues and I (*Spiegel 1957*) have found evidence that the type of consultant used for help with problems in normative structuring of roles varies with the class and ethnic position of the family. In the American working class, families of Irish background use priests, families of Italian background use doctors and neighborhood authorities, while Yankees deny having any normative problems of their own but comment on them in others. Middle-class families are well aware of normative problems and consult a wide variety of experts. We have had no experience with upper-class families. What is interesting is that none of these groups use the school teacher as a consultant for this purpose, and yet it is he who is socializing their children. The teacher is apparently not seen as a suitable expert by anyone. These impressions are based on a small number of cases. The topic would seem well worth studying systematically from the point of view of reference-group theory.

124

pist may find himself confronted with a choice of Transitional roles. Should he become a friend and partisan on behalf of his patient, supporting his views, taking his side against the other participants? The desirability of accepting these role assignments, which are always explicitly or implicitly tendered by the patient, may loom large, especially if the patient has been the "victim" of a coalition on the part of the others. In such a case, allying himself with the patient may seem to be the only way to neutralize or break up the rigidity of the role system which has been harmful to the patient. Or should he, rather, take the neutral role of counselor and interpreter, staying out of the conflict itself in order to help the patient, and ultimately help his role partners, to sort out the discrepancies in the explicit and implicit roles involved in the conflict? How the therapist will decide this issue will naturally depend upon many other variables — and especially the cultural values — present in the situation, so that no general rule can be given for it. However, both of these possibilities are loosely included in the vague psychotherapeutic technical jargon known as "being supportive" or "supporting the patient." These phrases are good examples of the evils attendant upon the common practice of appropriating an ordinary English word and attempting to give it a special technical meaning without giving thought to the nature of the interpersonal process the word is meant to stand for. "Being supportive" can mean either taking the patient's side in a polarized conflict or simply reversing roles with the patient so that he knows the therapist understands how he feels. But role reversal — the ability to identify with the patient's position within the role systems to which he is most intensely committed — is the *sine qua non* of psychotherapy. Without it no rapport or meaningful relationship can be established. Since it is so general to the establishment of a psychotherapeutic relationship, it should be distinguished from the many other roles and functions occurring in the therapeutic relationship, and particularly it should be separated from the practice of forming a coalition with a patient in the context of a polarized conflict.

In the usual course of role modification, when conflict formation has not been too intense and polarization has not occurred, the intervention of a third party as a consultant helps along the explorations already in progress so that ultimately the role partners are in a position to establish the compromise which will resolve the conflict. In role modification procedures, compromising is always the basis of conflict resolution. When prior polarization of conflict has taken place, or when the role manipulation techniques discussed below

125

have complicated the role conflicts, then compromise must be preceded also by conciliation and reconciliation procedures. These are all acts which function to restore complementarity in the role system, and it is a pity that we don't have more systematic information about them. We all know that conciliation and compromise are the way out of any complicated problematical issue — whether in the realm of international affairs, legislation, or interpersonal relations. However, they tend to become contaminated with value judgments and frequently acquire a bad name in contrast to such presumably sterling qualities (really acts) as "uncompromising," "matters of principle," "moral fibre," and others, insinuating that progress and fortune favor those who never give way. Compromise is probably the basis of all permanent social change, and it is the solution of the neurotic problems of the individual. Here a neurotic compromise gives way to a reality-oriented adjustment. But as psychotherapists we have concentrated so intensely on the conflict situation that, when the time of its resolution arrives, we heave a sigh of relief and pay little attention to the exact steps by which it is achieved. In this connection, a detailed knowledge of the processes of conflict resolution in mental illness would provide an answer to those critics of psychotherapy who claim it *merely* succeeds — if it is successful at all — in adjusting the individual to his environment and thus turns out another sample of conformity. The desirable outcome of psychotherapy is not a submission to the environment but a compromise with it, which needs to be kept continuously in repair.

ROLE INDUCTION

Although so little is known about the concluding steps of conflict resolution through role modification, one thing can be said. It results in a novel rearrangement within the role system. Each of the role partners has had to renounce some of his goals, omit or rearrange some of his acts, and substitute new ones. A new pattern emerges out of the old conflict (in a manner reminiscent of the Hegelian dialectics). This is the kernel of truth in the Marxian formula for general social change, and it applies as well to small-scale processes. It is the novelty and flexibility in the solution of the conflict that predominantly distinguishes role modification from role manipulations. The latter are designed to make the overt manifestations of the conflict disappear without effecting any fundamental changes in the underlying discrepancies which have brought it about. In role manipulations the partners attempt to manipulate,

126

persuade, or influence each other in such a way that either they don't have to face the conflict or else it gets settled in favor of one or the other contending versions of how the roles should be enacted.

Role induction is the first of the two groups of activities characterized by attempts to manipulate the roles. It consists of the various ways in which Alpha tries to get Beta, Gamma, and Delta, his role partners in the system, to pattern their roles in accordance with his version of the solution of the conflict. If his maneuvers are successful, the conflict will naturally disappear, since it is handled under the formula "Control or be controlled!" It is obvious that these issues are the ones usually handled under the concepts of power relations or dominance within the group. My quarrel with such concepts is not that they are inappropriate but that they are static and qualitative and thus are poorly designed to deal with the process on which the various positions in a power or dominance hierarchy may be based.

Since role inductions are techniques or strategies to gain compliance, they can be met with counter-strategies designed to resist or neutralize their impact. Such neutralizing techniques are specific for each induction strategy. They do not solve the conflict but merely prevent the particular induction technique from being successful, leaving the conflict about where it began. The neutralizing procedure is usually accompanied by some general complaints about being the object of role induction — which we ordinarily call "a protest." A protest calls attention to the fact that a neutralization is about to commence. Such "struggling" within the role system is characteristic of the regulatory processes by means of which a relative homeostasis is achieved.

The first role induction technique to be discussed is the familiar one of *coercing*. The colloquial description, "getting pushed around," can be given an operational definition. It consists of the manipulation of present and future punishments, in order to gain compliance. The punishments can range through such acts as physical control limiting freedom of action, physical injuries, or deprivations, either instituted on the spot or threatened in the future. The "threat" included in coercion can be delivered in a variety of ways, from vivid descriptions of what to expect to mere implications registered in the tone of voice. It would be helpful to know more about the process by means of which tone of voice becomes linked to threat, but we lack information about it and don't even know to what extent the process may be innate rather than learned. Coercing becomes institutionalized in the military, police, and legal systems, where it serves as a reintegrating mechanism for whole social systems. It is present informally in all situations of giving a command or an order. However, here one must be careful to distinguish that part of the order which is *merely* a prescription for action from the admixture of coercion which contains the message: any questioning, neglect, or failure to comply will be punished.

The specific neutralizing technique for coercing is *defying*. Defiance, as is the case with all neutralizers, implies no particularly emotional tone. It is merely a resistance or holding out against threat, which is often called "passive" or "non-violent" resistance. Since coercing usually stimulates various degrees of hostility in the role partners, defiance per se may be difficult to maintain, in which case it is replaced either with counter-coercion or submission. It is interesting, however, that patients who use defiance as a manipulator in the course of psychotherapy have usually experienced a great deal of coercion. For this reason they see therapy as a hopeless struggle for control in which they face the unhappy choice of neutralizing the therapist's power to help or else of submitting to it before they fully understand it and have lost their fear of it.

Coaxing is the next role induction technique, and it can be defined as the manipulation of present and future rewards. Offering gifts or blandishments, making promises of services or favors and the like are all designed to gain compliance through arousing and satisfying a need in the role partners. Many public relations and advertising techniques are based on this technique. Although it is said that one can catch more flies with honey than with vinegar, human beings differ from flies in having the ability to resist honey and other temptations. The neutralizing mechanism for coaxing is simply *withholding*. Children are expert coaxers, probably because of their low position in the family hierarchy, and frequently assail their parents with such rapid-fire heart-twisters as "Please, Mom, will you get me a sled for my birthday, please, please, please, PLEASE! I'll practice the piano every day for an hour if you do. Please . . . ." To which the mother may reply, combining protest with withholding, "Why do you keep on asking me when I've already said No twenty times?" The child who persists like this knows that his mother is potentially corruptible, and patients who coax persistently during psychotherapy are usually trying to find out whether the therapist, like the parent, can be bribed.

Another role induction mechanism is *evaluating*. This can be either positive as in praising or negative as in blaming or criticizing. As a process it entails placing the role partner in a class of rewarded or punished objects in order to gain compliance. Evaluations by the parent are internalized by the child and become the basis of much of his self-picture. It must be stated that not all evaluations are to be regarded as role inductions, since they may be made for other reasons. Alpha, for example, may ask Beta or Gamma for an evaluation in order to discover how his performance looks in someone else's eyes. Evaluating is institutionalized in the role of the art, literary and theater critic. It should be considered a role induction only when Alpha attempts to force Beta or Gamma to change their role performance in accordance with his prescription. In psychotherapy, patients almost universally impute evaluations of their conduct and personality to the therapist and make various attempts to get them confirmed. The therapist, however, seldom responds to such efforts by making an evaluation, since it is more important, especially at the beginning of therapy, to discover the origins of the patient's self-evaluation in previous or current role systems. In addition, if the therapist were to attempt to evaluate, the patient might very well respond with the specific neutralizing technique, namely *denying*. Praise as well as blame can be denied if it is suspected that role manipulation lurks behind it. Since patients have frequently been subjected to unrealistic praise and to cruel and destructive criticism, nothing is to be gained by the therapist's entering into such activity. There are, of course, exceptions to this rule. For example, there are patients who can enter into a relationship only on the condition that the therapist accept the role of critic, for it is the only role system to which the patient can commit himself. Such a patient knows only conflict. He experiences a harmonious role system as one in which there is no role for him. In such cases, the therapist has to "act out" with the patient, waiting for the conflict-laden role to depolarize so that other roles can be permitted into the relationship.

Negative evaluating is a complicated way of resolving a role conflict. For example, in order for Alpha to be successful with it, Beta and Gamma have to accept the criticism or blame, offer an apology or explanation, and make a promise to reform. Getting Beta and Gamma to do all these things may require Alpha to expend more and more energy, increasing the force of his criticism until his role partners are overwhelmed with guilt and shame. Gamma and Delta may even decide to form a coalition and conduct a counter-offensive campaign of criticism against Alpha. The question arises as to why Alpha should be willing to use up so much energy in such a complicated and frequently unsuccessful strategy when others are at hand. The answer to this question can be found in psychoanalytic theory and learning theory in psychology. For example, Alpha may not actually wish to resolve the conflict, either consciously or unconsciously, but may have an interest in prolonging or extending it. Under such circumstances even an apology will be accepted with bad grace. In addition, if Alpha has experienced evaluating as the primary mechanism of conflict resolution in his childhood, he is likely to find it easier to use than some other method. Finally, if Alpha has been dealing with an equivocal or implicit role within himself, by projecting it to Beta and Gamma, his efforts to control them represent in equal part an effort to control himself and to rid himself of an inner feeling of guilt and shame.

Masking is a fourth technique of role induction. The term refers to a method of avoiding role conflict by concealing the behavior which would precipitate it. There are many methods of this type, ranging from insignificant lies to evasions to the major triumphs of deception practiced by imposters and spies. Masking has deep biological roots, being found among all species characterized by protective coloration or some other method of concealing their presence from enemies or predators, on the one hand, and from prey on the other. Camouflage, whether for military or cosmetic reasons, is a form of masking. Masking is neither good nor bad, neither functional nor dysfunctional, except with respect to the availability of other methods of conflict resolution. J. B. Priestley's play of some years ago, *Dangerous Corner*, made the point that continuous masking was infinitely preferable to the unmasking of dangerous truths — on the model of "Let sleeping dogs lie." In T. S. Eliot's *The Cocktail Party* this moral point is reversed on religious grounds, and unmasking becomes the means by which the protagonists solve their dilemma. *Unmasking*, the exposure of what has been hidden, is the specific neutralizing technique, and when it is applied suddenly, the concealed conflict is likely to erupt with explosive force.

Masking and unmasking are continuously operative in the psychotherapeutic situation, for masking is the role system equivalent of repression. Just as repression consists of an internal instruction to deny the admission of a specific piece of information to consciousness, so masking constitutes an instruction within the role system that a particular message is not to be delivered to the participants. There are many subtle ways in which this instruction itself can be disguised. For example, when Alpha says to Beta,

"I just don't understand what you're saying," his remark may well mask the implicit message, "I don't like what you're saying. Please don't repeat it. Say what I want to hear, not what you want to say." If Alpha is a parent and Beta a child, after a few exercises of this sort Beta will unconsciously get the point and stop bringing up what his mother won't listen to. But, at the same time, Beta will not realize that masking has taken place. Instead, the banned topic will simply not occur to him in her presence. Thus masking is one example of an as yet unspecified class of "repressors" occurring in the role system. This process is reversed in the course of therapy. In conducting a gentle, low-pressure, campaign of unmasking, by judicious interpretation of what the undelivered message may be, the therapist shows the patient that any piece of information is acceptable in the role system. The gentleness of the therapist in stripping the patient of his defenses is achieved through the particular allocative structuring of his role discussed earlier. Since unmasking is always painful, even though helpful, the therapist can reduce the pain only by recognizing that the roles which are laid bare are not real or directly intended. In treating them as Imaginary roles and welcoming their assumption on that basis, the therapist legitimizes both the mask and what lies behind it, allowing the patient eventually to choose which he prefers. Left to himself, the patient will probably choose neither, since both are involved in the conflict which he has yet to resolve.

If masking and unmasking are so important in psychotherapy, does the role structure permit the patient to unmask the therapist? Patients often spot the pretenses of the therapist and on occasion attempt to unmask. There is no practical or theoretical reason that I know of why the patient should be denied this privilege. To refuse it would indicate that the therapist's mask is untouchable. Neither is there any reason for the therapist to admit the reality of what the patient sees behind his mask. He may do this and should, if what he thought hidden has actually slipped out. But he may have very good reasons for supposing that what the patient sees corresponds less with what he has concealed than with what the patient needs to find in him. In this case he needs only to disagree with what the patient attributes to him, not with the act of unmasking.

The final induction technique is that of *postponing*. This technique handles the conflict through avoiding it for the time being. For example, Alpha may say to Beta something like, "Let's not talk about it now. I'm too busy to argue with you. Go outside and play, and we'll discuss it when Daddy gets home." This sounds like an innocuous way of dealing with a conflict. But Beta, being a child, has a faster tempo and less patience than his mother. Besides, waiting until Daddy comes home has all the implications of a possible coalition. Having experienced this strategy before, Beta is likely to keep right on arguing in the hope of getting the conflict settled, even if this only provokes his mother. For *provoking* is the specific neutralizing technique to be used when confronted with a postponement. It is highly effective, and there is practically no way to forestall it short of direct coercion. Patients who are unusually provocative in the therapeutic relationship have probably experienced a rich combination of postponing and coercing in the past. They are expecting the therapist to try them both and are well prepared for the experience. The therapist can meet these intensely disruptive techniques only by doing everything possible to bring the underlying discrepancy in the role system to the surface so that it can be identified and possibly resolved in some way.

It is evident that all the role induction techniques come into play in psychotherapy just as they do in other role systems. I have called them emergency techniques because they are employed when conflict in the role system is high and anxiety among the participants has passed the level where role modification procedures are possible. Role modification is present as a regulatory or homeostatic mechanism only when conflict is at an optimum level and role reversal can still take place. In addition, role modification is a process that takes a long time, too long for the time span of many conflict situations. When the threshold composed of the time span, the level of internal anxiety, the level of external conflict, and the capacity to reverse roles has been passed, the regulatory mechanism jumps a step, and either role induction or role dislocation appear as ways of averting the disintegration of the role system. Nevertheless, it is important to emphasize again that role manipulations do not solve the conflict. When successful, they stabilize it so that some form of contact remains available to the role partners. Eventually, however, the conflict must be resolved through the role modification procedure. Without this, it will remain present (though hidden) in the role system itself and in the personalities of the participants.

ROLE DISLOCATION

Role dislocation is a process for avoiding conflict in a role system by rearranging the role partners' position vis-à-vis each other rather than changing the roles themselves. Participants in the system change

132

places with each other or trade off roles as a way of limiting the conflict without facing the issues involved in the role discrepancy. As a temporary expedient, such methods are often successful, but, as with role induction, the conflict remains buried and troublesome. What I have to say on the subject of role displacement has grown out of studies of interpersonal relations within the family, but it is only recently that we have begun to make any rhyme or reason out of these subtle shiftings, about faces, and unexplained gaps in the role system. They have proved difficult to perceive and to conceptualize, and I have very little confidence in the formulation of them presented here. It represents the best I have been able to achieve in the way of naming and classifying these elusive functional processes.

Role dislocations can tentatively be classified under three headings which seem to group together relatively independent variations on this general theme. These are role repudiation, role transposition, and role attenuation.

Role repudiation consists of processes in which one role partner tries to back out of a role to which he has been committed or attempts to squirm out of a new role assignment, leaving his role partners to deal with the situation. There are only three possible strategies open to the role partners in this event. They may try to prevent or forestall the repudiation. They may try to persuade someone else to accept the vacant role. Or they may have to withstand the deprivation if neither of the previous strategies are successful. When a role repudiation is about to take place, there is an increased amount of tension and struggling in the family. This tends to subside after it is determined which of the three strategies will crystalize out of the situation. With all the turmoil that boils up and around this process it is difficult to get a transactional or field description of the attendant events. To date, I and my colleagues have been able to settle on a description only of the second strategy. That is, we have located three different kinds of role repudiation in terms of the attempts to draft some other partner into the vacated role.

The first of these is *abdication-surrogation*. This designation applies to repudiation of a Biological or Semi-biological role. The word "abdication" was selected for this designation because Biological and Semi-biological roles to which one has been committed can't be abandoned without dire consequences. For example, a mother who abandons her child, whether in fact or simply by withdrawing from effective contact, not only disrupts the role system but also seriously harms the child, especially if no arrangement has been made for someone to take her place. In the cases where this happens, other members of the family or the child if he is old enough have to find someone to fill the gap, and it is to this relocation process that we have given the name "surrogation." The surrogate mother may or may not fill the bill, but she is probably better, in most cases, than no mother at all. However, a mother who remains physically a member of the role system but withdraws from contact with her child in a variety of more specific Informal and Imaginary roles may be described as showing partial abdication. It will be recognised that this is what is ordinarily meant by the expression "maternal rejection" or the so-called "rejecting mother." I think the description in role terms has the advantage of enabling the observer to describe the specific roles which the mother has renounced in the context of the patterning of the maternal role in the particular subcultural group to which the family belongs. This provides more objectivity and less observer bias in what has so far turned out to be a tricky and predominantly subjective judgment. It has the further advantage of enabling the observer to generalize his observations. In other words, abdication-surrogation can be studied within the family as it applies to age, sex, ethnic, class, and domestic roles in general.

The second sub-group under role repudiation is *resignation-substitution*. This refers to the same process as occurs in abdication-surrogation, but now confined to institutional and informal roles. It has seemed worthwhile to call the process by a different name for the informal roles because the consequences are so different. The different outcome is correlated with the type of Allocative Structure within the role orders. Because biological and semi-biological roles are ascribed, commitment to them is in deadly earnest and rejection of them is very serious. Institutional roles, however, are taken by achievement, and Transitional and Character roles by adoption, so that rejection of them is less disturbing. Where Institutional roles are concerned, resignation-substitution is an everyday affair from the point of view of the organizations which make up the educational, religious, occupational, and other spheres of activity. From the point of view of the family, however, the resignation may not be so routine. If the father gives up his job, the mother or someone else may have to take over the financial support of the family. If he renounces his religion and gives up his church membership, the mother will have to go to church alone or find some other companion.

For our purposes, the most interesting aspects of resignation-substitution have to do with Transitional and Character roles. Here the connection between the events in psychotherapy and the interpersonal relations within the family become most evident. For example, when, during successful psychotherapy, the patient gets ready to give up his sick role, it frequently turns out that the family is not at all prepared for this. If the patient insists on being released from his role as the sick member of the family, some other member of the family may often be induced to accept it. This "substitute" patient will then function so as to conceal from the other family members their part in the underlying role conflicts within the family which the sick ones have expressed. This is one of the reasons why treatment of the family-as-a-whole has some advantages over treatment of the individual.

The same processes can be seen behind the manipulations of character roles in the family. For example, in one family which we have studied it is important that Alpha, a child, play the role of clever fool while Beta, his brother, has that of simple-minded impostor. The first is reputed by his parents to get away with murder while acting innocently and charmingly stupid, while the second attempts to pull the wool over people's eyes but is too simple-minded to succeed. The first is explicitly scolded but secretly admired, while the second is explicitly pitied but implicitly scoffed at, badgered to change, and depreciated. Now, whenever Beta attempts to resign from his Character role by adopting intelligent and responsible behavior, and is partially successful, then Alpha's charming foolishness, which is usually treated as a clever mask, becomes a serious misdemeanor. When Beta resigns, Alpha substitutes in Beta's role, which is superimposed on the one he usually has. We were surprised to find that Alpha accepted this situation with his usual clown-like imperturbability. He said, smiling, "Now I'm in hot water, but by next month, he'll be back in trouble." This statement indicates a connection between role repudiation and role exchange, to be discussed below. Note the apparent immortality of a character role which functions to relieve a role conflict in a family system. Someone has to occupy it, or else the underlying conflict will break loose.

The third type of role repudiation is called *refusal-replacement*. It is applied to a Transitional or Character role which Alpha is attempting to get Beta to commit himself to, as a substitute for a role partner whom Alpha has lost. Thus it is coordinate with and necessary to resignation-substitution. Since Beta has not previously

135

been involved, he is free to accept or to reject the role assignment. If he accepts, then Alpha has found a substitute and solved his problem, though Beta may find that he has inherited one. This process is continuously in evidence in the course of psychotherapy. If Alpha is the patient, he will try to get the therapist to substitute for his lost or fantasied objects — or, in our terms, role partners. If the therapist refuses these assignments — as he will in the usual case — then the patient may seek replacements outside the therapeutic situation.

Role transposition, the second group of Role dislocations, contains two sub-groups, *role exchange* and *role displacement*. Role exchange occurs when Alpha and Beta trade roles with each other. This has often been called "role reversal." But I have used the expression "role reversal" to designate, in the words of George Herbert Meade, "taking the role of the other" — in other words, identifying with someone else. A different designation is required for the situation in which the role partners trade off with each other in actual fact. Role exchange can be a see-saw affair, the role partners trading back and forth continuously. In other instances, it is the basis of a permanent settlement of a role conflict. For example, a husband stays home, looking after the house and children, while the wife is the wage earner. As in the example of the two brothers just cited, role exchange frequently follows upon a role repudiation. The working wife, for example, may have had to take a job when her husband resigned from his occupational role.

Role exchange is frequently encountered in the doctor-patient relationship, not just in psychotherapy, but in general. The sophisticated patient, properly primed by the educational efforts of the medical profession, may attempt to make his own diagnosis and prescribe his own therapy. Since we all know that a little knowledge is a dangerous thing, the connection of this role manipulation with an anxiety-induced role conflict is obvious.

Role displacement is the second of the two sub-groups under role transposition. It can be described only in terms of a role system composed of three or more participants, since it seems to represent a complicated and tandem form of role exchange. Suppose that in the system composed of Alpha, Beta, and Gamma, Alpha has been taking an adopted character role to which Beta has been playing the complementary assigned role. In role displacement, Beta now adopts the role which Alpha had taken and assigns the complementary role to Gamma. Gamma, of course still has the choice of accepting or repudiating the role assignment. Alpha may or may not have resigned from and Beta may or may not have repudiated their original set of roles. For example, in a certain family of Italian background the wife had in her childhood experienced a Character role which, for lack of a better name, I will call the incompetent and unattractive child. This role was assigned to her by her mother, with the mother in the complementary role of competent critic. Because of the mother's induction techniques, the wife could find no way to resist this role assignment as a child. After her marriage, however, she put her husband into the role of the unattractive incompetent one and took her mother's role, the competent critic toward him. She copied her mother's induction techniques, which the husband found very difficult to cope with, although he never overtly accepted the role assignment. On the other hand, the wife's mother, who was still living, never repudiated her role as critic of her daughter. She now merely included the husband with the wife as another incompetent person. Meanwhile the struggle between the husband and wife revolved around the issue of who would get whom to take the incompetent role. At no time were they able to share such Character roles. That is, they were unable to say: "We are both incompetent in some ways and both competent in other ways." The unresolved role conflict which both had brought into their marriage from their childhood situations was too strong for a resolution through this realistic compromise.

Role displacements are central to many of the complicated shifting and defensive processes experienced by the doctor and patient during psychotherapy. During the development of the transference, the therapist is repeatedly asked to serve as a replacement for a lost role partner or as a displacement for a role position which the patient previously occupied, while the patient himself takes the role of one of his objects from the past. Untangling these transposed roles requires all the skill and alertness available to the therapist, plus a good deal of patience. The roles which have become crossed up, so to speak, require a long time to be teased apart.

Role attenuation is the last major group under role dislocations. At least three sub-groups can be detected in this division. They are *exclusion-reservation, segregation,* and *attrition.* What all these have in common is the impoverishment of the number and quality of the roles available to the participants in a role system. In exclusion-reservation Alpha tells Gamma that he is to stay out of a certain number of roles which he would like to take with Beta, the reason given to Gamma being that these are reserved exclusively for the

Alpha-Beta subsystem. This process is so general, not only in small groups but also between major groups in the social system, that it merits little comment here. Segregation is a very similar process which shows up only in a four-person or at least a somewhat symmetrical role system. Alpha not only tells Gamma to stay out of the Alpha-Beta relationship but in addition tells him to take these same roles with Delta as his partner. This process, of course, describes the issue of segregation between races and ethnic groups, but it is also seen in families. For example, in one of the families I have studied, composed of mother, father, and two sons, all the recreational roles and many of the domestic roles took place between father and one of the sons, while mother and the other son shared these same roles separately. We have become accustomed to describing such family situations by saying the father was close to one child, the mother to the other. But more than closeness is involved in this process, and in any case description in terms of role segregation has the advantage of requiring the observer to specify roles that have been segregated in the subsystems, as contrasted with roles that can still be shared within the family system.

Role attrition is probably not so much a process in itself as the outcome of a number of processes. When the role system in the family has been dislocated by a great number of previous repudiations, exclusions, and segregations, the number of roles which can be shared between the partners becomes so small as barely to sustain a relationship. What relations are maintained are exceedingly rigid and brittle. The fragility of role systems which I mentioned at the beginning of this chapter has under these circumstances become the crucial characteristic of the system. The potential conflict has invaded so many roles that the participants face the unhappy choice either of separating completely and thus breaking up the system or else of withdrawing further from each other while maintaining the mask of unity. Masking of this situation is such a strain to all concerned that it usually is associated with major pathology among the participants. Both Lidz and Wynne have commented on the presence of such impoverished role systems in the families of schizophrenic patients. *(Lidz 1958 and Wynne 1958.)*

I have not completed the description of the functional aspects of roles as they serve to maintain the intactness of the role system. I have unfortunately not been able to show, except through occasional hints and implications, how the analysis of the role system through the specification of role structure and function can be applied systematically to the pathogenesis of mental illness among the role partners. If this could be done, we would be well on our way to a basic science of social pathology, coordinate with our theories of psychopathology. However, this must remain for the future. In the meantime, I hope that I have been able to demonstrate that the concepts which I have called role analysis can be useful for the observation of the flow of events in psychotherapy which are so similar to the interpersonal events within the family.

Part III

Transactions in the Family

In this section the "value orientation" construct developed by Florence Kluckhohn is introduced. Spiegel's use of this theoretical construct is also dictated by transactional considerations. It makes possible the ordering of the broad range of variation in values characteristic of individuals within a single culture. The variations in value orientation are related to the differential patterning of social roles within the family as a sub-system of society.

The ethnic family undergoing the acculturation process in the United States is an ideal area in which to examine transactionally the interrelationships among cultural, social, and psychological events. Previous researchers have focused on only two of these dimensions at a time. Some have examined the social characteristics of the family as a small group and related these to the individual psychological functioning of its members. Others have studied the interrelationship of cultural values to family social role structure and functioning. The concurrent examination of these three dimensions as "foci" of a transactional field results in a new "gestalt," a broader and more comprehensive understanding of the family.

This becomes especially evident in Spiegel's clinical analysis of two Italian-American families undergoing the acculturation pro-

cess. The intrapsychic stresses experienced by members of these families take on new meaning when they are viewed within the context of the family structures and the cultural value orientation systems in which they are functioning. Members of the "sick" family, for example, had widely varying value orientations reflecting their movement from old world Italian to American culture. This value orientation discrepancy is related to the intense interpersonal and intrapsychic conflicts that characterize this family. In the "well" family, there is more interpersonal harmony and less individual pathology which is reflected by a corresponding congruence in value orientations.

FIVE

Integration and Conflict in Family Behavior

In 1950 the Group for the Advancement of Psychiatry formed a committee to look into the subject of family behavior. Although an extensive literature already existed in a number of fields *(See Waller and Hill 1951.)*, the committee's job was to bring the subject specifically into psychiatric focus. This chapter is taken from a report which Florence Kluckhohn and I prepared for the committee. *(Spiegel and Kluckhohn 1954)*

The difficulty at the outset was how to derive data and materials based not on the study of sick or well individuals but on the study of family processes. It is easy enough to study individuals against a family background in which the dynamic principles are never clearly specified. The influence of the father, or the mother, or the sibling on the individual being examined can be studied without consideration of the totality of relationships. To change the object of inquiry from the individual to the family, however, means the employment of different methods of observation and of different conceptual tools.[1] From an altered perspective, the family is seen as a fairly well-defined, organized entity with a life history and

---

[1] The committee was much influenced and guided by the research work and point of view of Dr. Erich Lindemann, who served as advisor in the

dynamic principles of its own. Because of this altered perspective, we found ourselves faced with a new problem. We had set ourselves the job of finding out something about the normal and pathological physiology of the family, so to speak, without knowing anything about its anatomy. It seemed fruitless to acquire extensive observational data without undertaking this fundamental step in self-education.

Thus we decided that the first step toward our goal would be to inform ourselves with regard to the structure and function of the family. But this apparently simple task brought us face to face with a whole new series of complications. Instead of finding a clear-cut definition of the family easy to achieve, we discovered that families exhibited the most astonishing variance in their structure and function. If one examined only variance dependent upon ethnic, class, and regional difference in the United States and excluded the variance found in other societies, the range was still quite remarkable. It was found that differences in lateral extension (the range of collateral relatives such as aunts, uncles, and cousins) and in vertical extension (the range of generations such as grandparents, great-grandparents, and grandchildren) made it difficult to know where to locate the boundary of "The Family."

In seeking for factors to correlate with this variation in lateral and vertical extension, we found that the structure of the family was inextricably associated with the structure of the society of which it was a part. Small family groups were associated with the urban middleclass and its continuous demand for maximum mobility, both geographical and social. Continuity of generations was found in the upper-class families with their family portraits, traditions, and hierarchical systems. Collateral relatives proved important in rural areas and in certain ethnic groups. In brief, it turned out that the family could not be identified as a structural unit except with reference to the surrounding social system.

This aspect of the complexities involved in a study of family dynamics became even more prominent when we considered the topic of the functions of the family. Not only were various and differing functions assigned to the family in different social milieu, but even those functions which were apparently universal, such as

preliminary stages. For his ideas on the relationship between family and community roles and the physical and mental health of individuals, see *Lindemann 1950,* especially the chapter entitled "Modifications in the Course of Ulcerative Colitis in Relationship to Changes in Life Situations and Reaction Patterns."

the socialization of children, the satisfaction of sexual needs, or the biological and material maintenance of the members of the family, were carried out in such various ways with such differing implications that it proved impossible to obtain meaningful patterns without reference to the surrounding social system. The responsibilities and attitudes of a father toward his child, his wife, and his mother-in-law could not be divorced from his other roles in the society in which he lived. For example, it was possible for him to perform differently, and somewhat different functions were expected of him, depending on what his occupational role was—whether he owned a farm, worked in a factory, or piloted an airplane. A mother's attitude toward and relations with her children varied, among other factors, with her ethnic origin as well as with her decision to stay at home or to increase the family income by going to work.

Since it was obvious that no generalizations regarding the structure and function of the family could be obtained apart from an understanding of the particular social structure with which it was integrated, a new dimension was added. The job of self-education was broadened by the need to become familiar with contemporary concepts and fundamental assumptions involved in the understanding of social systems. The structure of a social system, however, especially a system as broad and complex in development and in current function as that of the United States, proved to contain as much variance as can be found in families and in individual personalities. In pursuing our task, we discovered that the similarities and variations in our social patterns were related to a fourth level of human behavior — the variations in values of a culture and subcultures. These values are reflected in the social system. For instance, the significance and structure of the U.S. occupational system only became clear when considered in the light of the tremendous value placed on planning for the future, on personal achievement based on hard work, and on individual initiative. Relations between parents and children, in our own country, frequently reflect a belief in the potential for goodness, dignity, and worth of the individual. There was no escaping from the ubiquitous and penetrating effect of cultural value orientations on every aspect of human behavior. We had no choice, especially in view of the mixed and confused nature of our cultural heritage, but to add this area to our stock of information and to familiarize ourselves with the conceptual tools necessary to an understanding of this field, so far from our home base in psychiatry.

The process of self-education necessitated by the ramifications

145

of the inquiry had an advantage beyond that of extending the individual horizons of the members of the Committee. It focused attention upon a way of viewing human behavior which is not easily perceived in the context of purely clinical work with emotionally disturbed individuals. In clinical work one tends to study the distortions of a reality known to the observer and the maladapted behavior based on such distortions in psychologically disturbed individuals. The field of observation is intra-personal and inter-personal in the sense of a series of small two- or three-person clusters composing the social relations of the patient, including the relation with the therapist. In this setting, fairly satisfactory explanations of human behavior can be derived from conceptions based upon purely intra-psychic mechanisms, such as those of integration, defense, and disintegration. As soon as the area of observation is widened, however, to include larger human groups such as the family, the environment as a given constant disappears. In its place there emerges a *field of transaction* which is not intuitively known or easily discoverable by the observer, especially insofar as the observer is a part of the field. The structure of the *field* at any given moment is dependent upon components contributed by: (1) the physical universe, (2) the biological situation of the individuals transacting within the field, (3) the intra-psychic status of these individuals, (4) the small groups formed by these transacting individuals, (5) the extended social system, and (6) the system of values existing at that time and in that place. The extensiveness of this field of transaction, and the variety and intricacy of the network of interlocking systems of which it is composed, constitutes a cognitive problem for the observer. The attention falters in trying to span so large an area, and common sense and intuition fail to supply adequate and easily summoned cues for a "definition of the situation."

As psychiatrists, we lack *gestalten* for perceiving phenomena of such magnitude and complexity. We have to construct conceptual patterns for ourselves which can encompass the *field of transaction* as the necessary background for a complete and realistic description of human behavior. This means that we must add to our already existing stock of concepts related to physical, chemical, biological, and psychological events a new cluster of concepts, of equal scientific rigor and seriousness, related to the group-dynamic, sociological, and cultural-anthropological descriptions of events. Such an aim would go further than what is usually meant by the term "inter-disciplinary" or "multi-professional." The aim requires that the concepts basic to other disciplines must really be integrated so

146

that they become a part of the psychiatrist's cognitive orientation toward reality — or at least as much so as physical, chemical, and biological concepts are at present.

POINTS OF REFERENCE FOR THE ANALYSIS OF FAMILY PROCESSES

Our purpose, then, is to analyze family life with reference to the processes responsible for the mental health or illness of its individual members. For this it is necessary to develop a system of operational concepts. "The Family" must be defined. Since we have all lived in families, it is easy to assume that we know what we mean by the word. Yet, as with many other common-sense notions, rule-of-thumb definitions are likely to exhibit so much variation as to be practically useless for analytical purposes. Furthermore, insofar as the family is associated with the mental health of the individual, then it can be safely assumed that there are some states or conditions within the family that favor good or bad health. We need to develop concepts to detect and describe such states. Lastly, not all families are the same. If we compare them even within the same country or city, we find the most bewildering variety. How to distinguish the normal — dominant or variant — from the pathological or deviant states conducive to illness is a primary task.

To work with many concepts new to psychiatrists, we need a frame of reference within which to locate them. This can be constructed from a set of points of reference which will here be only briefly sketched.

1. The family is a collection of individuals. One point of reference, therefore, is the individual, including everything we know about his somatic and psychological functions.
2. The family, however, is not *simply* a collection but an organization, a group. Another point of reference, therefore, is the small primary group, with its characteristic action processes and group dynamics.
3. The family is in addition always a major unit of the total social system. As such, it has structural and functional characteristics which ramify throughout the whole social system in a network of articulation with other subsystems such as the occupational and educational systems. Thus a third point of reference is the social system.
4. The family is also an agency for the transmission of cultural values. Furthermore, its very form and function are

147

intimately connected with the specific value orientations of a given culture. Accordingly, a fourth point of reference is the system of values characteristic of the social system in question.

5. Finally, a family exists in a particular locale, or territory — a spot on the map. For example, the contrasts between a rural and urban environmental setting may be of considerable significance for variance in family structure and function. The geographical setting is thus a fifth point of reference.

These five reference points provide a convenient descriptive conceptual frame, making it easy to identify the point of view from which the family is being considered. It is a part of our thesis, however, that they can be considered as more than simple reference points. They can be viewed as a system of interrelated and more or less integrated component parts. When looked at this way, the individual, the group, the social system, the cultural values, and the geographical location are all foci of organization in one integrated system or field of transaction.

Thus, a married woman may or may not be a mother. Whether she is or not probably will depend on her biological and psychological state. But if she is a mother, her parental attitudes will vary according to her geographical location and status in the social system; she will have different techniques for taking care of her child if she lives on a farm with her husband usually within hailing distance from those she will develop if she lives in a city as the wife of a traveling salesman who is gone for long periods. Not only geographical location and occupational status but also the size of the primary group will produce variations in the parental attitudes and child-care arrangements. The farm wife who has ten older children will delegate much more responsibility than the traveling salesman's wife who has two children under five.

In spite of all the differences between these two mothers, they may yet resemble each other in their attitudes toward disciplining and "spoiling" their children. These attitudes will be strongly influenced by the cultural value orientations of the two women. For example, if both mothers derive their values from one of our more severe ethics, it is quite likely that they will consider their offspring basically evil little brutes who need to be severely trained and repeatedly punished in order to be turned into reasonable human beings.

148

The primary point to be made in this connection is that the foci of organization in the total field do not vary independently of each other. No matter where the focus of observation is directed — whether at the individual housewife, the family as a group, the family within the larger social system, the value orientation of the individual, family, subgroup, or total social system, or the geographical setting in which events of human behavior occur — all the other foci of organization are always implied. Because they are in a state of transaction and reciprocal influence, they cannot be divorced from one another, and any description of human behavior must take account of the contributions of all these foci of organization.

We intend in this report to confine ourselves to two of these foci, which seem to us to be of the greatest strategic importance. These two are: the social system, and the cultural value orientations. To a lesser extent we shall treat some of the effects of the geographical setting of the family.

THE RELATION OF THE FAMILY TO THE SOCIAL SYSTEM

Extensive cross-cultural surveys have shown that some form of family is found in every society. *(See Murdock 1949.)* There is no known society which has not institutionalized sexual and parental roles in a formal pattern of small nuclear groups integrated with other nuclear groups in an extended kinship system. The patterns vary with respect to size and kinship lines, but the basic structure is universal. Furthermore, in all societies the family system is structurally related to all other units of the social system. It is universally integrated with other systems such as residence, or community organization, the stratification system (i.e., the class structure), the occupational system, the educational system, and the religious system of the society. More often than not it is integrated with the power structure or political system of the society.

A familiar set of examples may be cited. Let us examine the relations of the family in American society with the occupational, social class, and educational systems. In the main the class position of the family in the United States — especially the middle-class family — is dependent upon the position held by the father in the occupational world. But it is also true that his job depends upon certain qualifications attained through education and training. Further than this, everyone knows — democratic ideologies notwithstanding — that what education one receives is in large part dependent upon the social and economic status of the family. This

149

is to say that family status, class position, occupational position, and educational attainments are all interdependent. However, the smooth functioning of these interdependencies in the time axis depends upon the individual and his personal qualities. Let us take the example of the child of the well-established upper-middle-class family who lacks the intelligence to obtain the training necessary for any job commensurate with the status of his family. If on this account he loses occupational status, then a strain is likely to develop in his family. It is to be expected that one or another member of the family will object to or at least be unhappy about his more menial job. On the other hand, if ways are found to maintain his occupational status without his demonstrating any ability for the job, then strains of another kind are produced. There is a serious threat to the structure of the whole social system in passing on occupational positions to persons who are not qualified for the jobs.

There is also a universal connection between the family, the rules of residence of the community, and the composition of ethnic groups. The members of a nuclear family group (by which we mean husband, wife, and their children) in almost all societies live together in the same residence. Whatever the physical or architectural nature of the dwelling place may be, it is nevertheless a *place* — a territorial location. Thus, from the point of view of the individual, it is the family primarily that determines where he lives and what he calls "home," with all the implications for the sense of personal identity that local, regional and national sentiments contribute. From the point of view of the social system the family is thus the basic unit of regional organization of the community, state, or nation.

Particularly important for our objective is the structural relation between nuclear and extended family groups, rules of residence, and ethnic groups. The nuclear or primary group, as stated before, consists usually of husband, wife, and their children. A kinship system integrates such nuclear groups both through vertical extension — that is, by continuity of generations in time — and through lateral extension — the collateral relatives of the present generation. The residential patterns of the group or sub-group prescribe what permutations and combinations of nuclear vertically or laterally extended relatives shall live together. In our American society, for example, especially for urban groups of an industrial community, the prevailing pattern prescribes residential isolation of nuclear families from all relatives, collateral or generational. The husband

150

who has to house and feed his mother-in-law, or the wife called upon to find room for a sister-in-law — to say nothing of more distant cousins, aunts, or grandparents — feels sorely abused, as a general rule. In other societies, however, the sharing of household facilities by a wider assortment of relatives, near and far, is regarded as a natural design for living.

The relation between the family — whatever its kind — and the system of residence is also structurally integrated with the ethnicity of the community. An ethnic group is in one sense a system of extended and related family groups. Any concept of race based on clearcut distinctions has now been shown to be invalid in any strict sense, and specific traits are found to be diffused through many different ethnic groups. Nevertheless, it is also true that the members of an ethnic group tend to be more closely related to each other, biologically, than they are to members of other ethnic groups. Thus the composition of the family is of structural significance to the related ethnic group, and, conversely, the ethnic group frequently determines the structure of the family. This reciprocal relation is also integrated with the residential structure of the community. Families that are ethnically related frequently tend — for some generations, at least — to live in the same location; a fact which in crowded urban communities often leads to considerable strain if not outright social conflict.

Clearly, then, the universality of these structural interrelations would seem to indicate that the family has functions of fundamental importance to the total society. They meet certain requirements which cannot be satisfied in any other way.

Of the many interrelated functions which the family supplies both to the individual and to the social system, two are apparently allocated specifically to the family. The rest are shared to varying degrees by other organizations. The first two functions are reproduction and socialization of the children. The survival of the species requires a mechanism for the constant introduction of new members. The biological processes of humans, which would in themselves, apparently, satisfy this prerequisite, are not intrinsically sufficient. The social organization which supports the species requires for its perpetuation that the new members be recruited in an orderly and systematic fashion. There is no doubt that every society universally ascribes a rank order — a destiny — to its children at the moment of birth through the mechanism of the family. Children cannot be potentially anybody with a perfectly random, anything-is-possible kind of future ahead of them. In order that the structure and function of the social system be maintained, children have to be introduced into it with an ascribed social status — a place to begin and a range of selection of future goals from out of the myriad possibilities of the total system of roles of the particular society.

This extensive selectivity and ordering of possibilities is accomplished through the legitimization of the parents. *(See Malinowski 1930.)* It is not the children, actually, who have to be legitimate, but the parents, so that the raising of children within families can be assured to the social system. Thus the invariant insistence on the legitimacy principle is not primarily for the sake of controlling sexual behavior. In many societies extra-marital and pre-marital sexual intercourse are positively sanctioned. The legitimacy is invoked primarily to preserve and transmit the entire system of status relations and the integrative mechanisms which maintain its structure, by allocating the newcomers to the appropriate status.

The second aspect of the recruitment prerequisite is the socialization of the children once they have arrived and have been legitimately assigned their initial status — whatever it may be. This functional prerequisite is closely associated with an important aspect of the biological focus of organization, namely, the prolonged dependency of the child. The dependency is actually both biological and psychological and stands in a reciprocal relation with another established biological fact: the apparent lack of innate behavior, and the extraordinary plasticity of the human child. Because our children bring so little predetermined behavior into the world with them, and have so much to acquire, they need a great deal of time to learn how to play their roles in life. By the same token, they can be taught a wide variety of behavior. And since much of it is mutually exclusive, once it has been learned, it cannot easily be unlearned or relearned or transferred to a different kind of social system. Plasticity diminishes with maturation.

This functional requirement, determined by the prolonged immaturity of the child, is apparently better satisfied by the family system than by any other institutional arrangement — at least to this point in the history of mankind. Efforts have been made to socialize children exclusively in institutions, where the parental roles are shared by a number of different individuals. By and large, these efforts have not been as successful as some form of a family. The very diffuseness and discontinuity of the roles does not permit the child to develop a clear idea of his status and identity. The child's need for a stable and enduring relationship with significant parent figures based on affection (a need which is assumed to be basic) is not well met.

It is within the framework of mutual love and interpersonal security — that is, relations relatively free from anxiety, exploitation, and intimidation — that the child can best learn the social role behavior and the techniques of adjustment to the situations he will meet as an adult. These roles are learned on the basis of imitation and identification. Assuming that the family is not itself a deviant one, the roles thus acquired will turn out to be appropriate for the social system in question.

At this point it is necessary to be more specific about the use of the concept of role as a conceptualization of human behavior. If one is describing the behavior of an individual in a known situation, anyone with common sense and intuition immediately apprehends and judges the behavior as either appropriate and realistic or as inappropriate, mal-adaptive, or unrealistic. This immediate cognitive ability to relate behavior to situations is possible only for experiences within one's own culture. Under such circumstances, the observer or the participant intuitively assigns the culturally appropriate roles to all who are participating in the situation. No need is felt for analytical dissection of the behavior patterns. In a strange situation, however, as in a foreign land, lack of prior experience makes such automatic allocations of behavior patterns impossible to achieve, and therefore the observer does not know how to define the situation. He does not know how to "understand" what is going on until it can be explained to him in terms of the roles being played, the motives activating them, and the goals implied in them.

The primary structural components of the social situation — so far as its human participants are concerned — can be conceived as a system of roles. *(See Neiman and Hughes 1951; Parsons 1951, pp. 36-45.)* Any single individual obviously plays many roles — in the occupational system (school teacher), in the family (wife, mother, daughter), in the economic system (consumer), in the political system (citizen, party member, voter), and so forth. *Each particular role is culturally patterned*, i.e., it is tailored to fit the needs of the social system or subsystem in question. This is to say that there are norms for each role which all persons in the role are expected to follow, in outline at least. There is, of course, always individual variation; no two people ever perform exactly alike in any given role. Role expectations orient the responses of the participants somewhat as a magnet orients previously randomly distributed iron filings in the lines of magnetic force. The limited range of response, analogous

153

to the field of force, results from the reciprocal roles the other participant or participants are forced to assume in relation to the one who initiates the new situation. The initiator, who plays the lead and structures the role situation, may be doing something as innocuous and informal as changing the subject of conversation, asking a question, or greeting another on the street. Nevertheless, by so doing, he specifically orients and limits the possible behavior of the others in the transaction. Although the process of learning new and more appropriate role responses is never finished, it is in childhood especially, that roles appropriate to the various statuses are learned through reciprocal transactions with the parents.

Another significant aspect of role playing is that it is a form of communication. As such, it is dependent upon a system of cues, signs, symbols, meanings, and values shared by the participants in the situation. Without such sharing, communication in the sense of meaningful interpretation of, and response to, the roles of the others would be impossible. Because of the cognitive and evaluative aspects of such a shared system of meanings and values, each role is accompanied by a set of complementary or counter-roles based on reciprocity within the cognitive and evaluative systems. In other words, the enacting of a role is associated in the individual with a set of expectations of reciprocal role responses on the part of others. The particular responses in the others then determine further aspects of the role playing on the part of the originator. To a certain extent, the role responses of the others either gratify or frustrate the expectations of the initiator. To this extent the counter-role is interpreted as approval or disapproval of the role behavior of the initiator. What is an expectation on the part of the initiator — i.e., how he expects the other to respond to his role behavior — is a sanction on the part of the participant — i.e., he approves or disapproves the role of the initiator, and vice versa.

It can be seen, then, that role behavior on the part of two or more individuals involved in reciprocal transaction both defines the situation and regulates it. The regulation is established in two ways: first, by the effect of the sanctioning function implicit in the counter-role response; second, through the functioning of the shared system of meanings and values which orient the actions of the participants.

The reader may wonder why so much attention is given here to the significance of role playing. There is probably no difficulty in perceiving its central importance to a description of the socialization of children. This topic can also be approached in terms of learning theory and in terms of the psychoanalytical theory of character development. Role theory, however, bites into the problem of child training from the point of view of the social system, especially as it is embodied in the family. Its specific contribution is that it makes it possible to describe the development of the child from the point of view of a *plurality of object relations*. Because it is based on a transaction system, inclusive of the self and others, it can prove to be a useful link between the intra-personal systems of id, ego, and super-ego, and the inter-personal systems of primary groups, such as the family, on the basis of which the former derives its characteristic stamp. Such a link also provides a mechanism whereby cultural value orientations can be described simultaneously from the point of view of the individual and from that of society. Because of this it opens up immense vistas for cross-disciplinary collaboration and research.

There is one other way in which role theory is significant to the aims of this report. As was stated above, it provides a method for defining the structure of a situation in terms of the roles of the participants. In this way it establishes the possibility of analyzing the state of a transaction system. The system may be stable and persistent, changing in an adaptive fashion, enduring with difficulty because of inner conflicts, or disintegrating. Where families are the system under scrutiny, it is our stated intention to discover methods for detecting states of deviance and pathology and to distinguish them from various states of stability or adaptive change which have healthier implications for the emotional adjustments of the members. The description of the family in terms of the roles of its members supplies an analytical method for approaching these variations in structure and function. The roles can be inspected for incompatibility and conflict both as an internal system and in relation to the integration of the family with the other parts of the social systems.

Some roles are general in character, others are specific. An example is the difference between the general role — woman — and the specific role — wife or parent. *(See F. Kluckhohn 1940.)* Furthermore, sociologists, as well as anthropologists, have shown that some roles are ascribed in accordance with invariant points of reference such as age, sex, or membership in a particular social group, such as a caste or class, whereas other roles are acquired through effort, achievement or failure throughout the lifetime of the individual. *(See Linton 1936, ch. 8.)* It is in family transactions that age and sex and other ascribed roles are initially learned. Apparently no other organized group can supply the variety and interplay of ascribed and acquired roles allocated to so few individuals. In residential institutions for children, in contrast, the roles are strung out among a wide variety of parent substitutes who have attained their position by achievement. The lack of ascriptive foci for the roles undermines the emotional poignancy of interpersonal relations. No one really "belongs" to anyone.

It is this factor of "belonging," by "right" of membership that underlies a group of functions which the family shares with other parts of the social system. These include the satisfaction and integration of biologic and psychologic needs, the performance of subsistence and maintenance functions, the observance of cultural and religious rituals, the more formal education of the children, and recreational activities.

There is enormous cultural diversity in the degree to which these functions are allocated to the family or shared and assigned to other institutions. In the United States, for example, education and recreation are shared with the schools, subsistence activities are shared with the occupational structure. The middle-class, urban family — as a whole — participates very little in these functions. Individual members of the family, taking advantage of the elaborate division of labor in the industrial community, enact these roles through group membership in other organizations or through purchase of services. In all societies, however, all these functions are performed to some extent by the family. Even in our highly specialized communities, there is always cleaning, mending, laundry, cooking, care of the sick, picnics, helping with homework, watching television, and so forth to be done in the home.

It can be seen from this method of analysis that social roles are a method of conceptualizing behavioral processes of transaction between individuals from the point of view of the social system. It is only by looking at the whole social system that one can segregate parental roles from occupational and recreational roles. Looked at from the point of view of the individual, however, these same social roles now appear related to inner needs and drives.[2] A role is a

---

[2] Actually the use of the terms *needs* and *drives* involves a non-transactional language. The alert reader will probably discover many other deviations from transactional concepts throughout this presentation, but this particular departure is so dramatic as to deserve special comment. It is evident that the concept of need and drive fractures the totality of the field of transaction and locates processes that occur *between* the organism as a system and the environment as a system as if they existed wholly within the organism. A *need* is presumably a "pull" from within the organism toward

socially regulated way of satisfying instinctual needs in an organized system of action. If this is true, then any discussion of the functions of the family must include not only the description of the particular configuration of roles which characterizes this primary group — depending upon the social system in which it functions — but also it must deal with the way these roles satisfy certain crucial needs of the individuals composing it.

Unfortunately, a consideration of this dual nature of the family — or of any primary group, for that matter — as the organized bridge between the individual and his needs and the social system and its needs precipitates us into the middle of a thorny theoretical problem. There is no uniform conceptual system for characterizing the needs of the individual. Instincts, drives, or needs are differently conceived and assembled in various schools of thought. The underlying assumption in all the various theories is that organic functions and "instinctual" processes are transformed in some way into the deferred aims and symbolic goals characteristic of role playing. The difficulty is that currently there is no easy way of dovetailing these conceptual systems with the theory of roles on which we have based our analysis of family processes. It is necessary, therefore, to by-pass this important theoretical problem and to discuss individual needs in a more general, non-specific fashion.

The socialization of children is an expression which covers — from the psychological focus — a cluster of intimately related individual needs. The biological need of the child for continual nourishment and physical maintenance during the prolonged period of dependency has already been mentioned. The family is certainly not the only agency that can satisfy this need in our society, but it is the most important one. More important, perhaps, is the child's

---

a prescribed "goal" in the outer environment. The goal is what is needed. A *drive,* on the other hand, is a "push" from within the organism representing a presumably definite quantum of energy which must be "expressed"—that is, manifested by some output of the energy in the form of an action process or behavior. In both of these concepts the environment is conceived on the basis of a concealed assumption as if it were entirely passive to all the activity within the organism. It is simply "out there," standing by, so to speak. Yet, if the area of observation is broadened, it then appears that the environment itself is not so passive, but, to pursue the metaphor, has its own needs and drives with respect to the organism. The organism cannot behave in any old random fashion for very long (and continue to exist), because it is continuously being pushed and pulled by the drives and needs of the environment. At this stage of the conceptual system, the metaphorical principle is reduced to the absurdity: which has the drive and which has the need.

need for love, approval, and security. This latter need can tentatively be further specified as the need for a consistent pattern of rewards and punishments in the context of a basic emotional acceptance and understanding of the child by its parents or parent substitutes.

These needs of the child cannot be adequately discussed without simultaneous consideration of the individual needs of other members of the nuclear family — siblings, mother, and father. The mother-child patterns of transaction are the process which have been most extensively studied in this area. The early symbiotic nature of the mother-child relationship and the gradual loosening and differentiation of the relationship with the changing needs of both mother and child have been stressed. *(See Benedek 1949.)* The significance of the child as an emotional object for the mother and also the unconscious identification of the child with various significant objects from the mother's past life have also been emphasized. The mother-child relationship, however, is not isolated from other family processes. Here especially the needs of the father vis-à-vis both mother and child, and of mother toward child and father, introduce complexities into family processes. Mother and father "need" (according to the specific cultural patterning) love, security, understanding, and sexual satisfaction in their relations with each other. But this system of needs is continuously modified by the competing systems of mother-child, father-child. Where there is more than one child, further imbalance is introduced by multiple assemblies of such triangulated need systems. Some of the most pressing problems in the etiology of mental health and ill health arise from degrees of good or bad "fit" among the triangular relationships which constitute the internal structure and function of the nuclear family.

It is evident that the conceptual items in the theory of social roles are not made up out of whole cloth but are already embedded in our everyday language as a sort of pre-conceptual wisdom. It is impossible, for example, to make generalizations about the distribution of needs or drives among the various members of the family without referring them to the social role of the individual member under observation. We have to talk about the generalized father, mother, daughter, or son in order to have a way of locating the observed drive in time and space. This is to say that needs are already specified to social roles in the ordinary currency of our discourse. Our problem, then, is to distinguish the various social roles from the point of view of their adequacy, their capacity for integrating particular needs. This may turn out to be something of an artificial problem created by a concealed value assumption, since we do not as yet know the degree to which the needs or drives which we can perceive (as well as the very act of observation) are shaped by the cultural patterning processes of a particular society. It is well to remind ourselves repeatedly that the observer is himself a part of the total field and is influenced or thrown off balance by it at the moment of observation as well as later in moments of reflection and conceptualization. Nevertheless, so far as one can discern in the present state of our knowledge, roles can be matched for the degree of satisfaction they provide and for their manner of organizing particular needs.

From this point of view it would appear that the family role relationships of husband-wife, father-mother, parent-child, and so forth are the most appropriate ways of organizing and satisfying the particular needs of the individual discussed above —at least, for our society. At the same time it is quite clear that these role relationships do not exhaust the ways of organizing the satisfaction of the same needs. So far as its total function in the social system is concerned, the family shares this function with other social structures characterized by variant social roles. In the matter of sexual satisfaction, for example, the husband-wife roles parallel other variant or deviant role relationships such as that with prostitutes, the brief "affair," or homosexuality. We have already mentioned social structures which share with the family some of the aspects of the socialization of children such as orphanages and the "foster" family. The strategic importance of the school system for the more formal cognitive and group oriented aspects of child training has also received comment. Obviously much more could be said about the relations between individual needs and role structuring, but for our present purposes it is only necessary to emphasize that although the degree of sharing of these functions varies from society to society, in every known society the family remains the central and apparently indispensable agency for satisfying such individual needs.

In order to account for the various forms which these universal aspects of family structure take in different societies and sub-groups, it is now necessary to discuss cultural value orientations. Not until this focus of organization with the total field of human behavior has been presented will a groundwork be laid to frame a typology of families — i.e., to make descriptive comparisons between various types of families within a society with a view to isolating unhealthy and deviant from healthy dominant or variant types.

THE FAMILY VALUE SYSTEM

Credit must be given primarily to the cultural anthropologists for calling our attention to the tremendous variability in human behavior, as determined by cultural patterns. This variation not only includes moral standards and mores but also extends to the subtler issues of motivation and patterns of interpersonal relations. The variations in existential judgments and systems of belief, such as are found in various religious orientations, philosophies, and science, while not new to us, have been integrated by the cultural anthropologists with other cultural patterns such as child-rearing practices, in a new way. As a result of the novel synthesis, we now have a clearer understanding of the relationship between the psychology of the individual and the culture in which he develops and to which he is adapted.[3] Owing to their work, it is now no longer possible to assume that generalizations based on observing individuals in one culture have a universal applicability.

A number of anthropologists have developed slightly varying concepts for dealing with the generalized meanings in a cultural tradition and have shown the significance of the differences in these meanings for the understanding of the differences in the behavior of individuals trained in varying cultural traditions. Almost all of the concepts also stress the critically important fact of the individual's lack of conscious awareness of most of the cultural values which so greatly influence his motivational system and action patterns.[4]

But in spite of the new insights provided by the concepts, most of them have had a limited usefulness in the analysis of the relationships between psychological and cultural processes. For the most part, the difficulties in using them arise from an absence of a

---

[3] For an excellent discussion of the relationship, see the work by C. Kluckhohn and H. A. Murray. (*Kluckhohn and Murray 1953*) Another approach is found in the writings of A. Kardiner and R. Linton. (*See especially Linton and Kardiner 1939; Linton 1945; Kardiner 1945.*) Still another work that deserves mention is Lawrence Frank's *Personality and Culture.* (*Frank 1948*)

[4] The most familiar names among the anthropologists who have been concerned with the problem are: A. L. Kroeber, Edward Sapir, Ruth Benedict, Clyde Kluckhohn, Margaret Mead, Laura Thompson, Gregory Bateson, and Morris Opler.

Some of the concepts developed to designate basic values are: "unconscious canons of choice" (Sapir); "unconscious system of meanings" (Benedict); "configurations" (Kluckhohn); "cultural themes" (Opler); "core culture" (Thompson).

systematic theory of cultural variation and the consequent tendency to rely too heavily upon mere empirical generalizations. The concepts have been both too empirically particularized to single cultures to permit systematic comparisons between cultures and too grossly generalized to allow for an analysis of variations within cultures. All too frequently the persons who have ably demonstrated a uniqueness in the value systems of different societies have ignored the fundamental fact of the universality of human problems and its correlate that human societies have found for some problems approximately the same answers. Also, in most of the discussions of the common value element in the many patterns of a culture, the *dominant* values of peoples have been overstressed and *variant* values largely ignored. These two concomitant tendencies have produced interpretative studies which are, in spite of their brilliance of insight, over-simplified and static representations of social structures and processes. Variation for the same individual when he plays different roles and variation within whole groups of persons in a single society have not been adequately accounted for. Yet it is precisely this kind of variation which is crucial for the conceptual integration of psychological and social or cultural processes.

The classification scheme and theory of variation in basic cultural values we shall use for our treatment of family patterns stems from all these previous concepts of variability, but it differs in that it rests upon several assumptions which postulate a systematic variation in value orientations both between and within cultures.[5]

Before presenting these assumptions, it is necessary to state the meaning of the term "value-orientation." In the main the definition of it being followed is that stated by Clyde Kluckhohn:

> It is convenient to use the term value-orientation for those value elements which are (a) general, (b) organized, and (c) include definite existential judgments. A value-orientation is a set of linked propositions embracing both value and existential elements . . .
>
> Since value elements and existential premises are almost inextricably blended in the over-all picture of experience that characterizes an individual or a group, it seems well to call

___
[5] The theory of cultural value orientations used here was formulated by Florence Kluckhohn. For her first statement of the theory, see *F. Kluckhohn 1950*. A further development of the theory appears in her "Dominant and Variant Value Orientations." (*F. Kluckhohn 1953*)

this over-all view a "value-orientation," symbolizing the fact that the affective-cognitive (orientation) elements are blended. More formally, *a value-orientation may be defined as a generalized and organized conception, influencing behavior, of nature, of man's place in it, of man's relation to man, and of the desirable and non-desirable as they relate to man-environment and interhuman relations. . . .* Like values they vary on a continuum from the explicit to the implicit. (*C. Kluckhohn 1951, pp. 409, 411*)

The first of the major assumptions for our classification and theory of value-orientation variation relates to the number of value-orientation areas: *There is a limited number of common human problems for which all peoples at times and in all places must find some solution.*

The second assumption is that, although *there is variability in solutions of the problems, it is neither limitless nor random but is a variability within a range of possible solutions.*

The third assumption, which provides the key for the analysis of variation, is that *all variants (all alternatives) of all solutions are in varying degrees present in the total cultural structure of every society.* There will be, in other words, in every society not only a *dominant* profile of value orientations, which is made up of those orientations most highly evaluated, but also *variant* or *substitute* profiles or orientations.

Four problems have been tentatively singled out as the crucial ones common to all human groups. These problems are stated here in the form of questions, and each is answered with the name which will be used henceforth for the range of orientations relating to the question.

1. What is the relation of man to nature? *Man-nature orientation.*
2. What is the temporal focus of human life? *Time orientation.*
3. What is the modality of human activity? *Activity orientation.*
4. What is the modality of man's relationship to other men? *Relational orientation.*

The ranges of variability suggested as a testable conceptualization of the variation in the value orientations are given in Table 2.

Man-Nature Orientation: The three-point range of variation in the *man-nature* orientation — Subjugation to Nature, Harmony

162

TABLE 2

Value Orientations

Orientations	Preferences		
Man-Nature	Subjugation to Nature	Harmony with Nature	Mastery over Nature
Time	Past	Present	Future
Activity	Being	Being-in-becoming	Doing
Relational	Lineal	Collateral	Individualistic

NOTE: Since each of the orientations is considered to be independently variable, the arrangement in columns of sets of orientations is only the accidental result of this particular diagram. Any of the orientations may be switched to any one of the three columns.

with Nature, and Mastery over Nature — is too well known from the works of philosophers and cultural historians to need much explanation. Mere illustration will demonstrate the differences.

In years past at least, Spanish-American culture in the American Southwest gave us an example of very definite Subjugation to Nature orientation. The typical Spanish-American sheep herder in a time as recent as fifteen years ago believed firmly that there was little or nothing a man could do to save or protect either land or flocks when damaging storms descended upon them. He simply accepted the inevitable. In Spanish-American attitudes toward illness and death one finds the same fatalism. "If it is the Lord's will that I die, I shall die" is the way they express it, and many a Spanish-American has been known to refuse the services of a doctor because of the attitude.

If the conceptualization of the *man-nature* relationship is that of man's Harmony with Nature, there is no real separation between man and nature. One is but the extension of the other, and both are needed to make a whole. This orientation would seem to have been the dominant one in certain of the past centuries of Chinese society.

A third way of conceptualizing this relationship is that of man's Mastery of Nature. With this view, which is clearly charac-

163

teristic of many Americans, natural forces are something to be overcome and put to the use of human beings. We span our rivers with bridges, blast through our mountains to make tunnels, make lakes where none existed, and do a thousand and one other things to exploit nature and make it serve our human needs. In general, this means that we have an orientation to life which is that of overcoming obstacles. It is difficult for us to understand the kind of people who accept the obstacle and give in to it or even the people who stress the harmonious oneness of man and nature.

Time Orientation: Concerning the definition of the human being's place in *time,* it should again be apparent that there is always a Past to be reckoned with, a Present time in which we live, and a Future which lies ahead. No society ever does, or even can, completely ignore any of the three time periods. Yet how greatly societies differ as to which of the three dimensions they stress or make dominant!

Spanish-Americans, whom we have seen take the attitude that man is a victim of natural forces, are also a people who emphasize Present time. They pay little attention to what has happened in the past, and regard the future as a vague and most unpredictable period. Planning for the future or hoping that the future will be better than either present or past is not the Spanish-American way of life.

Traditional China was a society which puts its main emphasis upon Past time. The ancestor worship and the strong family tradition were both expressions of this orientation. So also was the Chinese attitude that nothing new ever happened in the present or would happen in the future.

Many modern European countries have tended to stress the past. Even England — insofar as it has been dominated by an aristocracy and traditionalism — has voiced this emphasis. Indeed, one of the chief differences between ourselves and the English is to be found in our somewhat varying attitudes toward time. We have difficulty in understanding the respect the English have for tradition, and they do not appreciate our disregard for it.

Americans, more than most people of the world, place an emphasis upon Future time — a future which we anticipate to be "bigger and better." This does not mean we have no regard for the past or fail to give thought to the present. But it certainly is true that no current generation of Americans ever wants to be called "old fashioned." We do not consider the ways of the past to

164

be good just because they are past, and we are seldom content with the present. This makes of us a people who place a high value on change.

Activity Orientation: The modality of human activity is the third of the common human problems in the value orientation system, and the range of variation in solutions suggested for it is the threefold one of Being, Being-in-becoming and Doing.

In very large part this range of variation has been derived from the distinctions made long ago by philosophers. Moreover, the three-way distinction is to some degree similar to the classification of personality components made by the philosopher Charles Morris. The component which he labels the Dionysian and defines as being the personality component type which releases and indulges existing desires is somewhat the meaning of the Being orientation. The Apollonian component which he defines as being self-contained and self-controlled through meditation and detachment has some similarity to our Being-in-becoming orientation. Similarities can also be noted between his active, striving Promethean component and the Doing orientation.

However, the accordances with the concepts of philosophy are far from complete. In the conceptual scheme of value orientations the terms Being and Becoming, which are expanded to a three-point range of Being, Being-in-becoming, and Doing, are much more narrowly defined than has been the custom of philosophers. Furthermore, we hold to the view that this range of orientations varies independently of those which deal with the relation of *man to nature,* with *time,* and with basic *human nature.* The tendency of philosophers, writing with different aims, has been to treat these several types of orientations as relatively undifferentiated clusters.

The range of the three preferences centers solely on the problem of the nature of man's mode of self expression in *activity.* Each mode is definitely considered to be a type of activity. The differences between them are not, therefore, those which the dichotomy of active-passive, for example, distinguish.

In Being the preference is for the kind of activity which is a spontaneous expression of what is conceived to be "given" in the human personality. As compared with either the Being-in-becoming or Doing orientations, it puts a stress upon a non-developmental conception of activity. It might even be phrased as a spontaneous expression in activity of impulses and desires; yet care must be taken not to make this interpretation a too literal one. In no society, as Clyde Kluckhohn has commented, does one ever find a one-to-one relationship between the desired and the desirable. The concrete behavior of individuals in complex situations and the moral codes governing that behavior usually reflect all the orientations simultaneously. A stress upon the "isness" of the personality and a spontaneous expression of that "isness" is not pure license, as we can easily see if we turn our attention to a society or segments of a society in which the Being orientation is dominant. Mexican society, for example, is clearly one in which the Being orientation is dominant. Their wide-range patterning of fiesta activities alone shows this. Yet never in the fiesta with its emphasis on spontaneity is there pure impulse gratification. The value demands of other orientations — the relational orientation, for example — make for codes which restrain the activities of individuals in very definite ways.

The Being-in-becoming orientation shares with the Being a great concern with what the human being is rather than what he can accomplish, but here the similarity ends. In the Being-in-becoming orientation the idea of development, so little stressed in the Being orientation, is paramount.

Erich Fromm's conception of "the spontaneous activity of the total integrated personality" is close to the Being-in-becoming type. "By activity," he states, "we do not mean 'doing something' but rather the quality of the creative activity which can operate in one's emotional, intellectual and sensuous experiences and in one's will as well. One premise of this spontaneity is the acceptance of the total personality and the elimination of the spilt between 'reason' and 'nature'." *(Fromm 1941, pp. 258-59)* A less favorably prejudiced and, for our purposes, a more accurately limited statement would be: the Being-in-becoming orientation emphasizes the kind of activity which has as its goal the development of all aspects of the self as an integrated whole.

The Doing preference is so characteristically the dominant one in American society that there is little need for an extensive discussion of it. Its most distinguishing feature is a demand for the kind of activity which results in accomplishments that are measurable by standards conceived to be external to the acting individual. That aspect of self-judgment or judgment of others which relates to the nature of activity is based mainly upon a measurable accomplishment achieved by acting upon persons, things, or situations. What does the individual do, what can he or will he accomplish, are almost always the primary questions in our scale of appraisal of persons. "Getting things done" and finding ways "to do something" about any and all situations are stock American phrases.

Fromm also considers this orientation to be different from the one he defines in his concept of spontaneity, but he does not accord it an equally favored position. Instead he actually condemns it as a fertile source of neurotically compulsive behavior. While few would disagree that the Doing orientation of Americans leads to a comparison and competition with others which is often extreme and intense, we do not as yet know just how often the competition either leads to or reflects compulsion in the technical sense of the term.

Relational Orientation: The fourth and last of the common human problems treated in the conceptual scheme is the definition of man's relation to other men. This orientation has three subdivisions: the Lineal, the Collateral, and the Individualistic.

It is in the nature of the case that all societies — all groups — must give some attention to all three principles. Individual autonomy cannot be and is not ignored by the most extreme type of collectivistic society. Collaterality is found in all societies. The individual is not a human being outside a group, and one kind of group emphasis is that put upon laterally extended relationships. These are the immediate relationships in time and place. All societies must also pay some attention to the fact that individuals are biologically and culturally related to each other through time. This is to say that there is always a Lineal principle in relationships which is derived from age and generational differences and cultural tradition. The fundamental question is always that of emphasis.

For some types of problems it may be sufficient to differentiate only between the individual and the collectivity. In most cases, however, it would appear highly important to know what *kind* of collectivist preference is being stressed. A society which places its major emphasis upon the Lineal preference — as do, for example, the Japanese and some upper-class Americans — will have quite different evaluations of right and proper relationships from the society which puts a first-order emphasis upon the Individualistic preference (e.g., most Americans).

There will always be variability in the primacy and nature of goals according to which of the three preferences is stressed. If the Individualistic preference is dominant and the other two interpreted in terms of it, individual goals will have primacy over the goals of either the Collateral or Lineal group. When the Collateral

167

preference is dominant, the goals — or welfare — of the laterally extended group have primacy for all individuals. The group in this case is viewed as being moderately independent of other similar groups, and the question of continuity through time is not critical. When the Lineal preference is most heavily stressed, it is again group goals which are of primary concern to individuals, but there is the additional factor that an important one of those goals is continuity through time. Both *continuity* and *ordered positional succession* are of great importance when Lineality dominates the relational system.

How the continuity and ordered positional succession are achieved in the Lineal system is separate from the preference as such. It does in fact seem to be the case that the most successful way of maintaining the stress on Lineality is through mechanisms which are either actual hereditary ones based upon biological relatedness or ones which are assimilated to a kinship system. The English, for example, maintained into the present time a strong Lineality by consistently moving successful members of their more Individualistic middle class into the established peerage system. Other societies have found other but similar mechanisms.

In this delineation of the ranges of value orientations attention has been focused mainly upon dominant orientation emphases. But however important it is to know what is dominant in a society at a given time, we shall not go far toward understanding the dynamics of that society without paying careful heed to the variant orientations. That there be individuals and whole groups of individuals who live in accordance with patterns which express the variant rather than the dominantly stressed orientations is essential to the maintenance of the society.

Variant values are, as has been indicated in our third basic assumption, not only permitted but actually required. It has been a frequent fallacy of many to treat all behavior and certain aspects of motivation which do not accord with the dominant values as deviant behavior. Lack of adequate criteria has often led us to confuse the deviant, who by his behavior calls down the sanctions of his group, with the variant, who is accepted and indeed required. This is especially true in a society such as ours, where beneath the surface of what has so often been called our compulsive conformity there lies a wide range of variation. The dynamic interplay of the dominant and the variant is one of the outstanding features of American society, although it has been little analyzed or understood. We laud or condemn the "melting pot" ideology, accept or reject what we frequently term the contradictions of our society, but have not examined carefully the processes which create what we so readily judge.

We cannot in this report treat the kinds of variation or the reasons for them. However, it is a central theoretical proposition in all that is to follow on the analysis of family systems, that there is an ordered cultural variation (a web of variation) in all social systems.

INTEGRATIONS IN SPANISH-AMERICAN FAMILY PATTERNS

We have now completed sketching in the main elements in the theoretical framework we propose to use for the analysis of the family as a system of behavior. It is to be remembered that we consider this behavioral system to exist in a transactional field of interdependent systems. However, for the sake of simplicity and convenience we intend to confine this report to an examination of the interdependence of only four of the multiple systems transacting in the total field: (1) the geographical place or territorial reference of the transacting systems, (2) the system of cultural value orientations, (3) the extended social system, existing in that place with reference to the particular system of cultural value orientations, and (4) the family, as a system of social role patterns, interdependent with the place, the values, and the social system.

Since the transactional field is a unity of interpenetrating processes, each of these four systems is molded by the others; each one is reflected in all the others. There is no linear causal chain of events connecting them, but only reverberating processes taking place between and among all of them. In order to bring out as clearly as possible how this happens, we propose to compare two very different assemblies of these systems. The first is the patterns of family life among the Spanish-Americans of the American Southwest. The second is the role patterning of family life in the dominant middle-class large urban center in the United States. We believe that the contrast is sufficiently vivid to reflect clearly both the invariant and variant relations which we would like to make explicit.

The Spanish-Americans of the Southwest — a people who are, of course, a part of total American society — have had until quite recently, an order of value orientations which is in startling contrast with dominant middle-class American values. *(Adapted from F. Kluckhohn 1952.)* Ignoring for the moment the variant

169

TABLE 3

Contrasting Value Orientations: Spanish-Americans and Anglo-Americans

Subculture	Man-nature	Time	Activity	Relational
Spanish-American	Sub	Pr	Being	Lin
Anglo-American	Over	Fu	Doing	Ind

and deviant values within each of the groups, we can outline the contrasts in dominant value orientations as shown in Table 3.

Now, let us see how the Spanish-American system of value orientations is reflected in and maintained by a certain kind of social system and family role structuring. The first point is that to a large degree the whole social system and the family system coincide. The social system is formed to a much larger extent than in other communities by a network of interrelated families. Although the pattern is now slowly changing, the Spanish-Americans lived characteristically in small village units. Recently, economic and other pressures have served to push many of them out into the cities as laborers and have thus disrupted some of the old patterns. Yet, even in towns and cities today, they still tend to live, wherever possible, in some kind of interrelated group.

In the villages most of the persons are related to each other by blood and marriage ties. In fact such villages are little more than a large group of interrelated families. In one well-known village in New Mexico every family has the same surname. Within this network of biologically related people the occasional unrelated person is apt to have none too easy a time. Until he can establish some kind of relationship, he remains an outsider about whom there is always some concern and even suspicion. In part, such hostility results from the fact that social control in these villages is exercised mainly through the family. It is not shared, as it is in other communities, with such agencies as the police and law courts.

The extensive interrelatedness of the Spanish-American village community is achieved by wide-range recognition of kinship ties both vertically, through the generations, and laterally, to include fifth and sixth degree cousins, and finally, by a general extension, to include all who are however remotely related. Neither the pattern of relatedness nor the actual number of relations differs greatly from the situation in other communities. What is different is the strength of the ties which bind them all together. The basic nuclear family of husband, wife, and children exists just as it does in all societies. Yet, a true Spanish-American would feel extremely impoverished if the only relatives he had about him were his wife and children. His nieces and nephews are almost the same to him as his sons and daughters, and his cousins are very little different from his brothers and sisters. Everyone disciplines nieces and nephews as readily and as efficiently as he does his own children — to say nothing of feeding and caring for them in addition. There is a general and almost casual sharing of children. Since it is felt that a family without children — four to eight or ten of them are preferred — is not a family, the unfortunate family without children will usually take one, two, or three of those belonging to sisters or brothers or even other people who have too many. Some ten to twelve percent of all the children in one village, for example, were found to be living with persons other than their parents. It can readily be seen that the Spanish-Americans do not have the anxieties about adoption which many Anglo-Americans have. It can also be seen that such relative unconcern about who gets which child could not take place if they placed as much value on individualism as Anglos do.

The authority lines — the Lineal accenting of *relational values* — in the Spanish-American family system are definite and firm. The old people are the rulers; the male sex is clearly dominant. Respect for and obedience to age are bred into the Spanish-American child at an early age and are never forgotten. Sons do not expect to become independent upon reaching maturity. Only one son — the eldest — is permitted by custom to have any kind of authority and responsibility. Even he must remain subservient to the father's control until death or infirmity of the father makes it necessary for him to take over the family affairs. This special training of the oldest son is so pointed that the younger brothers and sisters treat him more as a father than as a sibling. The social mechanism which shapes the role of the oldest son is concerned

171

with preserving the continuity of authority by age. With such large families it often happens that the father dies before all the children have reached maturity. The oldest son then moves into the father's position, and all is supposed to go on as before.

The authority relations centered about age and other ascribed roles are not confined to the family system in the Spanish-American community. They are generalized and extended to include a kind of feudal relation called the *patron-peon system.* One powerful and dominant family, the head of which is the *patron,* rules the whole village in much the same fashion as fathers rule the families. Those under the control of the *patron* are sometimes called *peones* — or more frequently simply *la gente* (the people). Between *patron* and *peones* there is a relationship very similar to that which existed between the lord of the feudal manor and his serfs. Furthermore, beyond the *patron* there is still another authority — the village saint. The Spanish-American Catholic's interest in his own particular *patron* saint is far greater than it is in the more abstract aspects of the religion. It is he who is considered most responsible for everyone's welfare and for whom the big annual fiesta is given. In this way, the Lineal accenting of relational values is synchronized with the man-nature range of value orientations, with regard to which the Spanish-American views himself as subservient to and dependent upon forces in nature.

We have already mentioned the dominance of the men in the Spanish-American family system as an example of the importance of ascribed characteristics. It is true that in the larger towns and cities the Spanish-American women today do take jobs and assume many of the achievement aspects of the Anglo-American women. In the villages, however, the Spanish-American woman has only one career to look forward to — that of wife and mother. There is none of the equality between the sexes which is so significant in the Anglo social system. Instead there is a clear-cut division of labor and of rights and obligations. The lives of most of the women in the villages were, until recently, so circumscribed that they were not even permitted to market in the village store. The store was a meeting place for the men — hence neither safe nor proper for the women. Men and children bought all supplies.

Yet, for all the restrictions, which to us seem great, the feminine role offers the Spanish-American women great security. They expect their marriages to be permanent, and they usually are. They know exactly what is to be expected in every aspect of their roles. By the age of twelve almost every village girl is quite well trained for her future job of housewife and mother. She moves into her adult role through an easy transition without having to face such vexations and anxiety inducing problems as the question of what sort of a boy to marry or whether to choose a career instead of marriage.

According to dominant American standards, the Spanish-American patterns of living undoubtedly seem exceedingly repressive. Seen from the point of view required by the Spanish-American orientations, the picture looks quite different. Familistic ties — both Lineal and Collateral — bind them on every side and keep them dependent. Yet in that very dependence there is a definite security and safety. Even the *patron*, who has so much authority to demand obedience to himself and his commands, has many obligations to his people. It is he who often manages the economic affairs of the many families, who guides and counsels in times of crisis, and who has the major village responsibility.

Within individual families great stress is placed upon group cohesion. Each member of the family is responsible to all the others in accordance with his particular position. Without this extensive interdependence the Spanish-Americans could not long maintain their *Present time orientation* to life. It is one thing to accept each day for what it is and to enjoy it when one has many relatives to depend on if things should go badly. Such an attitude may be quite destructive, however, if independence and responsibility for self are prevailing rules. An example to the point is a case recorded by Florence Kluckhohn in 1936. The families of a father and two married sons constituted a single economic unit. Once they had been a land and livestock owning family in which all members had worked at a common task. By 1936 all property was gone, but the old patterns persisted — even though from our point of view each of the individual family heads was now an independent wage earner. All three families maintained a common larder, and all continued to contribute to the support of all. At no time did all three of the wage-earning men work simultaneously. At any time that two had moderately good jobs, the third was certain to be on a trip or vacation of some sort or simply resting at home. Since two could make all that any of them required or needed, why should all three be driving ahead? Indeed, there was nothing in particular to drive toward. For, as we have already pointed out, Spanish-Americans seldom expect that the future will be bigger or better than the past. That which *is* is good enough, and most show small concern for the future.

Correlated to this point of view, and of equal importance, is the acceptance of the inevitable. The whole system of relationships — those of family, but especially those of *peones* to their *patron* — tends to preserve what exists and leaves little room for achievement or ambition. Change is not expected, and improvement is scarcely even a dream. The family's standard of living remains the same generation after generation, with only microscopic alterations. *Peones* remain *peones*, younger brothers stay in their places, and for a woman to challenge masculine dominance is unthinkable.

Thus we see that Spanish-American value orientations are — or at any rate were — fully expressed in family patterns. It is also evident that, reciprocally, the family patterns foster and maintain the value orientations. This is to say that both systems participate in a transactional field. It is central to our thesis, however, and to our search for factors responsible for mental health in families, that the transactions between the two systems are not always well integrated. There is undoubtedly security in the Spanish-American patterns, but there are also definite strains and inadequate "fits" among the tightly knit relationships. The child is accepted for himself as few American children are. He is not driven or urged to be independent and ambitious. On the contrary, the training is consistently — except in the case of the oldest son — for a lack of initiative and responsibility. There is much evidence that this emphasis is too rigid. Although we are not considering the impact of biological variation on family patterns, there is no doubt that the Spanish-American values work a hardship on those children constitutionally endowed with greater reactivity, vigor, and energy. The most frequent conflicts occur in the relation between the older and younger brothers. Recent research in the area has shown that the family relationships have undergone considerable change in the past fifteen years. Especially is this to be noted in the breaking down of the oldest brother-younger brother relationship and the consequent intense conflict within or disruption of the family.

There has been an increasing shift from Lineally organized relationships to Individualistic ones, but as yet little or no change has occurred in any of the other Spanish-American value orientations. Disorganization within the structure of the family and in the personalities of family members is the striking result of the process. Delinquency among adolescents has increased rapidly, divorce has become more common, in-group taboos have broken down, and perhaps most important of all one notes in many of those who are middle aged or older attitudes of bewilderment and hopelessness.

174

Only a very few at any age level have become thoroughly acculturated in the ways of Anglo-American life. A majority are seeking new patterns of adaptation which it would seem certain will not be free of strain for individuals, because an Individualistic relational orientation simply does not fit well with either a Being activity or a Present time orientation. It is one thing to live in the present and act in accord with feelings when one has a Lineal family system which assures both economic support and firm regulatory norms for the impulse life; it is quite another when the individual or the small nuclear family lives alone.

INTEGRATIONS IN AMERICAN MIDDLE-CLASS FAMILY PATTERNS

The Spanish-American family patterns — as they were until quite recently — are good representatives of what is often termed a "familistic" society. In examining the contrast with Anglo-American family patterns it is important to keep in mind that the Spanish-American situation is not atypical. On the contrary, a majority of the peoples of the world tend to be familistic to some degree. They tend to emphasize either the Lineal or Collateral relational principle rather than the Individualistic one. It is the American pattern that is more atypical — if for no other reason than its reflection of the extreme stress on Individualistic relations. However, there are other ways in which the dominant American ensemble of value orientations is unique. We have already mentioned the extraordinary emphasis on Doing in the range of the activity orientation and the accenting of Future time. Indeed, this latter orientation goes so far that we often appear to have forgotten how to enjoy the present for its own sake. Perhaps this accounts for the existence of what David Riesman has called our "fun morality" — a compulsive search for enjoyment through ritualized and institutionalized "entertainment" in which having fun, having-a-good-time, has to be planned for and "achieved." *(Riesman 1950)* The difficulty here is that if one has to "plan" to enjoy the future, spontaneity tends to be vitiated by the time the future becomes the present.

That there may be some other difficulties flowing from the severe stress on these value orientations, will be taken up shortly in our examination of American family patterns. Here it is sufficient to point out that there is a good deal of harmonious interlocking of the value orientations in the ramification of roles that constitute the social system. The emphasis on achievement requires a considerable planning for the future, a step-by-step thinking out of the means-ends patterns by which future success may be secured. At the same time, this preference for far-flung and distant aims tends to place a great premium on the young — those with the most future ahead of them. Overlooking, for the moment, in what position this accent on youth may leave those who have long since lost it, we can nevertheless recognize that it is the individual who reaps the rewards and around whom all the planning centers. Without a selective sanctioning of Individualistic over Lineal and Collateral relations, the individual would never be free to realize his plans, to leave his family, his home town, or his job for a better situation. Along with the planning and achievement values is synchronized the optimism derived from the emphasis on man's Mastery of Nature. The conviction that we can always improve matters by thoughtful care and planning and the belief in "progress" through "scientific achievement" give our industrial, job-centered society its characteristic stamp and thus support the system of mobile occupational roles through which the plans for achievement are to be realized.

If we now observe how the dominant American value orientations are reflected in the patterns of American family life, we face problems of selectivity and special emphasis. For it is possible to speak of *The American Family* only if we realize that we mean the ideal or typical family of the dominant middle class. Actually there is no such thing as a single family type which can be said to be representative of all America. We have the kind of variation in families which results from our having within one nation large groups of people with quite different cultural backgrounds — groups which still have recent memories of other countries. There are also all the families which are midway between those of rather clear-cut ethnic background and those dominantly American. Differences of another kind can be distinguished in the families of the several economic class levels. Furthermore, aside from all such differences as these, there is much more diversity in individual families — even those of the middle class — than is commonly the case in most societies.

It is this very diversity which leads to the stressing of the dominant or "typical" family pattern. We could not long hold together all our differences if there were not at the same time a strong sense of conformity and oneness. Thus there exists a kind of consensus regarding the relationships and roles that should exist in the "Good Family." There is, in other words, a kind of model family according to which all others tend to be judged and like which many others are striving to become. It is this model which is the typical family of the middle class.

The typical middle-class family of today is a small nuclear family. A father, a mother, and two or three children, at most, has been the numerical pattern in recent years. Very recently, to be sure, the birth rate in such families has shown something of an increase. As yet, however, there is no way of predicting whether this upward fluctuation is to be permanent, or is merely the result of a wartime situation. Whatever the cause, it seems doubtful that the typical family size will be greatly enlarged. In addition to being small, this typical family is in many ways an isolated one. This is to say that it is an independent unit, both economically and socially. Even though its members always recognize the fact of relatives — grandparents, uncles, aunts, and cousins — the relational bonds with these relatives are not, in most cases, strong ones. Although personal preference may, and often does, make them strong, there are no binding rules — such as there are in Spanish-American society — which make it necessary always to accept and get along with relatives.

Let us take the relations between siblings in the typical American family as an example. It is easy to assume that the bonds of affection and antagonism experienced by the siblings as they grow up will gradually even out in adulthood and appear as permanent attachments. Yet an honest scrutiny of this assumption will reveal that by the time they are thirty-five or forty years old, many of the members of the typical middle-class family will be closer to their associates and friends than to their brothers and sisters. The actual separation and emotional distancing may be screened by sentimentality and fitful, last-minute gestures on birthdays and anniversaries, but it is there all the same.[6] It is frequently reinforced by the actual physical separation incident to the vigorous geographical mobility of middle-class Americans. But it is not only the ceaseless moving about that divides the members of the family. Quite frequently the gulf is widened by a social distance. One sister's husband is successful, another's is not. As a result they live in different social orbits and seldom meet. Even if the two sisters maintain their relationship, it is unlikely that their children will have much in common or have many contacts with each other. In other cases, the dividing agent may

---

[6] Sentimentality in this context means an increasing emphasis on the symbolic aspects of relationships which are simultaneously losing substantive content.

be merely that the interests of the family of one sister are professionally focused and those of the other concentrated in the business world. With relationships as distant as cousins the instances of weakened bonds are still more numerous and more frequent.

If this is the situation where Collateral relationships are concerned, the weakening of the Lineal bonds among the generations is still more poignant. The son or daughter who moves away from parents both geographically and occupationally comes to sense an ever-deepening emotional chasm in the relationship. In part this is linked with the deep strain on the dependent needs against which the child must strenuously defend himself if he or she is to fulfill the demands for independence and self-reliance occasioned by our value orientations. In part it is associated with the general sentimentalizing of family relations which serves as a substitute for the lost closeness of parent and child. "Mother's Day" is an example of one such sentimental bridge which helps us ignore the chasm below. A "rite of atonement" is what an analyst of American life has called our Mother's Day customs.

It is not our intention to shock with what may seem to be cynical objectivity, nor yet to place a value, positive or negative, upon our own value orientations and the customs in which they are reflected. Nevertheless, in all fairness, it must be pointed out that in some ways American family patterns put quite severe strains upon individuals. Since our aim is to present a method for dissecting out the mal-integrations in family patterns of living which underlie the mental ill-health of the individual, it is necessary to attempt to pinpoint some of these strains.

A prominent source of difficulty is the situation of older people in our society. Excluded from living in the homes of their children, often retired from jobs merely because of age and thus cut off from the occupational interests which have absorbed their creative energies for so many years, older people tend to become increasingly isolated from meaningful relationships. As the life span grows longer and longer, the interest span for such persons tends to shorten. We have to some extent overcome the hazards of their inability to rely financially on their children through social security measures and the tremendous elaboration of insurance devices. But the gap which severs dependent relations between the generations makes it impossible for the aged to rely emotionally, as well as financially, on their children. Whereas the Spanish-American or Chinese parent would expect not only to live with his children but to receive their continued respect and devotion, older people in our society can expect to be told that they are old-fashioned, their opinions out of date, and their capacity to give helpful advice based on long experience with life strictly limited. With our impatient march into the future and our restless pursuit of change, the wisdom of an older generation is not likely to count for much. The Council of Elders is notable for its absence, and the role of elder statesman finds hardly an applicant. Thus the rewards of intense planning for the future — if a person lives long enough — follow the law of diminishing returns.

Space does not permit an inquiry into the complicated effects of this required separation between the generations on individual personality structure or on behavior disturbance in the individual. This is an area of intense research activity in the field of personality study, most of which is highly fruitful, even though the relation between cultural value orientations, social structuring, family patterns, and the individual's adjustment is frequently not recognized. The sequence of relationships observed by Parsons and others with respect to the so-called American "youth culture" point to another kind of strain in the society. *(Parsons 1949, chs. 10-11)* It is not generally understood that the behavior of the more or less typical American adolescent is not universal. In many other societies adolescence is a period of fairly smooth transition to adulthood. The wild fluctuations between extreme dependence and disdainful or defiant independence, the gyrations from idealism to cynicism, from lush romancing to hard-bitten, stripped-down sexual aims, and from cringing conformity to last ditch non-conformity are attitudes largely unique to our own social system. Threaded through all the adolescent attitudes is the power of the gang, or the adolescent peer group with its own, unique and frequently spectacular behavior patterns.

Parsons points out, discussing the origin of the power of the peer group, that the adolescent in our society is caught on the horns of a dilemma. On the one hand, he grows up in a small, nuclear family in which all his dependent needs must be satisfied in relation with a very few persons. Consequently the libidinal attachment, especially to the mother, grows very strong. On the other hand, the child is expected to become an adult in whom extremes of self-reliance and independence can be easily mobilized. How is he to resolve this discontinuity between childhood training and adult expectations? The shadow of this dilemma is seen in almost every form of the neuroses of adult life. Adolescence is the hour when the first tentative solutions of pre-adolescence must be forged into workable instruments. If the individual waits until he attains adult status, it may be too late, the solutions may not be forthcoming, and shame at not being able to make the grade may wither further experimentation. He may then become increasingly trapped within his family, wooed, perhaps, by a mother who cannot let him go and scorned by father and friends who cannot tolerate his staying.

The adolescent peer group, then, is the mechanism through which the most workable solutions are provided. Instead of having to rupture his ties to his parents through a violent wrench as adulthood approaches, he can transfer them in part to his peers. Where his own lack of experience and uncertainty make it difficult to get along without the support of his parents, the solidarity of the peer group will back him up, whether or not his parents approve or disapprove his behavior. Furthermore, the adolescent in our society is considerably inhibited in his attempts to try his wings and discover his own abilities and natural bents — in the words of Erik Erikson, to determine his personal sense of identity — by the prolonged tenure in the school setting. *(Erikson 1950)* School is considered by most people to be chiefly a preparation for life, rather than an experience in its own right. Because of the technical requirements of our culture, it must be continued long after the adolescent has reached the point where he must determine his identity. As a result, however, the adolescent is sealed off from many of the aspects of the adult world which he is expected to be able to identify with and soon to master. This is perhaps the reason why so many young people develop neuroses, or at least discover their existence, after graduating from school, or at the point of graduation. At any rate, youth culture provides a framework of behavior half-way between the world of the child and the world of the adult. The roles in the peer group are distributed between those aimed at pleasure, play, and fun and those whose goal is a serious "project." Even where the latter occasionally or frequently verge on delinquent or deviant goals — depending on the nature of the group — they nevertheless feature the orientation toward planning, organization, and achievement which are so important in our system of values.

Another source of strain in our family patterns can be found in the role of the father. One aspect of his role is the tremendous responsibility he must bear for the welfare of his wife and children. In many societies — the Spanish-American, and Chinese, for example — no man is made to feel that he, and he alone, is solely responsible for the well-being of his family. There are parents, brothers, even uncles and cousins, to be called upon in times of crisis. Many American men feel that they would rather borrow from a friend or even a stranger than from a relative — so strong is the push toward independence. The proliferation of welfare agencies and other community mechanisms for absorbing the slack between emotional and financial income and output are becoming more acceptable but still encounter the resistance toward "accepting help" or "charity" associated with our value system.

The great resourcefulness and responsibility required in the father role is well integrated with the Doing aspects of his orientation toward life. As a result he is apt to be highly concentrated on his business or occupational role. There are several ways, however, in which this concentration is not so well integrated with other family roles. It means that he must, in the usual case, spend an enormous amount of time away from his home and family. Thus the amount of sharing of roles — of real companionship — between husband and wife comes to be reduced frequently far below the optimum, and the marital pair find themselves driven increasingly apart as their marriage progresses. Another strain arises with respect to the father-son roles. With father out of the home so much, the son is thrown very much together with mother. Not only are the mutual bonds thus intensified, but also the mother must then carry the lion's share of the training of the children and instituting of controls. She tends to assume a disproportionate amount of the moral authority for the whole family. For the son this means that the distribution of internalized traits which compose his psychological identifications with his parents is heavily weighted toward mother. The resulting feminine identification — especially the feminine superego — as well as the strong affective tie toward her then constitute mechanisms difficult to integrate later on with the initiative and aggressiveness demanded by ego ideals in accord with our value system. This situation is not helped by the fact that father's occupation often remains a mystery to the son. His occupation is obviously a focus of great interest and value and, therefore, an important way of identifying father and of identifying with him. Yet middle-class occupations take place, for the most part, far from home and are difficult to describe operationally. How many middle-class sons know what their extremely active fathers really do on the job?

But none of these strains are as severe as those found in the wife-mother role. Indeed, if we were asked to point to the most strategic spot in the American family system for an effecting of constructive change in it, we would certainly single out the feminine role. The reasons for the choice are many, and the whole of the feminine role problem which obviously includes the difficulties in both the husband-wife and the mother-child relationship is exceedingly complex. Here we shall point out only a few of the major strains which relate to the differential participation women are permitted in the patterns which express the dominant American value-orientations.

Compared to the masculine role, that aspect of the total feminine role which we label the wife-mother role is not well geared into the dominant value system. The mother of a family is not expected to express herself in an individualistic autonomous role in the way the father does in the occupational system. Instead she is expected to have a *collateral* orientation in which she puts the interests of the group as a whole above whatever individualistic interests she may have. She is, much more than the father, expected to play a "representative" role in her relations outside the family. She may, for example, be representative in the sense of being a husband's status symbol. Thorsten Veblen pointed this fact out long ago when he remarked that the American woman, in certain strata of society at least, is the symbol of a husband's or father's ability to pay and is in herself an item of conspicuous consumption. More often, today, the representativeness is found in the expectations we have that mothers will be the ones to represent the family at parent-teacher meetings, in the community churches and in a host of other community affairs. There is even a rapidly growing trend, especially in suburbs, for women to take a far more active part than men in community governmental affairs. Everyone is aware, for example, of the work that groups such as the League of Women Voters do in this field of activity.

Some women find a great deal of satisfaction in such roles. Some find satisfactions in the work of women's clubs, book clubs, music or art organizations. However, many do not. In the first place, the various activities have a diffuseness which do not permit to women the concentration upon central goals which is so characteristic a part of the dominant American achievement patterns. Second, almost all of the specified activities are mainly defined as women's activities in which men do not participate, and such a definition not only leads to an ever widening segregation of the spheres of the sexes but also tends to give to the activities themselves an evaluation of second-order importance. It is almost as if it were being said that men should tend to the truly important affairs in American life — those relating to the sphere of the economic — while the necessary matters of lesser importance can be safely left to women up to the point that issues become critical.

Even though there has been an increasing acceptance of women in the all-important occupational system — a fact which is evidenced by Labor Bureau statistics which record some 18,000,000 women in the labor force — there still is an expression of grave concern about the mother who works outside the home. Often a definite condemnation of the working mother is expressed. Delinquency, psychological disturbances of all kinds in children, and the divorce rate as well are frequently attributed in some large part to the fact of the mother being out of the home on a job. The American mother is not, in other words, expected to have an active part in those aspects of American life which best express the Doing activity and Future time orientations. Hers is a vicarious participation which depends upon what a husband, a father, or a son, and not she herself, accomplishes.

The frustrations which result from these variant definitions of woman's role would not be serious if it were not for the two facts that the domestic component of the wife-mother role has been increasingly demeaned as a prestige role and that women have been poorly trained to play that part of the total role.

In most respects American girls from babyhood through adolescence are trained to play individualistic and competitive roles which are very similar in nature to the masculine roles. Throughout childhood and youth the girl child goes to school with boys and competes for many of the same goals. True, little sister may find a doll and carriage under the Christmas tree while brother has a train, but in spite of this or other differences it is expected that the girl will learn to look after herself all through adolescence and beyond, even forever if need be. The hope is expressed that she will not have to remain independent and therefore need not use much of what she has learned. Instead — and this is the great problem — she is expected, upon marriage or certainly after children are born, to give her attention to motherhood and household duties for which she has had little or no training.

This lack of training, together with a lack of traditional methods for the rearing of children, creates in many women great anxiety about the mother role. Most American women desire children and most have definite aspirations to be "good mothers." Moreover, in the society at large the idealization of the woman is primarily an idealization of her motherhood. There is, in other words, considerable pressure for women to be good mothers and high prestige rewards for achieving the goal. But just what being

183

a good mother means or how to become one are questions many women find difficult to answer. All too often there is a slavish comparison of both one's self and one's children with those of friends or neighbors, or an anxious following of the prescriptions and suggestions of the latest theories of child care and training. Motherhood, like almost everything else in the society, becomes both competitive and instrumental. Or, as some have remarked, motherhood in many middle-class circles is fast becoming professionalized.

All of the difficulties encountered in playing the mother role are enormously increased by the low evaluation placed by most women themselves and the society as a whole on the domestic component of the wife-mother role. In earlier periods of American history the housewife and mother roles were a unitary role. Today in the minds of men and women alike the two components are fairly clearly separated, and the attitudes toward the housewife aspect of the total role are markedly negative. One has only to glance over the advertisements in current magazines to realize that the home as a house to be managed is constantly pictured as a mild variety of a penal institution. Almost everyone defines housework as drudgery — something which one does because one has to. The prestige rewards accorded domestic interests and accomplishments are not at all comparable to those which can be won in the occupational sphere or in other kinds of activities. Of all the evidence which supports this conclusion the most telling is the intoning of the phrase so common on the lips of women: "I am *just* a housewife."

Since being a housewife is an inevitable part of the mother role, it has not been at all unusual for mothers to convey the idea to children — whether consciously expressed or unconsciously made known in behavior — that mother deserves so much because she has given up so much and done so many things she really did not enjoy.

Even in the cases where women willingly accept the housewife role as a necessary aspect of motherhood one sees many instances of maladjustment when the time comes for children to leave home and go on their own. The mother's job in our particular kind of society and especially when families are small does not long endure. Margaret Mead has commented:

> Every social pressure to which she, the mother, is subjected tells her that she should not spoil her children's lives,

that she should let them lead their own lives, that she should make them independent and self-sufficient. Yet the more faithfully she obeys these injunctions, the more she is working herself out of a job. Some day, while she is still a young woman ... she will be alone, quite alone, in a home of her own. *(Mead 1949, p. 337)*

In an action-oriented, future-minded society, having no job to do engenders a feeling of uselessness which in turn creates emotional disturbance. Most of us have witnessed the disoriented behavior and emotional stress of women whose children have grown up and gone. Some respond by clinging to children; others try desperately to fit into jobs with the outmoded skills they learned and used years ago; others become unnecessarily fussy housewives; some are merely restless. But whatever the response or the degree of disorientation it should be plain that the demands of a role which is patterned rather inconsistently in terms of both dominant and variant value orientations are not easily met. There is considerable confusion in the minds of many women as to just what is expected of them, and the confusion affects all family relationships.

But in this instance as well as all others we have stressed the existence of problems not to demonstrate that the dominant family system is falling apart but rather to set up an analytical model for isolating some of the processes related to psychological strain and ill health. In fact, if it were our purpose, we could devote an equal if not greater amount of space to demonstrating successful integrations within family patterns, and among the family, the social system, and the system of value orientations. Given our basic values, the typical roles within the middle-class family structure appear, on the whole, to be well fitted to the functions of the family within the larger social system. The system of individualistic roles and autonomous functions within the family is remarkably well suited to, and good preparation for, the degrees of freedom and independence which our industrial society calls for. The weakening of ties between the generations is practically mandatory if the family is to be adjusted to the amount of freedom for geographical and social mobility which our occupational system requires.

It is wise to review what we have not attempted as well as what we have aimed for in this chapter. We have not attempted to give an account of the status of current research in family problems, useful as this might be. We have hoped, rather, that this necessarily schematic outline of a method for analyzing family problems will help to relate and correlate much of the vigorous research now going on. We hope that the demonstration of the interrelations between various parts of the transactional field within which family problems are set will help research workers coming from different disciplines and different approaches to become more aware of the importance and meaning of their work for each other. We have not attempted to set forth any practical approaches to the problems of integration which we have tried to isolate. Again many scientific and professional workers — psychiatrists, sociologists, anthropologists, social psychologists, social workers, and family counselors — are attacking these problems. Perhaps they will be able to draw from our report a widened perspective or a more definite view of the team-like nature of all their exploratory and therapeutic efforts. In our view the concept of "mental hygiene" should be widened to include a study of all the mal-integrations and strains that exist in all parts of the transactional field. Certainly mental health is not the responsibility of any one professional group.

Our story is very incomplete. We have described only a few aspects of the "typical" dominant American family. Even if we had taken the space to describe this family picture in greater detail, we would have produced a very distorted view of American family life. No particular family corresponds with this generalized model. If we were to take a particular family as a case study, we would have to locate it along some axis of transition from local, regional, class, and ethnic variables to the idealized dominant American pattern. In the meantime, we hope that we have presented a set of working principles and a method for isolating variance and conflict in family behavior. We believe that the description of such behavior patterns in terms of social roles is the crux of the method. We further believe that the relation of social roles to the specific variable items in the system of cultural value orientations, to the structure and function of the social system, and to the motivational processes of the individual constitutes a set of working principles.

SIX

A Functional Theory of Family Process

Elements of a transactional theory of behavior have been set forth. Values and roles have been identified as the keys for applying the theory to the interpersonal process in the family. In particular, Florence Kluckhohn's enlightening concept of value orientation has been mentioned. It is now time to speak in greater detail of a family study designed by Dr. Kluckhohn and myself.

Our overall aim was to maximize the possibility of observing the full range of cultural, social, psychological, and biological variables which are involved in the events of family life and the adaptation of the individual family member. This suggested to us that we ought to study families from various subcultural groups, in turn dividing each of the groups into two subsamples. The first subsample would contain an emotionally disturbed member, while the second, our control group, would consist of families in which everyone was in a reasonable state of mental health. Thus the first subsample was to consist of "sick" families, the second of "well" families. We believed that this division was important in that we could not think of any way of predicting which aspect of a culturally variant family pattern might be associated with emotional disturbance and which with healthy adjustment.

In addition, we decided that we would need a set of theories

187

for ordering and integrating the data of observation at the cultural, social, and psychological levels. As mentioned, for this purpose we selected the theory of variations in cultural value orientations which had already been worked out and tested by Dr. Kluckhohn, the theory of social roles for dealing with the social and interpersonal level, and psychoanalytic theory for dealing with the individual, intrapsychic area. But the question remained: could we modify or elaborate these conceptual systems so that they really composed an integrated approach instead of merely functioning as interesting and different ways of talking about the same phenomena?

Finally, we decided that we would require an interdisciplinary research team trained in the use of the concepts we wanted to employ. For this purpose, we selected two sociologists, two psychiatric social workers, two psychoanalysts, and a clinical psychologist to work with us in the gathering of data. For the first year we did nothing but meet frequently to talk over the virtues of one versus another type of research design and to iron out the biases and misunderstandings of each other's views — an inevitable part of interprofessional collaboration.

We decided to work with three different subcultural groups: Irish-Americans, Italian-Americans, and so-called "Old" Americans, or Yankees. We decided that the emotionally disturbed member of each "sick" family we looked at should be a child and that the "ethnic" families should be selected so that the grandparents were born in Ireland or Italy while the parents and *their* offspring, including the patient in "sick" families, were born in the United States. We believed that this design would give us the opportunity to study the effect of the change in cultural values as a family accommodates to middle-class American culture across the generations. Dr. George Gardner, Chairman of the Department of Psychiatry at the Children's Medical Center in Boston, kindly agreed to sponsor our investigation, and, as a result, our entire research team was appointed to the staff of the out-patient child psychiatry clinic with no additional clinical duties.

In its completed form, then, our research sample consisted of eighteen families: nine in the "sick" division and nine in the "well." In each of these subsamples, three families were Irish-American, three were Italian-American, and three were Yankee. In order not to complicate matters at the socio-cultural level, all families were working class. The members of the "sick" families were seen for the usual individual weekly psychotherapeutic interviews in the out-patient clinic setting. Work was divided so that the psychiatric social worker interviewed the mother, the sociologist interviewed the father, and the psychoanalyst saw the child-patient. The clinical psychologist tested all family members and occasionally treated a child when more than one child in the family required treatment. With these "sick" families, we held one conjoint family interview in the clinic and saw the entire family in their home from time to time. For the "well" families, this pattern was reversed. Two or three members of the research team visited these families in the home once a week in conjoint interviews, and occasionally one family member was interviewed in private, at work or in the home, in order to gather information that could not be revealed in front of the whole family. In these families, too, the clinical psychologist administered a battery of tests.

To repeat, the method we developed for formulating the nature of the pathological process in the family was through a description of the origin and the fate of role conflicts which disturb the harmonious functioning of the family as an organization. Since, in our approach, so much of the burden of the explanation of pathological function rests upon the social role concept, it may be well to review the way in which this concept was used.

A social role can be defined as a goal-directed configuration of acts patterned in accordance with cultural value orientations for the position a person holds in a social group or situation. This definition takes account of the fact that roles are developed within social systems for some purpose or end of the social system. The role of the parent is to bring up children. The role of a salesman is to sell, that of an educator is to educate. But the behavior assembled within the role in the pursuit of its goals varies greatly from one culture to another. English, Jewish, Arab, and Indian parents each behave differently toward their children and expect different behavior from them. For this reason, one cannot obtain an accurate description of any role without at the same time ascertaining the cultural values which pattern the acts included within the role.

Another important aspect of this definition of social roles is that it assumes that roles never exist in a vacuum but always in a social group or situation. In other words, the behavior to which the role refers always occurs between two or more people who may be defined as role partners. The behavior is then to be understood as occurring in role systems composed of the reciprocal, geared-in acts of the role partners. If the acts do not gear in with

189

each other — if they do not fit — then there will be conflict in the role system or, as we usually say, between the role partners.

We have found that once Formal role conflicts become firmly established in the family, they are likely to give rise secondarily to Informal role conflicts which drain the primary conflict away from the Formal role system in which it begins and deflect it in such a way that the real origin of these conflicts is obscured. Subsequently, communications take place around the secondarily involved Informal roles. Since these roles are not concerned with the real causes of conflict, such communications serve to increase rather than reduce tension.

In order to demonstrate how this process works, I will describe the classification of cultural values which characterize the Formal roles of the Italian-American families. For purposes of illustration, these cultural values will be contrasted with those of the American middle-class family toward which the Italian-Americans are moving in the acculturation process. The theory developed by Dr. Kluck-hohn states that value orientations are highly generalized solutions of common human problems. Secondly, the theory proposes that these solutions have an evaluative component — that is, they serve as principles for making preferred selections between alternative courses of action; an existential component, which means that the value orientations help to define the nature of reality for those who hold the given values; and, finally, they have an affective component, which means that people not only prefer and believe in their own values, but are also ready to bleed and die for them. For this reason, values, once formed, can be changed only with the greatest difficulty.

To repeat, there are four common human problems whose solutions form the classification schema of the value orientations. There are three possible solutions for each of these problems, and the theory states that each of the three possible solutions exists in every culture — though with a different ranking. For the sake of brevity, I will present only the first, or dominantly preferred, solution for each of the categories, illustrating first by reference to the American middle-class family, then passing to the Italian-American family. The value orientations to be described for the Italian-Americans are those characteristic of the native peasant cultures in southern Italy.

The first category involves the relationship between man and nature. *Man-nature* orientation preferences are Subjugation to Nature, Harmony with Nature, and Mastery over Nature. The last is the dominant preference of American middle-class families. Man is expected to triumph in any contest with nature in accordance with the optimistic confidence in the power of science and technology. For any problem encountered by the family, there is always an expert who can be found in the Yellow Pages. In contrast, the Italian families prefer the Subjugation to Nature solution. This, of course, accords with their religious ideology. Man is considered weak and helpless, and his only hope lies in recognizing this fact. He is dependent upon the deity and the saints and is also the prey of malevolent powers such as the evil eye and magical curses, spells, and incantations. The most common reaction we heard from the Italian-American faced with a severe problem was the fatalistic expression: "What can I do?" This means that it is better to recognize one's weakness than to have false pride and unrealistic hopes.

The second human problem, *time* orientation, breaks down into attitudes toward Past, Present, and Future. As discussed, the American middle-class family much prefers the Future for all sorts of choices and decisions. Prospective parents plan for their children's future before they are yet born, save for their old age, and are always watching the clock or inspecting their schedules and calendars to see what they will be doing next. The Italians, on the other hand, prefer the Present over the Past or Future. They live in an extended present in which the future is scarcely differentiated from the past. Accordingly, if change should come, it is usually for the worse. Time is demarcated for them not by the accusing clock or calendar, but by the leisurely cycles of seasons, religious celebrations, national holidays, anniversaries, and ceremonial occasions of all kinds.

The third category is concerned with the preferred mode of *activity*. The preferences here are Doing, Being, and Being-in-becoming. The Doing solution is preferred by Americans, who are always interested in each other's achievements. Parents train children to compete for success — in school, in sports, and in social life — and they anxiously review their own records as parents, comparing themselves in this way, as in every other, with their friends and enemies. Italians prefer the Being solution. Success and achievements aren't nearly so important as expressing one's moods, feelings, and desires. Children are impatiently scolded or punished one minute, effusively given affection the next. What is always expected is spontaneity of feeling. To the Italian, the self-control for the sake of achievement practiced by Americans, looks hypocritical and exploitive.

191

The fourth value orientation, the *relational* orientation, concerns relationships within groups and has three possible solutions: Lineal, Collateral, and Individualistic. Americans prefer the Individualistic solution. Parents train their children from an early age to stand on their own two feet, to control themselves, and to make their own decisions. Families live in small groups of parents and children and think nothing of pulling up roots and moving off to another part of the country, leaving their relatives behind. The Italians, in contrast, prefer the Collateral solution. They prefer to live in big families, in close proximity to relatives; and if anyone has to go away, it is a tragedy for all concerned. Children are trained to be dependent upon their elders and on each other. If anyone makes an independent decision, he is looked on as disloyal or uncaring.

This brief sketch of the two value orientation profiles reveals the extent of the cultural gap that confronts Italian families when they arrive in the United States. It is true that some families arrive with values that have already begun to shift in the direction of the American pattern. Even so, it takes a long time before the process of acculturation makes much of a change in the Italian's value system. As the shift takes place, however, the spouses in these families often find themselves in conflict with each other because the shift to the American value orientation has been unequal. Although some American values have been partly adopted, the old, native patterns have not been wholly relinquished. This produces an internal ambiguity or malintegration of values within the individual. One often hears the value ambiguity communicated in the expression: "Do as I say, not as I do!" Because formal roles are patterned by the value orientations, the relationship between the spouses becomes strained, and the strain then filters into other role systems. But, before the origin of this strain can be described, it is desirable to review the general classification of social roles which we have used to keep track of the role conflicts.

Social roles can be divided into three major categories: Formal, Informal, and Fictive. Formal roles can be characterized in several different ways. They include the major activities which every society needs to regulate in order to survive. Some, like age and sex roles, concern straight biological functions and are universally ascribed to every member of the society. Not for one moment can anyone safely step out of the behavior expected for his age or sex. Some, like domestic or family roles, are almost as universally and inevitably ascribed; for everyone is born into a family, and most people create new ones. Still others, like occupational, religious, and recreational roles, are more episodic. That is, one does not need to occupy all of them all the time. Nevertheless, they too are strictly patterned and required for most people.

Informal roles, on the other hand, are much more occasional and at the choice of the individual than are Formal roles. Some have to do with transitional occasions — that is, with getting out of one situation and into another. The sick role, for example, is such a transitional role (which the ill person may or may not agree to take). By the same token, some people, usually called malingerers, may take the sick role when they are not actually ill. At any rate, the sick role is informally patterned in every society in order to get the ill person back into a state of health. Visitors, guests, and travelers are also examples of transitional roles. Another group of Informal roles are the character roles. These include heroes and villains, liars and cheats, exhibitionists and voyeurs, sadists and masochists. Such designations are usually thought to result from traits of character, but a moment's reflection reveals that the given behavior can't take place without the reciprocal behavior of a role partner. Every hero must have his admirers; every exhibitionist must locate his voyeur; just as every masochist needs to find his sadist in order to enjoy his role in life. But such roles are not required of anyone by the social system. They may be adopted by one person or assigned to another — as when we assign the role of a fool to someone we don't like. Such adoptions and assignments, then, are parts of the informal workings of social groups.

The third category, Fictive roles, includes roles which are not pragmatically related to the ongoing work of any social system or group but serve the interests of imagination or play. For the most part, they are occupied quite deliberately on the basis of pretense, as when a girl plays the role of mother to her doll or a boy plays cops and robbers. All Fictive roles make room for fantasy behavior in everyday life and thus serve the purpose — for adults as well as children — of relief from the stress and strain of reality. Every society sanctions such roles provided they are accompanied by a communication that says in effect: this is not serious; this is in jest or play. When fictive or fantasy roles are taken without this accompanying signal — that is, in earnest — then we say that the person who shows such behavior and the group which accepts such behavior are pathological. I am referring to the difference between the person who pretends to be the prophet Elijah, for the sake of

193

amusement or satire, and the person who says he *is* the prophet Elijah and his followers accept this claim.

I would now like to illustrate the pathological relationships between value conflicts and role conflicts in the Formal category. Note that deflection of such conflicts into the area of Informal roles makes them almost uncontrollable without outside help. The reason for the pathological fixation of the conflict in the Informal roles system is that none of the family members is aware of the nature of the communication problem. They do not realize that they are involved in an incompatability of values, and they do not recognize that they have displaced their disagreements into the area of Informal roles. (Or, if they happen to realize it, they have too much anxiety about bringing the disagreement out into the open in the areas in which it really lies.)

What I am talking about was evident in the case of a second-generation Italian-American family given the name Tondi in our reports. Mr. Tondi was thirty-five years old; Mrs. Tondi was thirty-three, and they had two children, Timothy, six years old, and Antonio, Jr., (nicknamed Sonny) who was five. The family had been referred to the out-patient psychiatric clinic of the Children's Medical Center because of Sonny, who suffered from severe constipation of functional origin. In addition he was a stutterer. During the diagnostic workup of the family, it became clear that Timmie, the older brother, also had symptoms. He also was a stutterer, he suffered from a school phobia, and he had various eating problems. It was Mr. Tondi who had brought Sonny to the hospital, thus initiating the diagnostic process. It was from Mrs. Tondi that we learned, with some reluctance on her part, of Timmie's disturbances. This was obviously an unusual arrangement, since it is ordinarily the mother who brings a child to a clinic and who makes the complaints about the child. This reversal of roles, therefore, set the stage for our enquiry into the nature of the communication process in the family. Why was it the father and not the mother who assigned the sick role to Sonny, and why did he not assign the sick role to Timmie, who was equally, if not more, disturbed?

When the family was accepted for study, diagnostic and therapeutic interviews were held with the parents and with both children at the clinic and in the home. As our investigation proceeded, we discovered a number of other disturbances in the relation between Formal and Informal roles in the family. It turned out that Mrs. Tondi's definition of the nature of Sonny's bowel dysfunction was ambiguous and somewhat bizarre. Partly, she saw the constipation as a physiological dysfunction, partly as an act of wilful disobedience. For example, she believed that if Sonny would only agree to her giving him an enema every other day, his constipation would be controlled. On his part, Sonny was extremely frightened by the enemas and terrified of having a bowel movement, even though he knew he experienced pain if he withheld his stool. Accordingly, he lied frequently to his mother, saying he had had a movement when he actually had not. Mrs. Tondi was able to recognize the lie at the point where he was obviously in pain. Realizing what was coming, Sonny would attempt to hide. This was then defined by his mother as disobedience. She would become anxious about the damage he was doing himself and angry about his disobedience and would end up chasing him about the house in order to give him an enema, thus creating a scene which was frightening to both children. When he refused to take the sick role as she defined it, she perceived this as evil and assigned Sonny the role of rascal and troublemaker. In return, the boy saw himself in the role of victim of his mother's ministrations.

Sonny's role as the impulsive rascal was generalized to other occasions. For example, Sonny, though younger, was strong and well built, while Timmie was slender and poorly coordinated. When Sonny tried to protect Timmie in neighborhood fights, Mrs. Tondi would accuse Sonny of having started the fight in order to cause trouble. She repeatedly reproached him for not being a "clean fighter" and, in spite of his age, saw him as the future Italian cutthroat or thug. Sonny was, in general, treated by the parents as the older and stronger, while Timmie was given the role of the younger and weaker son.

What do these distortions of the Informal roles signify? What did they mean to the parents? How were they brought about? For answers we must look at the history of the parents' involvement in their Formal roles.

Mrs. Tondi's parents were born in Italy, and her mother considered herself socially superior to her father, as well as to most of the other Italian families in the North End of Boston. As an adolescent, Mrs. Tondi was not considered as attractive as her older sister, and later she had few boy friends. Mr. Tondi was the only man who asked her to marry him. Her family, however, considered his family socially inferior and discouraged the relationship. Since Mrs. Tondi's *Relational* orientation, like her family's, was Collateral, she followed their wishes. These values fit in with the fact that in Italy marriages are arranged by the parents.

When, after several years, no other prospect appeared, and Mr. Tondi refused to be discouraged, they finally gave in and sanctioned the marriage on the ground that she wasn't getting any younger.

Mr. Tondi was the youngest of the many children of his Italian-born parents. His father died when he was a small child, and the mother managed to support the family with the aid of the older siblings. Because of the hard economic struggle, because of his native intelligence, and because his older siblings broke a path for him, Mr. Tondi learned some of the middle-class American value orientations. He was able to plan for the future and to work for achievement. He was an airplane mechanic with good opportunities for advancement. But his family actually was somewhat lower on the socio-economic scale than his wife's, though not as much as her family claimed. To him, the social differences meant that his wife could help him on the road to success in American terms, and therefore the marriage represented an achievement, while to his wife and her family it represented a failure.

After several years of marriage, Mrs. Tondi continued to believe herself more American than her husband and superior to him. Actually, she was much closer to Italian values than he, as was manifested in the persistence of her Collateral ties to her own family and in the mixed Being and Subjugation to Nature values which she showed her children.

Because of her frequently derogatory attitude toward him, Mr. Tondi gradually began to respond with a bitterness and resentment which he was unable to express and was largely unaware of. He warded off these feelings by saying that his wife was irritable and nervous because of the constant demands made on her by her family. Thus his overt attitude toward his wife was calm and reasonable, if long-suffering.

Covertly, however, and unconsciously, he found a way to express his resentment and to communicate to his wife his criticism of her value orientations. How the Tondi boys became both pawns and participants in this domestic battle is related in the next chapter.

Up to this point I have described the Tondis from the point of view of the organization of the pathological behavior within the family process. I have spoken of the family as a whole, with respect to the interweaving of values and roles. Now it is time to ask, how does the psychodynamic process within the individual fit into the theoretical approach? How can the traditional categories of motivation derived from psychoanalytic theory be utilized?

To get at these questions our research group asked a new question of our data: what motivates the family members to take the Formal, Informal, and Fictive roles which we see them assuming and to assign the roles to each other that we see them assigning? For example, why did Mrs. Tondi assume that she was married to a husband inferior to her in terms of American values? Why did Mr. Tondi remain covertly so loyal and uncomplaining toward a wife who derogated him and gave him little affection? Why did Mrs. Tondi assume that Sonny is a dirty little thug, thus assigning him a Fictive role? Why did Sonny respond by withholding his bowel movement and by becoming his older brother's protector in the neighborhood battles?

These questions also are explored in detail in the next chapter. Let it suffice here to give some hints about the interconnections as they apply to Mrs. Tondi.

At the ego level Mrs. Tondi was genuinely confused about the nature of American middle-class values, and some of the social worker's activity with her consisted in helping her to clear up this confusion and to see that her definition of her husband and children was inconsistent with American values. Similarly, part of her shame about her husband and children stemmed from her ego ideals, which had been formed in terms of Italian values. Owing to the positive transference and strong identification she formed with the social worker, Mrs. Tondi was able to effect a change in her perception of her husband so that in the course of treatment her attitude toward him became more positive.

However, another part of the set of roles she assigned to herself and to her husband and children came from pre-genital and genital strivings and defenses which the value conflicts served merely to reinforce. For example, she herself had had difficulties in the control of bowel and bladder functions during her childhood. She was fascinated with dirt, with fecal products, and with aggressive behavior, and she was defensively determined to bring all of these under ruthless control. She spanked Sonny vigorously and with pleasure whenever he provoked her by being disobedient. Then she would ask the social worker, with a good deal of guilt, whether she had done "the right thing." She was able to justify this behavior in Italian terms with the formula: children need to be taught right from wrong. She felt guilty about it in American terms, however, on the basis that the child needs to learn for himself how to control his behavior. The difference between the ego-syntonic versus the ego-alien definition of her disciplinary behavior is clearly the product of which set of values she inclined toward. This, in turn, depended on which parental figure, her own mother or the social worker, she identified with. But the drive pressures behind the behavior stemmed from her childhood rivalry with her older brother, who had been preferred by her mother. Unconsciously, she both hated her brother and was libidinally tied to him. Consciously she had admired her brother during her adolescence and felt sorry for him later because as an adult he had turned out to be a troublemaker and a failure in life. Thus she had divided up between her son and her husband the roles which actually belonged to her relation with her brother.

If we traced the unconscious libidinal and hostile conflicts of the other family members, it would become clear how they fitted into the network of role relations which had become established in the family. Perhaps enough has already been said to put these interconnections into a brief formula: what are called object relations in terms of the unconscious intrapsychic process become Informal and Fictive role relations when manifested in external behavior. Just like the internal object relations, the role relations represent compromises between the drive pressure and the anxiety over gratification which fit, with more or less strain, into the cultural definitions of the patterning of the roles as well as into the overall organization of the family, with respect to its needs and goals. However, there is no one-to-one correspondence between object relations and role relations. The interconnections can be established only through a psychotherapeutic investigation.

The integration of value theory, role theory, and psychodynamics allows one to view the family process simultaneously with respect to its cultural, organizational, and individual determinants. To demonstrate however, that this approach constitutes more than an interesting way to talk about the same behavior viewed from these different frames of reference, it is necessary to compare the effects of cultural value strain between the different ethnic groups and between the sick and the well families. These comparisons are undertaken in Chapters Six through Nine.

The principal merit of this approach is that it permits us to detect the connection between cultural strain, family conflict, and individual pathology. These connections emerge only from the comparisons of the different groups. The second advantage of this approach is that it permits one to establish a therapeutic relationship with families who would, under ordinary circumstances, be very hard to reach.

Four general findings which grew out of our comparative analysis are:

1. We have found that each culture has its own, built-in, characteristic strain in value orientations. For example, the strain in the native Italian values lies between the *Collateral* orientation and the *Being* orientation. The collateral network can't take the strain of too much spontaneity, particularly when it involves hostile-aggressive behavior. The collateral network tends to split up, and violent feuds break out between the split groups, leading to personal tragedies. In the Yankee working-class family, there is a strain between strong *Doing* orientation and a *Present* time emphasis. The parents in these families expect of themselves and of their children individualistic achievement, in the American style, but since they are unable to plan for the future, the level of achievement is quite low, and the feeling of failure and bitterness is strong.

2. The built-in native strain becomes a point of vulnerability when the family undergoes cultural transition. For example, the Italian family is particularly vulnerable to threats to the maintenance of the collateral system. They may experience such a threat either because of the accidents of the immigration pattern which lands the family outside of an Italian community or because the family tries to change this orientation to the American emphasis on individualism prematurely. The lesson to be learned from this finding is that families can be taught which of their values they can safely change first and which had best be left alone in the course of cultural accommodation.

3. In the course of acculturation, some families attempt to change all their values rapidly and simultaneously. This produces chaos and anomie — a canceling out of the meanings and values which prevents anything other than a most cynical or delinquent adaptation.

4. All our families, both sick and well, showed value strains and role conflicts. But in the well group, typified by the Sirrentis in Chapter Eight, the strains and conflicts were handled by conscious communication and deliberate reworking and compromise around the Formal role problems. In addition, the conflicts were not so severe. In our sick group, the conflicts were more intense and the influences of the value conflict on the Formal roles was avoided or kept out of conscious

communication. As a result, the conflicts were shifted, as in the Tondi family, to Informal roles where they were immune to modification.

To what degree this difference between the sick and well families is a result of the intensity of the culture conflicts or of the biological limitations in adaptive capacity is a question for future research.

SEVEN

The Tondis: A "Sick" Family

I see the family in general as a system of reciprocal patterns and processes operating within a larger field of interpenetrating systems. Role and values are crucial in the workings of the system, and acculturation stress is potentially destructive. To illustrate the applications of transactional theory, the Tondis — introduced in the last chapter — are presented here in greater detail.

The Tondis, a nuclear family consisting of the parents and two small boys, were referred to our research project for the treatment of moderately severe symptoms of psychological disturbance in both children. Actually, it was Mr. Tondi who had initiated the diagnostic and treatment process. The youngest son suffered from chronic constipation with episodes of abdominal distress and severe pain on moving his bowels. He would go four, five, or six days with no bowel movement at all. The family doctor had ignored or minimized this condition. The father decided that his son should be seen by a specialist and brought the boy to an out-patient medical clinic for observation. There it was found that the boy had a moderately enlarged colon because of the retention of feces, but no organic cause could be found for the condition. The basic factor was considered to be psychogenic, and a psychiatric diagnostic study was recommended.

The family consisted of Antonio (Tony) Tondi, the husband, who was thirty-five years old; Celia, the wife, thirty-three; Timothy (Timmie), age six; and Antonio, Jr. (Sonny), age five. During the initial interviews it became evident that Sonny's constipation was not the only source of concern within the family. The parents were also worried about Timmie. He was subject to severe temper tantrums, stuttered badly, and could not go to sleep without rocking in bed at a tempo which alarmed baby-sitters, relatives, and friends. In addition, Timmie had great difficulty in separating from his mother. If she left him at home to go shopping, for example, he would become distressed, feeling that she would never return. Even when she remained at home, which she did most of the time, he could not play outside without returning to the house frequently to make sure that she had not gone away.

At first both parents were in a state of near panic because of Sonny's constipation, and, as a result, all other family problems seemed to be secondary. By the third and fourth day of constipation, Sonny was obviously in pain and quite tense and irritable. He also was clearly postponing going to the toilet because of fear — particularly fear of the pain which he experienced when he finally did have a movement. The parents were beside themselves when, no longer able to postpone the dread event, Sonny screamed and cried during the evacuation. They were also repeatedly astonished at the size of the stool which Sonny produced, a delivery of huge, stiff, hardened masses, which, on occasion, was said to have clogged the flushing mechanism of the toilet.

Mr. and Mrs. Tondi were beset not only by the pity they felt for their son and their inability to help him but also by the tyranny that his symptom waged over the family. Family events had to be timed to Sonny's abdominal state. If he had recently moved his bowels, there was freedom to plan visits to relatives or whatever activities might take them out of the house. But when he was in the tension phase of his constipation, it was necessary to stay at home. Sonny was afraid of using any toilet but his own. In addition, the parents were reluctant to expose him to anyone outside the immediate family when he was tense and irritable. They were ashamed of his condition and of their possible responsibility for it.

Fortunately, the constipation yielded rather rapidly to treatment. Soon after treatment was initiated, a more temperate rhythm of bowel movements began to be established, and the anxiety of the parents on this score began to abate. There then came into view a wider range of problems. Sonny also stuttered — not as

202

frequently or as severely as his brother but enough to cause the parents concern. Mr. Tondi, it turned out, had stuttered severely in his youth and still stuttered whenever he became excited. He felt very badly about the stuttering of his two sons, for he was convinced that his own speech problem had been an obstacle to job advancement and economic improvement. He said repeatedly that stuttering can hold a person back. The idea of being held back because of inner defects and initial disadvantages was a theme frequently expressed by both parents.

Tony Tondi viewed himself as a person who had struggled hard all his life to overcome the disadvantages with which he was initially faced — the large, impoverished, fatherless family in which he grew up, his stuttering as a youth, his shortness of stature, and his lack of educational opportunities. Though he sometimes wondered whether the struggle was worth the effort in view of the worries about the children, he usually maintained an air of optimism. His strenuous efforts to improve his circumstances had led, in his opinion, to a modest success. He was a skilled mechanic, and he believed that human problems, like mechanical ones, could be resolved through hard work and the application of the appropriate technology. This point of view had enabled him to hold a secure position for many years as an aircraft mechanic, to build a house for his family in an attractive suburban setting largely through his own efforts, and to give his children material satisfactions and personal attentions that he had missed in his own childhood.

When the possibility of psychotherapy for the children and weekly interviews with the parents was suggested, the father immediately assimilated the procedure to his views on technical solutions to problems. He believed that he and his wife must be making "serious errors" in their handling of the children. If these errors could be located and corrected while the children were still young, then they would not have to suffer from unattractive traits of behavior which, he believed, would make life difficult for them. If his own participation would help correct the error and overcome the children's handicaps, he was, as he said, "all for it." He asserted he had no complaints on his own account. He stated that his marriage was "perfect." There were occasional domestic quarrels such as one finds in any family, but these, he felt, were of no consequence.

This relaxed, optimistic view of the marriage was not shared by his wife. She soon unburdened a multitude of complaints about herself, her husband, her children, her home, her relatives, and her life in general. All her life she had felt inferior to others because of her short stature, poor complexion, unattractive figure, and inability to express herself. Now she viewed herself as a failure both as a wife and a mother. Her husband, she said, was also short and unattractive physically and was a very ordinary man who needed to be pushed in order to achieve anything. She wished she could encourage him, but the difficulty was that she had never loved him; and now she was afraid that she was becoming the same kind of nagging, unpleasant, critical wife that her mother had always been. With two such handicapped parents, it was not surprising to her that the children had so many defects. Still, this outcome was not what she had wanted or hoped for. Like her husband, she had hoped to rise above the circumstances of her birth and to bring up children of whom she could be proud.

Almost all the attitudes which Celia Tondi expressed were marked with ambivalence and ambiguity. She was ashamed of her low estimation of her husband and had never directly told him how she felt about him. Nor did she want him ever to hear of her actual feelings about her marriage. Though she tended to consider Tony ineffective, childish, and unattractive, she knew that he was well liked by the neighbors and respected by his associates at work. She said she could appreciate him only through the eyes of other people. He tried hard to be a good father and husband. But he failed to meet her standards for these roles. He left too many family problems up to her to handle. On the other hand, she knew that she compulsively criticized him so often for the decisions that he did make that it was no wonder he gave up trying to handle family affairs. Nevertheless, she secretly wished that he would overcome her tendency to dominate him; she wanted to be over-ruled and was happy when, on occasion, he would be firm and insist on having his own way as he did about bringing Sonny to the clinic. She was even happier if his decision turned out to be correct and hers wrong. And, in a reversal of her usual, sour view of her marriage, she sometimes described with pleasure her feeling of accomplishment on the rare occasion when they had been able to resolve some problem in collaboration with each other. She said that, if the family were to be accepted for therapy, she hoped she could learn how to be a better wife to her husband.

In her behavior toward her children, her usual ambivalence was complicated by nagging uncertainty. She felt that almost every-thing that she did with them was wrong; yet she did not know what was right. For example, for Sonny's toilet problem she had "tried everything" and "nothing worked." When Sonny threw rocks at other children in the neighborhood, she was especially upset. Unlike the Tondi's, most of the parents in the community were college graduates, and their children were "well behaved." She was horrified at Sonny's behavior and appalled at what the neighbors must think of his parents. She also believed that a boy who throws rocks at age five will throw knives when he is older. In her imagination, Sonny was already a budding Italian gangster, fated to a career of crime like so many of the boys in Boston's North End Italian community in which she had grown up. The behavior had to be controlled, in fact, expunged. Whenever it occurred, she spanked him vigorously and confined him to his room for several hours. If she caught him in the act of transgression, she was likely to rush out of the house, collar him, and hit him in front of his friends — to show one and all that this behavior was discouraged by his parents. She told the interviewer of her serious doubt of the correctness of her method of discipline. But how could one and how should one handle such disturbing behavior?

Similar questions of what to do and when to do it plagued her relations with Timmie. She wanted to help him with his stuttering. Her husband's stuttering had been cured, for all practical purposes, when he was fourteen years old. A sympathetic, kindly teacher, an expert in speech problems, had devoted a great deal of time to his stuttering and had taught him how to breathe and speak rhythmically by pounding out a regular beat with his fist. They had tried this with Timmie, forcing him to count regularly, breathe in time, and speak slowly. It had not worked, and Timmie now cried if forced to persist. Most of the time he could not persist because Sonny kept interrupting and talking when Timmie was trying "the method." Timmie could not tolerate his brother's intrusion into his talking time. He would abandon the method and attempt to gush out words as fast as possible to compete with Sonny. When Celia tried to slow them both down or silence them, Timmie would have a temper tantrum and retreat to his room, leaving the floor to the victorious Sonny.

To members of the project staff who were conducting the diagnostic interviews, the appearance and behavior of members of the Tondi family did not correspond to the views of either of the parents. Tony did not seem the ineffectual person described by his wife nor the calm, purposeful husband and father that he appeared in his own eyes. He was a short (5′ 4″), compact, muscular man, of dark complexion, with large brown eyes and a round face. Always neat and well groomed, he usually dressed in sport or working clothes. He had a genial smile, an alert expression, and a friendly manner. Though superficially relaxed and mildly deferential, there was an underlying tension in his behavior — as if, though basically guarded and cautious, he labored to make himself accessible and to be cooperative. He was intelligent (I.Q. of 113 on the Wechsler-Bellvue Test) and responsive in interviews, but it was difficult for him to express openly any personal feelings about members of his family other than concern for his children's behavior. He seemed to show concealed pleasure in Sonny's rebelliousness when, with a smile on his face, he said that Sonny had his mother "wrapped around his finger" over his bowel movements.

Celia's behavior corresponded neither to the perfect wife and dedicated mother of Tony's description nor to the dismal failure of her own. She was short (5' 2") and stocky, with dark hair and eyes, neatly and conservatively dressed, and carefully made-up with lipstick and pancake powder. When at ease and cheerful, she had an attractive sparkle, but most of the time her facial expression was tense and her manner urgent. She had difficulty restraining her emotions. Her eyes often brimmed with tears as she told what a poor job she was doing as a mother. In the waiting room before and after the individual interviews, she seemed quite anxious about the behavior of the children, tensely correcting them, supplying the word that Timmie was stuttering on or commanding Sonny to be careful with toys belonging to the clinic. Yet, behind her obsessive concern about appearances, there was a hidden warmth and a buried interest in the needs and personalities of the children. In the interviews, she too was responsive and intelligent (I.Q. 115) and eager to cooperate.

Six-year-old Timmie was of normal weight and height for his years. He had a thin, wiry build. His hair and complexion were lighter in color than other members of the family, and his movement was less heavy-footed. He was well coordinated and much interested in activities such as swimming, skating, building model airplanes, and modeling in clay. He stuttered so badly, distorting words, that it was often difficult to know what he was saying. Yet there were intervals when he could speak quite clearly. He was friendly and eager to please and rapidly formed a warm attachment to the female psychotherapist who interviewed him. His I.Q. was 103, representing average intellectual functioning. However, his vocabulary test score was low, and he was unable to admit not knowing the meaning of words. He made up fanciful definitions on the basis of clang associations.

Sonny was huskier and two inches shorter than his brother. He physically resembled his father, having the same large brown eyes, round face, and rosy, healthy appearance. There was a belligerence in his manner and an excitability of gesture which contrasted with Timmie's rather more shy and controlled conduct. He stuttered only occasionally, usually when he got into a talking contest with his brother in the waiting room. Despite a fleeting chip-on-the-shoulder attitude, he was friendly with the male psychotherapist who interviewed him. During interviews in the playroom, he alternated between exploring all the toys and other materials, examining them with great care, and gingerly putting everything back in place. He enjoyed painting and crayoning and was eager to display his products to his parents after the interview. His I.Q. was 87, but this score was considered to fall below his potential because of his inner conflicts. Both boys came to the interviews well dressed and immaculate.

In the course of the diagnostic procedure, both parents and children were given a variety of psychological tests. All the family members had considerable anxiety about the testing process. For both boys, the psychological tests revealed a greater impairment of ego functions than was evident in their relations with the interviewers. Sonny had difficulty attending to the test tasks. He frequently broke off, wandered around the room, opened drawers, and asked questions about what was contained in cabinets. But he could scarcely pay attention to the answers to his own questions. He seemed both to be running away from the test and to be driven by an insatiable curiosity. He expressed the idea that the tests would reveal whether or not he could go to school, and he seemed confused about his age. There was suggestive evidence that this confusion resulted from an imperfect separation of his identity from that of his brother, who was about to enter the first grade. To the last five of the Rohrschach cards he gave the single, identical response: pheasants. He said that he had recently seen a pheasant hiding in his back yard, and, it later turned out, he knew that his father hunted pheasants. Stories told to CAT and TAT cards indicated both a desire to destroy or mess up and a pronounced fear of the consequences of carrying out the desire. Considering his circumstances this fear was not unexpected. The defense against it, however, frequently consisted of a flight from reality or a distortion of reality. For example, in response to the spanking card of the CAT series, he reversed the actual situation and told a story of getting a mother's love through being clean and neat. In the summary of the psychological test responses, Sonny was described as being in an active and somewhat aggressive flight from a painful reality in which he experienced a temptation to destroy and to mess and simultaneously feared that he would be destroyed as a result. Still, the possibility of other than regressive solutions to his anal-sadistic conflict were seen in his desire to go to school and his active curiosity. It was considered that treatment was indicated and that he had sufficient intelligence and capacity for relations with others to be able to profit from it.

During the testing procedure Timmie was at first frightened, and at one point he was close to tears and asked for his mother. He was reassured by the tester that his mother was waiting for him, became calmer, and was able to complete the tests. Like Sonny, he had difficulty in paying attention to the test stimuli. His response to the vocabulary subtest of the Stanford-Binet has already been mentioned. He showed a somewhat parallel response to the Rohrschach cards. He began by responding specifically to the blot but rapidly went off into a series of free associations and fantasies. These excursions represented a flight from the actual percept, and he was unable to locate them in any features of the cards themselves. The fantasies were repetitious, containing an endless sequence of bombs, black clouds, lightning, jet planes, and black storms. These apparently represented natural and man-made forces of destruction of which he was frightened, both for their actual and for their symbolic meaning. In contrast to this "autistic" Rohrschach response, to the picture cards of the CAT he told conventional stories which were adequately related to the figures in the cards. The content of the stories involved a good deal of conflict between parents, in which he always chose to be on the father's side. In many stories he described an atmosphere of closeness between a father and son. (That this was a wish rather than an actuality was indicated by his fear of separation from his mother and by his father's statement that Timmie seemed to have little desire to be close to him.) In the summary analysis of the test responses, the psychologist stated that Timmie could be described as a phobic child with a tendency to autistic withdrawal under stress, particularly that of an unstructured situation. The boundary between reality and fantasy was indefinite and tended to disappear when his fears were evoked. However, there was also evidence of an attempt to turn back to reality through a counterphobic denial of fear. In consideration of his desire to master his fears and the warmth with which he could form relationships, a good response to therapy was anticipated.

Celia Tondi came to the testing sessions as a woman heavy with sorrow and guilt, the content of which was about to be revealed by the tests themselves. She sat primly, as before a judge, frequently readjusting her posture to an even more correct position. Anticipating exposure, she consistently interrupted the test procedures to make little confessions and excuses, perhaps in the hope of obtaining a lighter sentence. For example, she confessed to feeling guilty "to this day" for having somehow provoked "my gentle father into throwing a bottle at my mother which left a scar." Her responses revealed an excessive concern with what is proper and visible. In her TAT stories women were portrayed in a dramatic, almost soap opera fashion, as suffering from deep hurts and injuries, longing for an unobtainable freedom. A preoccupation with being damaged or causing bodily damage ran through her productions, most heavily concentrated in her view of mother-child relations. In the alternation between attacking and being damaged, there was a tendency to seek relief through withdrawal to passivity and helplessness, "like a kitty who is quiet and fed and cuddled and doesn't destroy much." She showed doubts about the completeness of the female body. Arms, legs, heads, and hands were variously missing from her drawings and percepts. Cleanliness and neatness were also emphasized, usually in the context of a cold, unsympathetic mother being stern with a child. That this was the way she saw herself and her own mother was indicated by the fact that it was in the process of reading these situations into the TAT cards that she talked about her own traumatic experiences as a child and her defective performance as a mother. Despite the conflict-laden material which was evoked, the tests did not reveal any serious distortions of reality or deficiencies in ego functioning. The diagnostic assessment was that of a neurotic character disturbance with hysterical and depressive features.

Tony Tondi was much less serious, more relaxed and matter-of-fact about the testing procedure than his wife. His anxiety was expressed in numerous digressions, jokes, and humorous attempts to disqualify himself: "I haven't done this since grammar school," and, in response to the TAT instructions, "I read non-fiction." In contrast to these disqualifications, he made known his competence in building houses, fixing cars, and sports. Unlike Celia, who spent a good deal of time defending and attacking herself before the tester, Tony was compliant in following instructions and sometimes asked for help. His productions were better organized than hers. In place of her pervading moralism, he displayed a practical common sense. However, he picked his words so carefully in the attempt to exhibit a sophisticated command of language that he often ended up with what sounded like a formal disquisition — for example, "This state going against his better judgment, he . . . ." (It later turned out that fear of being shown up as possessing an inadequate vocabulary was endemic in the Tondi family.)

Tony's reactions revealed a pervading passivity and a restriction of aggression. For him the Rohrschach cards principally suggested butterflies, insects, birds, and various other animals with open mouths. In his TAT stories there was little assertion, either by men or women, but signs of concealed anger toward women appeared in the frequency with which he depicted them sick or dying. Under a cover of conformity and compliance he showed evidence of covert rebellion toward authorities. For example, when asked what sort of an animal he would like to be, he said, "A dog because it's friendly and people like dogs, although some people might say because it tears up the boss's garden." Because of his desire to control aggression, his productions in general lacked spontaneity. His ego-functioning, however, though constricted in some areas, was considered adequate.

These test procedures plus the initial interviews disclosed the Tondis as a family seriously entangled in emotional conflicts between each other and within themselves. All had sufficiently intact ego defenses and appropriate orientations to reality so as not to be gravely threatened with a psychosis or some other mental illness too difficult to deal with in an out-patient setting. The diagnostic and behavioral data which we have presented so far are, of course, quite limited by the exclusion of the material on the past history and developmental course of each family member. These facts were gathered in the course of the assessment in the usual fashion. But, since we are dealing with a family rather than an individual, we believe it desirable to organize the data of the past in a fashion somewhat different from what is customary and to present them separately from this brief snapshot of the family's functioning.

BACKGROUND TO MARRIAGE

Up to this point we have said little about the issues involved in the social standing and cultural context of the Tondi family. Through a special effort these were gradually brought into focus.

Tony and Celia Tondi were both second generation Italian-

American Roman Catholics. Their parents had been born in Italy and emigrated to this country in their teens. Tony and Celia were both born in Boston's North End Italian community though they had been unacquainted with each other until they met as young adults.

Tony was the youngest of ten children in his family. His father had died when Tony was three years old, leaving his mother essentially without funds to support the large family. Nor were there any first generation relatives to help her. Tony was full of admiration for his mother's valiant efforts to keep the family going without becoming dependent upon public assistance agencies. She owned her own house, which was a large one, so that she was able to take in boarders. Thrifty and determined, she invested what she was able to save in real estate and eventually owned two other rooming houses. All the children were pressed into service in the maintenance and operation of these establishments, which were run like a small family business. Tony regarded her as a "pioneer woman" with a "good business head," and he attributed his desire to get ahead in life to the example that she set.

While the children were young and the mother alive, the closeness typical of the collaterally organized Italian family was maintained. There were conflicts among family members, which will be described later. After Tony's marriage, however, he and Celia took an apartment in the building owned by Celia's parents, and Tony's relations with his wife's family tended to take the place of the intimacy which he had formerly maintained with his own. He continued to visit his mother dutifully every day, running little errands for her and talking over the day's happenings, but he saw his brothers and sisters less and less frequently.

Just before Timmie's birth, Tony's mother died. He was depressed for several months after her death and then angry about a controversy which broke out between the siblings over the distribution of the mother's estate. Thereafter, his relations with his brothers and sisters became even more attenuated. By the time that we became acquainted with him, Tony's behavior toward his relatives was ambivalent. He maintained a formally "correct" attitude, paying visits on important occasions and avoiding outright rupture or conflict. But he was resentful that he had not received more help in times of stress, especially from his brothers. There were two sisters toward whom he still felt friendly. They exchanged visits frequently and sometimes served as baby-sitters for Tony and Celia. With the others he felt he had little in common.

As a result of Tony's attitude, there was no opportunity for project personnel to meet members of Tony's family, to see his personality through their eyes, or to determine, aside from Tony's and Celia's brief statements, what sort of people they were. Information about them is sparse. The eldest sibling, Ruth, was fifty-six years old at the time of first contact with the family. She was a widow with five children, living in a suburb remote from the Tondi's home. Her husband, a barber, had died several years before, leaving her in difficult financial straits. Tony had a special animosity toward this sister because, in his opinion, she had been disrespectful to his mother while demanding money from her because of her husband's difficulty in maintaining steady employment. The next born sibling, Carmen, was fifty-three years old. Her husband was a house painter. The couple had no children and lived in the North End of Boston, in the area in which the family had grown up. Arthur, age fifty-one, the oldest son, was unmarried. He was a chronic alcoholic whose behavior had troubled the family since Tony was a boy. A skilled mechanic, he was usually unemployed and dependent upon his family for help. Currently he was living with his younger brother, Robert, in the North End of Boston. Elizabeth, fifty years old, a widow with two children, also lived in the North End, but nothing more was learned about her. Nor were any details gathered about the next sibling, John, other than the facts that he was single, worked as a printer, and still lived in the North End. Alice, age forty-four, was single, lived alone in the North End, and worked for a curtain manufacturer. Maria, age forty-two, was married and had three children. She and her husband, a machinist, lived in the North End. Maria and Alice, who immediately preceded her, were the two sisters with whom Tony still maintained friendly relations. The youngest sister, Josephine, was forty-one years old and unmarried. She lived alone in the North End, supporting herself through odd factory jobs. Finally, there was Robert, age forty, Tony's next oldest sibling. He had attended M.I.T. during the evenings while working as a machinist and had graduated with a degree in civil engineering. He was the only one of the children who had attained a college education. Married, with two children, he lived, like the others, in the North End and was currently looking after Arthur, the unemployable, alcoholic brother. In spite of his superior education, his style of life, apparently, differed little from that of the other brothers and sisters who, unlike Tony, had never left the North End.

Under the matriarchal hand of the widow Tondi, functioning

as both mother and father for her large brood, the emphasis on economic survival was heavy indeed. With work so demanding, there was little time or occasion for the recreational pleasures, the food and drink and gaiety, even for the maternal succor and solicitous supervision usually found in the Italian-American family. During his interviews, Tony often commented on the material deprivation and the stern tone of his childhood. There was no money for toys — skates, bicycles, bats, and balls were non-existent. Birthday celebrations and gift-exchanges were minimal. His mother was usually too busy and too hard-pressed financially to attend to such things. During most of his childhood, it was his sisters, Alice and Maria, those with whom he was still friendly, who had looked after him, not his mother. The mother functioned more as the commanding officer, making the important decisions and giving orders for child care but leaving the execution up to the older siblings.

With the family system employed so much for the sake of work and sheer survival, so little in the interests of pleasure and gratification, the principle of maintaining close, collateral contacts inevitably suffered damage. There was insufficient emotional reward in it. Worse, still, was the effort made by the mother to maintain the prestige of the family in the extended Italian-American community by giving huge parties for friends and neighbors on important occasions, such as Easter, Thanksgiving, or local religious feastdays. That the money and the energy so hard to come by were used for this purpose gave rise to resentment among the children. As expressed by Tony, the children felt that, though a Rock of Gibralter against catastrophe and devoted to keeping the family together, she was more interested in winning love and acclaim from others by performing services for them than in gaining love and affection from her own children by paying personal attention to their needs. Thus a kind of isolated collaterality developed, lacking the warm support of a fully collateral group but nevertheless discouraging the children from seeking Individualistic or Lineal satisfactions instead.

As the youngest child, Tony felt that he had perhaps received the most attention and had suffered the least from this system of family life. Of all the children, he believed that he was the closest to his mother as he grew older, though she had been little in evidence during his earlier years. She had regarded him as the most reliable and stable of the sons and gave him a good deal of responsibility. Possibly on this account, he was the one who identified most with her desire for prestige and self-advancement. Like all the sons, who were heavily involved in maintenance and repair work in the mother's rooming houses, he became an able mechanic and contributed to the family income by working in a garage while attending high school. Under his mother's restrictive control, he even chose his friends at school from among those boys who were ambitious and not likely to become juvenile delinquents and common laborers. Later, with his mother's encouragement, while working full-time in a garage he attended night sessions at an aircraft technical school to be trained as an aircraft mechanic — the occupation which he then pursued up to the time of our contact with the family.

The key problem in Tony's growth and development — the one, at any rate, of which he was most consciously aware — was his stuttering. The onset of the stuttering, which was quite severe, was also associated with a period of nervousness and self-consciousness which persisted throughout his adolescence. In his own mind, these problems were the result of family conflict occasioned by the behavior of his oldest sister, Ruth, and his oldest brother, Arthur. Ruth's disrespectful, hostile attitude toward his mother, together with her constant demands for money, distressed Tony. From the age of twelve on, he began to stand up to Ruth, demanding that she show a more respectful attitude. He was the only child to do this, and the mother seemed peculiarly vulnerable and helpless in the face of her daughter's emotional assaults. Something of the same nature occurred with respect to Arthur's alcoholic episodes. This oldest son had been the mother's favorite child, the one upon whom she had placed all her hopes for prestige and success in her offspring. When he became an alcoholic in his youth, she was utterly helpless and continued to favor him and protect him, even though the scenes he made when he arrived home drunk and abusive harassed the entire family. Again, Tony was the only child who was able to stand up to Arthur, attempting to control his wildness by threatening to call the police. On one occasion of particularly combative behavior, Tony did notify the police, and Arthur was jailed overnight. He recalled the episode with a combination of guilt, for having humiliated his brother, and pride, for having taken a step to relieve the family of a menacing situation. He was then eighteen years old, and, though the youngest son, found himself acting in many ways the role of the eldest son. Indeed, it was after this episode that his mother finally renounced all hope for Arthur's rehabilitation and transferred her expectation of success in a son to Tony.

Having partly relieved his stuttering, with the help of a sympathetic speech therapist, and having partly stabilized the family situation through his domination of Arthur, Tony's attitude toward the mastery of problems and the wish for success was now crystalized. He was angry with Arthur and Ruth for producing so much stress within the family, and he was angry with the other brothers and sisters for not getting together and putting a stop to their depredations. Because of their default, he had had to take the unpleasant, necessary steps on his own responsibility. He had not had the help due him, but he had nevertheless been at least moderately successful. The effort and the strain involved had made him "nervous" and left him with a desire to get away from the family, to find some new, collateral group which would be more satisfying.

It was in this mood that he met Celia and her family and began a courtship which was to stretch over a six-year period. To understand both the strengths and the strains built into the marriage at its inception, it is necessary to review the social situation of Celia's family and the circumstances in which she grew up as a child.

At the time of therapeutic contact with the family, Celia's family of orientation, the Succis, consisted of her father, Enrico, age sixty-one; her mother, Angela, age fifty-three; her married older sister, Frances (Francesca), age thirty-six; and her married younger brother, Henry (Enrico, Jr.), age thirty-one. Her parents lived in the North End of Boston in a three-family house which they owned and in which the children had been brought up. Frances, her husband Joseph, and their two children lived in their own house in a suburb, while Henry, his wife, and their three children lived in an apartment in the North End, not far from his parents' home. Enrico, Sr, had been in the oil and ice business, making deliveries in the neighborhood in which he lived. Since he was ill with diabetes and partly retired, the business was now mainly in the hands of his son. Joseph ran a dry-cleaning establishment, and he and Frances lived on a somewhat higher economic plane than the others in the family.

In contrast to the polite but distant behavior existing among members of the extended Tondi family, the Succis were heavily involved with each other. Their social relations, however, were burdened with tension. Quarrels and flare-ups, acute and chronic resentments, reconciliations, restitutions for real or imaginary injuries, and constant exchanges of gifts, services, advice, and admonishment were the fabric of their family life. Both Celia and Tony participated, often painfully, in the volcanic eruption of her family's affairs, though Tony had made efforts to diminish his wife's and his own involvement. In fact, one of his main reasons for building the house in the suburbs was to be at least physically removed from her family. In the course of therapy, it soon became evident that to help the spouses either loosen these ties or else make them more endurable would be an important aim of treatment.

The turbulence in the Succi family was usually precipitated by Angela, Celia's mother. She was a blonde, with a fair complexion, abundant energy, many skills, and a fiery temperament. According to Celia, she had been beautiful when younger and was renowned in the neighborhood for her hospitality and her excellent house-keeping and cooking. She was a competent midwife whose services had once been much in demand, though now the younger Italian-American mothers in the neighborhood preferred to deliver their babies in a hospital. In addition, she was active, throughout Celia's childhood and to the present, in caring for recent immigrants from Italy, housing, feeding, and grooming them for life in the United States. In fact, one of Celia's prominent complaints about her childhood was that her mother did more for others than she did for her own children, a feeling reminiscent of the resentment expressed in the Tondi family about their mother's exhibitionistic hospitality.

Though Angela agreed that she gave much time and energy to doing things for persons outside her family, she also thought that she gave more than enough attention to her children. In any case, she was seldom happy with the outcome of her devotions, whether in or outside her family. No matter how much she did for people, they always managed to disappoint her. She was chronically critical of her husband, who, in her view, was passive, ineffective, and unable to earn enough money to give her the social position in the community which she would have liked. She believed that what status they had attained was wholly the result of her own efforts. She was bitterly disappointed in Henry, who had, in her judgment, all but ruined the reputation of the Succis by making what she insisted was a bad marriage to a woman of loose morals and unsavory family background. She had never expected much of Celia and took a dim view of Tony and the children. As for Tony's family, she regarded the Tondis as unstable, unrefined, and altogether beneath the social standing of the Succis, sullied though the family's honor was by Henry's marriage. Even Frances, the favorite child and the one who had come the closest to satisfying Angela's wish for success through social advancement in her children, had lately been a disappointment. Frances had a poor relationship with her children and quarreled with her husband, accusing him of not earning enough money. The couple were frequently on the point of separation. Angela felt let down by the domestic careers of all her children, as well as by her own.

According to Celia, her mother was incapable of believing that she had any responsibility for the many disappointments inflicted upon her. Nor did she regard her troubles as problems to be solved. They were deemed to come from bad luck, the innate wickedness and irresponsibility of others, or from evil magic. Possibly from all three combined.

When her son fell in love with the girl of supposedly loose morals, whom he later married, he was in his early teens, and Angela was convinced that this girl's mother had administered a love-potion to him. She and her friends consulted with each other about the most effective form of counter-magic to dispel the influence of a love-potion. Many things were tried — spells, incantations, and brews of various sorts — but the desired apotropaic effect never came off. Angela was furious and stormed at her son, vilifying the girl and her family and forbidding him to continue seeing her. These emotional scenes also misfired; Henry only shouted back his defiance of his mother's opinions and orders. When, in spite of her efforts, the marriage was scheduled to take place, Angela refused to attend. Then, as the wedding procession passed through the street below, she stood at the open window of her apartment, screaming down blood-curdling curses on the newlyweds, the bride's family, their future progeny, and all who attended the ceremony.

Angela's bad luck, it seemed, had begun in Italy before her emigration. Her family lived in a village near Naples and operated a small cheese factory. Their standard of living was higher than that of the farmers and residents of the villages in the area. Angela was quite aware of differences in social status, from an early age. Unfortunately, in her early teens the family suffered a business setback. As a result, her two brothers emigrated to the United States, and, somewhat later, a marriage was arranged by her family between Enrico Succi and the seventeen-year-old Angela. Enrico, then twenty-five years old, had emigrated at age sixteen to the United States, where he had worked on a railroad in the West. Now he had returned, briefly, to the region of Italy in which he had been born, to find a wife. Some weeks after the wedding, he returned to the United States alone with the intention of sending for his wife after he had found a better job and established a home. When, after a year and a half, he did send for her, the oldest child, Frances, had already been born.

Although Enrico had seemed enterprising, resourceful — even

217

dashing — in Italy, in the new environment Angela soon discovered that he was good-natured but slow. Her sisters and parents were in Italy, her brothers somewhere in the Midwest, and she found life in the North End of Boston lonely and difficult. Only gradually did her beauty and talents establish a place for her in the community. She realized that the doubts which she had entertained about Enrico's family background and fate in Italy — his parents were farmers — were justified. He was not destined to make much head-way in the land of opportunity, though he was reliable and would always work hard to support his family. Improvement of her social position would without question be up to her. And social status was, for Angela, the whole point of life.

It was in this atmosphere of social striving that Celia grew up. Her memories of childhood were stocked with examples of her mother's pushing behavior toward her children. The children were always being compared with other children in the neighborhood who were described as more attractive, competent, or intelligent. Although her mother displayed little physical warmth, such as cuddling or kissing, to any of the children, Celia always felt that her sister and brother received preferential treatment. Frances had her mother's beauty and talent, while Henry was an only son from whom great things were expected. Her father left the whole care and disciplining of the children in the mother's hands, and Celia recalled this with resentment. She felt that her mother's constant prodding and comparing them with others gave all the children the feeling that they were "no good." Her father was kind and gentle but could not be relied upon for support because of his subservient position in the home. And it was Celia who needed his support the most, for her mother regarded her as the most inferior of the three children, almost as a lost cause.

During her childhood, Celia's greatest worries centered upon her body and sex. Angela was constantly concerned about constipation. She, herself, suffered from constipation and was alert to its occurrence in her children. Celia recalled with distaste the many enemas she had received throughout her childhood. She regarded herself as the ugly duckling in the family. Her mother teased her about her unattractive nose and squat body. Fortunately she was well coordinated and good at sports. Her more beautiful sister, having had rheumatic fever in early childhood, was restricted in this area. Also, Celia was a good student and at least held her own with her sister and brother in school competitions. Sex was never discussed or mentioned in the home except as something

218

bad; yet it was often on Celia's mind as a dirty and shameful aspect of human nature. Between the ages of nine and fourteen, an adolescent boy who lived across the street and was a brother of one of her best friends repeatedly made sexual advances to her. She fended him off but never spoke of the episodes to anyone, since she felt that they were caused by some unnatural impulse within her which this boy had sensed. The incidents made her feel sullied and degraded. Even before these incidents began, her mother had caught her reading a book about sex which had been given to her by a friend. She was soundly thrashed. On other occasions, a salesman, who was often in the neighborhood, exposed himself to her. All these preadolescent sexual contacts remained in her mind as traumatic events about which she felt ashamed.

During adolescence her guilt about sex and her anxiety about her competence in feminine skills increased. She developed facial acne and believed that this was somehow related to her sexual impulses. As her breasts developed, she was ashamed of them, and felt all the more that she was ugly and repulsive. She obtained no information about sex or menstruation from her mother and had to make the best sense she could about these matters from what she gleaned from her sister and in the street. Yet, her information was beclouded with the admixture of facts and fiction about childbirth related by her mother in the course of recounting her ministrations as a midwife. Compulsively clean, Angela always described "the mess" attendant upon delivery of the baby and the afterbirth with a certain relish and in unnecessary detail. At the same time, her mother repeatedly scolded Celia for carelessness in carrying out housecleaning chores and incompetence in cooking and sewing, comparing her unfavorably to her more competent sister.

Celia recalled her adolescence as a time of unhappiness. She often had "black moods" during which she locked herself in the bathroom and daydreamed about running away from home in order to make everyone feel sorry. In high school she had few dates. Oddly, she found herself unwittingly encouraging a boy to make advances until the moment when he touched her. Thereupon she would feel a revulsion and shrink away. She also longed to have a romantic relationship with a boy who was "tall, dark, and handsome" but somehow managed to avoid this possibility by dating only short men. Her explanation was that she felt too inferior and unattractive with the tall men of her daydreams.

After high school and secretarial training, she worked in various business offices and encountered a surprising success. She

219

was efficient and reliable and much liked by her co-workers and bosses. She blossomed under encouragement, feeling that she possessed more competence than she had been given credit for and that she understood the workings of a large commercial concern. Though her mother was not impressed, her father, for the first time, praised her, stating that she had a good head for business and that she "would always know how to make a dollar."

It was at this time of her life that Celia met Tony, who immediately took a liking to her. He saw in her the efficiency and knowledge, the family loyalty and trustworthiness that he wanted in a wife. She saw in him just another short man, not too exciting or promising. After a few dates, Tony insisted on meeting her family. Celia explained that this was impossible. Her parents were of the Old World type who believed in arranged marriages. She was forbidden to bring any boy home unless it had already been settled that they were engaged. What she did not tell Tony was that her parents took no notice of what she did with her time outside the house, whereas they scrutinized her sister's and brother's behavior carefully — another discrimination which she resented. Either they trusted her completely or else they never considered her a risk, being too unattractive. In any event, she felt unprotected.

Paying no attention to her concern, Tony simply turned up at her parent's home and introduced himself as a suitor. For the next six years he continued to press his suit, interrupted only by a two-year stint in the Air Force during World War II. In the service, away from his family for the first time in his life and enjoying his work as an airplane mechanic overseas, he gained increased confidence in himself. Both before and after his absence, Celia steadily postponed making a decision about his offers of marriage. She was influenced by her mother's attitude. Though Angela tolerated Tony as a suitor, she had no great liking for him. She regarded him as a nervous person who stuttered when excited and who, like her husband, had little ability or drive. Celia's father, on the other hand, became quite fond of Tony and began to think of him as a prospective son-in-law. Tony, in turn, liked the old man and responded to him as the father he had missed during his childhood. In fact, he adopted Celia's family as his own. He performed services for them of all sorts, repairing the apartment and running errands to display his value as a candidate for Celia's hand.

In the course of Tony's long wooing of Celia and of her family, several events occurred which gradually tipped the balance in his favor. First, Frances was married. Celia had been telling Tony

220

that she could not marry before her older sister was married. Actually, Celia was quite dependent upon her sister and felt the loss through marriage keenly. Equally important to the change of atmosphere was the outbreak of severe quarreling in the home precipitated by Henry's announcement that he intended to marry the girl his mother detested. The household was continuously wracked with violent emotional explosions. Celia was torn between sympathy for her brother and her mother. She thought that her mother tended to take too seriously the gossip about the girl's immoral family, and she was reduced to tears when Henry said to his mother, "You never thought that I was any good; so how can I marry a girl who's good in your eyes?" Celia desperately wanted to escape from the turbulent environment of her home, and Tony was still urging her to marry him. Finally, when Angela, feeling pressed on all sides, irritably announced that Celia was not getting any younger and no more promising suitor was in sight, Celia accepted his proposal.

For Tony, the marriage was a triumph — a victory after a long campaign. In bringing off his success he had neatly managed a compromise between the Italian tradition of the arranged marriage and the American custom of an individualistic choice based on love. In effect, he had arranged his own marriage, conducting the negotiations between his family and Celia's with a skill that finally surmounted the obstacles on both sides.

For Celia, the marriage was a now-or-never affair. She still longed for a "tall, dark and handsome" lover but had no faith in her ability to capture the interest of such a man. In view of the shortage of suitors, it seemed practical to marry Tony even though she was ashamed of taking a husband whom she did not love. She felt that he would probably be kind and considerate toward her and a good father. Perhaps she could make something out of him if she tried hard.

On returning from a brief honeymoon in Canada, Tony and Celia took one of the apartments in the building owned by her parents. For the next two years they continued to live much as they had in the past, Celia working as a secretary and Tony as an aircraft mechanic. They worked hard, and in the evenings their lives seemed to blend with those of the Succi family. There was not too much communication between the young couple, but neither was there any strife. Celia was disappointed that she could not experience any pleasure in their sexual relations. As usual, she did not know whether the difficulty was due to some problem within

221

her — she still felt ashamed of her sexual feelings — or to Tony's ineptness. Since she said nothing about it, Tony was not aware that Celia had such a problem and thought that this part of their life was going smoothly. He and Celia were both upset by the continuing fights between Angela, Enrico, and Henry and his wife. As an aftermath of Angela's venomous behavior in regard to the wedding, the dispute had spread into the neighborhood. Pro-Henry and anti-Henry factions feuded with each other and with Angela. Tony attempted to maintain neutrality and to function as a peacemaker, but his efforts met with little success. Angela demanded total allegiance to her point of view. She now had, in fact, some new complaints against Tony: he did not support her in her feud with her son. And, to make matters worse, he continued to be attentive and respectful toward his own mother, as if, by contrast, to highlight her miserable relationship with her own son.

In their third year of marriage, Celia and Tony decided to have a baby. Despite the teachings of the Church, they had used contraceptives. Though they regarded themselves as good Catholics, they both believed that the position of the clergy on this matter was unreasonable, as did many of their friends. Accordingly, the pregnancy was carefully planned. When it occurred, Tony was exuberant. Celia was somewhat depressed but concealed her feelings from him. She was ashamed to tell her mother and her sister that she was "carrying Tony's child" and concealed the fact of her pregnancy as long as possible. Then Tony's mother died, unexpectedly, and he became mildly depressed for several months. The prenatal period was not a happy one for either of them.

Timmie was born in normal physical condition but only after a difficult, prolonged, wearing delivery. As soon as she set eyes on the baby, Celia thought that she saw all her suffering on his little face. He looked wrinkled and weak to her, as if worn out from the struggle of the delivery. Above all, he did not seem attractive or appealing. However he may have seemed, Celia was in no condition to pay attention to him. She told the interviewer that "for forty days and nights" thereafter she experienced severe discomfort and pain from hemorrhoids and that the only thing she wanted was to die. Celia's expression was in keeping with an ancient tradition. Like the forty days of Musa Degh, the forty thieves of Ali Baba, the forty days that Jesus spent in the desert and Moses spent on Mount Zion, or the forty years of wandering of the Children of Israel, her forty days and nights of pain was not meant as an accurate count. For her, as for the folklore tradition, the number forty signified an impressive quantity of suffering or effort. During this period, the baby was in the care of her mother and sister.

The research staff, in discussing this phase of her life, debated whether Celia might not have been severely depressed immediately following the delivery. However, the episode was hazy in her memory; she was never able to be specific about the thoughts and feelings associated with it.

On recovering her physical health, Celia took charge of the baby with many misgivings about her competence in child care. The idea of breast-feeding was repellent to her. Timmie was given a bottle propped up in the crib beside him. Holding and cuddling her baby was not something Celia could do spontaneously or easily. An even more difficult matter was what to do when the baby cried. Tony thought that Celia should pick up the infant and comfort him until he stopped crying. Angela labeled this as nonsense, in fact dangerous. The baby would soon be spoiled beyond all reason. She insisted that he be placed in his crib and left alone until he learned that crying would not be an effective way to get what he wanted. Celia, having no firm opinion of her own, was torn between pleasing her mother and satisfying her husband. She vacillated, but most of the time Timmie was left to cry it out alone, which meant that he cried until he went to sleep. Tony also thought that the baby should be fed when he was hungry. Celia's mother, sister, and girl friends, regarding Tony's opinions as old-fashioned, recommended feeding on schedule. Still trying to keep peace with his wife's family, Tony did not veto their decisions, but he was not happy about them.

In the following months, Tony's discontent with his mother-in-law's rules and regulations and general behavior gradually increased until he and Celia were almost constantly arguing about his complaints. She tended to defend her mother or, at any rate, was unwilling to oppose her. Tony was angry because he felt that Angela did not give his wife enough help with the baby — and what help she gave was wrong.

At first he was reluctant to voice his complaints too forcibly, because he wanted peace and Timmie seemed to be thriving. But when Timmie was six months old, the head-rocking in bed began, and shortly thereafter Timmie became "sickly." He ate poorly, had frequent colds and sore throats, and was underweight. Tony blamed the regime set up by Angela for Timmie's poor physical condition. Furthermore, Angela gave Celia practically no help at all with the diapering, washing, feeding, or general care of the baby. She was reluctant to look after the baby so that Celia and Tony could go out together to visit with friends. On the occasions when she did agree to babysit, Celia and Tony sometimes returned to find that Angela had gone downstairs to her own apartment, leaving Timmie alone.

Painfully, Tony had come to the conclusion that Angela was neglectful, not only of his son but of his wife as well. As his disillusion and resentment mounted, he began to make plans to move his family out of the apartment, then out of the neighborhood — as far away as possible. He had heard that there was property available at inexpensive rates in a distant suburb, still partly rural and awaiting development. He became fascinated with the idea of buying some property and building his own house. To be a home-owner, to have a place in the country where his children could grow up away from the turmoil of city streets and family interference — this would come close to his dream of a better life. His savings were insufficient, but he could take extra jobs and borrow money to tide him over. Even Celia was impressed with his plan. Though she was not sure that she wanted to be so far away from her family, she too liked the idea of having her own house in the country. Unexpectedly, Angela fell in with the plan and offered to loan Tony part of the money needed to buy the land. The whole family drove out to inspect the property; it was found suitable by one and all, and the purchase was made.

Then, when Timmie was just nine months old, Celia discovered that she was pregnant again. This conception was unplanned. Celia felt that she had her hands full taking care of Timmie and was not pleased. Tony was delighted. But later, somewhat influenced by Tony's enthusiasm, Celia began to think that she might have a girl and felt cheered. Remembering her experience with Timmie's birth, she was frightened of the delivery. Her fear was unwarranted. The baby was delivered with dispatch and practically no pain. As soon as she saw her new nine-pound son, Celia was pleased. He seemed round and happy, "like a little butterball." She took note of his large brown eyes and admired his physique, saying to the nurse in attendance, "Just look at those shoulders!"

Now the trace of melancholy which had accompanied the newlyweds during their first years seemed to lift. Celia had no post-partum pain or discomfort and was in good spirits. Tony wanted the baby named after him, and she agreed — a notable concession, considering her previous feelings about carrying his

224

child. Everyone admired the new baby for his cuddlesome qualities. Celia picked him up and held him for display in a spontaneous manner that had been absent in her reaction to Timmie. Nevertheless, she again was unwilling to breast-feed him, and she used the propped-up bottle as she had previously. Recognizing the physical resemblance which the new baby bore to him, Tony had eyes for nothing else. He would rush into the apartment on returning from work, crying, "Where's my son? Where's my pal? Hi, Sonny!" The words "Hi, Sonny" were heard so often that "Sonny" almost automatically became the baby's nickname.

In the following months, the house-building project — the symbol of social advancement and emotional harmony — continued to bolster the morale of the Tondi household. Tony was very busy with his plans and purchases and arrangements for building. He took extra jobs repairing private planes on weekends and holidays. Discussing plans and solutions of problems together, he and Celia felt closer to each other than usual, though Celia was never confident that Tony was making the right decisions. She was also very busy caring for the two children. Timmie's poor health was a constant worry. In retrospect, she told the interviewer that perhaps she had neglected Sonny somewhat at this time because she was so concerned about Timmie and had to make so many visits to hospitals and doctor's offices with him. Still, Sonny appeared to thrive. His appetite was good, he gained weight, slept well, and, somehow, the question of isolating him when he cried never arose as it did with Timmie — perhaps because he seldom cried and always seemed to capture the affectionate attention of those around him.

When Sonny was a year old, the problem of his toilet training emerged. During interviews, it was difficult for Celia to recall facts in this area in regard to either of the children. She remembered that Timmie had been trained at one year but could not recall any of the details. It seemed to her almost as if he had trained himself. At twelve months, Sonny was soiling constantly, and her mother was complaining about the way he smelled. Celia had paid little attention, being so preoccupied with Timmie's health. She regarded Sonny as strong and healthy and had defined him as no problem. But when her mother, with characteristic impatience, said, "It's time that baby was trained!" Celia, fearing that she had been neglectful, switched the full force of her attention to Sonny's bowel functions. Abruptly and forcibly, she put him on the training-seat. He took an immediate dislike to it and struggled to get out. She then strapped him in. He screamed and refused to cooperate.

At eighteen months, Sonny had still made no progress and the situation was at a stalemate. Sonny seemed both to hate and to be frightened of a toilet. He would run away when he recognized signs of preparatory toilet-forcing in his mother's behavior. Then on one occasion, while a friend was visiting, Sonny appeared in pain and lay on the floor with his legs drawn up. The friend said that he must be constipated. In some anxiety, Celia got a syringe and administered an enema. The fear that Sonny suffered from a serious bowel disorder was from that time firmly implanted in her awareness. Angela, always concerned about constipation, tended to agree. And, in fact, Sonny's withholding of his stools over a period of days dated from this incident.

As Sonny's constipation was in the process of becoming a firmly established pattern, the parents relied more and more on enemas to bring about a bowel movement. They took the boy to the family physician, who made a rectal examination and asserted that there was no obstruction in the lower bowel. He advised them to pay less attention to Sonny's bowels. Sonny reacted traumatically to the invasion of his rectum and promptly developed a fear of doctors. Furthermore, from this time on he seemed positively terrified of being given a enema. When he knew that an enema was about to be administered — and he developed a sixth sense about this — he would attempt to hide. Experiencing a distressing combination of fear, anger, and guilt, Celia would search for him, find him, and, with Tony's help, forcibly hold the child down on the floor while administering the enema. Sonny kicked and screamed like a wild animal during this process. Yet, afterwards, having delivered himself of a large stool, he would relax and return to his usual, cheery, somewhat belligerent, good humor — to everyone's relief.

The house-building project was now nearing completion. Tony was working such long hours on the house — six to seven hours a day in addition to his regular job — that he was seldom at home. He attributed the symptoms and behavior problems which both his children had developed to the tension at home during this period. This inspired in him a frenzy of activity in order to finish the house sufficiently to move his family to the peace and quiet of the countryside. Celia felt increasingly burdened by her husband's absence from the home. She now had to make all the decisions and manage the affairs of the family under her mother's critical eye. Still, she continued to take heart at the idea of moving and even bragged a bit to her father and girl-friends about what a nice house

226

they would have — implying that she would be better off than any one else in the family. The making of such an overt bid for success — even triumph — was an unusual piece of behavior for Celia, and she almost immediately regretted it. What if her claims should prove false? Suppose the house should turn out to be inadequate, the children even more troublesome, and the neighbors cool or unpleasant? She would be the laughing stock of the whole family!

Timmie's "sickly" behavior at this time, when Celia felt so burdened, seemed to increase. His stuttering now came into evidence. But equally worrisome was his reaction to a short period of hospitalization for a tonsillectomy. He had awakened from the anesthesia to find his mother present, but shortly thereafter she was required to leave by the rules of the hospital. Timmie believed he was being abandoned and was panic stricken. When she returned the following day, Celia found him tearful and distrustful of her. She dated his clinging behavior and his chronic fear that she would desert him to this episode. Indeed, whenever he was asked why he was so afraid that his mother would not return on leaving the house for some routine errand, he would cite his terrifying experience in the hospital.

Finally, after Tony had been working on the house for two years, the long-awaited move took place. The strain of preparation had been intense though relieved by the pleasure both spouses took in the prospect of fulfilling their wish for a better life. But at the last minute their pleasure was reduced by a sudden switch in Angela's attitude. Just before the move was to take place, she abruptly dropped her supportive behavior and began to complain about the impending separation. She was losing her daughter and grandchildren, she was being deserted, the house was much too far away — these and similar reproaches were heard day after day. Angela combined a martyred attitude with coldness and refused to be of any help with the actual moving.

For Celia, her mother's change of mind about the separation functioned almost like a prophecy. Having taken up residence in her own house, furnished it, and set up her housekeeping routines, she did not find that bliss in suburban living which she and Tony had anticipated during moments of euphoria. If anything, her problems seemed to increase. She was often lonely; she felt uncomfortable with the neighbors; she was more than ever conscious of her husband's inferiority; and her children seemed determined to embarrass her in the community. There were times in the following two years when her anxiety and depression were so severe that she thought she might be losing her mind. Even Tony recognized her "nervousness," though as usual he blamed it on her mother's behavior. In general, however, and with his customary inclination to ignore difficulties with his wife if at all possible, he continued to regard Celia as a good wife and mother who was doing as competent a job as possible under the circumstances.

The suburb to which the Tondis moved was about thirty miles from the center of Boston. In the past it had been a small, sleepy New England town. Now, with the new industrial expansion which had invaded the perimeter of the Boston metropolitan area, it was undergoing a fairly rapid change. The families of skilled workers, technically trained managerial personnel, and some junior executives were moving in to its still semi-rural environs. As a consequence, real estate prices were continually rising, and tracts of land all around the town were being dotted with new housing, of the one-story ranchhouse variety. The demand for services created by the influx of new residents tended to exceed the facilities of the community.

The lot which Tony had purchased was in a semi-rural setting with nearby open spaces, fields, ponds, and wooded areas. A few large farmhouses and barns lay scattered about in the distance. In the immediate neighborhood, newly constructed one-story houses lined a still unpaved, rather dusty street. The Tondi's half-acre lot was on a corner of a block on this street. Like the properties up and down the street, the grounds were partially landscaped. A well-cared for vegetable garden stood in the rear. There were scrubby shrubs around the house, a sandbox and barbecue stand at the side of the house, and a driveway leading to a garage attached to the house.

On the interior, only the first floor had been completed. It consisted of a kitchen, a bathroom, two bedrooms, and a living room. The rooms were rather small, with low ceilings and, to the observers, seemed crowded with over-large equipment and furniture and decorated with garish colors and florid ornaments. Religious paintings and statues, plastic flowers in huge, ornate vases, and other objects inappropriately scaled to the size and shape of the rooms produced a hemmed-in feeling. The boys slept just off the kitchen in a room which had originally been designed as the dining room but was being used as the children's bedroom because the rooms on the second floor were not yet completed. An aperture for passing dishes between the kitchen and the dining room had been covered with a wooden grill. Thus the behavior of the boys in their bedroom was open to inspection from the kitchen, and the entire arrangement produced the effect of a prison cell.

The unfinished rooms on the second floor consisted of two bedrooms and a bath. Since Tony had felt so exhausted from the effort of bringing the house to a state of completion sufficient to set up housekeeping, he kept putting off the work of finishing the upstairs rooms — much to his wife's discontent. Structurally, what had been completed was well done and a testament to Tony's skill and doggedness. In describing the house to visiting research staff members, he often said, "It isn't much, but I did it all myself. I never could have afforded to buy a house like this; so I had to do it myself." He estimated that he had invested seven thousand dollars in the house and lot over the two-year period of construction and that he could easily sell the property for fourteen thousand dollars. This was three years later, during the period of therapy. Although he liked to picture the construction as a one-man job, in fact he had received help in specialized areas of building. For example, his brother Robert, who was a civil engineer, had designed and installed the heating facilities. A neighbor who lived across the street was a plasterer and had carried out the plastering of the interior. Yet, for all the energy and enterprise that had gone into the construction of the house, Celia constantly complained that it was much too small and inconvenient because of Tony's failure to finish the upstairs rooms.

FAMILY ROLE CONFLICTS

Concerning the Formal roles enacted by the Tondis, the presence of open or concealed complaints characterized much of their day-to-day behavior. For both Tony and Celia, actuality failed to live up to previous hopes and expectations. The ever-present note of disappointment had many sources but chief among them was the frustration which they both experienced in regard to their hopes for a better life. In part, this frustration had to do with not feeling themselves to be at home in the new community. In part, it was concerned with disappointment in themselves, in each other, and in the children.

The switch from the kind of supports given to social mobility in the native Italian culture to the pattern of values preferred in American urban culture is a difficult one, not to be encompassed in a short time. For different reasons connected with their families of orientation, both Tony and Celia were in a hurry. As a result, they were attempting to realize their hopes before they had made an adequate transition from their native Italian value patterns to the dominant American patterns. Their understanding of each set of values — and thus of their worlds and of themselves — was imperfect and confused. In implementing their values, they were often at cross-purposes, though hoping to arrive at substantially the same goals. The value profile giving rise to their behaviors in their various roles is illustrated in Table 4, where each of their patterns is contrasted with native Italian and American patterns.

A glance at the value orientation profiles in Table 4 reveals that Tony had actually moved much closer to dominant American middle-class values than had Celia. Although she had shifted some of the native Italian value choices in the second-order and third-order positions, her first-order preferences were still typical of the Italian group. Her view of the world — of rights and wrongs and of how people behaved — was pretty much that which her family had brought to this country from their native Italy. On the other hand, with the exception of his preferences in the *Relational* orientation, Tony's value choices corresponded almost precisely to the American pattern. This is not to say that his implementation of these patterns was at all times in line with the avowed order of preferences. Facility at implementing a newly gained pattern of values takes a good deal of time as well as freedom from internal conflict, a freedom which had not been available to Tony.

In many respects, Tony's reliance on his wife to help him obtain a better life was in error. He had mistaken her sensitivity to social status — and her mother's — for a knowledge of how to gain it. But her value patterns made her a poor helpmeet for this purpose, all the more so because she had so little insight into the real nature of his or her strengths and weaknesses. In spite of his difficulty in recognizing the fact, Tony had a better knowledge of what was required for upward mobility than did his wife.

This poignant misunderstanding between the spouses consistently showed up in their interpersonal relations. In the *Time* orientation, for example, Tony was able to visualize and plan for gradual change in the future. For Celia, if a desired change did not occur immediately and visibly, then it was never going to occur. And, if an undesirable change occurred, then she was likely to view it as a permanent state of affairs. In the matter of undesired and undesirable change, especially where the children were concerned, other value preferences made cooperation between the spouses difficult. Tony's understanding of the Doing > Being > Being-in-becoming activity pattern led him in the first instance to judge

230

TABLE 4

Differential Transition of Husband and Wife from Italian to American Value Orientations

Orientations	American	Tony	Celia	Italian
Man-Nature	Over>Sub>Har	Over>Sub>Har	Sub>Over>Har	Sub>Har>Over
Time	Fu>Pr>Pa	Fu>Pr>Pa	Pr>Fu>Pa	Pr>Pa>Fu
Activity	Doing>Being>Bib	Doing>Being>Bib	Being>Doing>Bib	Being>Bib>Doing
Relational	Ind>Col>Lin	Col>Ind>Lin	Col>Lin>Ind	Col>Lin>Ind

Abbreviations: Fu, Pr, and Pa stand for Future, Present, and Past; Ind, Col, and Lin stand for Individual, Collateral, and Lineal; Bib stands for Being-in-becoming; Sub stands for Subjugation to Nature, Har for Harmony with Nature, and Over for Mastery over Nature.

desired or undesired behavior as an external performance which should be appraised on its merits. Celia's first-order emphasis on Being led her to view either desired or undesired behavior more as a reflection of the inner person and to become excessively emotional about it. Given her belief in a basically evil human nature, it is understandable that she should, at the same time, have regarded undesirable behavior in herself or others as a reflection of inner wickedness. Thus, in the case of all her interpersonal relations, it was hard for her to decide whether the undesirable outcome — whatever it might be — was caused by the badness within herself or within the other person. Lastly, her inclination to take a subjugated view of the *Man-nature* orientation was correlated with a sense of hopelessness or even of panic about the possibility of improving the situation. The forces that she was up against were too much for her. With her sense of hopelessness and her belief in her bad luck, it was almost impossible for Celia to convince herself that she could improve her way of handling matters. The upshot of these value interrelations was that she "tried" continuously but chaotically, always with the feeling that she was only making things worse.

Though it may sound paradoxical, this dismal view of herself and her world could be replaced on occasion with a more optimistic appraisal which was correlated with some of her second-order value choices. There were times, especially when she was not so depressed, during which she was able to believe in the Doing, Future, and Mastery over Nature views advocated by her husband. It was during these times that she saw herself as able to help him, even to teach him how to succeed. And it was these moments of her interpersonal style that he took to represent her "real" self. This act of perception constituted partly a rationalization (it was what he wished her to be), partly a projection (they were *his* first-order values), and partly a correct assessment (they *were* her second-order choices, and she was in conflict about moving them up into a first-order position). Tony was sure that problems between man and nature could be mastered and tended to take an optimistic view of difficulties. Accordingly, he did not regard the problems which he experienced either with his wife or with his children as resulting exclusively from a badness within them but saw them as troubled individuals whose behavior could be corrected. As a result, it was easy, as well as convenient, for him to regard Celia's first-order value preferences as a product of her "nervousness" rather than a representative of her "real" self.

What was most highly correlated with Tony's misperception of his wife's values was their agreement on the first-order choice in the *Relational* orientation. They both consistently upheld Collaterality, though they differed on its application. They were in agreement that they should stick together and support each other as man and wife and that the nuclear family should function as a collateral group aligned with other collateral groups. They differed, however, on what groups to align with. Celia wanted to remain close to her family and relied heavily on her dependent relations with them. Tony wanted to get away from all extended family connections and to find new collateral relations in the community to which they had moved. Because of his collateral views, Tony could not readily perceive his wife as an individual — nor his children — but tended to look at them as representatives of family needs and hopes. The same was true of Celia. Because of the Collateral emphasis in both of them, neither could view Tony's success strivings — nor their hopes for their children — as a matter of achievement for the sake of the individual concerned. Success in the new environment was needed and demanded as a sign of the family's prestige, almost as if it were a matter of removing a stain on the Tondi family name. In this fashion, the American achievement pattern was largely torn loose from its individualistic moorings and assimilated to the ancient Italian wish to keep the family honor bright and its reputation free of blemish — fighting issues in Italy from time immemorial.

The agreement on this issue between Tony and Celia was so solid that it might well be regarded as the pivot around which all other matters of interpersonal behavior rotated. It accounted for the solidity of the marriage itself: Tony and Celia and the children would stick together in spite of mutual disappointments, in the shame of failure, in the tragedy of defeat, in the joy of success if ever it should arrive.

In contrast to the agreement on the first-order preference in *Relational* orientation, their divergence on second- and third-order choices in this category gave rise to considerable strain. When Tony was faced with conflicts within the family which disturbed its collateral base of operations — for example, disciplinary problems in the children — he was inclined to deal with them on an Individual basis. Celia's second-order Lineality clashed forcibly with this method of procedure. Faced with a conflict of wills or expectations, she became authoritarian and asserted her dominance. Where the children were concerned, she tended to accuse Tony of spoiling

233

them. She would reproach and goad him until, his wish to individualize the problem undermined, he would lose his temper and yell at the disobedient child or hit him or threaten some dire punishment. Then she would accuse him of having gone too far, implying that, in spite of her wish for him to take charge, she understood these matters better and they had best remain in her hands. Yet, because of her belief in her bad luck and the evil nature of her basic impulses, she was never able to maintain sufficient self-confidence to carry through a consistent program of disciplining for the children. Sooner or later, she would resume her plea to Tony to take charge when there was an infraction of her hastily composed rules and regulations, only to undermine his handling of it all over again.

The question of who was in charge of decision making in the family was thus seriously confused and subject to see-saw struggles. Responding from his *Individualistic* orientation — imperfect as his understanding of it was — Tony wanted to find out how his wife felt about the issue which needed deciding and to arrive by discussion at a mutual decision. Regarding the same matter from the viewpoint of her hierarchical, *Lineal* orientation, Celia took Tony's outlook as a sign of weakness. She thought he could not make up his mind. Since any decision was something of an emergency for her, she felt that what was required was a firm decision — almost any decision would do so long as the question was resolved quickly. It was difficult for her to communicate to him her inner feelings on any subject and often impossible for her to know how she really felt. Accordingly, discussion and the airing of problems was beyond her. Besides, she believed that it was the responsibility of a man to make the difficult decisions. Having interpreted Tony's procedure as a sign of weakness, she usually ended by feeling that she *had* to make the decision. Celia would abruptly make decisions and take action only to feel, after some time had passed, that she had been wrong and that Tony, in his bumbling way, had probably been right. It was then that she would feel reproachful toward him, holding that he should have asserted himself and overruled her in the first place. The net effect of such to-and-fro swings was that though Celia won most of the short-term decisions, any line of action proposed by Tony usually won out in the long run.

We are now in a position to see how the congruent and divergent aspects of the values held by the spouses introduced complementarity or conflict into the manner in which they took their

234

formal roles. Starting with the Biological roles — age, sex, and body management — as enacted by the husband and wife, we immediately observe the effects of a value discrepancy: the partial conversion, under stress, of Formal roles into Informal or Fictive roles. For example, the disagreement between Tony and Celia about how decisions were to be made affected, as we have seen, both their ability to relate harmoniously to each other and their perception of the role ascribed to the role partner. Celia could not adapt her need for a quick decision to Tony's more deliberate and thoughtful approach. The complementarity of the roles, as taken, was very low, and Celia responded with a role induction maneuver: she coerced, forcing a decision by contemptuously criticizing his views. At the same time, considering Tony indecisive and vacillating, she assigned him a set of distorted age and sex roles. She perceived him as immature and unmanly. Having reduced his age to that of a child — and a rather backward child, at that — she then adopted a role which, to her mind, would be complementary to the Informal role which she had assigned him. She became the protective parent who had to criticize and take care of her dependent child-husband. She often told the interviewer that she had not two but three children on her hands. Since Tony appeared to go along with her procedure, the Informal role which she had assigned him was confirmed, as far as she was concerned. He had accepted his assigned role.

On his side, of course, Tony knew that he had done nothing of the kind. If his wife had to be so critical, bossy, and protective as to treat him like a child, it was due to impatience caused by her "nervousness." There was no point, as far as he could see, in directly attacking her, that is, in showing counter-coercion. One does not attack a person who is in a disturbed state. By assigning her a quite different Informal role from that which she had assigned him — that of a sick or harried person — he managed to dodge the issue. He also managed thereby to conceal from himself the anger he felt because of her depreciation of him. What became of this unconscious resentment we will consider in a moment. It is enough, for the present, to note that the Informal, Transitional, sick role he had assigned to her required of him only that he adopt an Informal complementary role which would not upset her further. He attempted to mollify her by becoming the patient teacher or advisor, waiting for her to recognize her error and to accept his recommendations.

These undercover Informal roles were introduced into their

transactions with each other as a way of avoiding further strain and its associated anxiety. Communication by indirection, however, is no adequate substitute for a thorough airing and discussion of underlying issues. In this case, the conversion of the Formal age and sex roles between husband and wife into distorted and implicit Informal roles was re-enacted, but now revengefully, in the arena of parent-child roles.

Before examining these displaced effects, we wish to point out that Celia and Tony shared a problem in body tempo, or psycho-biological rhythms, as related to distance in contact with others. Celia's rhythms were characteristically fast, sometimes explosive; Tony's slower, more deliberate. However, he exhibited an underlying tension which gave observers the impression that he was holding in and controlling himself. On rare occasions, the excitation would burst through, and he would, in interviews, wave his arms around, gesticulating forcibly and talking rapidly. Most of the time he sat quietly, in forced self-possession. Because of this contrast between them, Celia considered her husband "slow," while he considered her "impatient" or "nervous." With respect to physical distance, the contrast between them was equally vivid. Tony wanted to be physically close, almost literally in touch with his role partners. Walking toward the interviewing room with his male therapist, he tended to touch or bump into him somehow — not quite deliberately but not by accident either. He stayed in physical contact with his children — especially with Sonny — enjoying the acts of touching, holding, putting his arms around them, or even manipulating them in the course of demonstrating some activity. Celia remained at a greater distance from everyone. She frequently drew herself up as if shrinking from contact. This posture produced a strained, un-relaxed effect, certain nuances of which could easily be interpreted as guardedness — that is, feeling defensive and ill at ease — while other nuances gave the impression of unspoken disapproval.

From their varying positions vis-à-vis their role partners, how-ever, both of them engaged in a similar pattern of sudden inter-vention, either physically or verbally. To the observers, these rapid intrusions were more easily detected in behavior with the children than between each other, but they occurred in both situations. Celia, from her withdrawn position, would suddenly insert herself into an ongoing activity of Sonny or Timmie, breaking it up and taking control of it. For example, in an early clinic contact, the family was assembled in a waiting room equipped with a black-board. Timmie, the center of attention for the moment, was showing off his newly acquired skill in printing words on the blackboard. Celia had remained in the background, looking tense, as usual. When he had misspelled a few words, Celia could no longer contain herself. She dashed to the blackboard, seized an eraser and rubbed out the misspelled words, snatched the chalk from Timmie's hand, and printed out the words correctly, all the while verbally expressing criticism and distress at Timmie's inability to spell correctly. Timmie responded with a temper tantrum, screaming and protesting at being interfered with.

There was always an element of the surprise attack in such interventions. But, whether anticipated or not, they were forcible enough to disorganize whatever behavior was in process unless the object of the intervention was remarkably resistant. Among the research staff, these episodes received the label of "the interruption pattern." Indeed, interruption, as an interpersonal style, seemed to characterize all family members. Tony erupted into unexpected activity when his children annoyed him or Celia goaded him out of what she considered to be his passivity. From his closer physical distance, he would turn on one of his sons or his wife, suddenly imposing a line of action or a punishment which no one had expected. To the observers, "the interruption pattern" was highly correlated with the uncertainty of behavior and the tendency to stutter among the family members. Celia and Tony interrupted each other and the children — even themselves — to the extent that it was sometimes hard to hear what was going on. When Timmie had the floor, Sonny interrupted him. When Timmie stuttered, Tony tried to slow him down, while Celia attempted to speed him up — both maneuvers having the identical aim of getting the message out. When Sonny was the center of attention, Timmie had a temper tantrum or withdrew with an angry outburst.

The effect of such interferences with biological rhythms was to block the integration of a behavior process within the ego of the child. This effect was most noticeable in the case of Timmie's rocking in bed in order to put himself to sleep and in Sonny's constipation. In each case, a biological rhythm which required sensitive handling on the part of a caretaker had been ignored. What Celia did — often under pressure from her mother — was to attempt to coerce the child or to provoke him into emitting the desired behavior. When Timmie was an infant, it had been decided that he should learn to stop crying and go to sleep in a room by himself. Any physiological or psychological process which may have been interfering with his sleep-wake patterns was thus simply ignored.

When it had been decided that Sonny should learn to evacuate into a toilet, he was made to sit and was spanked if he did not produce; but the sitting and spanking were not timed to coincide with a peristaltic process in Sonny's colon. From the standpoint of the most naive principles of learning — to say nothing of the most sophisticated — such maladroit training practices could not be expected to lead to a good result. What, then, prompted them?

The chief, but not the sole, instigator of such coercive training was the aspiration within the Tondi family for higher social status, an aspiration which led to the scrambling of Italian and American value orientations. Celia like her mother wished her husband and her children to exhibit behavior consistent with the American success pattern. Every bit of behavior was judged — on misguided lines, to be sure — as to whether it fit or did not fit this pattern. Since it had been learned that American children are supposed to be self-reliant at an early age, the Italian pattern of close, warm, emotional attention to infants and children was simply reversed. Timmie was taught to rely on himself by being given no attention at all in going to sleep. It was understood that American children, unlike Italian children, learn to be clean and neat and to go to the toilet by themselves, at an early age. Ergo, Sonny must rapidly acquire these habits. What was not understood was that middle-class American parents did not expect their children to complete the acquisition of body management roles so early or so quickly. Nor was it understood that middle-class American parents handle the training process on an individualistic basis, studying the particular child to determine his needs. Rather, the Tondis assimilated the new training procedures to the old Italian Collateral>Lineal> Individualistic orientation. For the sake of the family's honor, the correct habits must be acquired; and, if any resistance crops up, then authoritarian handling is in order.

This widespread confusion in two areas of child training illustrates the significance of the connection between cultural value orientations and cognitive issues. Celia literally did not understand what was required. In her interviews, she constantly asked her therapist for instruction in the care and training of the children and for confirmation that what she was doing was right or wrong, depending upon how guilty she was feeling at the moment. She could not construct a sensible plan for child training — whatever her unconscious motives — because she had lost the coherent cultural orientations on the basis of which such plans are built.

Ego-psychological problems are involved here which, though

238

of interest, are not central to the present context. For the moment, our purpose is to trace further the relations between the patterns of values in the family and the prospects for complementarity of roles, both Formal and Informal. It is this prospect which governs the organization and integration of the family considered as a whole. And it is the fate of the integrations and conflicts in the family as a group which we wish to describe. While pursuing this end, however, we shall also pay attention to the fact that Formal and Informal roles inevitably reveal the motivations of the persons involved in them.

The purely Biological roles in the family — age, sex, and body management — were so distorted and chaotic as to preclude a smooth gearing-in of behavior among the family members. We have attributed the lack of harmony to ill-fits between the value orientation patterns. Furthermore, the presence of compensatory mechanisms through the elaboration of informal roles has been cited as one way in which formal role strains were temporarily neutralized. It was suggested, however, that the *implicit* suppression of the strains and the formation of compensatory mechanisms was not the best way to handle them. *Explicit* communication would have been preferable, but it was not available. Therefore one could expect the strains to produce effects in other role systems.

The underlying strains did indeed show up in other domestic roles and in the relation between them and roles in the various behavior spheres. Let us consider, first, the fate of the strains in the body management roles on intrafamily relations. The "interruption pattern" had led to the development in Timmie's behavior of bed-rocking, temper tantrums, stuttering, and a regressive tendency to cling to his mother like a much younger child. In Sonny, it was correlated with constipation and a degree of defiant belligerence. But these responses were not simple products of the strain in the body management roles. They were gradually inserted into informal Character roles to which the children were assigned on the basis of the wider strains in the Biological roles as a whole. We noted above that, although Tony consciously adopted the informal roles of teacher, advisor, or therapist when his wife treated him as an effeminate boy, he still experienced an unexpressed feeling of injury and resentment for being made to look so dependent and weak. And, we asked, what happened to this sense of resentment, where did its energies go?

Injury, injustice, and the resentment to which they give rise are very easily incorporated into a set of three informal Character roles which are logically related to each other: the Victim, the Oppressor, and the Protector. A variant of the Oppressor is the Persecutor (he is more vicious), and a variant of the Protector is the Rescuer (he must act faster). Tony took his revenge for his sense of injustice and injury by a skillful but displaced manipulation and assignment of these roles. Almost from the moment of birth, Tony had identified Sonny with himself, calling him "my pal" and "my son" and showing him attentions which he did not give to Timmie. Timmie responded with increased clinging. Regarding Timmie as hopeless and, in any event, inseparable from his mother, Tony took Sonny with him when he visited his relatives or went fishing or to a ball game — never Timmie. Similarly, if Celia went shopping or visited her relatives, she took Timmie — because he would not be left behind — but seldom took Sonny with her. Even on the face of it, Tony had become Sonny's protector, mentor, and companion, while Celia had the same roles toward Timmie. But why?

The explanation lies in the complementary, assigned roles. Tony had implicitly assigned to both of his sons the role of the Victim — of their mother's (and grandmother's) poorly disguised hostility toward men and of their erroneous notions of child care. By taking Sonny under his wing, he was sending an unacknowledged message to his wife. He was saying, in effect, "It's too late to rescue Timmie from the ill effects of your attitudes toward men (toward me), but I'll do my best to protect Sonny. Timmie will therefore represent the failure and injustice of your ideas, while Sonny will stand for the rightness and fairness of mine."

In this fashion, Tony made Timmie the symbol of injustice endured, Sonny the symbol of injustice defied. Both were projections of his own attitudes. In acting out these contradictory attitudes indirectly and in splitting them between his sons, he achieved several goals at one blow. He relieved himself of the internal pressure of feelings which he could neither wholly repress nor express directly. Thus by keeping the opposed attitudes apart he avoided the pathogenic consequences of an internal conflict. In addition, his revenge was accurately aimed at its target. For Celia did indeed feel guilty and responsible for Timmie's troubles and experienced them as a burden which, in all fairness, she alone could carry. As a result, she was defenseless against Timmie's clinging. On the other hand, the defiance which Tony indirectly encouraged in Sonny provoked her alternately to violent attacks and fits of remorse, deepening her concept of herself as a mother who had failed.

240

It is important to emphasize that these transactions were arranged, and the bargains made, outside of conscious awareness. When the therapists first picked up the clues regarding the Tony-Sonny, Celia-Timmie partnerships and called them to the attention of the parents, they expressed surprise and indignation. They had attributed the arrangement entirely to Timmie's clinging to his mother and did not think of it as something that they might be fostering. As, under the continued probing of the therapists, they began to consider this a real possibility, they soon made attempts to alter the arrangement. Tony made a greater effort to show interest in Timmie and invited him with increased conviction to come along when he and Sonny went out on an expedition. Celia began to control her feeling of anxious responsibility for Timmie and urged him to join his father and brother. This new tolerance for threesomes in the family, however, sat badly with Sonny. Dethroned as crown prince in his father's eyes, he became more openly rivalrous toward his brother and, like a miniature Iago, employed various stratagems to put Timmie in the wrong with his parents.

While this account of the effects of a therapeutic intervention takes us ahead of our story, it nevertheless throws light on an important issue: the consequences of disturbing a pathological equilibrium which has been set up in a family. A pathological equilibrium is an unrealistic and hostile balance of forces within the family which is (1) unconscious for the key members involved, (2) unmodifiable (without external intervention) because it is not susceptible to reality testing or new learning, and (3) conducive to psychopathology in family members because of the role distortions of which it is composed and the improbability of their taking effective action about the matter. Under the influence of their incongruent value orientations and the associated strains in their formal roles, Celia and Tony had become entangled in such a pathological equilibrium. What was out of balance in the area of Formal roles was made up for in the category of Informal roles. While Tony had permitted himself to be put down formally as an incompetent husband by Celia, he arranged, through the children, and with her help, to put his wife down as an inadequate and oppressive mother.

This tit-for-tat transaction had certain advantages and certain penalties for all concerned, though its disadvantages outweighed its benefits. Celia could continue to gain sympathy from her mother for being married, just as she was, to an ineffective man. But she also had to take the shame of losing out in her rivalry with her sister who, on this view, was married to a more successful man. The guilt which she experienced through being defined by Tony (and herself) as an inadequate, oppressive mother was neutralized during visits to Angela, who blamed Tony for the problems with the children. Angela claimed that the children were disturbed because all the Tondis were disturbed; it was in their blood! It had nothing to do, according to Angela, with Celia's capacity as a mother.

The trade-offs built into the pathological equilibrium served others a similar mixed diet of pain and pleasure. Though severely hurt by his wife's attitude, Tony was pleased with his more rational (and modern!) approach to her problems. Although unaware of it for the most part, he derived pleasure from his revengeful maneuvers and was only occasionally pained when, provoked by Celia, he was brought down to her level through an explosive outburst against the children. Timmie's role as Victim, while painful enough, entitled him to more attention from his mother than anyone else in the family. Considering Celia's tendency to pull away from contacts with the children, this was a triumph in itself. Meanwhile, Sonny, ensconced as his father's deputy, lorded it over Timmie, though he had to put up with his mother's disapproval.

Given the intricate, unconsciously established bargains of a pathological equilibrium, it is no wonder that any change wrought by therapy releases protest somewhere along the line. The wonder is that change can occur at all. But the reason that change does happen is because the system is out of balance to begin with and only secondarily — and clumsily — brought into a seemingly stable state. If relationships are founded upon a set of strains, any external impingement that dislodges the secondary compensations will tend to bring the primary imbalance into prominence. For the same reason, the secondary compensations tend to be endlessly ramified. We have touched upon only a few of them in the Tondi family. To examine all of them would require an unjustified amount of space. But there are behavior spheres into which the pathological equilibrium had spread whose importance requires some discussion.

One area was that of the Tondis' relations in the neighborhood and the wider community of the suburb in which they lived. Since Tony had made friends with his neighbors while he was building the house, he had a head start, so to speak, over Celia and the children. His easy-going manner, his technical facility in fixing cars and equipment of all sorts, and his willingness to do favors for people in anticipation of deferred returns all made him an accepted member of the local neighborhood community. He took a good deal of pleasure in this neighborly setting, regarding it as a network of collateral relations which could well function as a substitute for the extended family relations which he had rejected. He was pleased with the idea of introducing his wife and children into the local network so that his immediate family could feel at home in their new surroundings.

But he had not reckoned with the effects of the pathological equilibrium on Celia and the children. Soon after the move to the suburb Celia began to miss the daily contacts with her mother and sister and other family members. She required the contacts because her Collateral > Lineal > Individual pattern was not easily realized in the new community. Also she needed the compensatory reassurance (that she was superior to Tony) and criticism (that she had not achieved as much prestige as her sister) which her mother always offered her. Her extended family was actually the only agency which could satisfy her desire for the constant, dependent relationships which her previous experiences and her psychological makeup had prepared her for. Accordingly, she felt tied down in her new home, confined in cramped quarters with troublesome children and little adult company. Since Tony used the car to go to work, it was difficult for her to go to town to shop or to see her family.

Tony's solution for the problem was simple. He thought that Celia ought gradually to loosen her reliance on her family while she busied herself with making friends and becoming involved in activities in the community, in the classic suburban pattern. Though she half-heartedly agreed, she was unable to carry out such a program. In addition to the strong pull exerted by her relatives in town, the chief obstacle was her sense of inferiority vis-à-vis the neighbors. She tried to justify her feelings of inferiority in accordance with her mother's views — that her husband had not obtained the prestige which would qualify him as a successful American — but his manifest acceptance by the community made this disqualification increasingly difficult to maintain. Furthermore, it was undermined by a growing awareness of presumed disqualifications which she thought that she shared with her husband but which did not inhibit him. Celia was acutely conscious of being a Catholic Italian-American from the working class and of being surrounded by better-educated Protestants of muted national origins. On request, she would prepare Italian dishes for neighboring housewives; but, instead of being able to take the pleasure in this activity which would have been justified, she felt that it set her apart and called attention to her marginal position. So far as the research team could determine, there was no evidence of ethnic or class prejudice in the neighborhood, at least not in relation to Italian-Americans. In this area, her lineal beliefs served her particularly ill: she always had to place herself on the vertical scale of social importance, usually in its nether regions.

But the core of her inferiority feelings in the neighborhood centered on the behavior of her children and the reflections which she thought they cast on her qualities as a mother. We have already referred to Sonny's belligerent behavior with other children as one of the complaints which Celia brought to the diagnostic interviews. Episodes of this sort usually began with scraps between Timmie and other children in the neighborhood. If Sonny thought that Timmie was getting the worst of it, he would become Timmie's protector, acting out the role which his father took toward himself. Stormy, threatening to hit or kill Timmie's assailants, he sometimes grabbed a rock and threw it at the head of the offender, all the while screaming oaths and curses in words which he had heard from older children in the city streets. Celia, who believed (perhaps correctly) that the neighborhood children were unused to such language and behavior, would become horrified. What would the parents of these children think of her and her family?

On one occasion Sonny heaved a rock with such accuracy that it lacerated the forehead of a boy who lived next door. The boy ran home to his mother, streaming with blood. That evening the boy's father spoke angrily to Celia about controlling Sonny's agressiveness in the future. Though she was terribly upset, she managed to blurt out that she knew Sonny's behavior was inexcusable but that she was taking him to a psychiatric clinic to have it corrected. The next day the man apologized profusely. He felt badly for having shown such anger toward a "disturbed child" whose parents were doing their best to help him. His change of heart was small comfort to Celia. To have an emotionally disturbed child was almost as bad as having a delinquent one; in either case, the family was responsible. She feared that all the neighbors would hear of this and look down upon her. Although the neighbor and his wife tried their best to be hospitable and friendly thereafter, until near the end of her therapy Celia was unable to feel comfortable in their presence. Tony, on the other hand, saw nothing in Sonny's behavior beyond the ordinary and thought Celia's reaction part of her general difficulty in adjusting to the neighborhood. Privately, he was pleased that Sonny would stand up and fight for his brother.

The determinants of such behavior obviously had their roots

in the pathological equilibrium. Having been inducted into the role of victim at home, Timmie was prepared to find his persecutor abroad. And, while Sonny was willing enough to be Timmie's oppressor indoors, outside the house he enjoyed being his protector and rescuer, making himself a hero in his father's eyes, an embarrassment in his mother's. Whether he was defined as hero or scoundrel depended upon the perception of the Formal roles from which these Informal roles derived. According to Tony, Sonny was defending the masculine honor of the collateral family in the neighborhood; according to Celia, he was dramatizing the ethnic and class inferiority of the collateral family. Given the choice between the aggressive activity which his father wished him to present in public on behalf of manliness and the passivity or self-control which his mother wanted enacted in the interests of "good manners," Sonny naturally sided with his benefactor and ally — his father.

Once a pathological equilibrium has become established in a family, it acts like a magnet; the most diverse aspects of the biographies of the individual family members become aligned within its field of forces. For example, the cluster of Informal roles which Tony was encouraging his children to enact resulted in a reversal of age roles among the two boys. Sonny behaved like the older, stronger brother, Timmie like the younger weaker one. The role exchange served Tony well in his unconscious plotting to pay Celia back for the wrongs she had inflicted on him. They demonstrated plainly enough (to his mind) that his principles of child care and his notions of competent masculinity were more correct than hers, since Sonny was his child, while Timmie was hers. But, there was another motive for Tony's secret pleasure in the role exchange. Like Sonny, Tony had been a youngest son. He, too, had struggled to catch up with and overthrow a weaker, older brother, the alcoholic Arthur, becoming the hero of the family. In encouraging Sonny's behavior he was repeating a piece of his own life history. But he would not have needed to act out this fragment of his past had he not become involved in the hidden power struggle with his wife which was the nucleus of the pathological equilibrium.

From her side of the transaction, Celia accepted the age role reversal as part and parcel of the unconscious bargains within the pathological equilibrium. If Tony wanted to make her responsible for Timmie's weaknesses, let him. She was prepared to agree that she was guilty of faulty motherhood, as long as Tony accepted her version of his failures as a husband, a man, and an American. The bargain required that she also accept Sonny's domination of Timmie at home. But she could not accept Sonny's belligerence outside the home, since it stood, in her mind, for the ethnic and class inferiority which she reproached in her husband. However, there was another reason for the anxiety which Sonny's aggressiveness and rebelliousness stirred up in her. It revived memories of her brother's rebelliousness and hostility toward her mother and the shame he had brought upon the family within the neighborhood. Thus in attacking the aggressiveness in Sonny, she was repeating her own mother's behavior toward her brother — the boy who had been the light of Angela's eyes, just as Sonny was for Tony.

REDEFINITION AND CHANGE

Psychotherapy of the family is inevitably directed at both individual and group processes.

Even during the first diagnostic contacts the Tondis began to expose and to explore the nature of the pathological equilibrium in which they felt trapped. Celia treated her therapist — a middle-aged female social worker — as a confessor, a confidante, and a teacher. In her initial interviews she poured out the details of her life history with considerable emotion: her resentments against her mother, her envy of her sister and brother, her feelings of inferiority as a woman, and her shame over the shortcomings in her husband and children. These were feelings of which she was perfectly aware but which she had never openly communicated to anyone. The experiences of talking to someone who listened sympathetically and uncritically, with an eye to being helpful, was new to her. After the second interview, she spontaneously attempted to carry over in talks with her mother and her husband this new-found freedom to express herself. Tony was surprised to learn for the first time of her intense, long-standing inferiority feelings. As usual, he blamed her mother for them, while expressing sympathy toward her problem. By the time Celia saw her mother, the previously suppressed resentment for past injustices was strong. As Celia brought out complaints of ancient wrongs, Angela flew into a rage, denied everything, blamed Tony and his "crazy family" for all of Celia's shortcomings, and then elaborated upon them in great detail. Celia left in tears; she was depressed and apathetic for days afterwards. During this period, Sonny went through severe cycles of constipation.

These events constituted a "symptomatic episode" — that is, a clear and dramatic snapshot of some aspects of the basic conflict in the family. Such episodes always contain an important message for the therapeutic team. In this instance, although it was too early in the treatment process for the full significance to be appreciated, the symptomatic episode was understood as showing the desire on Celia's part for an Individualistic definition of her behavior and feelings as opposed to the Collateral > Lineal definition which so much of her training had emphasized. It was as if she were saying to her mother, "Look at me as an individual rather than a cog in the family machinery or a representative of the family's interests. Pay attention to my feelings." This wish, which had been evoked by the therapist's receptive attitude, was interwoven with feelings of guilt over the unacceptable desires which might attain expression were her personal feelings to be credited. Therefore, at the same time that she indirectly conveyed to her mother the sense of how she would like to have been treated, she exposed herself to her mother's predictable wrath and received her expected punishment. In the following days she was depressed, withdrawn, irritable toward her children's demands for attention, and antagonistic toward her husband. Having put herself in a position with her own mother where she could be defined as the disloyal, unloving, disobedient child, she subsequently assigned a similar set of Informal roles to her own children, especially to Sonny, who became chief villain in the family because of his attempts to deceive her about his bowel movements. This projection of the sense of wrongdoing undoubtedly relieved Celia's internal burden of guilt-feeling and remorse. However, it increased her external difficulties. Sonny was willing enough to adopt the job of protector-persecutor toward Timmie and of mischief-maker in general. But he could not bear the isolation and anxious accusations that were part of his role as villain-in-chief. In revenge, he extracted from his mother the pity, anger, and horror that always accompanied a withholding of bowel movements. And the shared anxiety in the household was raised to a nearly intolerable level.

That Sonny's behavior was quite explicitly governed by motives of revenge and counter-attack was revealed by Celia in the following interview. She told how on a previous occasion, when he had been punished for some misbehavior by being deprived of a toy, he threatened never to have a bowel movement again in his whole life unless the toy was restored to him. To be sure, Sonny's threat on this occasion was more indicative of the secondary gains which he derived from his symptom than of its primary determinants. Nevertheless, the circular transactions — from Celia's pleasure at the Individualistic reception of her complaints by her therapist through her masochistic request for similar treatment by her mother to her subsequent provoking of the constipation behavior in Sonny — provided the therapeutic team with a clue for the initial management of the symptom, in terms of the family process.

It will be recalled that Individualism was in the third-order position in Celia's *Relational* orientation. The events of the symptomatic episode showed that this last-in-rank position was not a simple matter but was a locus of intense emotional conflict. To oversimplify a complex matter, Celia unconsciously longed to shift Individualism from its third-order position to at least second place, if not a first-order position. The desire for the shift was governed by complex considerations, among which may be included her perception of the importance of Individualism in American culture and her feeling that she had been exploited by the Collateral > Lineal orientations so deftly deployed by her mother. But this desire was strenuously opposed, also unconsciously, by the guilt and the associated anxiety which attached to any expression of Individualism. The fantasies of revenge to which a possible Individualistic reorientation gave rise was too frightening. Yet, this was the problem which the therapeutic encounter could not avoid dealing with. It centered directly upon her handling of her relations with her mother and her children; and it was directly at issue in the transference situation. The lesson emerging from all these considerations seemed to be this: Celia's striving for an Individualistic reorientation was to be encouraged, but always within the constraints of a Collateral definition of the therapeutic relationship. The constraint and the control exercised by the therapist would constitute a protection against premature and self-punishing releases of Individualistic self-assertion, especially aggression. The therapist, in other words, was best advised to function for Celia partly as a mother — but a mother who, this time around, would honor Celia's individualism (and her competence) while exercising some controls over her behavior.

In view of the end result of the symptomatic episode, it seemed wise to center this strategy squarely around Sonny's symptom. This was, in any event, the focus of Celia's and Tony's interest. They both repeatedly requested advice on how to handle it, and Celia, in addition, constantly voiced her fear that Sonny had managed to damage himself in some irremedial fashion. These fears were understood by the therapist as indicating the nature of Celia's unconscious sadistic wishes toward Sonny. She had already been told by several physicians that Sonny's constipation was functional and that there was no sign of organic damage. Therefore, every time Celia expressed such fears, the therapist assured her that no harm had been done and sympathized with her concern. When Celia asked for explicit directions for managing Sonny's behavior, the therapist asked her what thoughts she had on the subject. This was done not for the sake of maintaining neutrality or with a view toward eliciting material for interpretation. Rather, its purpose was to establish a collaborative relationship. Celia reviewed various possibilities that had occurred to her, and then she and the therapist discussed the wisdom of one versus another of these possibilities. Among the variety of suggestions brought up by Celia, one seemed particularly promising. This was the possibility of Celia's offering to sit with Sonny whenever he felt like having a bowel movement, staying in the bathroom with him and distracting him from his discomfort in some way.

To everyone's surprise, Celia negotiated this transaction with considerable adroitness. Sonny was caught off guard by the offer and immediately took it up. As it turned out, he was ready to accept almost any offer of attention from his mother, especially one proffered in good faith. And Celia was enthusiastic about her "experiment." She sat on a chair opposite Sonny on the toilet, reading to him or singing or playing some game. He did not always have a movement; nor did he always draw her attention to the times when he had a spontaneous urge. There were repetitions of the constipation pattern; but these repetitions of the old pattern were increasingly punctuated by stretches of smooth sailing in which the reciprocal behavior of mother and child led to a successful and comfortable evacuation. Eventually, toward the midpoint of the therapeutic process, Celia told Sonny that she thought he had reached the point where he could go to the toilet by himself and that perhaps he would not need to tell her every time he wanted to go. Although concern over constipation had long since evaporated, the symptom was now officially a thing of the past.

It would be an error to conclude that Sonny's symptom disappeared exclusively as a result of this one maneuver. Other changes were ricocheting around the family at the same time. Meanwhile, in his own therapy, Sonny experimented with the manifold possibilities of making a mess. Policed at home, he gloried at the clinic in squeezing and pounding clay, smearing water colors, chalk, and crayon on receptive surfaces, exploding a ping-pong rifle at the therapist, and teasing him with riddles ("Guess what I'm thinking!"). At first Sonny's experimenting was abruptly concluded with scrupulous cleaning-up and putting-in-order: restoration on a grand scale. Later, with the help of the therapist, he was able to define his play less as offensive messing and more as investigating or making. His role gradually changed from that of the little-slob-in-the-parlor to that of the little-explorer-in-the-playroom. It was impossible to determine what factor played exactly what part in his improved bowel control. The fact, however, that the improvement set in so early and, apparently, in response to a solution conceived by Celia with the help of her therapist put the whole therapeutic enterprise in good standing with the Tondis.

While Celia and Sonny were learning to sort out their impulses and feelings with the help of their therapists, Tony took a different stance in his treatment. He defined the relationship as purely a matter of technical or pedagogical instruction, as if he were back in school. He asked for information about what caused his children's symptoms and directions for solving the problem. He took the position that mistakes had been made in child care and training which could easily be corrected in exactly the same manner as he corrected faulty equipment in an airplane. He was immensely pleased with Sonny's prompt response to Celia's handling of the toilet-training situation and expected all the other problems in the family to vanish with equal dispatch, once the key had been found. But it had never occurred to him that his personal feelings and impulses, as well as his own childhood experiences, were a part of the problem. Although his therapist often asked him how he felt about various events in the present or past, Tony was able to give only the most meagre response. Sometimes he was "happy," at other times "disgusted," depending upon how the children were behaving or what past event was under discussion. Where Celia's behavior was concerned, he was always satisfied that she was doing her best under difficult circumstances. Nor could he understand why the therapist wanted him to talk at greater length about something so irrelevant as his own feelings. Aside from the problems of the children, he presented himself as entirely content with his lot in life. And even in regard to the children he was mostly concerned with the significance of their present problems for their success and happiness in the future. If he could have convinced himself that they would ultimately outgrow their behavior problems of their own accord, he would have rejected treatment altogether. It was only the slender thread of his anxiety about the children's future that attached him to the family therapy program.

It seemed evident that the therapeutic problem presented by Tony was that of a "technological defense" against inner anxiety, something roughly parallel to an "intellectual defense"

250

in a more highly educated person. The denial of affect was intense, and it was rationalized and justified by his view of the almost mechanical perfectibility of human conduct. In his experience, he had found unwanted behavior correctible if the right person came along with the right method, as had happened in the case of his own stuttering. To be sure, every defense has its adaptive aspects. Tony's technical approach made him optimistic of success. He was willing to try any rational method, and he tried hard to understand and cooperate with the method of psychotherapy. He delivered long, completely neutral accounts of the latest happenings in his family or at work. Still, so long as the defensive side of his behavior kept his feelings so rigidly out of the therapeutic relationship, little insight into his motivations could be obtained. And, without insight, not much progress could be expected.

Frustrating and confusing as the therapeutic problem was, one thing was crystal clear: Tony was not going to change his position on the expression of emotion as a result of encouragement or interpretation. After six months of the therapist's probing for feelings he once said, "Oh, I see. You're interested in how *I* feel about this!" But the illumination was not a prelude to change; he kept right on with his denials that he was much affected, one way or the other, by family events, and, as usual, he asked for a prescription for handling the particular incident. On the principle that "if you can't lick 'em, join 'em" it was tempting to yield to Tony's requests for specific direction and advice. The difficulty with this strategy was that, without a better understanding of the meaning to him of any particular behavior, it was impossible to know what advice to give. With Celia the problem was simpler because she revealed her feelings and her fantasies without much urging. Tony wanted to know, for example, how he should handle Timmie's temper tantrums. Should Timmie be punished? If so, how? Should he ignore the outbursts? Was there some other method for putting a stop to this behavior? What caused it in the first place? And what about the rocking in bed? The therapist responded to all such queries with the statement that the answers were not yet known — in fact, that psychotherapy consisted of a long process in which one studied and worked with the children in order to discover the solutions. In the meantime, it was important to know how the parents felt about it.

A potential therapeutic stalemate of this sort is often — though by no means always and never exclusively — the result of an imperfect comprehension of the value orientations and role relations

251

of the patient. The therapist's procedure would have been appropriate had Tony displayed a dominant American middle-class value orientation. The hitch occurred because Tony seemed in some ways a typical American. He had, as a glance at Table 4 reveals, adopted all but one of the first-order American value choices. Certainly he had moved a considerable distance from the native Italian-American value profile. His doubly atypical values — conforming neither to the American nor to the Italian patterns — underscored the problem of how to procede therapeutically. It also raised the interesting question of the relation between value orientation and intrapsychic defense in a particularly pertinent context.

Had Tony's value orientations conformed more exactly to the American, middle-class pattern, his resistance to therapeutic exploration would have taken a different form. Because of long-standing repression reinforced by various character defenses, he might have had just as much difficulty in revealing his feelings. But he would have understood this difficulty as an obstacle to therapy, have become interested in it and willing to inquire into its meaning. The key to the difference lies in the first-order emphasis on Individualism. The American would have been more inclined to ask himself such questions as "Why do *I* have so much trouble showing my feelings?" and "What is *my* relation to my family, apart from what others expect of me?" Tony's first-order emphasis on Collaterality tended to make such questions irrelevant. In his own mind, his personality was not well distinguished from that of others in his family, and the choices, the decisions about actions, had not seemed, in the first instance, to be so definitely in his own hands. True, he had moved Individualism into a second-order position. But this happened partly in response to his perception of the importance of Individualism everywhere in American culture, partly because the Lineality of his own family systems — which had been the second-order choice of his childhood training — had led to so much anxiety and disappointment. Individualism, accordingly, had been installed in the second-order position as a *reaction-formation* against the anxiety and the sense of shame that accompanied the Lineal choices. Behind the defense, therefore, lurked the hidden desire for the devalued Lineal satisfactions: to be told what to do, to have an assured place in an hierarchy, to be loved for his obedience by a more powerful person. This was the problem that got him into difficulties with his wife and that produced the hitch in therapy.

When a switch in value patterning is the result of a defensive reaction-formation in a single value orientation category — even one so sensitive as the *Relational* orientation — it can usually be isolated and brought under the scrutiny of the therapeutic process. In Tony's case, however, switches in other categories were also the result of reaction-formations. The first-order position of Doing, for example, was held in place by the not always successful repression of Being, while the primacy of his Mastery-over-Nature position was barely maintained against strong pressure for the fatalistic acceptance of the Subjugation-to-Nature position. It was the defensive combination of these positions that gave his technical approach to problem solving its mechanical and unrealistic optimism.

A pattern of values which is rank-ordered along such defensive lines will, quite obviously, be difficult to modify; in addition, a precipitous alteration will run risks of severe personality disruption. It must be handled with care. Therapeutic interventions must be carried out within its structure rather than in opposition to it. In Tony's case, an added problem was that the very character of the defense made its elucidation difficult. It was not until many months had passed that the pathological equilibrium previously described came into view. Only then was it possible to see how the feelings which he kept out of the therapeutic interviews were expressed in action, how the formal roles in the family had been distorted through the segregation of the family into two subgroups, and how in this fashion and in other ways the tensions in the family had been transferred to a set of inappropriate Informal roles. Once the significance of the role segregation was understood, it then became clear that this was an area in which Tony's desire for human engineering could be satisfied along adaptive lines, thus putting only a small strain on his defensive systems.

Tony was asked why the family always did everything in two's rather than in three's or with the whole family together. The question startled him, and, although he gave an indignant justification, he was not entirely convinced of its truth. The matter had hit home — that is, his behavior now looked to him like a violation of his first-order *Collateral* orientation. He took immediate action. He began to invite Timmie along on various excursions with Sonny and to take the whole family on outings. At first Timmie resisted, displaying his phobic pattern of inseparability from his mother. When his behavior was discussed by Celia with her therapist, she was able to see that she was aiding and abetting Timmie's avoidance of his father by her over-cautious attitude. She then understood that she wished to keep control over Timmie because she felt so guilty and responsible for him. With this insight established, she was able to insist that Timmie accompany his father and brother, and the pattern of avoidance was broken.

If a pathological equilibrium is loosened, the feelings formerly used to solder it in place begin to appear in verbal communications and in protest reactions, as stated above. It was now that Tony began to verbalize his envy of his children, to whom he gave so much and with whom he tried so hard. Such expressions of feeling were, however, quite brief, and he was completely unable to admit that they had anything to do with his actions. It was also at this time that Sonny, having lost his exclusive position with his father, became more aggressive toward Timmie, attempting constantly to put him in the wrong. And Timmie, having been pried away from his mother and not yet feeling secure with his father, seemed only too willing to be put in the wrong. He, rather than Sonny, now became the chief family problem.

One might have expected that with the elimination of the distortion in age and sex roles formerly imposed upon him, Timmie would have blossomed. In fact, in some ways this is what happened. In activities concerned with physical coordination, in sports and games, he developed quite impressive skills. But other problems which had been hidden behind his phobic behavior now came to the fore. One of these was a tendency to tell tall stories in which he figured either as hero or victim. Timmie usually told these tales with such a mixture of excitement and stuttering that it was difficult to hear exactly what he was saying. More difficult was the problem of distinguishing fact from fiction in these adventures. There was no doubt that, whatever the core of truth in his stories, the greatest part was fantasy. Many of his accounts were so preposterous as to raise the question of his ability to discriminate his fantasies from reality. For example, he called himself "Sky King" — a role borrowed from a television show — and related his adventures in outer space and the dramatic rescues he carried off for earthbound creatures. He told his therapist many tales of his working on planes at the airport with his father, of planes that he had piloted, and of underwater adventures in submarines in which he had participated. At other times he depicted himself falling out of trees into ponds and having to be rescued from the threatened attacks of underwater monsters. However, his role as victim or rescuer was unstable; in the same story he might alternate several times between these two roles.

254

Timmie's behavior represented a fascinating psychosocial problem. The unconscious determinants of the manifest content of his fantasies were fairly easy to interpret. Quite obviously, he was satisfying a wish to reverse his lowly status in reality as the weak, rather effeminate, mother-bound child by assuming dramatically masculine roles in' fantasy, in which his association, indeed his identification, with the father from whom he was so distant was clearly portrayed. The fantasies also incorporated the punishments for seeking to gratify the wish — the fall from glory and the reversion to the victim's role. The person he most often rescued in the stories was either his brother or some symbolic substitute for him. But the chief behavioral problem was not the content of the fantasies or the unconscious wishes which gave rise to them. Rather, the significant question was: why did Timmie tell these stories? Did he really expect others to believe them? Was he aware of the distortion of reality?

The answer to this question was contained in the status of Fictive roles in the Tondi family. Fictive roles are elaborated within all societies — as well as in persistent small groups — to allow the individual some escape from reality with its often grim necessities. Where children are concerned, each culture elaborates a set of Fictive roles which the child can assume in play. Within a particular culture, these roles vary for the age of the child, younger children usually being permitted much more inventiveness and freedom in the choice of Fictive roles. Between cultures, variation proceeds along different dimensions; but the two most significant variations are the differences in the choice of role for same aged children and differences in the cues exchanged between adults and children (or between children and their playmates) when Fictive roles are being assumed. These are subtle matters that have not been systematically studied in the context of cross-cultural comparison. For families undergoing acculturation to new customs, the cues often become confused and ill-understood. This is what had occurred in the Tondi family.

Let us recall that in the native Italian culture Fictive roles, especially in the sexual or aggressive areas, are well understood and expected behavior. Bragging, dramatic impersonation either by impromptu "acting" or the telling of long, circumstantial tales and histrionic exaggeration are part of the bill-of-fare of everyday behavior. In Italy and in Italian-American communities life would seem colorless without these touches of the *commedia dell' arte* and of theatrical display in general. The behavior of Angela, for example, when she delivered her "mother's curse" while viewing the wedding procession of her son could have been taken from the libretto of an Italian opera. The key to the assumption of Fictive roles in Italian culture is ambiguity. The observer, or participator, should be left in a certain doubt as to whether the role is really a Fictive one; otherwise the display is no fun. Part of the entertainment consists in calculating and gossiping about what part of the behavior is serious, what part merely for the sake of putting on a good show. To make such discriminations requires experience with the culture in general, the local group in particular, and the individual himself, since the cues are almost indefinable.

The behavior of the Italian in assuming Fictive roles is guided by the preference for Being in the *Activity* orientation, supported by the general configuration of values in Italian culture. For the middle-class American, Fictive roles have an entirely different status — one confined to particular recreational or informal occasions which de-emphasize successful performance of a job. The cues, in these circumstances, are much more definite, and the observer or participator wants to know "for sure" whether or not the behavior is serious or in jest. When children play, it is considered "good for their development"; and when adults joke or play, their fun is believed to have been "earned" because they have worked so hard. The hard-and-fast distinction between work and play leaves no room for ambiguity. This much of the American approach to Fictive roles both Celia and Tony had learned. But they had not learned how to place their children's behavior within these rules. They did not know how to determine when the boys were showing behavior which ought to be taken "seriously" and when the behavior could be taken "lightly," as childlike or amusing by-play.

When Timmie embarked on one of his epic tales, for example, Celia would listen, unbelieving yet fascinated by the excesses of his youthful imagination. As he became more and more wound up in the dramatic effect he was creating, she would make a great effort to control herself while experiencing a sense of panic about how to control him. Self-control — the calm, urbane behavior exhibited by the families surrounding her in the neighborhood — was what she desperately wanted for herself and her children. Yet self-control somehow always eluded her. Goaded to distraction by what seemed a deliberate confabulation, she would end up screaming at Timmie: "Stop telling lies!" Deflated, Timmie would retire in a confusion of stuttering and ineffective protest. Still, there had occurred that subtle, mutual participation in a dramatic encounter — a catharsis — which both mother and child had unwittingly enjoyed and to which they would both return.

We can now see why Timmie told his far-fetched stories. He was a poet, indulging in hyperbole and poetic license. Although he made up his tales out of phallic exhibitionistic materials which were of the greatest importance to him psychodynamically, he *told* them for the sake of their effect upon an audience. He was not interested in their accuracy but in their ability to generate interest. In the presence of his mother, he received the accolade most desired by a poet: attention and appreciation, even though the appreciation had to be concealed behind an admonition.

The problem for psychotherapy, then, was how to deal with Timmie's muse, the internalized mother imago. The therapist decided that it was a question of establishing ground rules for the appreciation of fantasy. She listened patiently and with unfeigned pleasure while Timmie displayed his dramatic talents. For he was almost irresistible in the role of bard. He twinkled with mischief, glowed with courage, and shuddered with terror while staging his miniature spectaculars. After he had finished, she reviewed the account with him piece by piece, to discover what was fact and what fiction. At first Timmie had little patience with this procedure. What he wanted was an effect on an audience, not an analysis of his performance. Gradually, however, he fell in with the practice — as if to say that he liked her and, if this interested her, he would try to cooperate. Later the therapist attempted to explore the content of his stories and offered some interpretations. Timmie never seemed to respond to this sort of probing. His interest turned to making and doing, especially to making model airplanes. As he became more involved in this activity, in active mastery of his physical environment, his fantastic stories both at home and in the therapy diminished in quantity and stayed closer to reality, though they never completely lost the aura of the fable.

Unfortunately, Timmie's status as the family problem was not confined to his feats of myth-making. As this problem behavior subsided, another took its place. His school reports began to show unsatisfactory progress in reading and spelling. Again, this was something that neither Celia nor Tony could take lightly. To them it meant one more injury to the family's reputation. If Timmie was an incompetent student, then his parents were also intellectually inferior. They responded with a flurry of home instruction. Timmie was made to read aloud to his parents, who alternated between correcting his reading or his stuttering while reading. Meanwhile they both brought the problem to their therapists, asking how to handle Timmie's learning difficulty.

The questions which this newest piece of symptomatic behavior posed for the therapists was how to determine the actual severity of Timmie's learning defect. They had the impression that the anxiety of the parents was wholly out of proportion to the seriousness of the problem. Normally, this would have been established by a conference between Celia and Timmie's teacher. But Celia was terrified of a meeting with the teacher. She made and canceled appointment after appointment. On one occasion, when she thought that she saw the school principal walking down the street toward her house, she hid in the bathroom and refused to answer the doorbell.

It was clear that Celia's fear of teachers could not be resolved in therapy in time to discover the nature of Timmie's reading and spelling difficulty. The information could be obtained only by direct contact between the therapists and the school. With Celia's permission, the therapists talked to both the principal of the school and Timmie's teacher, as well as the teacher of remedial reading with whom he had begun to work. He was regarded as somewhat slow but not gravely deficient. The teaching staff was unaware of the parents' anxiety, and they believed that the home instruction was unnecessary and possibly harmful. All the teachers commented on the charm of Timmie's personality and said that, although his stuttering was occasionally noticeable, it was not a serious problem. As a result of the visit, however, they promised to pay more attention to his individual needs.

Armed with this information, the therapists advised the parents to discontinue home instruction. In addition, summoning up all their credentials of authority, the therapists told Celia and Tony that Timmie was not a backward or stupid child and should not be treated as one. Furthermore they said that Timmie should not be put under constant pressure to achieve better grades in school, since, in the normal course of events, the teachers expected him to perform adequately and saw no reason why he should not be promoted at the end of the year.

This maneuver did relieve Timmie of some of the parental pressure, though he was not immediately released from his role as "family problem." After all, the authoritatively delivered advice did nothing to alter the pathological equilibrium in the family but only diluted some of its force. Though they were reassured, Tony

258

and Celia continued to await the school's next report on Timmie with fear and trepidation. Timmie still occupied the role which symbolized the parents' projected inferiority and marginality in their middle-class community. The pathway toward the further loosening of the pathological equilibrium was not yet available.

Now two events occurred which prepared the way for a more effective exposure of the pathological equilibrium. One concerned Tony and the other Celia. Tony had from the beginning brought up in therapy the problems he experienced in his job. They concerned his lack of promotion after so many years of working for the same company. He was still a line mechanic; though younger and newer people had been promoted to the position of foreman, he had remained stationary. For a long time he attributed his lack of advancement to factors completely beyond his control: the constantly growing complexity and increasing impersonality of the airline company, the cliques that formed within the line personnel, and the personalities of various foremen with whom he did not get along. Gradually, his therapist was able to show him that some of the factors which blocked his progress were within himself. They mainly concerned his first-order Collateral value preferences. Tony actually could not push himself forward as an individual or fight a competitive struggle for self-advancement. He felt that people who pushed were selfish and unfair to the company, caring only about their own benefits, while he always had the interests of the airline — the whole organization — at heart.

It was clear that Tony's *Relational* orientation was not well suited to the American occupational setting which places so much emphasis on Individualism. Since values are incorporated into the superego, he felt ashamed at the idea of pushing himself forward and could not include such acts in his concept of his occupational role. He treated the airline company as if it should be, ideally, one, big, happy, collateral family. Even the anticipation of becoming a foreman caused him some anxiety because a foreman was a boss, the head of a Lineal chain of command. Lineality was in last place in Tony's hierarchy of values.

As these matters were talked over in therapy, Tony began to see that in his job, at least, he was not a typical American. He also began to understand that Celia's constant pressure on him to obtain a job promotion was not simply a matter of her "nervousness." As a result of the slight change in his self-concept and in his concept of others, he was able to make demands on the company's management personnel for an improved job status. We have

259

already described Tony's weak Individualistic preferences as the result of a reaction-formation. Therefore it should come as no surprise that he experienced much anxiety when he had his talk with the personnel supervisor. He had rehearsed what he would say for days, using Celia as an audience. On her side, she did her best to be uncritical and supportive. Still, Tony was afraid that he would begin to stutter or that he would forget what he had intended to say. The result was not an overwhelming improvement in his career; Tony was not promoted to the position of foreman. But he was given a great deal more consideration and recognition on the job. He was sent to London to obtain training in the use and maintainance of a new piece of equipment. Then he was sent to New York and Florida to train others in the necessary procedures. As a consequence, his pay checks were larger, and his status in the company, in his family, and in the neighborhood was higher.

The further removal of Celia from her involvement in the pathological equilibrium was brought about through the therapist's cooperation with a sudden insight which she achieved. She had been repeatedly discussing her conflicts about visiting her family or having them visit her. She wanted to see her mother or her sister on Tony's day off, when he could look after the children at home. She regarded this arrangement as a vacation from childcare, as well as one of the simple courtesies to one's relatives which are to be expected in an Italian family. Tony objected to these weekly excursions, both because she took the car in order to cover the long distance to the city and because he wanted her to be home on his day off. But Celia became aware that there was more to this situation than an external conflict with her husband. She had begun to realize that she herself was not of one mind about her obligations to her extended family. Visits to her mother usually ended in some sort of unpleasant disagreement, while seeing her sister made her feel envious and dependent. She had reached the intellectual insight that there was no longer any reason for feeling inferior to her sister, who was experiencing even more severe domestic problems than Celia herself. However, she was unable to shed the long-standing though now unreasonable *feeling* of inferiority. She had also recognized that her mother was helpless against an inner need to deprecate the persons and things closest to her.

While struggling with this quandry, looking for a way out of the traditional Lineal compulsions within her behavior, Celia one day had a brilliant idea. She proffered the idea that Angela's unpleasant behavior had grown worse over the years as she had increasingly been separated from her children and her activities in the Italian community. There was no longer any need for her services as a midwife and little call for her talents as a hostess, entertainer, and trainer of the newly arrived Italian immigrant. Perhaps, thought Celia, her mother was suffering from unemployment. Having been impressed with the effectiveness of the therapists' intervention in the school situation, Celia wondered if something could be done to provide her mother with a job.

Celia's therapist, a social worker, thought the idea well worth considering. She asked Celia whether her mother would enjoy the job of homemaker or housekeeper in families troubled by the illness or absence of the mother. Celia proposed this possibility to her mother. Angela was at first surprised, then uncertain, and finally offered to try out such a job if she did not have to travel a long distance. Celia reported Angela's response to her therapist, and her therapist reported it to the research team, whose members enthusiastically endorsed the plan. A position was soon found for Angela, and, to everyone's relief, she took pleasure in it. She liked taking care of a house and the small children in the family, she enjoyed being in control of the situation, and, above all, she was pleased to feel useful and to be earning money again.

A definite change in Angela's moods and behavior now took place — an alteration which reverberated throughout the extended family system. She was more cheerful, had fewer criticisms of her husband, children, and grandchildren, and made fewer demands upon them. It seemed clear that a longstanding but clinically masked depression had been partially relieved through her involvement in an activity which was in accord with her ego ideals and which satisfied her need for contact with and control over others. As a result of the lightening of Angela's mood, family gatherings became less harassing. Celia reported with amazement and delight that a get-together for a Thanksgiving meal had taken place in an atmosphere of harmony, for a change. Furthermore, since Angela now had less need for contact with her own children, Celia was freed of the responsibility for ritual visiting.

The unexpected loosening of the Lineal bond between Angela and Celia now put Celia in a position to spend more time with her husband in Collateral activities. They began to plan together for the completion of the unfinished rooms in the house. Not only did they plan together; they actually discovered how to work together in the building process. To be sure, there were still see-saw struggles for dominance between Tony and Celia, with Tony

261

exhibiting his celebrated patience while Celia learned, to her dismay, that she had been wrong about a structural detail. But as the rooms took shape, Celia began to feel somewhat more comfortable about her house and its overcrowded feeling. Now that her pride in her house was partly restored, she was able to feel a bit more relaxed in the neighborhood. And, feeling more acceptable, she was able to be more active in the community. In fact, the most striking change in the Tondi family was the increased participation in community activities. Celia joined the P.T.A. and discovered that she had some organizational ability along with her known tendency to be bossy like her mother. Tony, having had a head start in the community, now indulged his desire to join as many organizations as he had time for. Collaterality, which had always been Tony's first-order *Relational* preference, became dominant for Celia, bringing their domestic and community roles into better consonance with each other.

Though still not completely resolved, the loosening of the pathological equilibrium which now took place resulted in a considerable increase in the level of mutual appreciation and self-satisfaction in the nuclear family. Tony, feeling that he was "beginning to live for the first time," bought himself new clothes to celebrate his rebirth as a suburbanite. Celia appreciated his "dressed-up" look. She went on a diet, lost ten pounds, and was quite pleased with herself. The "new look" was also shared by the children, who began to do better in school, fought less with each other, and seemed to feel more comfortable with playmates in the neighborhood. Above all, the parents and the children were able to give up the need to put someone in the role of family scapegoat or "problem." The problems were still there, but they tended more and more to be defined as "family problems" rather than the result of the undesirable behavior of one or another member.

The easing of tension in interpersonal relations was so noticeable that both the parents and the therapists began now to talk of the possibility of terminating the therapeutic work. As one might expect, the prospect of severing the dependent relations and the collaborative teamwork so painfully established in the course of therapy brought about a recrudescence of family tension. Symptomatic episodes reappeared as a probable date for termination was agreed upon. What was interesting — and different — was that the conflicts remained visibly imbedded in the Formal roles of the family without being displaced to distorted Informal or Fictive roles. As a part of this new mode of conflict resolution, Celia and Tony were much more able to discuss the emerging problems with each other, with persons in the community, and with the therapists.

For example, a typical conflict developed over the purchase of a new car. The family's old second-hand car was constantly breaking down and required extensive nursing. Tony was embarrassed because its deficiencies seemed to reflect on his mechanical aptitudes. No matter how much he fussed with it, the car refused to remain in good running order. Celia was embarrassed because its shabby appearance made an unpleasant contrast with the shiny, well-cared for cars of the neighbors and seemed, thus, to symbolize not-making-the-grade-with-the-neighborhood. She wanted Tony to buy a new car. Tony, his eye on the state of the family finances, wanted to buy another second-hand car. To bolster her position, Celia told Tony about her mother's teasing description of Tony as a man who always gave his family second-hand things. Tony was wounded by the kernel of truth in this remark and decided, in desperation, to buy a new car. Whereupon Celia reproached him, as usual, for not sticking by his guns — essentially, for not being a man.

There was much in this family transaction that reflected the old disorders in the sphere of cultural values. Celia's inability to plan for the future versus Tony's emphasis on caution and careful planning; Celia's emphasis on "appearances" and symbolic representation versus Tony's interest in functional mastery at the expense of "externals"; Celia's equating of masculinity with dominance versus Tony's notion that decisions should be made mutually. But, instead of the dissociation in formal roles that these value discrepancies would have produced in the past, Celia and Tony now argued the matter out with each other and actually did reach a mutual decision: that it would be best to buy a "good" second-hand car, shiny enough to please Celia and cheap enough to satisfy Tony. The compromise attained by confrontation and explicit communication was reached soon enough to avoid having the children become involved in a displaced role conflict.

The ability to cope with conflict through discussion was steadily maintained in the final weeks of therapy. Individual gains in performance and insight were also recovered. Celia held steadfastly to the difficult insight that her dissatisfaction with her husband and her children were colored by her dissatisfaction with herself. This insight enabled her to be more content with them, on the one hand, and more direct and less emotional about disagreements, on the other. As she gained self-confidence, she began to see Tony's good points for herself rather than through the eyes of others. Feeling encouraged, Tony accepted a job promotion which had given him considerable anxiety when it was first proposed. He became a "company man," a teacher of advanced mechanical techniques. The position demanded that he give lectures to trainees, an activity which evoked his fear of stuttering in an intense fashion. Nevertheless, he mastered his fear, worked very hard, and eventually felt proud of his promotion, as did Celia. At the point of termination, they both expressed satisfactions with the gains achieved in therapy; they also expressed keen awareness of the problems which they had not been able to resolve. But they thought that they would prefer to work on these problems by themselves. Celia expressed their attitude in the words, "I can see now that there is no magic to solve our problems; it's up to us." Although they had been told that they could get in touch with the therapists at a later time if they wished for more therapeutic consultations, they did not do so. A follow-up inquiry several months after termination revealed that the mutual satisfactions were being maintained.

EIGHT

The Sirrentis: A "Well" Family

The Sirrentis — the family we meet in this chapter — were, like the Tondis, changing some of their traditional Italian values in the direction of dominant American orientations. Thus they experienced cultural strain. Unlike the Tondis, however, they dealt with their problems more or less successfully through their own efforts.

The nuclear Sirrenti family with whom our research team came into contact consisted of the husband, Benito, age forty-one; his wife, Consuelo, age thirty-five; and their three sons, Natale, thirteen, Rudolphe, eleven, and Benito, Jr., two years old. Project interviewers were introduced to this family through the agency of a graduate student who was a friend of one of Benito's first cousins.

Benito, Sr., called Ben by his family and friends, was employed as a waiter in a hotel restaurant located in Boston. There was no mistaking his Italian facial characteristics. He was active and agile. Whenever the interviewers visited, he busied himself with their comfort and plied them with food and drink. He was frequently unshaven and wore an old sweater with threadbare slacks. His manner toward the interviewers was open and cordial. At the first visit to the family, not long after the introductions, he poured a drink for everyone and proposed a toast to the newfound friendship.

265

Consuelo Sirrenti, or Connie as she was known to her family, was short and rather plump, very lively, and quite expressive in speech. Like her husband, she made a great effort to feed and entertain the interviewers. She had black hair and an animated smile, somewhat marred by a partly decayed, gold-filled front tooth. The interviewers usually found her wearing a flowered house dress and apron. It was obvious from the outset that her husband and children were the most important and absorbing of all her day-to-day interests.

The oldest boy, Nat, was almost fourteen at the beginning of contact with the family. He was tall and lean, with his father's olive-colored skin. He had thick black hair and a rather prominent nose. His manner was usually reserved, though on occasion, when thoroughly interested in what he was saying, he could become quite voluble, savoring, like his parents, the possibility of telling an entertaining story. He was ambitious to make a good record in the parochial high school which he attended, both in sports and in academic subjects. During the visits he was usually studying, watching television, or out playing sports with his friends in the neighborhood.

Eleven-year-old Rudy was physically at the opposite pole from his older brother. He was short and chubby — in fact, corpulent. His hair was dark, and his facial characteristics — indeed, his whole physical aspect — resembled his mother rather than his father. Rudy had the reputation of being a big eater, but it was difficult for the interviewers to determine what part of his larger-than-normal intake was due to his appetite and what part to his mother's pleasure in seeing him eat. He was not as active or as overtly ambitious as his brother, although his academic record was fully as good as Nat's. Rudy was an altar boy in the church attended by the family and spent much of his spare time doing odd jobs for the priests at church. He participated very little in sports. He was less reserved than Nat, usually presenting a cheery, good-natured attitude.

Benny was a two-year-old of average height but rather thin and pale. He was extremely active, and, since he had the run of the house, he was often underfoot. It did not take him long to overcome his shyness in the presence of the interviewers, but during visits he usually preferred to sit in the living room watching television with his brothers. On the first visit, his mother described Benny as "a nervous child" because he was fussy about eating. He never ate enough to please his mother, and, if too much food was placed before him, he would refuse to eat at all. He had been toilet trained before his second birthday. In the month or so before the visiting began, Benny had lost ground and now frequently wet his pants. No one in the family regarded this as of any particular consequence.

The Sirrentis lived in a four-room apartment in Boston's North End. The neighborhood was almost wholly Italian, the buildings were shabby, and the streets narrow and crowded with parked cars and pedestrians. The wooden structure inhabited by the Sirrentis had been put up at the turn of the century and was now owned, along with the neighboring tenement, by Benito Sirrenti's father. There were fourteen apartments in the other building and eight in the one in which the Sirrentis lived. On the first floor were several stores, only intermittently used for commercial purposes. The dark wooden stairway in the building was dimly lit. The entrance way and stairs, however, were always clean. A pungent odor, which greeted one on entering the building, was not noticeable on the fourth floor, which the Sirrentis occupied along with one other family.

The apartment consisted of a central kitchen, on one side of which was a living room and the parents' bedroom, on the other side the boys' bedroom. All the floors were covered with linoleum. The windows were fitted with plain white cloth curtains. There was no central heating in the building, and the apartment was heated by an oil stove. Nor were there any bathing or toilet facilities. An ancient and rather dirty toilet which the Sirrentis shared with the other family on their floor was located in the hallway. A gas hot water heater in the kitchen led to a sink which was used by the family for shaving and washing the face and hands as well as for the dishes and food. In addition, the kitchen contained a four-burner gas stove, several steel cupboards, a table and chairs, a refrigerator, and a telephone.

The central position of the kitchen was figurative as well as architectural. This was where the family entertained their guests, the focal point of all important social events in the family. The living room was used by the parents for watching television and by the boys for studying — activities which usually occurred simultaneously. It was furnished in a worn, maple "Colonial" set consisting of a couch, upholstered chair, table, and desk. There were no closets in the apartment, but several large wardrobes in the bedrooms took their place. Nat and Rudy slept together in a double bed; their room, which was small, also contained a dresser, ward-

267

robe, and two chairs. The parents' bedroom contained a double bed, a wardrobe and dresser, and the crib in which Benny slept. In addition to the human occupants, two parakeets carried on their social relations in a cage on top of the refrigerator.

Since the Sirrentis frequently had other visitors in addition to the interviewers, the place had an atmosphere of crowded conviviality. If the living arrangements lacked convenience in some ways, substitutes or compensations were to be found in the immediate environment. For example, though the apartment building lacked bathing facilities, a public bathhouse was available just a short distance down the street. Ben Sr. took his showers at the hotel where he worked, and Connie and the boys used the local facilities. A grocery store across the street supplied ice cream and soft drinks for the boys, freeing Connie's refrigerator for more weighty foods. Another store, next door, was a gift shop which made the frequent exchanges of presents easier. Grandma and Grandpa Sirrenti lived in the apartment immediately below, so that mutual services were easily rendered. The Catholic church which the family attended was just around the corner, connected with the parochial high school and primary school used by the boys. Nat was a member of a boys' club associated with the church, and Rudy had a circle of friends in the neighborhood. In short, the Sirrentis could satisfy most of their needs for material supplies and services, companionship, entertainment, education, and religious worship within the small compass of the surrounding community.

The social position of the Sirrentis in the community was intimately related to the structure of the extended family. Benito's parents and his brothers held definite positions in the neighborhood, and their relative status in each other's eyes affected everything that happened between Benito and Connie and their own children. Connie's family and their social standing likewise played a part in the interpersonal events of the family, for reasons that will become evident later.

Opportunities to meet Ben's relatives never seemed to be lacking. Grandma and Grandpa Sirrenti showed up from downstairs during the first visit, joining the family circle and exchanging jokes in mixed Italian and English. Neither of them spoke English with any facility, and they were both short, stocky, graying and wrinkled, obviously Old World people. Ben's father, Rudolpho, after whom Rudy was named, was still active at age sixty-five in the care of the two tenements he owned. He had a reputation in the family for being "deep" — a man of few words but full of wisdom and humor, so that everyone listened when he chose to express himself. He was born in a small village near Naples and came to the United States when he was thirteen. Most of his life he had worked as a tailor, but he had saved enough money to purchase the two buildings for his "retirement." Ben's mother, whose maiden name was Maria Gondo, was born in the same village in southern Italy as her husband and emigrated to the United States with members of her family when she was eighteen. She was now sixty-three years old. She was honored within her family and in the community for her skill as a "native healer." She attended to broken bones, sprains, wounds, and a variety of diseases with a combination of physical manipulations, herbs, concoctions, magical formulae, spells, and incantations that she had learned from her mother as a child. She was a figure of importance in the local community not only because of her healing arts but also because of the high status of her sons, all of whom were considered to have done well. Their success was largely attributed to her intelligent, forthright, moral character.

Vito, Ben's oldest brother, was forty-three years old at the time of introduction to the family. A college graduate, he now operated a small insurance agency and was regarded as a successful businessman by the family. His wife, Louise, a blonde Sicilian, owned a beauty parlor, and their combined income was said to be about $40,000 per annum. They had three sons and lived, according to Connie, in an attractive house in the suburbs. The family usually consulted him with respect to any business dealings. They were particularly proud of the fact that Vito's agency wrote insurance in several foreign countries, including Italy.

Benito was the second son, and after him came Carlo, who was thirty-six years old. He attended a Catholic college and seminary and had been ordained a priest when he was twenty-four years old. Father Carlo was esteemed and loved by the family and the community, to whom he was well known. He had said his first Mass in his local parish, and for several years he taught in the elementary school in his own neighborhood. During the time of our contacts with the family, he was posted in various cities and held different duties, all of which indicated a steady upward career within the Church. Like Vito, he was looked upon as more Americanized than Benito, and this view corresponded with the interviewers' impression on the few occasions that they had the opportunity to meet with him. He was a slender, energetic, intelligent man who talked without a trace of Italian accent or manner.

269

The family also thought of him as a "good sport" — a person who, in addition to his ambition and ability, could be as informal and entertaining at family gatherings as was the Sirrenti custom.

Dominic, the fourth son, age thirty, was a musician who played in a small jazz combo. His group obtained engagements in nightclubs in the New England area and in Florida, depending on the season. Accordingly, Dom, like Father Carlo, was seldom at home. In the family's eyes, he had made a tragic marriage. His wife had been a cardiac invalid, unable to bear children or do much housework. After six years of marriage, his wife had died. They had been very much in love, and for a year following her death Dom had been griefstricken and withdrawn. He had not attended college but had finished high school and had been working in a factory before and during his marriage. After a year of mourning, he had decided to turn his musical talent to professional account. Since then, he had been continuously on the road, coming home only for brief visits. He had not remarried, and his parents were upset at the lonely, wandering existence which his life represented to them. At the same time, they realized that he now seemed more cheerful and contented than in the anguished time following his wife's death.

The youngest son, Eduardo, was often referred to as Grandma Sirrenti's change-of-life baby. He was twenty-four years old, unmarried, and a senior in medical school, clearly the young hopeful of the family. His school record had been outstanding, and his ability to concentrate all his energies on his work was held to promise a fine career in medicine. He lived with his parents when he was not working as a clerk or interne in a hospital. He was already regarded as Dr. Ed and was called upon to diagnose and treat the minor ailments of family members. He was also appreciated for his strong family feeling and for the attention he gave to his parents and to the children of Ben and Connie. He was held up by Connie to Nat and Rudy as a model of scholastic dedication and achievement.

The five sons of Grandpa and Grandma Sirrenti had each chosen a career line which represented an activity practiced to some degree by their parents, a fact which was recognized by the Sirrenti clan and was spoken of with some pride. The first-generation Sirrentis were, in their fashion, shrewd and economical in the handling of money. They had managed to finance a college education for three of their sons and, in addition, save enough money to purchase the two apartments so that they did not have to worry about poverty in their old age or become dependent upon their children. Vito's business interest and ability seemed to flow naturally from this aspect of his parents' behavior. They were also dedicated to their religion,. and Grandma Sirrenti was active in various religious organizations, fund-raising efforts, and other affairs which represented the intricate penetration of the church into the daily life of the family. Father Carlo's career represented a crystalization and professionalization of this organic part of the Sirrenti's life style. The grandparents' facility in hospitality, accompanied by music, dancing, and singing, seemed to have been differentially distributed between Dominic and Benito. In his role as a jazz musician, singer, and occasional master-of-ceremonies, Dom turned these informal family recreational pursuits to professional advantage. Ben, too, had musical ability. In his youth he had played the violin and at one time considered being a professional violinist. Now his violin was in a state of disrepair, but he frequently strummed a guitar and sang for the amusement of his children or guests. As for Eduardo, the connection between his interest in medicine and his mother's local reputation as a native healer was so obvious that the family continually remarked upon it.

In all this differentiation and individualization of family pre-. dispositions among the career lines of the children, the outcome for Benito was atypical. All the other sons had entered occupations which represented some degree of upward social mobility and dis-tillation of the life style of the parents. Vito, the oldest son, had gone the farthest in the direction of American middle-class patterns, though Eduardo promised to equal or overtake him. Father Carlo's career as a priest showed some of the typical American success strivings worked out within the constraints of the Church. Dom had established his freedom and independence of the family even while expressing a recreational interest which the whole family shared. Only Ben had stayed, so to speak, in the bosom of the parental family and in an occupation not much different from that of his father. At no time did any member of the family express a sentiment indicating a feeling of disappointment or derogation in regard to Ben's occupation or style of life. On the contrary, he was valued as the loyal son, the considerate husband, and the attentive father. He seemed to fulfill adequately all the expectations held for him.

Connie's family originally lived in the West End of Boston — a district which in recent years had been torn down and subjected to urban renewal. In her childhood it had been populated by a mixture of ethnic groups, predominantly Italian and Jewish. Her father, who had worked as a common laborer, had died thirteen years ago but her mother, age seventy-two, was still alive. There had been sixteen children born over a period of twenty-six years, of whom eleven survived. Of these, seven were girls and four boys. Connie was third in the birth order. The interviewing did not uncover the cause of death of the non-surviving children, but it was learned that the father died of a cardiac condition which became aggravated at the time his youngest son was drafted for service during World War II. The father was said to have been extremely upset because he did not regard this son as able to make the adjustment to army life. Unfortunately, none of the four boys in this family ever became distinct as individuals to our research team.

Although the interviewers hinted, suggested, and finally openly pressed Connie for an opportunity to visit with her mother, they made no headway at all. At one point, the interviewers went with the Sirrentis to watch a religious feast-day celebration in the West End neighborhood not far from where her mother lived. When Connie said that she was going up to visit with her mother for a while, the interviewers suggested that they would like to accompany her. At that she stiffened and said that her youngest sister, who was pregnant, was visiting her mother, and she would be extremely embarrassed were we to show up. There was little substance to this remark, for the interviewers had met this sister, Louisa, at Connie's apartment, not too long before this occasion. A month following this episode, the interviewers pressed Connie harder over their desire to see her mother, and she put up a blank wall of opposition, saying that her mother was seventy-two years old and not a well woman and no longer as friendly a person as she had been in the past. She found it difficult to keep up a conversation with others. On inquiry, it was learned that her mother had a cardiac condition, with dependent edema and occasional fluid in the abdomen. She still lived in the West End apartment where the family had always lived, but when her cardiac symptoms were severe, she stayed with one or another of her children.

Whatever the source of her opposition to interviewer contact with her relatives, Connie herself visited her mother and sisters frequently and apparently with enjoyment. Although the interviewers could obtain practically no information about them through direct questioning, through information that emerged inadvertently it was learned that two of her sisters had been married, had borne several children, and were now separated from their husbands. One of these, one who still lived in the West End near the mother, was receiving twenty-five dollars a week from her absentee husband and was also receiving public welfare payments for the support of her three children. This sister maintained a sexual relationship with a man who lived openly in her apartment — a relationship of which Connie strongly disapproved. Since the man contributed food and other material help to the deserted wife, Connie's mother and her sisters had accepted his presence. The other sister, who had four small children, lived in the North End not far from the Sirrentis. She was also a welfare client and was considering obtaining a divorce and remarrying.

The reader may now be able to visualize the setting of Ben and Connie's nuclear family in the bilateral family field. We have presented a roll call — a dramatis personae — so that the reader may engage each of a rather large cast of characters, both as to his individual attributes and as to his position in the extended family. Yet the family is more than a catalogue of individuals. It is an organization undergoing perpetual, slow transformation, characterized by a history, a structure, a pattern of values, and a way of functioning in its community setting.

THE NETWORK

The dominant overt tone of husband-wife relations between Ben and Connie was one of home-centered contentment — a devotion to each other and to the children. This phrasing of family solidarity and satisfaction was more apt to be put into words by Connie than by Ben, who nevertheless, manifested in his behavior what she tended to articulate. In an early interview, in response to a description of our search for families that were handling their problems in a reasonably satisfactory manner, she said:

> Oh, we're happy all right; we're as happy a family as you'll ever find. I love my boys, and I love my family, and they all want to stick around here. You don't find my boys wanting to go out all the time.

Connie often mentioned how fortunate it was that after sixteen years of married life she and her husband still loved each other. She did not regard this wholly as an act of fate but also as a result of wisdom, effort, good humor, and tact.

As to wifely wisdom, Connie's strategy emerged during a discussion of women, including her sisters, whose husbands had deserted. She began by speculating what she would do if her

273

husband should desert her. She wondered especially would she look for another man?

> I don't think that's the way I'd do it if my husband left me. I got my kids, and I think I'd spend my life with them. And I'd look after them and go places with them. People would say that it isn't right and that I'm young and should get another man. But I don't think I would. It doesn't matter, because my husband would never leave me anyway. The secret is you gotta let men have some freedom. All men want their freedom. If you keep after them all the time, they feel they haven't got any freedom at all; why, they're just gonna get up and walk out. I know that with my husband I go just so far, and then I don't bother him any more.

The theme of mutual attraction was frequently acted out by Ben and Connie under the cover of teasing about sexual jealousy. For example, Connie said that when they went to dances, Ben wanted to dance with her all the time because he was afraid to let her dance with other men. Ben played into this, claiming that she made eyes at all the other men. On the other hand, Ben liked to arouse Connie's jealousy by talking about the attractive waitresses at the restaurant and the adventurous women customers at the bar. These provocative exchanges, always carried out with expert timing, were partly done for conventional reasons. They were in line with Italian male and female sex roles. Seductiveness on the part of the woman and attempted seduction on the part of the man were expected to take place — at least symbolically — on any public exposure of the two sexes. Even Grandpa and Grandma Sirrenti, deep in their sixties, made sexual jokes in the interviewers' presence, kidding each other as well as visitors. On the very first visit there was a shortage of chairs when the senior Sirrentis came up from their apartment to be introduced. The female interviewer asked Grandpa Sirrenti to share her chair, and he replied, "In a bed, two can sleep, but not in a chair." There was uproarious laughter all around.

Just how conventional — indeed, fictive — the role of the sexually seductive female was for Connie was revealed on an occasion when the interviewers accompanied her and Grandma Sirrenti to a party at a nightclub, given to raise funds for a new church building. The affair held no interest for Grandpa, and it had been decided that Ben would stay at home to look after Benny, the baby. There was music and dancing, and though the male interviewer asked Connie to dance on several occasions, she always made some excuse. Furthermore, she avoided the possibility of being asked to dance by other men by holding intense, animated conversations with various female friends throughout the evening. Yet, on the occasion of the next visit, she asked her husband, looking provocatively at the interviewer, what he would think of a man who ignored all her hints and suggestions that she would like to be danced with.

The festive, recreational element was always implicit in Connie's definition of her married life, and it was interesting, along the lines described above, that fun-making could reach its fullest expression only during a party given in her own home. For example, when plans were being made to go to the fund-raising party at the nightclub, someone suggested that everybody return to the Sirrentis' afterward so that Ben could participate in the festivities. At that point Connie said:

> Oh, we've had some wonderful parties here. You should have known me when I was younger. When I only had two kids, why, I had all the energy in the world. We'd have parties here until two o'clock in the morning, and I'd still be raring to go.

On another occasion, Connie emphasized the solidarity between herself and her husband on the importance of home entertainment. This came up in an early phase of our interviewing, when the interviewers still worried that the frequent visiting might annoy the family. She said:

> But I love company. You can come any time you want. That's one thing about our house. Company is always welcome. That's what I admire about my husband. You know, some husbands, they come home, they just go and bury their heads in a newspaper. But not my husband. He says that when people come to see us, they want to be entertained. They're not gonna stay all night; they're gonna leave soon; so he says we should treat them right when they're here.

The Sirrentis had multitudes of friends who dropped in for impromptu get-togethers. Many of them lived in the neighborhood and the Sirrentis' home seemed to be an especially popular gathering place. But there was a note of anxiety, at least for Connie, in their popularity. For one thing, Ben worked long hours and on occasion took multiple jobs to increase the family income. Connie frequently had to play the hostess without his expert help. She felt uncomfortable about taking so much responsibility. In spite of her avowed pleasure in having company, she was not wholly sure of herself. The reason for her insecurity emerged during a discussion of Grandma's outgoing personality and high status in the community. Connie said:

It's just through her that I have my popularity, because I'm married to a Sirrenti. She's the popular one, and I borrow from it. Popular! Everybody around here knows her, and they all love her and respect her. Why, do you know when Dom's wife died, they had never seen such a crowd of people? And they were all friends of the Sirrentis.

Connie's dependence upon her husband and his collaterally extended family was not limited to social status. She relied upon her husband and her mother-in-law for guidance in various domestic matters. In the following conversation, she had been talking about her husband's interest in her clothes:

Why, I'd never go shopping without him. I just don't feel right if I buy something without him being along. He knows just what's right for me, and he'll *tell* you; he *should* be truthful like that. Sometimes I don't like him to say those things, but I know that it's the truth, and he should say it, and I want him to say it. Like I remember one time, just after we were married, I was making lentils, and I cooked them too much, and I said, "How do you like them?" "Fine," he said. "They're good." And he tried to eat them, but he just couldn't. Finally he said, "When my mother cooked lentils, you could count the lentils," and I was all upset. But I knew he was telling the truth, and I wasn't cooking them right. So I went to his mother, and I said that I cooked the lentils too much; so she told me how to do it.

Forthrightness about feelings — blurting them out, even if they hurt others — was a common practice in the Sirrenti family. It was held that one could not really know where one stood with others unless they were frank about their reactions. Frankness, for example, provided the cues for cultural change or resistance to

276

change through a continuing process of challenge and response. The appeals for change were out in the open, as much a matter of emotions and taste as of belief and principle, almost as if change were to be introduced through direct, somatic experience. An illuminating illustration of this approach to cultural change was provided by Connie in respect to food habits. During a discussion of the children's appetites in the general context of the skills of her mother-in-law in cooking Italian dishes (and her own moderate but growing skills) she said:

> You know what happened? Nat came to me one day and he said, "Mummy, can I ask you something?" I said, "Sure you can." And he said, "Can we have roast beef on Sunday?" (She paused for a moment to let this sink in, and the interviewer said, "You mean instead of spaghetti?") Yeah, he wanted roast beef and potatoes. So I said, "Sure!" So I got this roast beef, and they ate it all up in one serving. I think people should have meat. Meat's good for you; it gives you a lotta strength. So now we have roast beef on Sunday.

In a way, "roast beef on Sunday" epitomized the slow, deliberate pace of acculturation in the family. The energy in meat and the plain, American quality of beef were contrasted with the starchy, highly seasoned character of Italian cooking — but only on Sundays.

The unhurried pace of change was based on the orientation to time and activity. Connie's orientation toward Present time and Being emerged with special clarity on an occasion when we were talking about the possibility of our going to watch the children perform in a school play:

> *Interviewer:* I'll check my calendar and let you know.
> *Connie:* Don't it make you nervous to have so many things to do that you keep looking at your calendar?
> *Interviewer:* If I didn't check my calendar every day, I would be nervous.
> *Connie:* It's better to live from day to day except when you plan for the kids or weddings.

Connie's description of her value preferences corresponded exactly to what we observed: she and her husband accented the future only with respect to major festivities and the lives of the

277

children. Where the children were concerned, Future time was usually linked to Doing, as we shall see shortly. We might note in anticipation, however, that a future crowded with planned activities was also associated, for Connie, with the possibility of becoming "nervous" about it. We will not comment on the fact that, for the middle-class interviewer, the idea of neglecting the calendar was equally loaded with worry. Each to his own source of anxiety!

The same values were at work with reference to the speaking of Italian in the home. Connie and Ben spoke English with each other and with the children, but they spoke almost exclusively Italian with Ben's parents. Grandma Sirrenti wanted the children to preserve their ability to speak Italian, and this was an item of discord between the generations. The struggle of challenge and response in relation to cultural change was graphically described by Connie, in answer to a question as to whether the children spoke much Italian. She said:

> No, not very much. They know what you're saying, but they won't talk to you very much in Italian. My mother-in-law gets so mad at me! She tells me that we should speak Italian in the house, here, and that they should learn to speak Italian. It makes her so mad because Nat can understand her in Italian, but he always talks to her in English, and her English isn't too good. She really tells me off for not talking Italian, but why should I talk it all the time? We're in America. I'll talk English. I think it's easier for them on the outside, because they're going to have to speak English there, aren't they?

A primary emphasis on Collaterality, Being, and Present time was equally shared by Ben and Connie. Their agreement on these values kept their relations as husband and wife fairly well attuned. Their agreement was nowhere better seen than in their attitudes toward work, jobs, and the earning and spending of money. Their value orientations favored a relaxed, come-what-may point of view, in money matters as in other things. Though there could be emotional explosions during disagreements, the acceptance of the individuality of persons was very high. People should do what they want, what they like, and what they're good at. This position was upheld emphatically by Grandma Sirrenti as well.

Ben, it was learned, could have improved his job situation in the early years of his marriage, but he had turned the opportunity down. His attitude toward his previous and his current jobs emerged in the following way:

> *Interviewer:* How long have you worked at the hotel?
>
> *Ben:* Six years. But I don't know — being a waiter is no life. Your social life is a flop. You never see anybody. You lose contact with all your friends. When everybody else is off, you're working. On weekends we're busiest. That's when other people are off, and I've got to work all the time. It's no good, but that's all I know how to do.
>
> *Interviewer:* What had you done before that?
>
> *Ben:* I worked for a packing company. That was a wonderful company to work for. They moved their plant down the coast somewhere, away from Boston. They wanted me to go along. The job was there if I wanted it, and it would have been a pretty good deal, too. But, you know, we're a pretty close family. Connie didn't want to go, and when it comes right down to it, I didn't want to leave either; so we stayed here. I had to get another job, so I went back to the only thing I knew how to do — restaurant work. But that was a wonderful company to work for. I'd work for a big company any day. If we'd moved down the coast with them, why they'd have paid for everything — all the moving — and they'd buy you rugs and drapes and everything for the new place. You know they figure that when you move, the woman wants to get new drapes and rugs and curtains and things like that. Well, they pay for all that.
>
> *Connie:* Maybe it's too bad we didn't leave when they went down the coast.
>
> *Ben:* Yeah, isn't it?

But such regrets did not appear to be very strong. For both, a dependence upon one's family and community seemed preferable to dependence on a large industrial concern. Both of them expressed occasional envy of relatives who had wished for independence from the family and had struggled for better jobs and a house in the suburbs. But, when the chips were down, they both preferred to be exactly where they were. Sometimes one, sometimes the other, would express the dominant side of this ambivalence:

> *Connie:* What I say is, just because you got money doesn't mean that you're happy; and if you're not happy, what good

279

is money? Like my husband's always sayin' that he wished he had more money.

Interviewer: Why does he want more money?

Connie: Oh, he says if he had more money, he could buy more things for me, and he'd like to do that. But I tell him it doesn't matter. I know that I could get a lot more out of him than I do if I wanted to, if I was that kind of woman. I know I could get around him. It'd be easy. But do I care?

Interviewer: What would he do with the money if he got it?

Connie: Oh, he'd buy a new home with a bath and a shower, and a new car, and put some money away for the kids' education.

Interviewer: What does he want most?

Connie: Money — that's what he says. I tell him he's crazy. I say, "Look at those other guys. They got money, and are they happy?" So I said, "Would you trade places with them?" And he said, "Sure, I'd trade places with them. Then I'd have their money, and I'd be happy too."

At other times it would be Connie who would talk about how nice it would be to have a house with a bathroom and a yard for the children to play in. However, she would usually conclude by saying that neither she nor her husband nor the children wanted to move away. Similarly, on the score of ambivalent attitudes, Ben was not always so sour about his job as in the conversation reported above. He derived pleasure from his association with the other waiters and waitresses, and especially with regular customers. Some of the customers were local politicians, and his acquaintance with them, established in his usual open, jocular fashion, gave him a feeling of being a part of the political scene. It was these politicians who helped him to obtain a job on the state payroll when he needed extra money. Furthermore, the hotel, or rather its dining and bar facilities, kept his family well supplied with a varied stock of expensive liquors.

The economic advantages of an organized network of relatives and friends were evident in various exchanges of favors or services which saved the family cash expenditures. For example, all long-distance telephone calls placed by or made to members of the family were funneled through a friend who was a telephone operator in the central exchange. No charges were placed for these calls. The friendly telephone operator received gifts from the family in exchange for this service. Besides, she valued her association with the extended family and was particularly close to Connie. The relationship, however, had been initiated by Father Carlo, who had met this person through other mutual friends.

In a well-organized network everyone has his place, his appointed role in the system, especially in the system of command. Though the Sirrentis preferred to hold members within the system through mutual accommodation and the exchange of services, there was no hesitation in the use of force or intimidation if the situation seemed to warrant it.

At the time when we met him, Ben's relation with his parents was that of the dutiful son. He was still helping his father with the painting and general maintenance of the apartments in his odd moments of free time. Grandpa was clearly the boss in such matters. He would give orders and make peremptory demands, even in the interviewers' presence. A male interviewer occasionally visited when some household project was in process and would find himself included in the project. As low man in the hierarchy of maintenance skills, he received his orders from Ben. Although given in a pleasanter tone than the one his father used, they were nevertheless orders, not requests. Ben and his father often argued volubly; but, right or wrong, Grandpa always won the argument. Ben believed that because of his parents' age and the sacrifices they had made for their children he should not oppose them over minor matters.

A similar pecking order existed between Grandma and Connie. Ben's mother was sparing in her displays of dominance over her daughter-in-law — at least when the interviewers visited. There were occasional arguments, which Grandma Sirrenti usually won through superiority of energy, forcefulness, and stubbornness. Since they were usually conducted in Italian, the interviewers had difficulty following the ins and outs of the argument, but they noticed that, unlike Ben, Connie did not yield on the grounds of deference, and occasionally she emerged the victor. When talking privately about her relations with her mother-in-law, Connie showed considerable ambivalence of feeling. Sometimes she portrayed their relationship as predominantly close and pleasant, even though punctuated by vigorous disagreements. In this mood, she seemed to value her dependence on the older woman in ways that we have pointed out above. At other times she resented the older woman's peremptory, depreciative attitude. Indeed, at times there was a tone of contempt in Grandma's voice when addressing Connie. For example, when driving back to the Sirrentis' apartment after the party at the nightclub, mentioned above, the women were discussing shopping. Grandma had described how, in her younger days, she had done all the shopping for her large family, keeping a close eye on sales and making expeditions to the downtown commercial area of the city to get the best bargains. Connie responded by saying that, although she had formerly done this, since the birth of the baby she did her shopping locally. For essentials that could not be obtained in the neighborhood, her husband, she said, went downtown — frequently accompanied by her telephone-operator friend — to do the shopping. In the midst of this monologue Grandma suddenly burst out in Italian, "Lazy women!" She did not expand on her feelings, but the outburst effectively put a stop to the conversation.

There was one aspect of the "lazy women" accusation which was puzzling. On the one hand, Grandma could merely have been expressing her bitterness over the difference between the role of the Italian housewife of her generation and that of her daughter-in-law. The idea that women had it easier nowadays was frequently expressed in the home. Women no longer had so many children to take care of; they did not have to scrub hard wooden floors and pinch pennies the way they used to. Even though they had worked hard to make life easier for their children, women of Grandma's generation were not without considerable envy of the younger generation's easier lot in life. Such envy was more likely to be felt toward their daughters and daughters-in-law than toward men. The men were apt to be seen as still working hard to increase the family income and to make life easier for their wives. In this context, particularly since she had used the plural form, Grandma may have been expressing a general feeling of which Connie's conduct was simply seen as a particular illustration. On the other hand, Connie told the interviewers on several occasions that the biggest disagreement she had with her mother-in-law was over leaving the baby at home, either in Grandma's care or with the older boys if she wanted to go out. Grandma was opposed to the baby's being away from his mother, even for rare short periods. This attitude seemed odd to the interviewers since Connie was such a devoted mother. Now it seemed particularly odd that Grandma was criticizing Connie for not going downtown alone to do her shopping, when she also criticized her for wishing to go out and leave the baby. Grandma's attitude was not only inconsistent, but it also produced a bind for Connie. No matter which course of

282

action she chose, she was criticized. The exact meaning of the bind, however, did not become clear until later.

Connie's relation to her father-in-law was warm and untroubled. She expressed a great deal of admiration for him, emphasizing his shrewd common sense, good judgment, and fairness to members of his family. She said that whereas Grandma demanded compliance, Grandpa "used psychology" — meaning that his orders were phrased in less peremptory tones. She also described him as being supportive toward her in distinction to Grandma's predisposition to criticize her. Toward the other males in her husband's family, Connie was adulatory. Vito earned her praise for his well-deserved success in business, Father Carlo for his popularity as a priest, Dom for his charming personality and ability to entertain, and Dr. Ed for his dedication to his career in medicine and for his strong family feeling. She enjoyed the company of all of them and especially looked forward to Father Carlo's infrequent visits home. Toward her two sisters-in-law she was less sympathetic. Although she felt sorry for Dom's deceased wife — and for Dom's intense sense of loss after her death — she was highly critical of the girl for getting married at all in her sickly condition, especially when it was known that she would be unable to have children. For Connie, motherhood, potential or actual, was an essential part of the married woman's role.

It was more difficult to assess Ben's responses to his brothers. Unlike Connie, he seldom characterized his feelings toward anyone, and he consistently refused to be drawn out on the subject of his close relatives. He would tell objective facts about them on direct questioning, but with neutral feeling. In our experience, this was not a merely personal reaction. All the Italian-American males that we encountered showed a similar behavior, and some were able to express the opinion that to discuss relatives was not a proper way for a man to behave. It was all right for women — they were prone to gossip anyway. Also, women had stronger feelings on all sorts of subjects, especially the subject of religion and the family. A male was supposed to be more reserved — at least on that topic — though he could expand indefinitely on his attitudes toward his employer. Given this generalized cultural definition of the male's role, it was not surprising that Ben proved so stubborn about revealing his attitudes toward his immediate family.

As in the case of his relations with his father, it was possible to draw some inferences about his attitudes from direct observation of his behavior. He was respectful to his older brother, Vito, and sought out his opinion on business matters, such as the purchase of a new car. However, he did not appear to be eager to see him often. Rudy spent an occasional weekend at Vito's house in the suburb, and Ben appeared pleased at this opportunity for his son to have a different kind of family experience. Toward his younger brother, Father Carlo, on the other hand, his behavior was neither respectful nor disrespectful. He was not at all awed by his brother's priestly office. He treated Father Carlo, rather, as a good companion and a man of some wisdom about the world. There was, perhaps, a touch of cynicism about the precise amount of worldly wisdom possessed by Father Carlo. There was no opportunity to observe Ben's behavior in relation to Dom.

In relation to Eduardo, Ben was usually warm and appreciative of his youngest brother's closeness to Nat and Rudy. Eduardo was only eight years older than Nat. On one occasion, however, Ben showed an unexpected flash of envy and resentment toward Eduardo. Connie had been praising Dr. Ed to Nat and Rudy, telling them how bright he was and how well he did in high school, college, and medical school. She had been elaborating this theme at some length when Ben broke in, saying, in a rough tone of voice, "Well, he ought to have done well; he never did anything *but* study." This was the only observed sign that Ben might have felt somewhat belittled by his wife's habit of using his more successful brothers as ideal figures on whom the children should model themselves. At the same time, the remark may have indicated that, given Ben's preference for *Present time*, *Being*, and *Collateral orientations*, there was a limit to his tolerance of Connie's constant verbal emphasis, to the children, of the importance of achievement and planning for the future, as exemplified by his brothers.

Ample giving of food, affection, and care was one side of Connie's conception of motherhood. The other side consisted of equally generous doses of discipline. At one point, when she had just rushed into the living room to slap Benny for teasing and interfering with Rudy while he was doing his homework, she said, "I believe in teaching my boys what's right and what's wrong. Sometimes I yell at them; I have to do it. I don't like to do it, and sometimes I wish I hadn't done it afterwards. But you can't be a 'yes' mother all the time."

Connie's delight in the process of nutritional exchange paralleled and supported her belief in the moral value of maternal devotion. For example, in describing to an interviewer in the presence of Rudy her general attitude toward breast feeding, she became increasingly excited and spoke with explosive energy:

> I breast-fed Rudy for ten months, and it was wonderful.
> I tried to breast-feed Nat, too, but my milk ran out after three
> days. It was water; so I was over at the hospital, and they took
> me off it. The same thing happened with Benny. I breast-fed
> him for three months, and then I got an infection; so they took
> it away from me. Oh, that was great. I used to eat like a
> horse. I was eatin' all the time, and those kids were just takin'
> it out of me, especially Rudy. But I felt on top of the world.
> Why, we had more parties round here and people in than
> we've ever had.

On balance she believed that the children should be given the
freedom to develop in accordance with their own inclinations and
innate characteristics. But it was difficult for her to bring her behavior into conformity with this attitude. The difficulty rose out of
her concern about the boys' career choices. She worried constantly
that they would never decide on a career. Daily she asked the boys
what they thought they wanted to be in the future. Connie did not
understand that her pressure for a decision in this matter was premature, considering that Nat was in high school and Rudy still in
primary school. But the tone of anxiety was transmitted to the
boys, and each responded in his own fashion: Nat by repeatedly
picking a career and then changing his mind; Rudy by refusing to
commit himself, refusing even to discuss the topic.

Connie's specific view of Nat was that he was a good boy,
conscientious and hard-working, and considerate of her. He saved
money to buy her a birthday present and card. She was proud of
his academic record. He never received a grade under eighty-five
and was usually on the "principal's list." The nuns and priests who
taught him frequently praised his behavior, and Connie was not
reluctant to brag about him to her family and her friends. From
time to time, Nat won prizes at school, and once his picture
appeared in the papers when he received an award from the mayor.

Toward Rudy, Connie's attitude was less positive. Whereas
she constantly praised Nat in the presence of both boys, Rudy was
subjected to teasing and scolding along with faint praise. Though
his academic record was as good as Nat's, Connie seldom spoke of
it. She was pleased with his corpulence because she thought that it
showed how well fed he was. At the same time she felt that it indicated a lack of sufficient exercise. Though she did not press him to

get more exercise, she frequently teased him about his excess fat, pinching and prodding his flesh and asking the interviewers to feel it. She displayed a similar ambivalence about the amount of time he spent at the church. At times she appeared pleased with the idea that he might become a priest; at other times she grumbled about his being indoors so much and about the single-mindedness he showed — almost all his recreational spare time being given to his official duties as an altar boy and choir boy or helping with various chores at the church. Her irritation was increased by Rudy's habit of keeping his feelings and opinions to himself (in contrast to Nat, who confided in her). Though Rudy was cheerful and accessible on superficial matters, he was inscrutable about the things that meant the most to him. Furthermore, he was occasionally disrespectful; he gave his mother "fresh" answers when she scolded him, and now and then he ignored her demands or took his own sweet time in obeying them. However, he also remembered her birthdays with cards and presents, and, if she was tired or had been up most of the night with the baby, Rudy would offer to prepare his own breakfast and would try to relieve her of other pressures.

With the baby, Connie was affectionately effusive and punitive, depending upon her mood. She frequently picked him up, hugged him and kissed him, and told him how much she loved him. If he got too wild, she would hit him and tell him to calm down. She thought that Nat and Rudy spoiled Benny by letting him be too aggressive toward them. On the other hand, Connie herself had difficulty in regulating his rhythmic, physiological processes. This was most apparent in relation to his sleeping. Benny was always up when the interviewers arrived after eight in the evening and often was still up when they left at ten. Connie would tell him to go to sleep, but she never made any effort to put him down in his crib. She would wait until he fell asleep, exhausted, in a chair in the living room while watching television, then carry him to bed. As he got more tired, he would become more active and cranky; but she never perceived this behavior as a response to fatigue, nor did anyone else in the family.

Benny never was allowed to play outside and seldom got out of the apartment. It seemed possible that his over-activity and his pallor were related to his being confined indoors. Occasionally his father or one of the boys would take him for a walk outside. He had one playmate—a girl of his age who lived in the apartment upstairs. Connie attributed his confinement, in part, to the fact of his carsickness. He could not go any distance in a car without vomiting and thus had to stay behind when the rest of the family visited relatives. Connie herself felt confined by this problem, for, considering Grandma's attitude, she was reluctant to leave Benny in the care of her mother-in-law or with the older boys. Indeed, she often spoke with nostalgia of the years before Benny's birth when she and her husband had more time to themselves for recreation. In this mood, she felt that during the eight years between Rudy's and Benny's births she had become spoiled and that it was now difficult for her to take care of a young child.

If Benny was alternately a burden and a joy to his mother, he was a steady source of pleasure to his father. Ben, Sr. liked to play with Benny, to buy him gifts, and to hold him in his lap while he strummed a guitar, encouraging the baby to strum along with him. Benny always seemed quieter and less demanding toward his mother when his father was home. Ben's behavior toward Rudy was in considerable contrast to Connie's. He never teased Rudy, and, if Connie was praising Nat to the skies, Ben would manage somehow to draw Rudy out and make him sound as interesting and promising as his older brother. In general, the father seemed to act toward his children in a way that compensated for the mother's volatile behavior, without overtly criticizing her. If Connie disparaged Rudy's excessive concentration on activities at the church, Ben would get Rudy to tell about some feature of his daily work. Under the benign encouragement of his father, Rudy would wax more and more expansive and amusing until even Connie would get interested in what he was saying. With Nat, Ben was usually more matter-of-fact. He treated his oldest son as his deputy, delegating tasks and responsibilities and correcting him in a calm tone of voice.

There was a general feeling, shared by Connie, that although she barked and made demands on the children, Ben could get them to do things with only a word or a quiet request. His role as the authority was never questioned, and his attitude toward assuming control of the family was quite explicit. At one time the female interviewer mentioned that she had to study for an examination and would have to leave sooner than usual. Ben said, "You're still studying? Didn't you study enough already? It's all right for a man to study, but why does a woman have to study so much? A woman should be home with the kids. If you think too much, no one will want you. A man wants to feel he is the boss." Ben was teasing the interviewer, but Connie responded quite seriously, "You know my husband is boss in most things except sometimes he gives in to the kids."

287

In general, all three children had a warm relation with each other. Though there were mock battles, they had no serious fights. Rudy was deferential toward his older brother. He imitated his mother in praising Nat's accomplishments and his father in drawing Nat out to tell of his latest achievements. Nat was protective and played the more knowledgeable guide to both Rudy and Benny. He tried to get Rudy interested in sports. Toward the end of the visiting, as Rudy passed his fifteenth birthday, he underwent a sudden growth spurt, lost his corpulence, and became tall and husky. Now Nat's efforts were successful, and Rudy became as good an athlete as his brother. Both boys went to school dances and spoke about their girl friends but did not have steady dates. In many ways their lives were independent of each other. Yet, when Nat went to summer camp ahead of Rudy, the younger boy missed his brother and was impatient for a reunion.

Nat was fatherly and indulgent toward Benny. He comforted him when he was hurt, took him for walks, and played cards with him. Benny respected Nat and was quieter with him than with Rudy, whom he teased mercilessly. Rudy was not aggressive with Benny but often considered him a nuisance. When his irritation mounted — as when Benny's carsickness prevented the family from holding a planned beach party — he was likely to tell his mother that he wished Benny had never been born. Connie was sympathetic and patient with such outbursts. When both older boys were doing their homework in the living room, Benny played a game of also "doing his homework," scribbling on scratch paper and looking at a television program at the same time. This scene always delighted Connie. It represented a tableau of fraternal harmony symbolizing the group solidarity so important to the family.

There are three general areas of behavior in which the family's attitudes and their effect on each other have not yet been described. These are religion, illness and death, and sex. In a transacting system, such as a family, everything is interconnected. These three areas, however, were more closely associated than one might have expected. For Connie, the significance of each area seemed to blend into the other, whereas for Ben and the boys these areas were more easily distinguished.

Connie's feelings about religion always emerged around some concrete situation. There was nothing abstract or intellectual in her approach. The following excerpts are from a long, detailed account of her attendance at a mission.

Interviewer: Who is the priest they had for the mission?

Connie: Oh, it was Father R. He is really wonderful. What I like is these passionate priests. They can really make you cry. They carry this big cross when they're in church, and they point this cross right at you. I was sittin' up in the front row, once, and he pointed the cross at me; and I was watchin' him and tears came into his eyes. They really put it on, like a play, you know. They're wonderful, these passionate priests.

Interviewer: I don't know about these missions. Tell me about them.

Connie: You should have gone; it makes you feel so wonderful. I went to all eight meetings, and then I got the Papal blessing — the last one — and when I came out of the church I never felt so good in all my life. . . . And, oh, that priest! He really laid it on the line. They're not like ordinary priests, you know; they can be very outspoken. He said: "People, you're always coming in here; you make those vows, and down in your heart you know you're not going to keep them. I don't want to see you around if that's the way you're going to be. I know we're all hypocrites to some extent, but unless you really love God and feel it from right down in your heart, why you shouldn't darken the door of the church."

These priests can admit they do wrong. Like, this one priest told us, "When I'm driving along in my car and someone cuts in front of me, I want to swear too. But I gotta hold myself back. I owe it to God."

Connie's attitude toward the priests was not always so positive. As a member of the P.T.A. of the parochial school, she was often indignant because of the priests' constant requests for money. They did not sufficiently appreciate the fact that they were dealing with poor people. In her view, their greed got the better of them. They had no sooner built a new friary than they wanted fluorescent lights for the classrooms. Such temporary annoyances, however, did not represent a sense of disillusion. Priests had their good and bad sides, like everyone else, and the good far outweighed the bad.

On sex and marriage Connie took the church's line, as evidenced in the following conversation at which one of our interviewers was present:

Paula: Marriage is okay, sometimes, but take me — I'm almost forty, and I think I'm pregnant again. I'm so ashamed.

Connie: Oh, that could happen to anyone who's married.

Louisa: Perhaps you should try rhythm.

Paula: Rhythm is impossible. When your husband has the urge, you almost always have to give in or have a fight. So how can you practice rhythm?

Interviewer: How about a diaphragm?

Connie: You're only kidding — I hope. In the eyes of God, when you have relations with your husband, you take what God wants you to have. If it's his will that you should have another baby, then you should have one.

Paula: I guess you don't sleep with your husband very often then, Connie.

Connie: About once a month. Usually, I'm too tired; so I go to sleep before he gets home. But sometimes he catches me awake. And sometimes, when the kids make me nervous, I have to say, "Don't bother me. I'm too tired to sleep with you." He gives me a peck on the cheek and says, "I know you're tired. Have a good rest." See what a good husband I have. After all these years I'm still in love.

Whenever the subject of sex came up directly, Connie placed it in a religious context. For example, when Nat spoke to her in his usual confiding way about his dawning sex urges, Connie told him that God was preparing him to be a man and to get married and have children some day but in the meantime he would have to find a way of controlling his urges. It was all right to kiss a girl, but he should do it in the same way that he would kiss his mother or sister. As in the other instances of formal sex role definitions, this sketch of the adolescent male sex role was taken almost literally from the prescriptions of the priests, delivered at countless missions which Connie had attended.

In her responses to illness, Connie varied between two forms of behavior. If the illness did not threaten life or bring great suffering, it was treated partly as a technical matter, partly as a recreational occasion. For example, when Rudy suffered a minor knee injury, Grandma was called to the scene in her role as native healer. Despite her serious visual difficulties (she had cataracts in both eyes) and despite Rudy's reluctance to have anything done about it at all, Grandma manipulated the leg, scrutinized the sore knee as well as she could, made a diagnosis, and prescribed rest. To his great annoyance, everyone was solicitous to Rudy for a few days. Later, Nat broke his femur while playing football. He was taken to a hospital to have the fracture reduced and set. He was out of school for several months, reclining in splendor at home, visited by multitudes of his own friends and relatives and friends of the family. As an excuse for more company than usual, the accident was relished by everyone.

Where serious illness, suffering, or death were concerned, Connie's behavior was a problem to the family. She would become very upset, tearful, almost hysterical. She would repeatedly describe the illness or accident and deploy all her considerable dramatic talent to do justice to the description. Italian women in general have a taste for tragedy, but even Grandma, who was not above shedding tears at the news of a serious illness or the death of someone in the neighborhood, thought that Connie went too far. Ben lectured her on controlling herself at wakes and funerals and sometimes refused to accompany her. Although she tried to control herself for his sake, she was not very successful. At times she herself recognized that her emotional outbursts were beyond the average person's reactions, especially when she had to struggle against the desire to scream while attending a wake. In general, however, she felt that this was a thing that her husband simply could not comprehend — the strength and depth of a woman's feeling over the loss of friends and relatives, real or threatened.

STRAIN AND RECOVERY

The general description of relationships within the Sirrenti family presents a portrait of an extended family maintaining itself for the most part in smooth running order, nestled fairly comfortably in a local Italian-American community, while establishing colonies of its younger generation in middle-class outposts. However, the second-generation nuclear family on which we have centered our attention has not participated in the upward and outward migration. Having chosen to remain within the parental fold, Ben and Connie's children experienced certain strains and conflicts only lightly delineated in the general description.

It is now appropriate to examine these strains in greater detail. To put them in adequate perspective it is necessary to retrace the formation of the marital relationship during the period of courtship and early marriage. A husband and wife must cope throughout their married life with the conditions and conflicts obtaining at the time they decide to get married. The past is felt in the present as an in-

291

fluence which can be neither abolished nor denied though it can be modified. If unmodified, the present version of the conflicts of the past assert themselves within the otherwise smooth tenor of family life, cropping out from time to time in the form of "symptomatic episodes" — periods of turbulence accompanied by maladaptive behavior. It is to the incorporation of the past in the present that we now turn our attention.

Ben and Connie first met each other at a dance when she was sixteen and he twenty-two years old. She had stopped attending the public high school in her West End neighborhood after the tenth grade, her services being needed at home. But she loved to dance and was an expert; she taught dancing to boys and girls at a settlement house in the community and was a familiar figure at the settlement house dances. On this occasion, she went to the dance with a girl friend, for her parents were very strict and did not allow her to date. There she met Ben and one of his friends. The boys suggested that they take the girls home. The girls felt that these were nice fellows, and finally agreed. Connie's girl friend told her that she wanted the good-looking one, so Connie took the other fellow — Ben — whom she described as "a little quiet but very nice."

This encounter led to further meetings at dances. Connie was soon in love — in fact, she decided it was love at first sight. But the courtship was troubled by various difficulties. Connie could not let her parents know that she was dating at all, much less a boy who was a stranger to her family. She had to sneak out of her home to meet him, and, when she was caught, she was whipped.

Ben, on the other hand, was anything but ardent. When Connie told him about her interest in other boys in order to make him jealous, he told her to go out with them. Gradually, however, Ben's interest increased, and they began to meet regularly. Neither of them had any money; they usually just walked around or went to the movies. In order not to seem forward, the first time Ben kissed her she told him not to get fresh. To her dismay, he made no attempt to kiss her again for a period of many months! Then, finally, after they had been seeing each other for three years, he began to talk about marriage, but only to say he couldn't afford it. Taking this as a proposal, she offered to go to work if they got married. He would not hear of it. Nevertheless, they set a date to get married. Connie was now approaching her twentieth birthday.

The engagement had to be kept a secret from their families. By this time both families had learned of their interest in each other and were violently opposed to the relationship. Connie's parents wanted her to marry a man with a better job and a more promising future. Ben's parents, especially his mother, wanted him to marry a girl from a wealthier family — a rich girl who would have a good dowry. Furthermore, what Ben's mother had heard about Connie's family did not do anything to decrease her objection. Not only were they less well off than the Sirrentis, but the behavior of Connie's older sisters had tarnished the reputation of the whole family.

Given the custom of arranged marriages in the Italian community, there was little that the engaged couple could do about the opposition of their families. They could not even bring about a personal introduction to each other's parents. Connie decided not to buy a wedding dress for fear her mother would discover her plans, come to the church, and tear the gown off in the midst of the ceremony. They were married in a simple church ceremony with only a few friends and no members of either family present. Directly afterwards, they went to Connie's parents and told them about the wedding. Connie's mother flew into a rage and administered a physical beating, then and there. They fled to Ben's home. His mother threw them both out of the apartment. Having no place to sleep, they took a room in the neighborhood for the night.

After a few days, they found an apartment not far from Ben's family's home, and there they lived for the next five years. Ben obtained a job at a large packing concern, and Connie also worked.

For months there was no contact with either family, until Connie began to urge Ben to visit his mother alone, which he did. The atmosphere was cool up to the day he said to his mother, "Ma, I don't want you to think that I'm coming because I want to. I'm coming because my wife throws me out and tells me that you're my mother and I gotta come down here and respect you and see you. If it wasn't for her, I wouldn't come." His mother became upset and said, "You and your wife come down to dinner on Sunday." After that, relations between the young couple and Ben's parents gradually improved. Connie's contact with her own mother was reestablished when, after seven months of marriage, she became pregnant. Sometime after Rudy's birth, they moved into the apartment building owned by Ben's parents, where they had lived ever since.

Connie always felt that the opposition to the marriage came completely from Ben's mother. She felt that his father was on her side from the beginning; they had always gotten along well, and she found his attitude steadily supportive. But Grandma's feelings were much influenced by neighborhood gossips. According to Connie: "All those busybodies would say to her, 'Look at you. You are well off. You are a religious woman. You are a high muckety-muck, and your son runs off and gets married to a girl like that.' She was so embarrassed!"

In the intervening years, Connie felt, the situation had changed. She had been accepted by the whole family and was respected as a good wife and mother. Some of the children of the neighborhood gossips, on the other hand, had not fared so well in their marriages. Grandma was no longer embarrassed. The episode was a thing of the past and could be treated lightly, with no hard feelings to worry about. Or was it?

"Symptomatic episodes" in a family are parallel to transient neurotic symptoms in an individual. They show up the weak spots in the structure of the family's organization, the places where strain can have an effect, and the sorts of transactions that can produce stress. Since they are transient, they also demonstrate the types of defense or techniques for resolving conflicts which are available to the family.

The conflict in the Sirrenti family induced by Ben and Connie's decision to get married over their families' objections was a typical symptomatic episode. The young couple, a modern Romeo and Juliet, defied the collateral organization of their respective families. Regarding the marriage as too much the product of individualistic choice, the families reacted by breaking off relations. Though Ben and Connie would have had plenty of support for their right to marry for love from dominant American individualistic values, they chose — or rather Connie chose — not to make an issue of it. In sending her husband back to "respect his mother," she was avowing the importance of traditional Italian collateral relations. This melted Grandma's heart, and the split in the extended family system was repaired, on Collateral lines. One might say that it was a victory for the traditional value profile except that the product of the Individualistic choice — the marriage — was retained. After all, Romeo and Juliet's defiance ended in tragedy.

During the course of our visiting we observed the onset, elaboration, and resolution of several symptomatic episodes of varying degrees of severity. Sometimes one, sometimes another member of the nuclear family responded to these episodes with a form of maladaptive behavior which receded as the episode itself

294

subsided. We will describe three of these events in some detail in order to demonstrate their circumscribed nature.

There had been talk in the Sirrenti family for some time about the possibility of the whole clan making a safari to Canada to visit a nephew of Grandma's who had only recently emigrated from Italy. During the month of June the idea began to take definite shape. Ben bought a new car, suitable for the trip. Grandma was eager to make the journey because this nephew, Peter Martinneli, and his wife represented the only link to her sister, Theresa, who had stayed behind in Italy when the rest of the family came to the United States in her youth. Others welcomed the plan as an ideal vacation trip, to last about two weeks. Father Carlo said he would go along, as did Dom and Eduardo. Only Vito begged off, saying he had other vacation plans. Ben planned to go, and Connie expected to take the baby along, Nat and Rudy being at summer camp.

Then came the blow. Grandma ruled that Connie and the baby must stay at home. She had reasons: Benny was too little for such a long trip, he suffered from carsickness, and the car would be too crowded. Ben did not oppose his mother, nor did he decide to remain at home with Connie. He wanted to go along with his parents and brothers. Connie was heartsick and angry. To be faced with a hot summer alone in the apartment with just the baby for company was unbearable. When Ben tried to kiss her goodbye, she pulled away and told him that she hoped he'd never come back. Later he told her that he'd recognized that she was upset and was upset himself, not really enjoying the trip. He sent her a postcard every day, signed LOVE in large letters.

The interviewers knew nothing about this turn of events until the family had been away for over a week. Because of the summer vacation period, the visiting had been curtailed. They heard about it when Connie called the female interviewer on the phone, depressed and tearful. She badly needed someone to talk with and did not want to turn to her mother or sisters. She told the interviewer then that she was very depressed, had been unable to eat or sleep very much, even before the family left, and had lost a good deal of weight. Glad to unburden her feelings, she expressed a great deal of hostility toward her mother-in-law and toward her husband. She described Grandma as always trying to interfere and have her own way and Ben as a weak person unwilling to stand up to his mother.

What was most difficult for Connie to deal with during her depression was a fantasy of Ben's unfaithfulness. She partly recognized her thoughts as a fantasy but was partly persuaded of their

295

truth. She pictured her husband as having gone on the trip for the sake of sexual freedom. She visualized him going to night clubs, picking up women, getting drunk, and having sexual relations. In their most intense form, the fantasies expressed the idea that Ben had a woman with whom he was in love and whom he was meeting clandestinely.

In spite of her angry, depressed feelings and her somatic reactions, she was not physically or mentally retarded. Nor was she actually agitated. Clinically, she showed a mild depressive reaction with some compensatory features. Though she could eat very little, brooded a great deal, and felt very sorry for herself, she continued to take care of Benny without particular difficulty. Furthermore, she went out frequently, taking Benny along — to dinner with friends and on shopping sprees. Without really needing them, she bought herself a dress, shoes, a blouse, and underwear. The purchases improved her spirits, but only for a short time.

Then, at the end of two weeks, her husband called. The family had stopped, on the return trip, to visit the boys at their summer camp. The call was placed through the friendly telephone operator, and Connie talked to the boys, but she was brief and cold to Ben. He called her seven times during the next two days. Arriving home, Ben dropped the family off at the apartment while he went to a nearby garage to have a flat tire repaired. Father Carlo took Connie aside and talked to her for a long time about the rocky road of marriage. She told him how lonesome she had been, how much she missed her husband, and he told her how much Ben loved her. By the time Ben arrived, her spirits had improved; she accepted his kiss.

During the next days they had several long talks; they discussed matters which they had never talked over before. Connie told him how tired and held down she had felt all year, confined indoors with the baby. Ben told her how hurt he felt about her sexual coolness — it made him feel inadequate as a man. He swore that he would see to it that she got out of the apartment and had some fun. She promised to be more considerate in bed.

By the time of the interviewers' next visit, not only had Connie's depression lifted, but her ascription of responsibility for it had reversed itself. She now blamed herself entirely for what had happened. Not her mother-in-law's hostility or her husband's weakness but her own defects were the causes. She realized that she had been a nagging, sexually rejecting wife. Now things were changed. She and Ben had been out for rides in the car, were planning to go out for dinner and dancing at a night club, and were thinking of a trip together to New York. Never again would she allow herself to become a fussy, complaining housewife. Romance had been restored — at least for the time being — to the Sirrenti household, and this brought the episode to a conclusion.

Two other symptomatic episodes may be briefly described in order to show how the underlying strains focus on various family members and stimulate a maladaptive response in line with the emotional conflicts of the individual. Shortly after the vacation crisis, Ben gave up his job at the restaurant. The hotel was under a new management, and his salary had been drastically cut. While working on a politically obtained state highway job he formed the plan of opening up a laundry in one of the vacant stores in his father's apartment building. Connie opposed the idea on the grounds that running it successfully would involve more working time for both of them than if Ben had a steady job. She saw her precious recreational time being threatened. When Ben nevertheless vigorously pursued the plan, she persuaded the senior Sirrentis and others in the family to oppose the enterprise. Thereupon Ben gave up. Now his former enthusiasm was replaced with apathy and loss of confidence in himself. For the first time, he relied on the male interviewer in a personal way, expressing his feelings of inadequacy and asking for advice. He could not think of anything to do except to go back to waiting on tables. The pressure on him to do just this from Connie and the extended family was great, and he complied. Concomitantly, everyone gave him praise and emotional support for doing it, and he soon recovered his usual, buoyant spirits.

The other symptomatic episode involved Nat. During his last year in high school he applied for admission to several different colleges and universities. This produced a pre-admission crisis in the family. Nat had been tense and over-concentrated about studying and maintaining his grade record ever since his leg injury the year before. Connie, as usual, had been pushing him in the same direction. But now Ben, who had been a balancing force in the past, also applied pressure. The anxieties in the parents took the form of a concern that Nat did not yet know what career to choose (let alone which college to go to).

Nat leaned toward a local college which offered no scholarship, whereas his father thought he should choose a college which could give him a scholarship. The parents were worried about having insufficient funds to finance Nat's college education. Dr. Ed constantly tried to persuade Nat to choose medicine as a career, but

297

Nat feared the sight of blood and disliked the idea of working such long hours.

As the time of decision approached, Nat became increasingly anxious. Every week he would announce that he had made a new career choice, only to become discouraged about it. For the first time, Connie became openly critical of her husband for not earning more money, thereby producing so much concern about Nat's education. Finally, after a week of intense studying for exams, one night Nat lost control of himself. He began screaming that he hated the sight of books, and he violently threw his books around the room. His parents attempted to calm him and had some success. There was a general realization that too much was being made of achievement for college, and Nat was urged to get more recreation. Nevertheless, he continued to be agitated and depressed for some time and at one point said that he thought he would give up the whole college and career idea and just be a waiter like his father. However, when he finally received notification of admission to several colleges and decided upon the local institution toward which he had all along leaned, his tension disappeared. The matter was, in effect, resolved for all concerned.

The group portrait of the Sirrenti family is now sufficiently complete to allow us to penetrate beneath the phenomenal description of behavioral events to grasp the dynamic processes which support them.

The first step is to set forth the process through which the family relationships are integrated and maintained. What is the design — the formal pattern — which knits together into a going organization the tendency of human beings to behave at cross purposes? The postulate advanced throughout this whole study is that the pattern can best be represented as a profile of value orientations variously adjusted to the cultural traditions of the family and to its current environment.

As always, we are interested in the attitudes of the Sirrentis toward *Man-nature, Time, Activity,* and *Relational* orientations. Through testing we know that they had moved slightly from the value profile typical of Italian culture toward the dominant American middle-class profile.

In order to demonstrate the relevance of the profile of values to the integration of the observed behavior in the family, we must consider the patterning of the Formal roles. In particular we shall discuss age, sex, and body management roles.

Age roles throughout the family were delicately adjusted,

especially in terms of the respect owed by younger to older members. When the respect and obedience demanded and owed were not tendered to — as when Ben and Connie went through with the marriage over their parents' objections — the hostility of the older ones broke through revengefully and without restraint. The young couple were excluded from the collateral networks on both sides, having abrogated their right to belong to them. Restraint of strong emotion was not to be expected in a family placing primary emphasis on Being — on the expressive and the dramatic. Nor was it difficult for the parents to find an explanation of the young couple's disobedience. Since human nature was basically regarded as a mixture of good and evil, one had to take the bad with the good; Benito and Connie became the bad children, leaving enough good children within the family to console the unhappy parents. By the same token, when Connie wanted to re-establish her husband's and her own "goodness," she asked Ben to visit his parents and to pay his respects — with a view to being received back into the family circle.

Teaching respect for parents through physical coercion was a standard aspect of the learning of body management roles. Confronted with a conflict of wills, the parents hit or beat the children into submission. Access to the body-space of the child and control of his orifices was a privilege of the parents. As Connie said, she "gave" her children not only love and care but also discipline. Almost all body surfaces — even among adults — were presumed to be open for touching, grasping, and manipulations of various kinds, as if closeness and warmth in the family were to be maintained through physical contact. But, of all the avenues to physical exchange, the mouth and the digestive tract had first priority. In both a concrete and a figurative sense, one's mouth and oral intake were not one's own concern but were under the supervision of the whole collateral network. Accordingly, supervision, which worked so well for oral exchanges, was the model for all controls of impulse, of whatever kind. Not self-control but control administered by the group was the expected form of regulation. Taught early in life, this lesson guaranteed that dependency on the collateral group — if not the family, then some substitute for it — would be well learned.

One aspect of the collateral controls was that everyone's business was always in every way everyone else's. Nowhere was this *summum bonum* more evident than in the patterning of sex role behavior. Regarded as one of the more powerful and ubiquitous impulses, sex had naturally to be kept under strict supervision, everyone watching everyone else. It was better to stimulate a certain amount of sexual behavior so that it could be watched than to let it remain hidden, considering what a potential source of strain it could be. The sexual joking and the erotic provoking in front of others was a way of handling the strain. When this sort of control did not suffice — as was usually the case for Connie — then religious precepts were brought into play. The entire apparatus of the clergy, the scolding of the passionate priests and their approval for restraint, was deployed to enforce a strict monogamy whose rules would probably be broken anyway, out of human weakness and badness.

The various contradictions in the patterning of the traditional Italian sex roles were always difficult to resolve: what had to be done (confinement of sex to marriage) could not easily be done, and no one expected strict compliance even under the best of supervisory regimes. The flesh was too weak to cope with the contingencies of an arranged marriage formed for other than erotic motives. In the native Italian culture there were two possible attitudes to take toward the *cul de sac* of marriage. One could be prepared for unhappiness, even for its enjoyment, or one could look to romance outside of the marriage, premaritally, extramaritally, or both. Both attitudes, in fact, were consonant with the tragic view of life and the acceptance of man as subordinate to the inscrutable will of God and the mysterious forces of nature.

It was interesting, in view of this tradition, that Connie's response to the expected nature of American marriages was to insist that hers was both happy and romantic: a marriage in the new style. Yet the picture of the unhappy, deserted wife and the philandering husband was in the back of her mind, accompanied by a set of fantasies which were ready to emerge when the fragile concept of the American-style marriage was jeopardized. Since she had married for love over the objections of both sides of the family, she was partly justified in viewing her marriage as romantic. But since she had made her peace with the collateral networks, held the same values as others in the family, and lived in accordance with its demands, she was partly justified in viewing her marriage as subject to the traditional strains.

One of the aspects of sex-role patterning in the traditional Italian family was the subordination of the wife to the husband. Both Connie and Ben's behavior were in accordance with this tradition: as Connie said, "My husband is boss in most things." The reciprocal gearing-in of husband-wife relations — to which this acceptance of dominance was a key — was generalized in many other behavior spheres. The integration in the family, then, was maintained by the concordance of role expectations in a variety of areas. Connie was happy, for the most part, with Ben's occupation and financial status and satisfied with his conduct as a father. Ben was content with Connie's function as a housewife and mother. Though their activities were segregated in many ways, they got together for the recreational activities which were so important to both of them. Living so largely in the present, they did not have to plan — except where the children were concerned — for changes with which neither of them were prepared to cope.

Still, there were strains, as we have seen, within their system of values and these produced endemic if low-keyed conflict. Usually not visible, the conflicts were apt to erupt in short-term crises which we have called "symptomatic episodes." The strains lay partly within the Italian patterns themselves but were partly the product of partial accommodation to American expectations. For example, Connie's membership in the Sirrenti family system, though officially established after the reconciliation, was always somewhat questioned by Grandma. The privilege of age plus Connie's desire to belong to the collateral family system made it difficult for her to deal with the problem. Most of the time, her solution rested on the attempt to be the wife, daughter-in-law, and mother that her mother-in-law wanted her to be, even though this meant taking some abuse from the old lady. It also meant that her own family could never meet socially with the Sirrenti family.

Given the degree to which the collateral Italian family system is subject to sudden fission, this was the best solution possible. It worked so long as Connie could be assured of her official place within the family. Anything which threatened this status tended to undermine the whole solution of this conflict, bringing into question whether Connie had made the right marriage after all. Such a question tended to stimulate within her thoughts of a sexual or romantic relationship with some other man, as well as complementary fantasies of her husband's unfaithfulness. Since she was driven strenuously to defend herself against the fantasy of her own unfaithfulness, the wishes entered her awareness only in their projected form and only when she felt herself to be threatened with desertion. It was into this stressful situation that she felt herself thrust when the Sirrenti clan, accompanied dutifully by her husband, decamped for the summer vacation, leaving her behind with the baby.

The chronic family conflict which this event brought to the surface was not simple but was compounded of several elements. Its principal component, however, and the one that we wish to consider, was the strain endemic to all collateral systems. This is the tension of loyalty versus disloyalty which is stimulated when some members feel themselves to be unfairly disadvantaged by the way the system is working. It is this tension that leads to the frequent ruptures, feuds, and fissions in collateral systems. The rationale of the system is that everyone is in the same boat, experiencing shared advantages and disadvantages as the case may be. In accordance with Italian values and traditions, the advantages of the system are in the economic and recreational areas. If anyone is to be deprived of economic or recreational benefits, then all should be.

In the Sirrenti family there was chronic tension between Connie and Grandma about this matter. Connie believed that she was not getting enough of the recreational pleasure which was so important to her. She felt tied down with the housework and the baby, and Grandma would not help or permit others to share this responsibility. Grandma, on the other hand, felt that Connie, only admitted to the family on trial, so to speak, should be willing to make the sacrifices and do the hard work ("Lazy women!") that was the price of her admission. Ben, as usual, attempted to function as a balance wheel, to keep both his mother and his wife happy. For some time before the vacation episode, however, Connie had been feeling neglected and deprived by the degree to which her husband favored his mother's wishes over her own wish to get out of the house and have some freedom from child care. To be left behind with her child while all other family members went off to enjoy a vacation, then, was the blow that sprung the conflict into the open.

As stated earlier, conflicts in Formal roles are usually compensated for by a variety of mechanisms. In this instance, we can observe the suppression and diversion of the conflict in its chronic, concealed form, being maintained by methods of re-equilibration which we have called *role induction*, initiated principally by Connie. She brought into play the techniques which we have labeled "masking" and "positive evaluating." She concealed her unhappiness and discontent from herself and others by overemphasizing her happiness and through elaborate praise of her husband and his family. Her husband and other family members officially went along with her technique of handling the conflict, thus supporting its suppression.

Long-continued role induction leads eventually to the establish-

302

ment of either Informal character roles, Fictive roles, or both. In this case, a set of character roles was laid down under the title of "the happy family," with an aura of romance. With her propensity for dramatic enactment, Connie played the happy-housewife-in-love-with-her-husband to the hilt. Ben supported the role with complementary behavior in the presence of others. In private, his uncomplaining silence could be construed as acquiescence by Connie, though he actually defaulted the role of happy-husband-in-love-with-his-wife in a serious fashion.

These romantic roles were not "fictive" in the sense previously defined. They were sufficiently embedded in reality to have substance. But they did not take into account the negative side of emotional reality created by the actual balance of satisfaction-dissatisfaction in the marriage. The defensive nature of these character roles was revealed on their collapse, in Connie's mind, during the vacation episode. Helpless against the pressure of rising dissatisfaction, she could no longer maintain them. Nor could she prevent the emergence into action of the opposite set of roles against which she ordinarily maintained a defense: the unhappy, disappointed, and overworked housewife, deserted by her unfaithful husband.

Once out in the open, the conflict tended to evoke the full panoply of re-equilibrating devices and secondary defenses. They ran their course like the stages of a serious illness followed by recovery. Connie showed coercive hostility before and on Ben's departure. He coaxed (with a goodbye kiss); she withheld, unmollified. He continued coaxing by postcards and a phone call; she maintained a stony distance. On returning, he postponed facing the music by going to a garage to have a flat tire fixed. He sent his brother, Father Carlo, as go-between and peacemaker. Father Carlo, reversing roles with the dexterity of a professional counselor, interpreted her husband's behavior to Connie in a more favorable light while accepting the validity of her complaints. Result: husband and wife so prepared by role reversal for sympathy with the other that the feared encounter turns immediately into a reconciliation. Later, role modifications are rehearsed in the atmosphere of mutual acceptance of complaints. Connie hears for the first time his tale of sexual disappointment. Ben hears of her imprisonment with children and housework. Each vows to change for the benefit of the other, working on an effective compromise of differences. The problem appears to have disappeared.

We may be assured that the conflict has not and will not disappear so long as values remain unaltered and Grandma is still alive. But it has subsided into its constricted, suppressed form, somewhat alleviated by its having been aired.

We are now in a position to examine the personality structure of Connie viewed as an individual. What type of emotional conflict did she manifest, how much of the ego was involved in conflict, what sort of diagnostic label would be applied to her disturbed behavior — these are the sorts of questions which would ordinarily arise within a purely psychiatric context. Since our interest has been in the structure of the family and in its dynamic process as related to its environmental setting, we have come to the subject matter of personality process — of intrapsychic dynamics — later than is customary within the helping professions. Viewed from the standpoint of psychiatry in its traditional form, all that has been presented so far is merely background and setting, preparatory to the understanding of the individual case. Viewed within the framework of the transactional approach, the psychodynamic issues are merely one among a number of interdependent foci of behavior which need to be considered together in order to understand the difference between "sick" and "well" families.

Since "the psyche" has been among the foci which had to be considered all along, we have inserted statements about personality here and there throughout the previous discussion. Now that we are required to switch to a high-power lens focused more narrowly on psychodynamics, the question of vocabulary arises. How are the value patterns and role structures which we have used to analyze the process within the family to be related to the drives, defenses, and personality structures ordinarily used to describe intrapsychic process? The best brief answer is to say that the strategy will be to examine the chief roles and role conflicts in which the individual is involved and to relate these to the personality structures.

Connie's problem within her family was this: how to behave like the "good" wife, daughter, daughter-in-law, and mother (her Formal roles), which both she and the family wished her to be, when there were external and internal factors operating against such behavior. The external factors, represented by conflicts within the value and role systems of the family have been examined above. The internal factors were represented by an emotional conflict which we have now to consider, much more briefly than is desirable.

The "good wife" role for Connie had to be maintained against an unconscious desire to enact the role of an infinitely desirable, sexually free charmer for whose attentions men would vigorously compete while women looked on with jealousy and resentment. Because of her moral objections to this wish, the psychic energies which it would have satisfied were never expressed in the real world, though they did obtain a small victory in the fictive world of sexual joking. To help maintain the repression of this wish, Connie could use the unhappy example of her sisters who were living in sin, deserted by their husbands, and looked down upon by the community. For the wish was regarded, consciously and unconsciously, as very dangerous. Its enactment in the real world — even its admission into conscious fantasy — was associated with the inevitability of punishment, of which abandonment or death were the principal examples.

The fantasy of romantic attachment and mutual devotion was the central defense erected by the ego to stave off the claims of forbidden sexual urges and to deny the possibility of the expected punishment by banishment from a nurturing environment. That the fantasy could be materialized and maintained in actuality was attributable both to Connie's dramatic talent and to the actual supports for the role provided by her husband and family. Undoubtedly, she had the ability to draw others into her emotional orbit, even though they might not fully subscribe to the roles she assigned them. But, in addition, the actual feelings of her husband and her children toward her were not too far away from the fantasy which she attempted to realize. She exaggerated and improved upon but did not falsify the actuality. To the extent that the roles which she held in conscious fantasy corresponded to her actual situation, therefore, they were adaptive and sustaining. To the extent that they exaggerated the reality, they were defensive and thereby revealed her vulnerability.

For such a combination of adaptations and defenses we have no diagnostic terms. Because of the histrionic element in her behavior and the inhibition of genital sexual satisfaction, one might say that Connie displayed a neurotic character structure of the hysterical type. The label, however, contributes little to our understanding, and it obscures a great deal. It says nothing about the adaptive elements in her personality or about the way in which her family accepted and appreciated her defenses. Better, then, that we specify the nature of the strains to which she was vulnerable, along with those which she was able to master.

So long as she was able to believe that she and her husband loved each other and that she was considered a valuable member of the Sirrenti clan, Connie maintained an adequate emotional balance. In order to consider herself a representative member of the extended family, she also had to believe that her children would fulfill family expectations for loyal, obedient behavior and for a certain amount of achievement in the wider community. Given the belief in the reality of these conditions, she was able to satisfy both her personal criteria for adequate functioning and her views as to what the family expected of her. This concordance of ideal expectations kept her self-esteem at a fairly high level. On the whole she was behaving as she and they thought she should. At the same time, the exchanges of gifts and services throughout the family and neighborhood systems satisfied her need for sublimated oral supplies. Thus, when everything was taking place as usual, she had no occasion to face the feelings which would be aroused within her if she were required to be more independent and self-sufficient.

The family vacation trip forced just this situation upon her. Furthermore, since she was left behind, it was easy for her to feel that she had been deserted. She interpreted separation as abandonment: a catastrophic punishment for her forbidden sexual wishes. Feeling unmasked, she attempted to unmask her mother-in-law and her husband. It was her husband, she suddenly imagined, whose insipid dependence on his mother was responsible for her difficulties. It was also her husband whose unforgivable infidelity brought about the desertion. And it was her mother-in-law who was the agent of her punishment, activated by jealousy and revengefulness.

These projections, in which there was also some truth, relieved but did not abolish her need to suffer because of feeling guilty. Furthermore, she suffered from actual loneliness and the drudgery of housework and of caring for the baby. Deprived of sympathy, she sympathized with herself and ruminated on her husband's wrongdoings. Lacking appreciation, she bought some pretty clothes which she could appreciate on herself. The consolations were unable completely to ward off melancholy, but, as with her other tactics, they lightened the gloom somewhat.

These consolations also demonstrated the circumscribed, reactive nature of her distress — the quality that we have postulated for all personal responses to symptomatic episodes within "well" families. Her internal resources, while damaged, were sufficient to see her through the episode. Furthermore, she was successful in communicating the precise degree of her distress to the family while they were still away. The ego, in other words, was able to use its distress responses for secondary purposes, not only to gain

306

pleasure but also to make an indirect protest. The protest function of symptomatic behavior is usually overlooked. It is assumed that secondary gain, or the use to which symptoms are put, is inevitably maladaptive. But in this case, as in many others, the symptoms were useful. They called the attention of the family, and particularly of Ben, to the seriousness of her situation, warned that it had best be avoided in the future, and suggested that the factors underlying it be looked into, that she be protected where she was vulnerable.

That the protest was effective we know from the anticipatory responses in Ben and Father Carlo. Their behavior brought into play what we have called *organizational adaptations,* to be distinguished from *organizational defenses.* Organizational adaptations are secondary processes called forth within the group organization of the family to settle the role conflicts which have given rise to a symptomatic episode or crisis; they appear more frequently in "well" families than in "sick" families. They are characterized by the use of internal or external agents who perform as buffers for the disequilibrium, as go-betweens or referees, or as models for the solution of the conflict. In this instance, Father Carlo performed all three functions — go-between, buffer, and role model. His performance was effective, giving rise to the processes of role modification noted above, or, in less technical terms, to a reconciliation.

To return to the psychodynamic account, viewing the ensuing process from the standpoint of Connie's state of mind, we see that Father Carlo's actions followed by Ben's contrite behavior served as a partial acknowledgement of the legitimacy of her indirect and previously ignored complaints. One might have expected her to feel reassured and gratified, though still somewhat injured. What, then, accounted for her about-face? Why did she exonerate the key figures and take the burden of responsibility for the episode upon her own shoulders? Why did Grandma have to be reinstated as a loving and honored mother-figure and her husband defined as the injured party, sexually frustrated and insufficiently appreciated?

One answer is that Connie could afford to be generous in taking responsibility in that her husband was also admitting his share of responsibility for their mutual problems. If both parties to a dissatisfaction acknowledge responsibility for disappointing the other, then the way out of the difficulty is easier to find. But there was another reason for her response. By admitting that her sexual coldness had offended her husband and by promising to show greater warmth in the future she was able to deny once more any guilt for her unconscious sexual wishes. If she had anything to feel guilty about, seemingly it would be for her frigidity. Furthermore, her sexual participation in the future was not to be based on her own wishes for erotic gratification; it was for the sake of preserving the marriage. With Ben's interest in her now a matter of record, the atmosphere of romance could be restored to the marriage. Sex was, in this atmosphere, not an act of genitality or of erotic enjoyment, but something to be given and exchanged for the preservation of relationships. It was thus assimilated to all the other orally stamped behavior so meaningful to her emotional economy. In this warm climate of giving and receiving Grandma's peccadilloes could be overlooked. Connie could always — as she had in the past — win over the old lady, transforming her into the figure whose seal of approval, though somewhat forced, nevertheless kept the marriage an important segment of the extended family system. Meanwhile, having established a closer liaison with Ben and having received his assurance that her need for recreation and relief from household duties would be gratified, she could realistically assume that her influence over her husband was at least equal to that of her mother-in-law.

AN END AND A BEGINNING

With this analysis of the temporary stabilization of the dynamic process in the family and in Connie's personality, we conclude our discussion of the Sirrentis — a "well" family. They typify a collateral network of Italian-Americans in an urban American setting. The conflicts which they experience are not excessive and are usually under control, though occasionally they give rise to turbulence and crises. None of the family members is clinically disturbed. Those elements or foci of psychopathology which can be detected are embedded in a pattern of adaptive functioning. During times of turbulence, the psychopathology in one or another family member temporarily dominates his behavior, then subsides. What is ordinarily called mental illness can, with unusual clarity, be seen as a transactional effect. It is triggered by a confrontation between the psychobiological vulnerabilities of the individual and specific short-term stresses growing out of chronic strains in the family relationships. What is more difficult to specify — namely, mental health — can be seen as a smooth fitting together of the value orientations, roles, and personalities of individual family members. In this broad perspective, it is the coherence of cultural, social, group, and individual processes — their relative integration within a conflict-controlled field of behavior — that can be identified as the specific condition which must obtain if the person and his family are to function at an optimum level of behavior. The word "relative" is important. In the "well" family — as perhaps in most ecological systems — conflict is not absent but is regulated by mechanisms of control. It is held within constraints in such a fashion that the transacting systems are only occasionally thrown off balance and are soon brought back to relative equilibrium.

Considering the variety of systems within a family that must be kept in balance, we may regard it as a miracle that equilibrium is ever approached; no more so, however, than is the case for the body as an organization of anatomical and physiological systems, or the nation-state as an organization of political, religious, class, and ethnic systems.

Part IV

Transactions in Psychotherapy

In this section Spiegel focuses his inquiry on the individual in the psychotherapeutic situation. Transactional systems theory is here employed to order the complex interrelationships between patient and therapist. Freudian psychoanalytic concepts are employed to order intrapsychic events within the individual viewed as a "self action" system. It should be noted that these psychoanalytic concepts are not violated in any way when placed within a transactional framework. These intrapsychic events, however, are related to the social and cultural events occurring concurrently in the psychotherapeutic situation. The social role concept is employed to order the cultural patterning of these roles. It is the simultaneous viewing of these three "systems" in transaction which opens new avenues for understanding the complexities of the psychotherapeutic situation.

In Chapter Nine the major focus is on the social role concept and the doctor-patient relationship as a social system. The distinction between psychoanalysis and psychotherapy is explored in the light of social role considerations. In Chapter Ten the focus shifts to the value orientation concept as a tool for ordering the cultural system within which the therapist and patient interact. This conceptualization of the cultural dimension, which is often ignored by many theorists, provides new insights into the transference and counter-transference aspects of the psychotherapeutic relationship.

NINE

The Social Roles of Doctor and Patient

In recent years the question of the distinction between psychoanalysis and psychotherapy, in terms of their methods and goals, has received a great deal of attention. The discussion has had the effect of producing a great many different points of view without settling the fundamental difference in the two methods. Even among those who accept psychoanalytic theory and who are recognized analysts, there is some difference of opinion as to where psychotherapy leaves off and psychoanalysis begins. In the variety of theoretical and methodological issues that have been raised by the problem there have been two common and related themes: the fundamental importance of the doctor-patient relationship and the management of the transference.

It is with respect to the meaning of the doctor-patient relationship — especially as conceived in terms of transference — that I wish to apply the concepts of *transaction* and of *social role*. Transaction is a term introduced by Dewey and Bentley to describe reciprocal, reverberating processes which occur in any system of action or behavior. *(Dewey and Bentley 1949; Bentley 1950)* In such a system, especially if it is in equilibrium, there occur two-way phasic and cyclical exchanges which are largely self-regulating and self-correcting — that is, they keep the system going. A key

313

example of transactional processes at the somatic level is the neural and hormonal exchanges which keep the body at a constant temperature. As a concept, transaction is in contrast to interaction — which describes behavior produced by the effect of one object upon another — and to self-action, which describes the isolated behavior of one object activated wholly by inner forces. A good example of interaction is the effect of one billiard ball upon another, where no systematic relations are maintained once the force is expended. A clock is an obvious example of self-action behavior.

How can we describe the relation between two or more human beings in the light of these concepts? It seems clear that if two people relate to each other at all, they become involved in a system of transaction characterized by mutually regulative processes which we ordinarily term adaptation or adjustment. These processes are mediated by the exchange of information which is called communication. Thus if we want to describe the doctor-patient situation as systematically as possible, we will study the flow of communication — verbal and nonverbal — that occurs in the system of transactions as it becomes established by the incorporation of the doctor and the patient within it. If such a study is to be successful, we should be able to name and describe the mechanisms which disturb the equilibrium in the system as well as those which restore it. Furthermore, we should be able to assign responsibility for perturbations in the equilibrium of the system to either doctor or patient, as the case might be.

As the psychotherapeutic situation is ordinarily understood, the flow of communication refers to the statements and behavior of the patient and the "interpretations" of the doctor. The therapist's "interpretations," as a general rule, refer to "motivations" which govern the patient's statements and behavior but which are hidden from his awareness. Among the most important of these unconscious motivations are the patient's attitudes and feelings toward the doctor, and this is what is understood by the term transference. It is assumed that the patient's unconscious attitudes toward the doctor, insofar as they represent transference processes, are based upon experiences with significant figures in the past. They therefore constitute ways in which, without the knowledge of the patient, the past is distorting his current behavior and interfering with his ability to adjust to present reality.

According to this way of understanding the doctor-patient relationship, it is the transference which accounts, for the most part, for the perturbations in the equilibrium of the transactional

314

system. Thus the concept of transference comes close to satisfying the demand for a mechanism to locate the disequilibrium in the communication system. There are two ways, however, in which it fails to qualify as an adequate concept for such a mechanism. On the one hand, it is a relatively abstract concept. Because of its high level of generalization, it provides no concrete way of specifying or distinguishing what is unconsciously transferred from what is appropriate and realistically oriented to the current situation. The therapist has to rely, for such distinctions, on his intuitive judgment and experience. On the other hand, it provides no way of describing the real nature of the therapist's involvement in the behavorial system. The picture of the therapist making perfectly neutral comments or interpretations of the meaning of the patient's productions leaves out all the nuances and richness of detail, the multiple choice of response, and the interplay of processes which actually occur in the doctor-patient relationship — whether it is psychoanalysis or psychotherapy. Such a picture is based on an interactional rather than a transactional model of the system of relations.

A more concrete way of getting at the intricacies of the communication process, still consistent with the general aspects of transference, is through the concept of social role. Since the term role and the expressions role-playing and role-taking always bring up a number of misunderstandings, it is necessary to make some definitions of these concepts. As used in social science, the terms have nothing to do with artificially adopting a role as an actor does in the theater. Rather, the concept of role is concerned with a description of behavior from the point of view of a social situation. All behavior is patterned in accordance with cultural standards to fit some part that the individual plays in a social situation, and these parts are called social roles. *(See Neiman and Hughes 1951.)* Actually, it is impossible to describe behavior without referring it to the role played by the individual. Even in our clinical descriptions we are forced to refer to our patients in their roles as students, mothers, housewives, daughters, and so forth, in order to indicate what sort of behavior may be expected of them.

A role, however, is more than a descriptive term for the pattern of behavior which one may expect of an individual. Roles are governed both by motivational processes and by cultural value orientations, and it is important to keep these two aspects of role behavior distinctly separate. The distinction can be illustrated by an example. Let us contrast the patterning of roles in two doctor-patient situations. In the first situation the patient is an Eastern European Jew, and in the second he is an Englishman, but in all other respects the situation is the same. In the first situation the patient states his complaints with great drama, emphasizes his suffering with loud moans and groans, and considerably exaggerates the degree of disability. The doctor will most likely respond with tolerant sympathy and reassurance, telling the patient that he will take care of the difficulty and that his suffering will be relieved. In the second case the patient reports his complaint in an offhand manner and minimizes his suffering or treats it humorously. In this pattern, the doctor may very probably warn the patient that he must take better care of himself but that if he follows orders and keeps his appointments, the situation will be cleared up.

These two completely dissimilar people, both playing the same role of patient, are both actuated by an identical motivation — to solicit the interest and care of the doctor. The motivation is inferred from the effort each participant makes to induce his prospective role partner to play the desired complementary or reciprocal role of doctor-interested-in-his-case. The variation in the way the roles are played can be accounted for by the difference in cultural value orientations. For the Eastern European Jew, the dramatic and voluble exhibition of emotion, especially of suffering, has great value and can be counted on to elicit the interest of another person. For the Englishman, consideration for others and a calm attitude in the face of adversity have greater value than giving way to individual expressions of feeling. This contrast throws an interesting light on the way cultural values are built into the personality as a mechanism for the control of anxiety. The Jewish patient unconsciously fears that unless he presents a convincing picture of personal suffering, the doctor will not take his case seriously. *(See Bettleheim 1947.)* The Englishman fears that any undue show of feeling will make the doctor lose interest in his case.

A number of other important insights into role-playing as a system of communication can be gained from a consideration of this example. The chief homeostatic or regulative mechanism in the system is the complementarity of the roles. *(See Parsons 1951, esp. pp. 36-45.)* Roles are culturally patterned to dovetail or integrate with each other by means of reciprocal actions, verbal communications, or symbolic gestures. A question calls forth an answer, and the answer maintains the equilibrium in the system. Not to answer a question introduces tension into the system as does any failure of complementarity. Thus the equilibrium state of the system is directly proportional to the degree of complementarity in the roles. For example, if in the situation just described the doctor refuses to pay attention to the complaints of the patient — that is, refuses to play the complementary role — the system is in danger of disintegrating, with the production of anger or anxiety in the participants. Another way of describing this is to say that the doctor *declines* the role *assigned* to him by the patient. This phrasing calls attention to the highly significant fact that roles are consciously or unconsciously *assumed, assigned, accepted,* or *declined* in all human relationships. The to-and-fro play among these four transactions governs many aspects of the dynamics of the communication process.

Two other aspects of role relations remain to be considered before examining the doctor-patient relationship. One is the classification of roles into two general categories: *instrumental* and *expressive*. Instrumental roles are designed for solving problems, and emotion has little place in them. Expressive roles are patterned for the expression of feeling or emotion and are not concerned with getting anything done. The distinction is somewhat abstract since many roles have elements of both instrumental and expressive behavior, but the categories are nevertheless useful. For example, the role of patient is chiefly instrumental; he has to help the doctor solve the problem. But the Jewish patient just described may inject so much expressive behavior into the role that the doctor may be prevented from solving the problem. In psychotherapy and psychoanalysis, however, expressive behavior becomes a part of the instrumental problem to be solved.

The other aspect of role-playing concerns the interplay between *explicit* and *implicit* roles. If one focuses a high-power microscope — so to speak — on the processes inherent in role systems, it becomes plain that any two-person system is characterized by multiple, simultaneously enacted roles. Everyone wears many hats at the same time. For example, the Jewish patient we have discussed is wearing his patient hat, his Jewish hat, and his suffering hat. Under this array of millinery, he may also wear hidden hostile, affectionate, and anxious hats. It can be seen that this multiple, layered structuring of roles is arranged in an order of nearness and remoteness from the surface aspects of the social situation. The *explicit* roles are those that are closest to the surface and therefore closest to the observation and awareness of the participants. In addition, they are oriented to the most highly structured and therefore most stable aspects of the social situation. *Implicit* roles, on the other hand, are more remote from the sphere of awareness of the participants, and they are thus more subtle, complicated, and variable. Associated with their remote position in the role-structuring of human relations is the fact that the implicit roles are the seat of the chief emotional currents and dynamic trends in the social situation. It is the configuration of implicit roles assumed by a person that constitutes his "character." The life, the color, the vividness of any human situation is given by the interplay among explicit and implicit roles.

These structural relations can be brought into relief and applied to the basic distinction between psychoanalysis and psychotherapy if one studies the flow of explicit and implicit roles as they are delivered into the communication system established between doctor and patient. Let us dip into a clinical situation and take out a very small sample for study.

A twenty-three-year-old, highly intelligent girl came for treatment with the problem of feeling generally frustrated and "lost" in her adjustment to life and specifically unable to realize her ambition in her chosen career. She was constantly haunted by a deep and abiding sense of shame, on which account she was extremely shy and retiring in all her social relationships. She initiated the particular segment of the doctor-patient transaction that I wish to discuss by taking up the problem of her abilities and her career. She had a Ph.D. in mathematics but was unable to do much with it. Perhaps, she speculated, she had chosen the wrong field. Maybe she was more suited to the arts; she always found herself interested in aesthetic problems.

Up to this point I found myself, as the doctor, comfortably installed in my explicit instrumental role; the role assignment given me by the patient appeared to be concerned with her "problem." The system of roles was complementary and apparently well integrated. The next moment, however, the patient initiated a new role assignment. She asked me if I had seen a recent performance of "Don Juan in Hell" from *Man and Superman*. The question seemed a simple enough request for information regarding my playgoing habits. But since I did not know what role I was being invited to take, and because I suspected that behind whatever explicit role this might turn out to be there lurked a more important implicit one, I did not answer the question. The patient paused for a moment, and then, perceiving that I would not answer the question, she continued. She had already learned from previous transactions that I would decline implicit roles into which I was being

318

inducted through a question, and although she still resented my "rudeness," as she usually described it, the behavioral system was by now no longer subjected to intense strain by my declining to play complementary roles in this fashion.

In continuing after the pause, the patient delivered a highly perceptive account of Shaw's intention in the Don Juan interlude, of the actors' interpretations, and of her reactions. The account was so long that I finally interrupted to ask if she knew why she wanted to tell all this. At the point of interruption I had become aware that my new role was an expressive one — to play the appreciative audience to her role as a gifted art and drama critic. I could have accepted this role and made it explicit by complimenting her, since she had certainly done a first-rate job. Or I could have modified my role slightly by discussing with her the points she had made. Either of these two responses would have maintained equilibrium in the system by re-establishing complementarity. But to do so would have meant passing up the opportunity to get more information regarding the hidden, implicit role buried in this transaction and thus to learn more about her motivation for shifting out of her initial instrumental role in which she had started the interview.

Her response to my question was that she was just chattering because she felt like it and that there was no particular reason for her talking about the play. Now in her response, especially in the tone of voice, I was aware that she had assumed yet another role; she had demoted herself, within her value system at any rate, from the brilliant art critic to the idle gossip and chatterer. But why should the patient choose this new, depreciated role? Such sharp jumps in explicit role-structuring are always indicators of intense unconscious affect connected with the implicit role, against the expression of which there is strong resistance. The key to the shift can be found if the therapist puts himself in the complementary role assigned. If she was now the gossip, it must have been I that thought her so. In other words, she must have interpreted my question as indicating I did not appreciate her talents and that I thought she was just chattering. In identifying with my assumed view of her, she was able to control her intense disappointment and thus to maintain the feeling of closeness to me which was being threatened.

To make this transaction explicit, I now told the patient that I thought she must be feeling disappointed because she had hoped to interest me in the quality of her grasp of aesthetics. To this

319

description of what I assumed had taken place between us, the patient had an intense reaction. She immediately covered her face with her hands and declared herself to be horribly embarrassed. Her face felt hot and red, the whole room felt hot — so intense was her feeling of shame. She felt that I had reprimanded her, as if she were a child.

Although her description of herself in the role of the child brought the buried implicit role somewhat nearer the surface, an exact definition of the role was still lacking. Because of the intensity of her reaction, I waited some moments until she became calmer. Then I speculated aloud that her expectation that I would accept the role of appreciator — of one who puts great emphasis on artistic achievements — must have been learned in some previous experience. In response she told me that her father was greatly interested in intellectual and artistic pursuits and could seldom make contact with anyone except at this level. When she was a child, dinner-table conversations used to consist of long orations by father on some intellectual topic — conversations which she was hardly ever allowed to enter, on the ground that she was not qualified.

As she spoke, the similarity of the role relations that she thought she had experienced with me to the role she felt she had occupied in relation to her father became clear to both of us. She felt that she had tried to master with me a situation which she had never mastered at home, had failed, and had then felt presumptuous, exposed, and ashamed — just as she had all her life. Thus the implicit role which guided her in talking to me about the play had finally become explicit and clear.

I would like, now, to review the significance of this clinical fragment for the distinction between psychoanalysis and psychotherapy from the point of view of role theory. In psychoanalysis, as I understand it, the intention of the technique is to help the patient to become aware of his own motivations and of the self-constriction, the narrowness of the ego, associated with the fear and guilt attached to his motivations. Since motivation can only be expressed in social behavior, the motivations with which treatment is concerned are built into social roles, which, because of the fear and guilt, are either repressed or given only very disguised expression as hidden implicit roles. As a technique, psychoanalysis is a system of behavior or communication wherein the explicit permissiveness and acceptance of all communications associated with the doctor's role encourages, through complementarity, the eruption of the buried implicit roles. This is the general process denoted by the concept of transference, which is signalled by the forcible intrusion of an implicit role into the explicit role system. The expression "the management of the transference" refers, then, to the roles assumed by the doctor with respect to the emerging implicit roles of the patient. If the procedure is a psychoanalytical one, the doctor will not play a complementary role to the emerging implicit role of the patient. It is this refusal on the part of the doctor which forces the role and its motivation explicitly into the consciousness of the patient. The reason for this is that a person is much more likely to become aware of his role, his motivation for it, and the feelings connected with it when the transactional system is at an optimum disequilibrium. No one is likely to give much thought to a role system that is running perfectly smoothly. In this connection, the opportunities for "interpretation" by the doctor represent an instrumental role in which he reviews what has happened in the transactions subsequent to his declining the complementary role. At the same time, he helps the patient define the role satisfactions that were sought for and thus sheds further light on the patient's motivation. Looked at from the point of view of this definition, the procedure in the clinical fragment just reported was that of psychoanalysis.

In my view, the role of the doctor, when the procedures are those of psychotherapy, is in some respects directly opposed to the process just described for psychoanalysis. Overlooking, for the moment, the factors which may structure the situation, the situation which calls for psychotherapy, as here defined, is one in which the communication system is potentially disturbed by disequilibria of great magnitude. The role balance of doctor and patient is continually threatened by the eruption of explicit roles which seem inappropriate to the purely instrumental role of the doctor. Because of the great disequilibrium, the doctor cannot refuse to play a role reciprocal to the dominant explicit role of the patient. Only through the re-establishment of complementarity can the disturbance be quieted or averted. But this takes place at the cost of suppressing the implicit roles, and therefore the specific complementary role must be chosen with great care so that it results in redefinition of the explicit roles.

This principle can best be illustrated in terms of concrete procedures by discussing a further development of the clinical fragment presented above. At the moment when the patient discovered that the role she had wanted to play with me was identical to the one she had wanted to play with her father, I had to make a procedural choice. On the one hand, there was the possibility of exploring further her motivation in wanting to play an intimate intellectual role with her father. I suspected then, and subsequent events proved, that her motivation was to be the sole possessor of her father's attention and to have a revengeful triumph over her mother. To have pursued this goal would have required a continuation of the analytical procedure. But at the moment such an exploration would have been doomed to failure because the explicit role situation was wholly dominated by the persistence of her sense of shame. She kept her face averted from me, and her whole attitude was one of shrinking away, as if she desired to be invisible. The shame of having revealed her intention to me and of having failed was reinforced by the memory of failures in the past. It was clear that some activity on my part was indicated in order to help her to master the overwhelming shame. But what role was to be chosen for this purpose? In this connection the expressions "ego support," "ego strengthening," "reassurance," and many others easily leap to mind. It is also precisely in relation to such maneuvers that our concepts are at their weakest.

The role I chose was related explicitly to the management of her shame. What she was expressing, it seemed to me, was her feeling that she had had little value in her father's eyes, and that she had just now made the discovery that she had very little in mine. I could have reassured her directly by denying this picture, by affirming my appreciation of her abilities in the area which she had just attempted. In other words, I could have redefined the explicit roles by letting her have an insight into my actual opinion of her intellectual performance. This is a perfectly feasible transaction in a psychotherapeutic procedure. The objection to it was that under the circumstances it would have appeared artificial, as if applied only to ease her pain. Instead of this, I pointed out that by placing me in her father's position, she neglected to explore the possibility of my seeing any values in her personality other than intellectual achievement. I tried to show her how her involvement with her father narrowed her view of herself and, reciprocally, the view that she could see others taking of her. In pursuing this line, my intention was to broaden the perspectives of her self-valuation. To accomplish this, I tentatively accepted the role of "appreciator," but I enlarged its range of application. In role-theory terms, I was working on the connection between her cultural values and the anxiety about values built into her personality by her unresolved relation with her father. As we discussed this area, her shame visibly decreased. The psychotherapeutic procedure restored the equilibrium in our relations with each other.

In my view, this procedure illustrates one of the principal contrasts in method and goal between psychotherapy and psychoanalysis. Whereas in the psychoanalytic procedure the explicit role assignment is refused by the doctor, in psychotherapy it is accepted but is redefined so that the patient is able to take a new view of himself and of others. This may be called reality interpretation, reassurance, or ego support, but the general principle is the same. It does not lead the patient to a discovery of his unconscious motivation nor to a clear realization of what his implicit role is, but it puts him on more secure ground so that the discovery is more easily made at a later time.

According to my experience and what I have been able to observe of the experience of others, both psychoanalytic and psychotherapeutic procedures may be indicated in the treatment of any patient. This is what makes it so difficult to draw hard and fast lines and what makes the discussions so confusing. Partly because of structural relations within the ego, and partly because of the socioeconomic situation of the patient and the amount of time he can give to the treatment, it is possible to engage in predominantly psychoanalytic transactions with some patients, while with others psychotherapeutic procedures are what is principally required. In any event such quantitative distinctions are relative rather than absolute. If the concrete procedural distinction can be made exact, and if any treatment can be assumed to contain variable quantities of both procedures, then the choice of terms to apply to the over-all relation with any particular patient — that is, Is the patient "in psychoanalysis" or "in psychotherapy"? — becomes less controversial.

In conclusion, it should be said that this presentation of role theory overlooks many important technical and theoretical aspects of psychotherapeutic and psychoanalytic method. I do not know if it has anything to add to psychodynamic theory other than the possibility of greater precision in the examination of the details of the treatment process. But in view of the difficulties of assembling the vast array of data accumulated in the course of a patient's treatment and of relating the data to precise theory, this approach seems deserving of further exploration.

TEN

Cultural Aspects of Transference

In discussing some of the cultural aspects of transference and countertransference as these phenomena appear in the course of psychotherapy, I would like to leave out classical psychoanalysis. Readers of the previous chapters about the research carried on by Florence Kluckhohn and myself with a number of co-workers will understand why. My information regarding cultural influences has been gathered in a non-classical framework: mainly through the investigation of the impact of cultural variations on interpersonal relations within whole families and on the psychologic adjustment of family members.

In all cases we maintained contact with the families as a whole; and in the case of "sick" families in our research sample, contact was carried on through psychotherapy with the mother, father, and at least one child. Because of our interest in observing social role conflicts in the family, individual interviews in the clinic were supplemented by visits to the home. *(On role conflicts, see Spiegel 1957.)* These visits also permitted us to observe the functioning of the family as á unit. In addition, we at times attended family celebrations, accompanied the father to his place of work, and conducted therapeutic interviews in unusual places such as trucks and bars. It is apparent from this brief description that we have regarded the usual settings of psychotherapy — the office with its desk, chair couch, and other props — as merely one possibility for therapist-patient exchange. Thus the observations which form the basis for this report are drawn from a greater variety of therapeutic contacts than are usually included in the definition of therapy. The reasons for this flexibility will, I hope, become more evident after I have discussed the various cultural issues involved.

One other introductory point ought to be made, although it too has been touched upon in previous chapters. Namely, in recent decades cultural anthropologists have brought to everyone's attention the great variety in patterns of living and in basic values throughout the world. As Florence Kluckhohn stated, cross-cultural research demonstrates that, although people everywhere face much the same problems and choices, they do not choose the same solutions. *(Kluckhohn and Strodtbeck 1961)* Moreover, it has been shown that the cultural value orientations guiding these solutions are not superficial; nor are they present in conscious awareness. On the contrary, although they pervade every area of thought and activity, they can usually be formulated only in the most fragmentary fashion, if at all. They thus constitute an example of what has been called "behavior without awareness." *(Adams 1957)* This phrase refers to the making of an unconscious discrimination between two or more choices of behavior when the act of discrimination cannot be brought to the status of a conscious report because it has never at any time existed in consciousness. Since the value orientations of a culture are outside of awareness to begin with and are learned in childhood only through their indirect influence on conscious behavior, they can be expected to have a powerful effect on the therapeutic relationship.

Let us now turn to some of the considerations governing the appearance of transference and countertransference behavior within the psychotherapeutic situation.[1] The word transference generally denotes behavior which is clearly an inappropriate response to the behavior of the therapist and which functions as a resistance to therapy. It is understood to derive from some aspect of the child-

---

[1] I am here ignoring the confusions and controversies over the exact meanings of the words "transference" and "countertransference" which have troubled the literature on these subjects. Excellent historical reviews of the semantic and conceptual problems involved have been published by Orr in 1954 and by Zetzel in 1956. The topic is further complicated by the almost complete absence of any discussion of the countertransference in the literature of psychotherapy, as distinct from psychoanalysis.

hood relation with a parent or some other significant person. It is assumed that the memory of this earlier relationship has been repressed but that the patient hopes to recapture with the therapist some of the actual or hoped-for satisfactions of the original relationship. It is one of the aims of treatment to recover the repressed memory, wish, or fantasy and thus to dissipate the transference behavior.

There is little to be added to these considerations where the therapist's countertransference is concerned. Countertransference describes an attitude in the therapist — whether or not it is actually manifested in action — which is inappropriate and unrealistically related to the current behavior of the patient. It is therefore presumed to have its origin in an incompletely resolved childhood relation or wish. The principal difference is that the therapist alone has responsibility for identifying his countertransference responses and for exploring their significance.

An objection may be raised that these considerations have been developed in the context of the standard psychoanalytic technique and that they cannot be applied without modification to the therapist-patient relation in psychotherapy. The objection derives from the fact that the heightened activity of the therapist and the relative paucity of his information make it much more difficult to keep track of what aspects of the mutual transaction either partner may be responding to. I agree with this objection. However, the fact remains that transference and countertransference responses do occur in psychotherapy and must be dealt with in some way. I believe that the point of view which I am about to propose may represent an auxiliary tool for identifying and controlling such responses.

Let me first ask in what way are we to understand the meaning of the word "reality" as used in psychotherapy? Reality is a slippery concept, and the implicit assumptions buried in it are usually left unexamined. The best way of getting at whatever reality may mean in the context of psychotherapy is through an examination of the most general and standardized expectations established by professional practice for the behavior of the therapist and of the patient.

Looking first at the patient, I think it is fair to say that the person is expected to tell as much about himself as he is able. He is expected to work toward a recovery from his difficulties in a responsible way without depending on outside help from his family or friends. It is hoped that he will not withhold important information or refuse to discuss certain topics because of loyalty to external persons, beliefs, or institutions. It is expected that he will want, for the sake of his own emotional health and maturity, to become as autonomous and as independent in the making of choices and decisions as is possible, considering his life circumstances. In connection with this personal aim, it is expected that he will wish to have a future different from his past and present and that he will wish to take individual responsibility for seeing that it is different. It is assumed that he will perceive the therapist as a professional person who has no ax to grind and nothing to contribute to him but his technical ability. It is assumed that the patient either begins with or soon develops confidence in the benefits to be expected from communication, from insight into himself, and from the use of words rather than physical action in expressing himself. Finally, it is hoped that he will be able to limit his expressive emotional behavior, both within and without the treatment situation, so that he escapes neither from his thoughts and memories through too much overt action nor from his feelings through too much inhibition of action.

These are the goals set up professionally for the patient. Because of the operations of "resistance," it is not expected that the patient will actually be able to adhere consistently to these standards. On the contrary, it is believed that a large amount of treatment time will be spent in discovering why he is unable to behave in accordance with such goals. Nevertheless, it is hoped that by the time the treatment has ended, he will have *achieved* many, if not all, of them. For these are the standards, in this country, of what is called "mental health." It should also be clear by now that they represent, in vivid detail, the value orientations of the American middle-class family.

Now let us look at the expectations for the psychotherapist. It is expected that, like any expert or professional person, he will confine his activity with the patient to serious, responsible work on the patient's problems. In connection with the "work-oriented" relation he has with the patient, he is expected to exclude the ordinary social, recreational, and personal aspects of human relations. Though he is permitted a modicum of so-called "educative" activity, he is expected to refrain from influencing the patient in accordance with his own personal, as opposed to professional, goals, standards, or values. Indeed, he is expected to display a "benevolent neutrality" in this area, neither approving nor disapproving anything the patient says or does. In the place of a value

327

attitude, he is to substitute "reality testing," helping the patient to discover the actual consequences in "external reality" and in the "reality" of the treatment situation of anything the patient does, feels, or thinks. This neutral attitude with respect both to the good and the evil in the patient's behavior is maintained for the sake of helping the patient obtain maximum autonomy and independence in the formulation of his own goals and standards. He is expected to believe firmly in the patient's capacity to master his problems, neither overestimating nor underestimating the degree to which actual change is possible. Concerning the probability of change, the therapist is expected to keep a weather eye on the future but to concentrate mostly on the past and the present. There is some difference of opinion and even controversy as to whether the past or the present is to be given greater consideration, but most therapists would emphasize a balanced perspective between the two.

Such controversy, however, is indicative of a wider area of tension and indecision in the definition of the therapist's role. This has to do with the degree to which he should be free to change or modify the techniques he uses. On the one hand, he is expected to express his individuality in the moment-to-moment exercises of his technique. But on the other hand, he is expected to preserve the theories, concepts, and techniques inherited from the past. Accordingly, he inevitably experiences some conflict between the conservative and the experimental aspects of his role. Furthermore, the tension between these two contradictory goals is heightened by the structure of the organizations with which he is affiliated. These organizations, such as hospitals, clinics, and professional associations tend to be more hierarchically structured and more conservative of the past than is altogether congruous with the goals of scientific and technical activity.

If one scrutinizes this description of the standards for the "reality" structure of the therapist's behavior, it becomes evident that they, too, are guided by the American middle-class value orientations. Slight variations appear in the *Man-nature,* the *Relational,* and the *Time* orientations. The first emphasizes the intensely neutral attitude toward good and evil more than is characteristic of the American middle-class family at the present time. The relational orientation gives a stronger stress to the Lineal structure than one finds in middle-class values and is probably representative of a value conflict in this orientation. Similarly, the therapist is expected to carry on his technique in an independent and individualistic way but not to violate the canons of theory and practice imposed by the

328

hierarchically structured organizations to which he belongs. In the same vein the time orientation stresses the tradition and importance of the past somewhat more than is called for in American middle-class values.

In spite of these mild incongruities between the values governing the definition of "reality" for the patient and for the therapist, the fit is on the whole a fairly good one. The roles are matched to each other on the basis of their conformity with the dominant American middle-class values. On this basis, it can then be stated that transference and countertransference phenomena will be identified, insofar as they have cultural determinants, on the basis of their departure from these value orientations. This means that resistance, from the cultural point of view, is resistance against dominant American values. One might say, without being altogether facetious, that to resist is to be un-American!

Although this statement of the cultural determinants of transference and countertransference resistance may sound overgeneralized, it is certainly not unexpected, nor does it require any apology or defense. Psychotherapy is a scientific and technical procedure and it is only natural that it should be based on the same set of values which govern the socio-economic class most representative of the scientific and technical outlook of the society as a whole. It may even turn out to be the case that the slight incongruity in the values governing the two roles is necessary to the maintenance of an optimum tension between the patient and therapist.

Good as the matching of the roles may be at this professional level, there is abundant evidence that the goodness of fit is subject to several weaknesses which I would now like to examine. Theoretically, it could be expected to remain stable if both the patient and the therapist come from American middle-class families. In such cases there should be nearly perfect agreement about the "reality" toward which both parties are to strive. However, psychotherapists come from all classes and ethnic groups in this country, and, with the increasing development of mental health education and facilities, so do patients. So, one must ask, what happens when the value orientations of the family of origin of both the patient and therapist are discrepant with each other and with dominant American values?

There is a presumption that the therapist is spared from difficulties in this matter in two ways: through a personal psychoanalysis and through identification with the professional values and goals which I have just described. A personal analysis is designed to free the therapist from excessive bondage to his archaic superego, and for this reason he is supposed to be able to remain relatively flexible in the presence of values different from those in which he was trained as a child. Correlated with this lack of anxiety toward new or different values is the internalization of the "benevolent neutrality" and the other standards of the image of the perfect therapist.

Although there can be no doubt about the validity of both these assumptions, there is rightfully some skepticism about the extent to which the therapist can actually be freed of his original values. The experiences my colleagues and I have had working with patients whose cultural backgrounds differed greatly from our own suggest that the value discrepancy sets up a very complicated strain within the therapist. The conflict between the original values of the patient and the original values of the therapist stimulates a strain between the therapist's archaic superego and his new, professional identifications. A three-way conflict is precipitated in him which becomes fertile soil for the growth of countertransference difficulties. But before examining the details of such value conflicts and their consequences, let us turn to the patient and look at the difficulties he may experience on contact with the therapist.

For purposes of illustration, let us take a father in one of our Irish-American families. How will he perceive the "reality" of the behavior which the therapist expects of him? He is expected to tell everything he knows about himself. But his training is that one does not tell intimate details about oneself even to family or friends, much less a total stranger. If the details are shameful or guilt-ridden, one doesn't even admit such things to oneself. They are too suffused with evil, and there are only two ways to handle such things: either deny their existence or confess them to a properly constituted authority, such as a priest. But isn't the therapist such a properly constituted authority, somewhat different from a priest, perhaps, but a person entitled to hear such things? Certainly not. By virtue of what organization and what authorization would he possess such a right? I must confess that when we hear this question, which is usually implicit rather than directly stated, we are tempted to answer, "On the authority of Freud, the American Psychiatric Association, and the Children's Hospital!" However, even this answer would not help, since these authorities and organizations are already perceived as either unknown or possibly sinful. To the Lineal values of the Irish-American, any hierarchy is better than no hierarchy at all, but one that is unknown or remote is likely to be regarded as hostile until it has proved itself otherwise.

But, one might well ask, how about the "benevolent neutrality?" Won't this neutral attitude help to counteract the fear of sinfulness and its associated hostility to the sinner? Unfortunately, the answer is again no. In the perceptions of the Irish-American patient, such an attitude is hypocritical. It smacks of the benevolence of the upper classes toward the "deserving poor." It signifies merely that one's real feelings remain undeclared behind a concealing mask of condescension. Hiding one's real feelings is a familiar affair and, according to his experience, is inevitably followed by brutal frankness when it is least expected. So this "neutrality" is merely a matter of waiting for the ax to fall.

Still, looking at the problems this presents to the therapist, one might ask whether it is really so different from run-of-the-mill difficulties which always crop up at the beginning of therapy. Won't the suffering experienced by the patient encourage him to continue with therapy despite these hurdles? There are two answers to this question. In the first place, if the patient is the father of a disturbed child, he may very well not experience much suffering in his own personality. The only emotional disturbance he may be aware of is that caused him by his child's illness. But, secondly, even if he is aware of inner disturbance, this will probably not in itself be sufficient to make him want to work hard on the overcoming of obstacles. Hard work in an independent, self-responsible way for the sake of long-distance goals has not been a part of his value training. In this area, the Present time, Being, Lineal value structure are all firmly opposed to psychotherapy as understood by the therapist. Such a patient is not used to working on his own problems for the sake of vague future gains. He is accustomed to being told what to do, right now, in the present. Therefore he repeatedly asks the therapist what he is supposed to be doing, and, if he is not told, he is paralyzed. He feels that nothing is happening and he is wasting his time. And, even if the therapist, sensing this hopelessness, tries repeatedly to instruct him on how to conduct himself in the interview, this will prove to be of little help. For the Subjugation-to-nature and Present time orientation lead the patient to see little possibility of change or improvement in the future. What will be, will be, and evil must be punished. In fact, the only hope of the future, as he sees it, is to cling grimly to the sense of evil, wistful for forgiveness, but never abandoning the sense of the power of evil, since this is his only guide to realistic conduct.

Exposed to these responses, which constitute the "reality" of the patient, how will the therapist conduct himself? For a while he may identify the patient's response as "resistance" and keep on trying to use his usual techniques. However, after a variable length of time, he will feel intensely frustrated. This frustration will stimulate the three-way conflict which I have already mentioned. On the one hand, his therapeutic values will order him to stick to his technique. The strong Mastery-over-nature position will make him feel guilty if he wants to stop the treatment before the patient appears ready to quit. For the American therapist, unlike the European, feels that no patient or situation should be identified as "untreatable," at least until all possibilities have been exhausted.[2] But, if he continues under the guidance of these values, he will reach a stalemate, not being able to make progress or to terminate treatment. Meanwhile, the original values attached to his archaic superego tend more and more to assert themselves into the gap created by the stalemate. As this happens, a conflict develops between his original values and his newer therapeutic values. In addition, a conflict develops between his original values and the values on which the patient is acting. Since there already exists a conflict between his therapeutic values and the values which are guiding the patient, his ego is caught in a three-cornered struggle which in most cases proves too much for its integrative capacity. When this point has been reached, the archaic superego wins the struggle, though usually concealing its activity behind the facade of the therapeutic superego.

For example, suppose the therapist treating an Irish-American comes from a Jewish-American background. The values of this culture, insofar as they can be discerned at present, are characterized by the first-order position of Subjugation-to-nature, Future Time, Doing, and Collaterality. Thus his Doing and Future Time orientations clash violently, with the Being, Present Time behavior of the patient. The Subjugation-to-nature orientation of patient and therapist coincide. Therefore he comes to feel more and more hostile to the patient for not making a sufficient effort, and comes to characterize this default as evil, just as he would originally have characterized such a trend within himself. As the patient comes to stand increasingly for a rejected and bad part of the therapist, his ego tends to give in by finding a way to characterize the patient

---

[2] See, for example, the contrast between the contributions of an American analyst, Leo Stone, and a British analyst, Anna Freud. The difference between the two analysts in value orientations as they are related to therapeutic indications is striking. (*Stone 1954; Freud 1954.*)

as deserving of rejection. However, the therapeutic part of his sugerego will still be strong enough to insist that such a rejection be justified on technical grounds, or at least clothed in professional jargon. The final resolution of his inner conflict is obtained through a termination of treatment on the grounds that the patient is too immature, too narcissistic, too dependent, too well defended, or any of a multitude of expressions which indicate that he has found the patient burdensome.

Is this description too cynical or too cavalier in respect to the psychodynamic issues? The question is valid, because there is always a danger of explaining too much through the use of a cultural analysis. Certainly, much more is involved in the development of the transference-countertransference impasse than the value content of the superegos of the patient and therapist. I do not wish to ignore the complex questions of ego psychology with which the conflict in cultural values is also associated.

While it is perfectly true that one aspect of the Irish-American patient's resistance is associated with the Subjugation-to-nature value position, this is by no means the whole story. The value orientation accounts for the patient's resignation, his inability to conceive of the possibility of change, in the cognitive area. A real change within the personality has not been in his experience, and he just doesn't see that it is possible. However, there is an emotional as well as a cognitive side to this kind of resistance. On the emotional side it is associated with the identification with the angry, critical parents. The attachment to the internalized parental images is intensely ambivalent and masochistically satisfying. The treasuring of the sense of sin is, from one point of view, a conscious derivative of the highly libidinal, unconscious cathexis of the internalized, scolding parents. In addition, the scolding parent within becomes a tender forgiving parent whenever a confession takes place. The alternation between sinning and confessing is necessary to the maintenance of the internal, libidinal dynamics. Furthermore, sinning or the alerting of the sense of sin in the external object is the primary way of getting the object's attention.

These considerations are directly pertinent to the transference problem in the management of such a patient. It is not only that the patient remains cognitively unaware of the possibility of change. In addition he has no wish to change in the direction which the therapist expects him to. Giving up the crushing sense of sin means, essentially, renouncing the relation with the internalized parents. This might be possible if the therapist could capture the attention

333

of the patient. It is an accepted fact that psychotherapy cannot take place without the establishment of at least a minimum positive transference. But the neutrality valued by the therapist operates precisely at this point to prevent the establishment of a positive transference. The patient feels he cannot get the therapist's attention. Furthermore, he has no other reason to care about the therapist since the latter is not associated with any of his prestige systems or organizations. As a result he withdraws, and the therapist then realizes that *he* cannot get the *patient's* attention. This is the beginning of the therapeutic impasse.

There are several possibilities for handling this impasse. One can resign oneself to the acceptance of defeat. The conclusion then offers itself that not everyone can profit from psychotherapy and that it is important not to let therapeutic ambition overrule good diagnostic judgment. This view involves a shift from the Mastery-over-nature position which is difficult for most Americans to effect. Another possibility is to persist, doggedly, neither modifying the technique of psychotherapy nor abandoning the attempt to help. Some Irish-American families have made a sufficient transition to dominant American values so that they may be able to respond to the standard techniques. However, the payoff in success is low, and thus the price of sticking to the Mastery-over-nature position in this fashion is very high. It can be done only by extremely patient therapists who have a high tolerance for frustration.

A third alternative preserves the Mastery-over-nature position but abandons the Past time orientation insofar as this inhibits change and experimentation. This is the approach we adopted in our work with Irish-American patients. We experimented with various methods for overcoming the resistance and for establishing a positive transference so that we could be in a position to exert some psychotherapeutic influence. The steps we took, however, were not set up on the basis of trial and error, but arose out of our theoretic point of view. We had already become convinced of the close connection between the pathology of the individual and the interpersonal and cultural value relations within the family. But the modifications which we adopted were made primarily for the sake of carrying on research. Only gradually and secondarily did we perceive their relevance for the handling of transference and countertransference problems.

Our approach emphasized the importance of the extended family and the community to the functioning of the individual. Although therapy concentrated mainly on the mother, father and child, we attempted to see and make ourselves known to a wide assortment of relatives. This meant that we became assimilated, to a certain extent, in the Lineal chains of influence which bore upon the pathologic deviations in the family members. In addition, members of the therapeutic team became known, not simply as individuals, but also as members of a readily identifiable organization. This approximation of individuals and organizations reduced the fear of the strange, unknown group and, simultaneously, raised its prestige. At the same time, we showed our willingness to depart from the routine of regular office appointments whenever this was necessary. Seeing family members when and where they were available was closer to the Present time and Being orientations. Therefore it was more apt to be perceived as a valid act of attention than strict adherence to a Future-oriented appointment book and other bureaucratic routines.

In further validation of the Irish-American value orientations, we relaxed to a considerable extent the principle of nonreciprocity. We answered personal questions about ourselves and did not hesitate to reveal our own value attitudes upon a variety of issues. Although our therapeutic standards made us somewhat uneasy about such conduct, we gradually became more comfortable with it, especially as we came to understand how the Irish-American patient perceives nonreciprocity. Failing to answer a question, directing it back to the patient, or interpreting it are perceived as evasive maneuvers. Withholding a personal attitude is seen as having something to be ashamed of. Concealment, evasion, and denial are so ubiquitous in Irish-American culture that they are easily projected to the therapist. Such projections can be handled by interpretation only after the relationship has been established.

Finally, we came to reinterpret the meaning of "benevolent neutrality." As ordinarily understood, this principle involves the adoption of a strictly neutral attitude with respect to the matters about which the patient feels guilty or ashamed. We found that if the impulses of which the patient is ashamed would also make us feel ashamed if discovered within ourselves, it is best to be quite frank about it. And vice versa. That is to say that, if his impulses would leave us truly neutral and unmoved, we have to be frank about that, too. Since the sense of sin is a primary vector of interpersonal feeling, it cannot be hidden from those who are highly sensitive to its manifestations. Thus the reinterpretation of "benevolent neutrality" involves the recognition and admission that we all think of ourselves as sinners in some way. On this basis, denial is more easily renounced and the evil impulse more easily held in consciousness because the therapist is seen as someone who recognizes the patient's problem and has established his right to deal with it. This point of view also makes it easier to deal with the characteristic denial through the use of humor. Since the therapist is not denying anything through the assumption of "neutrality," he can appreciate the humor and still insist on the expression of the feelings it is meant to conceal.

These are the major modifications which we used in our research. While the results were not spectacular, we gained the conviction that we were able to establish and maintain therapeutic contact with patients who would otherwise have been rejected or would have dropped out of treatment. We were able to produce small increases in insight in individual family members. We were impressed with the fact that a small gain in one or two family members was registered as a large gain in the total functioning of the family.

I hope it is clear that the modifications in approach which I have described are not to be considered general prescriptions for the field of psychotherapy as a whole. On the contrary, the value of a cultural analysis of the psychotherapeutic situation is that it clarifies the relation between variations in technique and the specific transference (and countertransference) responses which can be expected from members of different cultural groups. The general principle that emerges from this point of view is that modifications in technique should be rationally adapted to the varieties of cultural value orientations which exist among patients. A corollary of this proposition is the need, in the future, to give as much consideration to problems of cultural dynamics as has been given, in the past, to purely psychologic processes. It is my firm belief that such a program is necessary if we have to extend the range of effectiveness of psychotherapy to groups who have, up till now, proved refractory in the face of our best efforts.

Part V

Transactions in Community Conflict

The directions Spiegel has taken in his current work are reflected in the four chapters which comprise this final section. Here he broadens his inquiry from individual and family pathology to the general disorder in contemporary society. The various theories brought forth to explain contemporary violence are reviewed. These theories invariably locate the cause of social conflict in either the inadequate "system" or in the pathology of individuals comprising it. Little attention is paid to the value discrepancies that characterize opposing segments of our society such as the "youth" and the "establishment." It is only when these differences in value orientation are identified that appropriate strategies can be designed to bring about conflict resolution and effect a reequilibrium in the social system. Efforts at reform that are limited to "system change" cannot be successful without a concomitant shift in values.

The implications of these considerations, derived from a transactional theoretical framework, are immediately relevant to the "social change" characterizing the mental health field in the United States. The shift to community mental health and "community control" involves radical value change that must be identified and dealt with if this movement is to be successful. A reorganization of the mental health delivery system alone, without an effort to deal *with the necessary and concomitant value changes on which it is based can only result in frustration and failure for those undertaking it.*

ELEVEN

Toward a Theory of Collective Violence

In our search for appropriate ways to define the main features of a historical epoch we often use the big, broad label. Thus the 18th century is called the Age of Reason, the early 19th century the Age of Romanticism, and the late 19th century the Age of Materialism. Continuing this imagery into the 20th century, we can, with some plausibility, characterize more recent times in terms of thirty-year periods. The period from 1900 to 1930 could be called, for the United States at any rate, the "Age of Optimism," reflected in self-confident national slogans as "Make the world safe for democracy." It was a time in which, despite the temporary setbacks of war, depression, or race riots, change always seemed to be for the best. In contrast, the period from 1930 to 1960 has been called the Age of Anxiety. Because of the Great Depression, the rise of Fascism, World War II, the collapse of the colonial powers, and the uneasy tension between the Communist and non-Communist worlds, national self-confidence was replaced with increasing self-doubt. Social change seemed now to be sometimes out of control and frequently for the worse. Though traces of hope remained attached to such worldwide efforts of reconstruction as the United Nations, the newly emerging nations, and aid to underdeveloped countries, the national mood was one of uncertainty and personal anxiety.

Since 1960, however, the increased turbulence both within and between nations has introduced a new note into national life — anger, recrimination, and aggressive behavior between individuals and groups. A corresponding change in national self-awareness gives rise to the notion that we are at this moment living in the "Age of Violence." Certainly, such a designation is suggested by the public media, in political oratory, and in the minds of citizens troubled by campus riots, civil disorder, and the fear of violence in the streets.

Although it may be plausible, from the viewpoint of national imagery, to call the period we are passing through an Age of Violence, the title may not necessarily be accurate or helpful. In fact, it raises many questions. What is meant by the word "violence"? What moral or ethical assumptions are embedded in such a characterization? What social and psychological processes can account for an increase in personal and collective aggression, if indeed such an increase can actually be demonstrated?

In this chapter I shall attempt some partial and temporary answers to these questions.

During the Age of Anxiety, a good deal of psychosomatic and psychiatric research was based on the concept of "stress," an internally experienced correlate of anxiety. Similarly, in the sociological and anthropological literature considerable emphasis was placed on processes of integration and equilibrium within social systems. Social change and the pathologies of social systems, if considered at all, were treated as instances of social "strain" to be overcome by a process of internal readjustment.

But in the current, somewhat more heated climate of research, both psychological and social research have shifted, in some degree, to more externally defined problems of behavior. Where individual behavior is concerned, there is an increased focus on drug use, on hippies and youthful activists or rebels, and on the relation of the person to his family, organizational, or community environment. At the social level, interest has shifted to a greater examination of social problems and the need for social change. Concurrently, we are acutely aware that we lack not only knowledge for determining desirable directions of such change but also the techniques for bringing it about.

Although the shift from internal to external problems and from adjustment to reality to changing that reality should not be

340

overemphasized, this transformation does highlight the need for new definitions and concepts. Just as, during the thirties and forties, it was necessary to define "stress" and "anxiety" as accurately as possible, now it is of the greatest importance to define what we mean by the terms "aggression" and "violence."

All definitions tend to sound dry and academic. Nevertheless, significant consequences flow from them. Although violence may be defined narrowly or broadly, we have chosen a narrow one which goes as follows: violence lies at the extreme end of a spectrum of aggressive behavior. It is characterized by acts of physical force aimed at the severe injury or destruction of persons, objects, or organizations. A second defining feature is concerned with timing and tempo, usually expressed as "explosiveness." Violent behavior, in other words, is aggression released fully and abruptly and usually in a state of high energy arousal.

The definition rules out much behavior often included when the word occurs in ordinary speech or in the popular press. For example, it excludes sin and evil in general as well as such particular forms of evil as injustice, exploitation, deprivation, defamation, and starvation. It excludes brutalizing social arrangements not characterized by the use of physical force.

Many people, particularly social activists, are unhappy with such a limited definition. For example, they prefer to describe our society as violent because it is responsible for so much social injustice. From the point of view of research, however, it seems preferable to restrict the behavior to be studied and to ask that other forms of undesirable social behavior, such as injustice and exploitation, be considered separately.

A more serious problem arising from the narrow definition concerns destructive force used in lower-keyed or nonexplosive ways — for example, torture, poisoning, and exile. Such acts could be conceived as lying within the spectrum of aggressive behavior just short of violence. A graphic or linear concept of this sort, however, becomes quite arbitrary in the absence of a definition of aggression, and we all know how difficult it has been, in the past, to define the word "aggression."

Despite the difficulties, the need for a workable concept of aggression geared to the concept of violence is so great that it seems important to formulate a definition for this purpose. Accordingly, the following formula is proposed: aggression is defined as behavior involving the use of force or its symbolic equivalent to effect an outcome in line with the intentions or goals of an aggressor acting against the intentions or goals of an adversary. It usually, but not always, occurs in an agonistic situation characterized by a conflict of interest.

This definition is by design quite broad. It leaves open the character, intensity, and aim of the force used to secure compliance from an opponent. Under these general terms, aggression can vary along a continuum from acts of simple assertion requiring a minimal use of force, at one pole, to violence, as defined above, at the other. It also leaves open the techniques — such as a formal challenge, a surprise attack, or a conspiracy — used to set up adversary relations. Finally, it leaves open the timing of the behavior with respect to securing compliance or noncompliance. For example, the show of real or symbolic force used to secure compliance in advance of a struggle we call threat-behavior, just as we call force used after the loss of a contest revenge-behavior.

Two significant consequences proceed from this formulation. First, a great deal of aggressive behavior is nonviolent in character. Even in the purely physical realm, such acts as pushing, holding, blocking, restraining, constraining, confining, and depriving, though aggressive, are nonviolent. Considering the heated debates over who has done what to whom in the streets of our cities — and on our college campuses — it is of the greatest importance to distinguish between violence, on the one hand, and aggression, no matter how disruptive, on the other hand.

The second consequence of our formulation consists of an avoidance of the question of whether aggression is to be regarded as instinctual or learned behavior. It must represent a combination of both elements. Vexing images — such as man the killer-ape struggling to control his innate violence, or man as the noble savage taught to be violent by an aggressive civilization — become irrelevant. Aggression as the use of force to overcome obstacles is innate behavior that man shares with most living species. Violence as the maximum arousal of aggression for destructive purposes, including the killing of members of one's own species, is by the same token, an innate behavior potentially capable of being aroused in all men. But the internal, biological conditions necessary for arousal are ordinarily under the control of external, environmental contingencies. If this view is correct, then what is sorely needed is research directed at investigating the feedback relations between the mechanisms of biological arousal, particularly in childhood, and the environmental controls, both instigating and inhibiting, over aggressive behavior.

I should now like to turn to the second part of such circular, feedback mechanisms: the question of environmental instigators and inhibitors. Clearly, the first level of environmental control over the behavior of man is based on morality and ethics. Ethical standards govern what is regarded as acceptable or unacceptable behavior, both for the individual and the group. Our question, then, must read as follows. Is there an ethic of violence, known and subscribed to by most members of society?

Despite an abundance of ethical statements from a variety of religious and philosophical contexts, there exists no systematic analysis of ethical principles in this area. What does exist, apparently, is a vast confusion — a state of contradiction bordering on chaos — which has been more or less internalized by most members of American society. Three ethical or quasi-ethical positions can be discerned within the confusion. The first can be called "negative absolutism." This position is taken by persons who say that violence is never justified. A moral posture of negative absolutism is quite familiar to Americans under the label of pacifism. It is also the position of Quakers and some other religious sects: for them, violence between nations, groups, or individuals is *never*, under any circumstances, justified.

The second ethical position, "positive absolutism," is not so directly known to Americans, but it has been well articulated by the French social philosopher Georges Sorel in his book *Reflections on Violence*. Sorel postulated that violence is a social good. Those who are fit to govern are those who understand and know how to use violence. The ability to employ violence intelligently is what separates the elite of any historical epoch from the dull, passive, decadent, and corrupt bourgeoisie. Hitler with his boast, "We *are* savages; we're proud of being savages!" was an intellectual offspring of Sorel, as was Mussolini with his advocacy of national "audacity," along with the Italian poet and political adventurer Gabriele D'Annunzio, who emphasized the creative, releasing functions of violence, daring, and militant pugnacity.

In contrast to these two absolutist positions, most Americans tend to endorse a relative one. According to relative principles, violence is generally condemned but can be justified under certain conditions — for example, in the service of "self-defense." Violence on behalf of an indisputably just cause — for example, a "war of national liberation" — is another possible basis of exemption. The guiding principle is flexibility; permission to use violence depends upon conditions, though there is often a notable lack

343

of consensus about just what conditions can be used to excuse the use of violence.

The paralyzing effects of confusion and contradiction are nowhere more conspicuous than in the confrontation of absolutist and relativist ethical principles. From the point of view of the relativist, the position of negative absolutism is exceedingly dangerous. How would any individual or group ever overcome injustice, escape exploitation, or overcome oppression if violence were not permitted? So far as the ethical position of positive absolutism is concerned, to the relativist this posture seems to promote perpetual destruction and killing as pugnacious aggressors flex their muscles and deploy their weaponry against each other, utterly without moral controls, in a state of constant vendetta.

But, to the absolutists, the relativist position seems equally dangerous; like a rubber band, it can be indefinitely stretched and extended to justify continuous escalations of violence. Today we have to fight in a just cause in Vietnam, tomorrow in China, the day after that the whole Communist world? If we exonerate ghetto rioters on the basis of "white racism" in Watts, won't the violence break out in Dayton, in Newark, in Detroit?

To such oppositions in ethical position at the overtly moral level, we must add a new component of environmental control: the recently articulated "therapeutic" positions. Here again we encounter an unyielding contradiction between positive and negative positions. The negative therapeutic position holds that an individual or a society displays violence because of illness. The violent society is a sick society; the violent person is disturbed. Thus professional help, on the part of psychiatrists or social therapists, is required. The positive therapeutic position, on the other hand, holds that violence itself is therapeutic, a position clearly articulated by the black psychiatrist Franz Fanon in *The Wretched of the Earth*. An oppressed people or a mistreated person, according to this view, will usually identify with the aggressor and as an inevitable result display depression, apathy, and alienation. If, however, identification *of* the aggressor is substituted for identification *with* the aggressor, then the victim will fight the oppressor and overcome both his depression and his social inferiority.

This contradiction of guiding principles again generates seemingly insoluble problems. From the viewpoint of the positive therapeutic principle, the negative position is both degrading and unrealistic. What is to become of our national heroes if violence is a sign of illness? Was George Washington sick because he led

344

the violent action which freed our nation from the English Crown? Were the colonies sick because they fought the British at Lexington and Concord?

To those who subscribe to the negative therapeutic position, however, the positive position seems a prescription for paranoia. How is a sense of reality to be established if any frustration or grievance or feeling of inferiority is to be ascribed to some real or fictitious oppressor? Doesn't this position sanction a wild spree of impulse gratification? Of the fight of all against all?

There appears to be no way of reconciling these moral contradictions. Ethical principles, it would seem, can be found to justify almost any line of conduct. Perhaps this means that morality and its embodiment in law is a primitive — or at least a prescientific — form of social control. If so, then we obviously must search for more rational or objective principles of environmental control. But is research, specifically behavioral research in this case, actually a realm in which it is possible to assume such a responsibility?

This question may be partially answered by briefly examining some of our more salient episodes of civil disorder. Shays' Rebellion, a revolt of poor farmers on the western frontier of Massachusetts in 1786, is typical of late 18th century violence. The farmers were resentful of the unjust tax laws passed by the Massachusetts legislature (and the subsequent jailing of many farmers for debt). Led by Daniel Shays, the farmers seized law courts and prevented the legal apparatus from functioning. Then, as now, the wealthy members of the legislature underestimated both the burden imposed upon the farmers and their capacity for resisting it. Surprised and frightened by the farmers' reaction, the power structure — as we say — got the message and passed fairer tax laws. Similar uprisings occurred in other parts of the Eastern seaboard, generally with a successful outcome for the protesting parties.

The years from 1830 to 1850 were particularly marked by attacks by Protestants upon Irish-Catholics. Led by the Native American Party, the Protestant establishment vilified Irish-Americans as papists — unpatriotic foreigners who were both an economic and a moral threat. Protestant rumor and press depicted Catholic institutions as havens for sexual license and abuse. Consequently, in August of 1834, when a disturbed nun left her Ursuline convent in Charlestown, Massachusetts, an aroused citizenry burned the convent to the ground — despite the knowledge that the nun had reconsidered and returned to the convent. In Philadelphia, the city of brotherly love, at least thirteen persons were killed and fifty injured during an anti-Catholic riot in July 1844.

Although reliable statistics are unavailable, the New York City Draft Riot of 1863 undoubtedly ranks as our most violent single episode. Angered by the exemption clause in the Conscription Act which permitted the wealthy to escape the draft by the payment of $300, poor people rose up in wrath directed not only at the Republican Party and the police, but also at the blacks, who were held responsible for the war in addition to their economic threat to working class whites. For three days the city was ravaged by mobs numbering in the thousands. Army units — some returning from Gettysburg — succeeded in quelling the disorder which claimed at least 300 lives and perhaps as many as 1,000.

Among California's poor white population of the 1870's, racism, combined with economic threats, led to anti-Chinese riots. During the riot in Los Angeles in October of 1871, eighteen Chinese were killed. Similar riots occurred in 1877 in San Francisco, and in 1885 in Rock Springs, Wyoming.

The long series of civil disorder arising from the movement for organized labor began in the 1870's, reached a peak of intensity in the 1890's, and disappeared only after the passage of the National Labor Relations legislation in the 1940's. At least ten people were killed and hundreds wounded during the strike at the Carnegie, Phipps and Company steel plant at Homestead, Pennsylvania in July 1892. During the Pullman Strike in June and July of 1894, 16,000 Federal troops were called out to control the disorders which, starting in Illinois, spread out over the country from Indiana to California.

The anti-Negro riots before, during, and after World War I were — taken as a group — probably the bloodiest and cruelest episode of American violence. In East St. Louis, Chicago, and elsewhere, whites viciously assailed blacks, clubbing, shooting, lynching, and mutilating while the police stood by and national guardsmen joined in. As in the West Coast anti-Chinese riots, racism combined with economic fears, and whites tried to drive black men, women, and children out of the neighborhood, out of the city, out of the way.

Since 1964 we have witnessed disorders involving black people seeking control of their ghetto communities and young people seeking more control over their own lives in their college communities. Though there has been less violence in this most recent episode of American violence — fewer deaths and fewer injuries

346

— the same themes of injustice, protest, and backlash which characterized previous episodes are visible.

Has the substance of protest varied over the years, or has the underlying problem remained the same despite its different manifestations? If we are to be concerned with the conditions governing the outbreak of collective disorder, this is an extremely important question.

The evidence would seem to suggest that civic disorder reflects a chronic social conflict, a basic flaw in the social structure of the United States. In previous writings I have described this strain as the incompatibility between our democratic ideals and our authoritarian practices. *(Spiegel 1968.)* The rights of man, equality among peoples, and the principle of representative government — the main items in the democratic ideology — have from the time of the Constitutional Convention in 1787 been pitted against an all-encompassing but largely masked authoritarianism modeled after the European social systems that the American Revolution was presumed to have broken away from. This concealed hierarchical structure of power has been maintained in two ways: (1) by the principle of exclusion of social groups from the decision-making process; and (2) by the operation of pyramidal, bureaucratic structures with power held at the top of the pyramid.

At the time of its formation, the American system of government was limited by six principles of inclusion and exclusion. Let us call this the WAMPAM structure of the social system. In order to have access to power one had to be:

1. White, excluding all who were red, yellow, or black;
2. Anglo-Saxon or of some closely related national background, excluding the Irish, the southern and central Europeans, and those from the Middle and Far East;
3. Middle-class or better, excluding the working class and the poor;
4. Protestant in religion, excluding all Catholics, Moslems, and Jews;
5. Adult, excluding all children and youths from the decision-making process; and
6. Male, excluding all females of whatever color, religion, or national background.

This was the political and social structure of our republic.

347

Whether a system so elitist in form and function can be called a democracy is doubtful. From the beginning these six structural principles were under attack from both sides — by the Reconstructivists who wanted to broaden them and by the Nativists who thought they were already too broad. The riot episodes I have discussed, including the present one, can be correlated with attempts by one or another excluded group to penetrate the elitist barrier in order to be admitted to the seats of power. In Shays' Rebellion, the poor began their struggle, one that has not yet been wholly successful. The anti-Catholic riots were meant to discourage the Irish from their bid for power, feeble as it was during the 1840's. In the New York City Draft Riot the poor and the Irish joined forces to limit the power of the wealthier Protestant establishment over the conscription issue. And so it went for the Orientals in California, for labor organizations all over the industrial North, and for black people in both the North and the South. A relatively weak Reconstructivist effort to enter the system was almost invariably met by a powerful and violent Nativist effort to keep them out. With the single exception of the Draft Riot, a more complicated case in any event, Reconstructivists have directed their violence mainly against property, such as buildings, equipment, and machinery. Nativists, on the other hand, have tended to direct their violence against persons, quite often in the form of frenzied and bloody massacres. Nativists have consistently held that the Reconstructivists "provoked" the violence, usually through nonviolent demonstrations and protests which were conveniently found to be illegal or simply annoying.

Though particular Reconstructivist efforts have been successful, they have not succeeded in changing the system. Irish and Italians, Jews and Catholics have been admitted into the power structures in ever greater numbers. Still, the Reconstructivists of one season become the Nativists of the next. Some Irish-American Catholics, some Jews, and some members of labor unions, forgetting the bitter struggles of their past, now resent the efforts of the poor, the blacks, and youth to enter the system and make their claim for power. The familiar objections of the past are leveled at each new group knocking loudly at the elitist barrier with their ever-present "demands." They are seen as upstarts, as unintelligent, unmotivated, lazy, untrainable, unmannerly, uncouth, and, above all, undeserving. The stamp of inferiority is pressed upon them, softened, to be sure, by humanitarian kindness, Christian forbearance, or therapeutic understanding. But to the excluded, a patronizing charity is little better, and may well be worse, than outright rejection.

This description may be slightly overstated. Not all Reconstructivists have turned nativistic after entering the system. There have always been some who, after having climbed the upper rungs of the social ladder, stretched down their hands to help those at the bottom of the heap, sometimes at considerable risk to their own positions. But such rescue operations, even when successful, have not changed the vertically stratified structure of the social system. They seem mainly to add new rungs at the bottom of the ladder.

When considering the conversion of Reconstructivists into Nativists in a previous publication, I asked why such a transformation should take place. *(Spiegel 1968.)* What psychological mechanisms, other than identification with the aggressor, could account for such a seemingly radical change? Before their penetration into the system, Reconstructivists of whatever historical epoch have usually been interested in adding their own cultural forms — their art, their speech patterns, their national heroes and holidays — to the native American stock of culture patterns. Such efforts have always been strongly resisted by the Nativists. To them, a broadening of this sort has meant a weakening, an introduction of un-American clannishness, at the least, the corruption of the moral fiber of the country, or, at the most, the "take-over" of the entire nation. Thus in the 1840's rumors were propagated by the Native American Party that the Catholic Church, including the Pope, was planning to take over the country. In the 1890's and again in the early 1920's, radical labor leaders — anarchists, syndicalists, socialists, or communists — were represented as planning the take-over. Today, radical youth and extremist student leaders are reported to be planning the destruction of the country in order to seize power. Let us grant that in the minds of a few revolutionaries these have been serious goals. Still, revolutionary or drastic change has never been a serious threat in our country. Therefore we must ask: how is it that, having had firsthand experience with the unrealistic nature of Nativist fears, recently arrived Reconstructivists can so quickly internalize these apocalyptic fantasies and direct them at the newest ranks of dissatisfied outcasts?

After much discussion and thought about this question, I have concluded that it has probably been wrongly posed. Rather than assuming that a change takes place, would we not be more correct to assume no change at all — that Reconstructivists have all along only wanted "a piece of the action," as it is phrased today? They have wished to penetrate the system but not to change it. In the process, to be sure, they have wanted to bring parts of their culture along while dropping or attenuating other parts. But, in the main, they have wanted to become as Americanized as possible as quickly as possible, to be given the chance of "making it" within the system as they view it. This would imply an easy acceptance, once entry was gained, of both the democratic ideological disguise and the authoritarian realities of the social system. If this is true, their protest all along was directed not at the elitist system per se but at their own exclusion from it.

If the foregoing analysis is correct, large-scale civil disorder will erupt whenever a group in an excluded category makes its historically appropriate bid for entry into the elitist system. There are, of course, particular determining conditions governing the local outbreaks of rioting. These have been dealt with in the Kerner Report and in previous publications from the Lemberg Center for the Study of Violence. But in general the environmental contingencies associated with the violence arise from the clash between a determined Reconstructivist campaign and an equally determined Nativist resistance. Since the resulting episodes of disorder produce no change in the underlying social conflict, their recurrence is inevitable. Given the tension between democratic slogans and elitist practices, oppressed ethnic and subcultural groups will initiate new episodes of disorder. There would seem to be no solution.

Recently, however, as if in response to such a pessimistic conclusion, various groups have pointed with increasing urgency to the need for dealing with the underlying social conflict. It is being suggested that what is usually talked about as social change, even rapid social change, is in fact an example of *Plus ça change, plus c'est la même chose*. For the most part, suggestions for real rather than delusory change are concerned with the need for remodeling the social and political structures which support the elitist system. While such a restructuring is of the greatest importance, current blueprints being offered for this purpose suffer from a certain vagueness combined with angry denunciations of the status quo. The New Left and militant student groups appear more certain about what is wrong than how to make things better.

The work of sociologists and cultural anthropologists has produced fairly convincing evidence that cultural value orientations and social institutions have reciprocal effects upon each other. I trust that earlier chapters about family structure and function as studied by Florence Kluckhohn and myself, using her theory of variations in value orientations, have demonstrated the importance of these interrelationships to family conflicts. It seems fruitful, therefore, to submit the chronic conflict between democratic and authoritarian values in our society to a more refined value analysis based on the Kluckhohn theoretical approach.

Of the four value orientation categories included in the Kluckhohn schema, only one, the Relational orientation will be used here. Although the Relational category is probably of key significance, I must stress that a full discussion of the current social conflict would require reference to all four categories.

The Relational value category deals with the issues I have discussed under the labels of democratic and authoritarian values but in a more complex fashion. It is concerned with the manner in which group decisions are arrived at and with the ordering of interpersonal relations within the group. To recapitulate, three possible arrangements for group decision-making are specified by the theory: the Individual, the Collateral, and the Lineal. Individualism is an arrangement in which each member of the group has the right — indeed, the obligation — to state his opinion, and the decision is made by a vote of the majority. In the Collateral arrangement effort is directed at reaching group consensus by a decision with which most group members can feel comfortable. In the Lineal arrangement decisions are made by the leader, then handed down through the chain of authority.

The interpersonal aspects of the three arrangements are in harmony with the decision-making process. In Lineal structures, each member must know his place in a system of leaders and followers, dominance and submission. Strict dependence on the hierarchy of authority is strongly emphasized. In Collateral arrangements, group harmony is stressed. Group members are mainly at the same level of importance; but the goals of the group are more important than individual needs or preferences. Individualism accents the importance of each member, of his own goals and needs, of his ability to make decisions by himself and to stand on his own two feet.

The Kluckhohn theory assumes that every culture or subculture ranks the three arrangements in an order of preference in accordance with its institutions. The ranking pattern which is dominantly preferred in the United States is first the Individual, second Collateral, and third Lineal. This pattern has been ascertained in several ways but primarily through the use of question-

naires. It is clearly a value pattern which is easily articulated —
a set of preferences close to conscious awareness. The importance
of the individual conforms to the ideal image Americans have of
themselves. For certain purposes, however, they will shift to the
second-order Collateral position — for example, in the case of
team sports and in a crisis, when individualism must be subordinated
to group goals. The least preferred Lineal position receives short
shrift. While he might be necessary in certain situations, most
Americans resent a boss who acts too bossy, and their sympathies
tend to lie with those who have to take rather than give orders.

Although there are many subcultural groups which vary from
this pattern of relational values, there is no doubt about its stability
for the nation as a whole when respondents are asked to make
verbal choices between alternatives. How then are we to reconcile
this pattern, especially its anti-authoritarian implications, with the
authoritarian practices and the hierarchy of power which we noted
earlier?

The first answer which suggests itself is that this value pattern
conforms to the official, democratic ideology of the nation. It
corresponds to the well-advertised American way of life, a view
that has been drilled into us from early childhood. Since it is so
strongly held among our ego-ideals, we tend to selectively screen
out, to repress, or to dismiss most evidences to the contrary in our
national affairs or everyday experience. As a result, we are forced
to falsify our own experiences and thus to maintain the hypocrisy
which the young, who are not yet committed to inauthenticity, so
easily spot in adult behavior. Furthermore, this official pattern of
values receives just enough valid support in middle-class styles of
life, particularly within the family, so that it is not wholly lacking
in substance. Thus we can afford, it seems, though at considerable
psychological cost, to shut our eyes to the entrenched Lineality that
characterizes our political institutions, our universities and hospitals, our business and commercial establishments, and our conduct
of foreign affairs.

But there is a more subtle and more unconscious fashion in
which the discrepancy between ideology and reality is obscured.
Individualism was first installed as a national value during the
Revolutionary War in order to rationalize the declaration of
independence from the Crown. "All men are created equal," said
Thomas Jefferson, and "are endowed with certain inalienable
rights." Among those rights were life, liberty, and the pursuit of
happiness. To justify the obtaining of liberty, Individualism had

352

to be elevated into the highest position while Lineality which would have required loyalty to the King had to be reduced. Collaterality, the value principle that united the colonies in common effort, was hardly mentioned in Jefferson's eloquent prose. The struggle was between tyranny — that is, Lineality — and liberty — that is, Individualism.

The value goals of the Founding Fathers were valid, for their time. But the formula of freedom versus tyranny in the absence of a strong Collateral value orientation too easily becomes a mask for the perpetuation of tyranny. Many would-be dictators have used the language of freedom to obtain power. Freedom from something — from the conqueror, from the sense of inferiority, from want, from lawlessness — becomes the slogan to rationalize the seizing of power for the purpose of subjugating someone else. Identification with the oppressor perpetuates the authoritarianism of the fighter for freedom. The Lineal principle, the unconscious or concealed endorsement of authoritarianism, persist behind the mask of Individualism. The institutions established in the name of freedom embody for the most part the hierarchical structuring of authority. Thus it seems fair to say that the *operative* pattern of relational preferences consists of first the Individual, second the Lineal, and third Collateral. This is, of course, in conflict with the officially acknowledged or *ideal* ranking pattern: Individualism first, Collateral second, and Lineal third. It is the inconsistency between the ideal and operative pattern that generates the strain in the system.

It has been said that the price of liberty is eternal vigilance. Vigilance against tyranny, of course. But this saying misses the mark. It seems more likely that any price tag attached to liberty would have to be labeled "Collaterality." Angry demands for the rights of an individual or a group would not be necessary if social structures were arranged horizontally rather than vertically — if all were in the same boat, on the same level. In the presence of pyramidal power structures neither vigilance nor protest can do much to preserve freedom. The most that can be accomplished is the effecting of "deals" and "trade-offs" between the power structures — the formation of temporary coalitions which gain a measure of freedom for participating groups. This is the "wheeling and dealing" which runs straight through our political and commercial life. The saying, "You can't fight City Hall," may or may not be true — truer in Chicago, for example, than in New York — but it illustrates the impenetrability of the pyramidal power structure.

The remedy, at the level of cultural value orientations, would seem, then, to consist of a rearrangement of the operative value priorities. Collateral values will have to be given preference over Lineality, in action, in the actual performance of our institutions, so that the operative pattern conforms to the ideal pattern. This requirement is hardly a new thought. The United Nations, the One World Movement, the slogans "Participating Democracy" and "Community Control" — to say nothing of time-honored appeals to the brotherhood of man — all represent structural rearrangements based on the Collateral principle. However, something may be gained by spelling out the needed direction of change in value terms. At the least, this approach can provide a test for determining whether a proposed change really meets the need. Beyond this, it may provide a steady image for the mobilization of the energy required to effect change.

I raised the question earlier of whether research can provide us with the information needed to determine directions of social change. If the above analysis is correct, then we can give a positive answer to the question. I also questioned whether behavioral research could have something to say about the techniques of change — especially on the score of nonviolent as opposed to violent techniques. This still seems to me more problematical. Any determined effort to remodel our social structures in the promoting of Collaterality over Lineality will meet strong resistance. It will be called "Collectivism" among many other epithets. Those who propose it will be perceived by many, particularly the Nativists, as un-American. Still, Collateral structures may contain the resistance by their inclusion of their opponents in the Collateral group. This possibility must be put aside for more study. For the moment, it is sufficient if we have been able to throw some light on the environmental conditions which give rise to outbreaks of collective violence.

TWELVE

Theories of Violence—An Integrated Approach

There is considerable need for a more systematic approach to the theory and the concepts used for explaining the occurrence of collective violence. Because the most recent manifestations of group violence — the urban riots in black communities and the student disorders in high schools and colleges — are novel in appearance and highly dramatic, many writers have tended to propose theories explaining these events. The profusion of theories, most of which are interesting and plausible, is currently tending toward chaos — a situation which is not very helpful in determining what steps might be taken to reduce levels of collective violence. Nor does the present array of assumptions and explanations serve as a good guide to further research.

The variety of theories currently on the market can be grouped under three headings. The first consists of what might be called "popular" or "non-scientific" theories, advanced by editorial writers, columnists, law enforcement officials, and some investigatory commissions. One such theory is the notion, proposed by the FBI, that the collective violence seen in urban riots is essentially meaningless, a simple breakdown in law and order. *(See FBI 1967.)* Another related theory holds that riots consist of the actions of a tiny minority of black people living in the ghetto. This so-called "riff-raff" theory further proposes that rioters consist, for the most part, of hoodlums and criminals plus a few disaffected or alienated slum dwellers. Moving a little further in the direction of a socially determined explanation is the assumption that riots are caused by "outside agitators," "communists," or other unnamed, probably left-wing "troublemakers." There is some disagreement, however, as to whether the troublemakers are politically motivated or whether they are out merely for fun, loot, and "kicks." Since such actions are considered by the popular theorists to be quite attractive, even seductive, another explanation postulates "contagion" as significant in the spread of rioting. The media, particularly television news broadcasts, have often been accused of stimulating contagion by showing inflammatory scenes of mob action to those who have not yet "caught the fever." Finally, urban crowding and the presumed tendency of crowds to behave irrationally can be grouped within the popular or commonsense theories.

The problem with these popular theories is not that they are necessarily wrong or unscientific, though some of them, such as the "riff-raff" theory, have been disproved by recent research. *(Sears and McConahy 1969)* The problems are: (1) that they are assumed by their promoters to be so obviously true as not to require proof or disproof; (2) that they are one-sided, explaining a complex process by means of one or two simple variables; and (3) that they invariably picture the collective violence of urban rioting as a pathological or deviant phenomenon — as exceptional, irrational, criminal, or purposeless behavior. As Grimshaw, Skolnick, and others have pointed out, labeling the phenomenon in this fashion tends to justify repressive action against actual or potential riot participants while it distorts or misdirects scientific inquiry. *(Grimshaw 1968; Skolnick 1969, Ch. 9)*

The second category of theories includes those that have reached scientific status through the process of scholarly or empirical research, Louis Masotti has grouped these more scientific approaches under four headings.[1] (1) Those based on the notion of absolute or relative deprivation. (2) Those based on the collapse of rising expectations when promises remain unfulfilled. Both of these explanations are related to the frustration-aggression hypothesis which has been confirmed by experimental procedures. (3) Theories

---

[1] See Masotti and Bowen 1968, including a contribution by Leonard Berkowitz on laboratory studies of frustration.

based on the breakdown of shared norms and values incidental to large-scale migration, industrialization, and other forms of rapid social change. The resulting fragmentation of the power elite makes it increasingly difficult for those in authority to maintain social control. The movement toward black power, community control, local autonomy, "youth power," anti-war protest, and student rebellions are usually cited as evidence for the breakdown of shared values leading to violent eruptions. (4) The scientifically oriented theories based on the theory of group conflict and conflict resolution. White racism, exclusion and discrimination practiced against black people, their justifiable grievances and mounting anger, especially against the law enforcement agencies of the dominant white power structures — all these evidences of group conflict have been well documented and have been used not only as explanations of urban rioting but as clues to the resolution of the conflict. Conflict is seen, according to this theoretical standpoint, as arising from the demand for and the resistance to social change. The greater the polarization between the two contending groups, the greater the likelihood of group violence.[2]

In addition to these rather more formal theories, the literature on collective violence contains a number of more empirical observations which have not yet been placed within a theoretical context. These are concerned with the nature, timing, and placement of precipitating incidents, the interaction between riot leaders, counter-rioters (trying to cool things off) and the police during a confrontation, the influence of weather, and the topography of one versus another ghetto community.

To be sure, any one research publication may combine several of the formal theories with empirical generalizations or even with some element drawn from popular theory. Still, those writers who are drawn to conflict theory are more likely to understand collective violence as a form of political protest necessitated by resistance to change through ordinary political processes, while those who use the frustration-aggression hypothesis and its derivatives are more likely to see riots as spontaneous outbursts of rage, with the politi-

---

[2] This is the principal message of the report of the National Advisory Commission on Civil Disorders: "Our nation is moving toward two societies, one black, one white—separate and unequal." The remedy follows from the diagnosis: "This deepening division is not inevitable . . . The alternative is not blind repression or capitulation to lawlessness. It is the realization of common opportunities for all within a single society." National Advisory Committee on Civil Disorders 1968, p. 1.

cal message added on later through interpretation after the fact.[3] Conflict theory tends to align itself with the notion of breakdown of shared values and social control by picturing collective violence as a form of rebellion, with possible revolutionary overtones. This connection then leads to some vigorous though often confusing discussion as to whether collective violence is a good thing or a bad thing, a device for overcoming repression or for reducing the social system to utter chaos and misery. *(Moore 1969.)*

The diversity of theoretical orientations, their contradictions, and their implicit involvement in value judgements about the purpose and utility of violence inevitably bring up the question as to whether it is possible at the present time to construct an integrated theory — one which takes into account most of the existing explanatory notions but relates them to each other in a consistent fashion, without making premature value judgements as to whether violence is good or bad. Given the existing state of knowledge, the chances of successfully constructing such a theory are not too good. Unless the attempt is made, however, research, values, and opinion will continue to be mixed together to such a degree that it will remain difficult to decide whether proposed solutions are valid or will only make matters worse.[4]

One problem which an integrated theory must embrace is the contradiction between psychological theories which, like the frustration-aggression hypothesis, focus on the individual and his decision to engage in or refrain from rioting, and political or sociological theories which focus upon groups, on the formation of movements, and parties to a conflict, such as the divisions between ethnic, racial, or socio-economic groups. Because of this problem it is important to select for our integrated theory, a concept which correlates the motivations of the individual with the possibilities for social action within groups, parties, and other settings. The concept of social role is ideally designed for this purpose. A key concept, widely used in sociological theory, it focuses directly on the intersection between the individual and the social system. *(See Dahren-*

---

[3] Cf. Skolnick 1969 and Fogelson 1969 with T. M. Tomlinson's contribution to Masotti and Bowen 1968, pp. 417-28.

[4] Consider, for example, a remedy proposed by the National Advisory Commission on Civil Disorders and repeated by the National Commission on the Causes and Prevention of Violence. These bodies recommended putting large federal subsidies plus private capital into the black ghettos. Some social scientists thereupon argued to the contrary that such measures might have a short-term calming effect but would make black communities more dependent and impotent in the long run. *(See Cloward and Priven 1969.)*

dorf 1969, pp. 19-87.) Because of the complexities of the social role concept, in addition to the vagaries of violence theories, our attempt here to build an integrated theory of collective violence will, perforce, be rather superficial. Nevertheless, we shall ask how it is that, given current conditions of conflict within our social system, black and white Americans come to adopt the role of "rioter," a person who engages in collective violence.

In Chapters Three and Four I defined a social role as a goal-directed pattern or sequence of acts tailored in accordance with cultural values for the transactions a person may carry out in a social group or situation. Since most such transactions occur in harmonious situations, roles are designed for reciprocal behavior among role partners, a form of learned behavior in which the acts of one person, say a husband, mesh with the actions of his role partner, in this example, a wife. Such reciprocal behavior maintains equilibrium and satisfaction within the role system. For a variety of reasons, however, conflict, especially a conflict of interest based on incompatible values, may enter the role system. The behavior of the role partners then no longer remains smooth and orderly. Arguments, threats of coercion, and actual coercion are then likely to disrupt the behavior of the role partners. This is a general description which applies to almost any social situation. Our question now becomes: how can we apply these ideas to the outbreak of collective violence in urban situations?

If social roles are organized in accordance with cultural values and if a breakdown of shared values is theoretically assumed to be a cause of collective violence, then clearly the first item in our integrated theory should concern itself with value orientations. Of the many value conflicts currently associated with the process of social change, I emphasize one value dimension as of key importance: the Relational area. In accordance with Florence Kluckhohn's theory of variation in value orientations this area is concerned with group structure and decision-making. *(See Kluckhohn and Strodtbeck 1961.)* It is postulated that the ideal (dominantly preferred) decision-making pattern places Individualism in the first order or most preferred position; Collaterality — that is, horizontal, consensus decisions — in the second place; and Lineal — hierarchical, authoritarian structures — in the last or least preferred position. Although this is the ideal rank order of values in which all Americans are trained to believe and even though it fits well with the American middle-class family structure, still it does not correspond to the actual value patterns of many of our major American institutions. International relations, business, government, education, welfare, and many community organizations operate in accordance with a discordant pattern or preferences — that is, with the Lineal rather than the Collateral in the second-order position. This means that behind our Individualism there is an intense but largely concealed emphasis on superior-inferior relationships — on "Who's on top?" or "Who is making it?" in terms of social position, power, and income. The accent is on elitism and on power relations between groups rather than the pluralism or equality between groups called for by our national ethos.

This ambiguity and conflict in value choices produces two types of strains disruptive of harmony within the social system. The strong influence of Lineality sets working-class and lower middle-class, ethnic whites and working-class or poverty-stricken blacks at each other's throats as each tries to gain or preserve a foothold on the bottom of the ladder of opportunity. So far, neither the civil rights push toward integration nor the black power movement for separate community control has enabled blacks to scramble up this ladder, despite (or because of) the fears of working-class whites. But the conflict generated by the Lineal strain becomes more and more acute.

The second type of strain is produced by the clash between the ideal value pattern and the actual or operative pattern. This inconsistency between political ideals and practice is perceived by many young persons, both white and black, as hypocritical. It is seen as a way of preserving exploitation and repression on the part of adult authorities who excuse their practices by constantly invoking their ideals, toward which, the authorities say, they are trying their best to move. An aging observer, such as myself, is bound to sympathize with *both* the youthful protesters and especially the black protesters, on the one hand, and with the adults on the other. The value conflicts are institutionalized, and institutions can be changed only with the most extraordinary pain and effort.

If the prospects for social change are constrained within these value conflicts, then there are four logically possible responses, each of which forms the nucleus of a social role. The first three responses are to the operative Individual-Lineal-Collateral pattern, while the fourth is in response to its conflict with the ideal Individual-Collateral-Lineal pattern. The first role response is termed "Nativist," and it includes all those who resist any new group's effort to enter the mainstream. The name is adapted from the

Native American Party's effort in the 1840's (and later the Know-Nothings) to prevent the Irish-Catholics from entering the power structure. The second role response includes all supporters of the status quo, whom, for lack of a better name, we shall call the "Standpatters." Whereas the Nativists would like to push the hands of time back to an earlier, more exclusive, and in their eyes "purer" vision of America, the Standpatters are content with the existing system or will, at best, settle for very slow change, involving the gradual admission of new groups to positions of power or prestige. The third role response includes those sufficiently committed to change so that they are willing to make strong efforts to help new or previously excluded groups climb up the ladder of power, prestige and opportunity. Such persons we term "Reconstructivists," on the analogy to the Abolitionists and other white groups who before, during, and after the Civil War took considerable risks to free the Negroes.

Nativists, Standpatters, and Reconstructivists vary only with respect to their attitudes toward groups inferiorized by Lineal values. The fourth role response to structural change differs sharply from these three previous role designates by the strength of a desire actually to institute the ideal Individual-Collateral-Lineal pattern of values. Whereas Reconstructivists, both white and black, accept Lineality and ask merely that, in the current racial struggles, blacks be given a "piece of the action," this fourth group complains bitterly about a social system that makes it necessary to struggle so hard for a "piece of the action." Since, as I said above, to institute our ideal values, to actually make them a part of "reality" will require a major and possibly traumatic overhauling of the social system, this fourth role response may be called the "Revolutionary."

Since all four of these role types feature behavior directed toward political goals while not yet formally connected with political parties or action groups, we may call them parapolitical roles. Being informal, such roles tend to be adopted or exhibited only as the occasion demands — in a political discussion, during an argument about racial affairs, in response to a local election, or in answer to a question asked in the course of attitude surveys. In order for such parapolitical roles to be connected with more formally political behavior, they must undergo a further refinement. Each of the four role types is susceptible of division into a "moderate" and a "radical" subgrouping. The distinction is based on the willingness to use force or violence as against the normal political process in the pursuit of the parapolitical goals. For example, radical Nativists will arm themselves and, like the Ku Klux Klan of a former era, kill blacks who seem to be challenging the white Nativist dominance. Moderate Nativists will, like many Southern senators, judges, and mayors, misuse the political and law enforcement processes to attain the same ends. Moderate Standpatters will espouse "law and order" programs, while radical Standpatters, like the Northside Citizens Organization in Newark, will arm themselves to prevent blacks from entering their white ethnic neighborhoods but will not harass or kill blacks as long as they remain within the ghetto. Moderate Reconstructivists will attempt to pass reform legislation, while radical Reconstructivists will seize buildings, resist arrest, and engage in other extralegal activities, including rioting, if necessary, to force change. Moderate Revolutionaries will write articles, give lectures, create ideologies and party programs describing the required revolutionary changes, while radical Revolutionaries will be prepared to use violence, though usually for specific ideological ends.

We can consider these parapolitical roles and their action-oriented derivatives as the second major item in our integrated theory. Clearly, on the one side, they are related to the conflict in values. But, on the other side of role formation and role adoption, they are related to three other factors which must be included in the integrated theory. One of these has to do with the personal motives for role adoption — a mainly psychological factor. For this purpose, the frustration-aggression hypothesis, though correct in its main outlines, is too simple. We need to know much more about the inner, psychological conflicts which must be resolved before a person can become a Nativist, Standpatter, Reconstructivist, or Revolutionary. Especially, we need to know about the mainly unconscious factors combined with personal experiences which are correlated with the adoption of a nonviolent, moderate position versus a radical, violence-prone position. In this connection, it would be important to investigate the process of conversion from one position to another, for example, in the cases of former communists who have become extreme conservatives, and vice versa. A beginning inquiry in this direction has been made for historical personages by Erik Erikson and for contemporary college students by Kenneth Kenniston. *(Erikson 1958; Erikson 1969; Kenniston 1968)* This area, which can be called the psychological determinants of role adoption, will be considered the third major item in our integrated theory.

Another side of role adoption concerns social backgrounds

and demographic factors. On the basis of common observation as well as specific research, we would expect to find more Nativists among Southerners and within older age groups, more Reconstructivists in the industrial Northwest and among the young. Revolutionaries tend to be drawn from the children of middle-class professionals who are also members of minority groups. It hardly needs to be said that a majority of blacks are Reconstructivists. These factors tell us a lot about the potential strength of the corresponding group formations in various regions and locales. We shall call this, the fourth major item in our theory, the social determinants of role adoption.

Still another factor correlated with role adoption is more complex. It has to do with the interaction, at national and local levels, between moderate and radical Nativists, Standpatters, Reconstructivists, and Revolutionaries. It is reasonable to assume that if the style of a particular city administration is largely and effectively Reconstructivist, the number of radical black Reconstructivists will decline in favor of the moderates while the number of radical white Standpatters and Nativists will increase at the expense of the moderates. Since the police are drawn largely from the ranks of potential Nativists in the South and Standpatters in the North, their behavior toward black people, so often characterized by disrespect and harassment, can be expected to promote the recruitment of blacks into the radical Reconstructivist role.

These dynamic interrelations vary from city to city, and yet we know very little about such variation from systematic studies. *(See Campbell and Shuman 1968; Masotti and Bowen 1968, pp. 187-200.)* Included in this area should be the kinds of communication about race relations provided by the local press, radio and television, the policies of school boards, unions, local industries, and the success or lack of success of civil rights organizations in pushing for Reconstructivist goals. Since the outcome of these interrelations is of the greatest importance to the polarization or defusion of conflict, we shall call this, the fifth major item in our theory, the interactive determinants of role adoption. It should be possible to devise assessment procedures in any city capable of determining at different points in time the proportions of moderate and radical Nativists, Standpatters, Reconstructivists, and Revolutionaries in a representative sample of the urban population.[5] In

---

[5] See Conant *et al.* 1969 for a start made by the Lemberg Center for the Study of Violence, Brandeis University, toward this goal.

this way a graph of the state of conflict and change in the city could be constructed.

If our integrated theory of collective violence is to be organized around the social role concept, then we are still quite a distance in our development of the theory from specifying the factors which lead to the actual adoption of roles in which violence can be expressed. If we use the not too accurate but nevertheless convenient designation "riot role" or "rioter," then we can ask what factors are conducive to the adoption of this role by an incumbent of one of the parapolitical roles. How does one person become inducted into this role while another person resists such induction?

To grapple with this problem we may distinguish between the preparatory factors which are conducive to riot role adoption and the circumstantial conditions which actually manufacture riot roles during an outburst of civil disorder.

It is not possible to present a complete list of preparatory factors at the present time. Among those that should be considered, however, are the following: (1) the levels of grievance, resentment, and anger among black and white incumbents of the parapolitical roles, or, roughly the explosiveness index within the city; (2) pattern-setting, or the images of successful riots in other cities (or of previous riots in the same city) which provide scenarios of how the riot will go and of what roles are available, with what effects on the prospects of change and at what risk to the rioters; (3) formal and informal leadership, both among those groups who would promote a riot and among the "counterrioters" who would seek to prevent the riot. Although the nature, quality, and effectiveness of leadership is difficult to ascertain in advance of the event, it still must be taken into consideration. We shall call this, the sixth major item in our theory, factors conducive to the adoption of riot roles.

Finally, we must deal with the events of the riot itself. Beginning with the precipitating incident, roles are manufactured through the transactions of city authorities, law enforcement personnel, and residents of the riot neighborhood, as the riot goes through various stages of escalation. There is considerable evidence that the provocative behavior of authorities and particularly of the police often leads to the adoption of riot roles by moderate Reconstructivists whose previous orientation had been non-violent. (*See Walker 1968.*) On the other hand, during the reciprocal escalation of conflict, rioters may actually provoke the police to acts of violence which are not included in their professional role expectations. Mutual and reciprocal provoking of aggressive behavior is a standard aspect of any role conflict. (Chapter Four) Its avoidance requires not only self control but, more important, confidence in non-violent strategies for the resolution of conflict. Such strategies are, of course, extremely difficult to maintain in the emotionally heated atmosphere of the riot situation.

Another important circumstantial factor is concerned with the reporting of events both by the media and through informal networks of private communication. Here it may be helpful to recall W. I. Thomas' dictum regarding "the definition of the situation." A situation becomes "real" and calls forth relevant behavior in accordance with the way it is defined or labeled. The media play a significant and sometimes unfortunate role in defining the riot situation by providing the public with false descriptions of the event, manufactured in the overheated atmosphere of the circumstances, and liberally sprinkled with fictive roles invented by spokesmen for nativist, standpat, reconstructivist, or revolutionary orientations. *(See Knopf 1969.)* On the other hand, it must be said that the concept of objectivity in reporting events is also a myth. Observers will always select and emphasize certain aspects of the event in accordance with their personal values and institutional affiliations.[6] It would be well for these sources of distortion to be understood by the general public so that a skeptical attitude and allowances for bias could more easily be maintained.

The circumstantial factors conducive to the adoption of riot roles constitute the seventh and final major category in our integrated theory. They are obviously of key importance to all those who are interested in riots for their own sake. However, in the context of our theory of the connection between role conflict and social change, the question of why the riot takes place subsides in importance. Explanations of the riot are not as relevant as the possibility of discovering what effect collective violence has had on the prospects for social change.[7] In terms of our theory, this means discovering the proportionate redistribution and location of parapolitical roles in the community and assessing the substantive changes in institutions following the riot.

Collective violence may be regarded as a social experiment — an experiment which has had some notable successes and failures

---

[6] Good examples of press distortions are given in Takagi *et al.* 1970; Rainwater and Yancey 1967.

[7] See Canty 1969, an audit conducted as a follow-up to the Kerner Report.

in the past. *(See Davis and Gurr 1969; Rubenstein 1970.)* Just as the threat of military violence is regarded as a deterrent to attack from abroad, so the threat of internal violence can also be regarded as a deterrent to decay and stagnation within the society. What attitude one adopts toward such experiments is a personal judgment that cannot be derived from research procedures. What science can possibly do, as we have attempted to demonstrate here, is to set forth the transactional, interdependent processes which should be taken into consideration in reaching such a judgment. *(See Runciman 1966.)*

THIRTEEN

The Group Psychology of Campus Disorders

There can be no doubt that the spectacular growth of campus disorders over the past several years has aroused intense interest and stimulated strong feelings. As one of the most rousing controversies of our times, the topic of student protest has generated a wealth of publication. Innumerable articles have appeared in the press, in national magazines, and in professional journals, expressing either hostility toward or sympathy with the student uprisings (or perhaps more characteristically a mixture of both feelings). Congressional committees have been urged by expert witnesses to pursue completely incompatible lines of inquiry and to establish quite contradictory national policies in the interest of terminating the disorders.

In all this varied comment, however, little attention has been paid to the group process and the dynamic interactions which create the various factions, on and off campus, and set them into such intransigent, antagonistic, and occasionally violent relations with each other. Especially prominent through its absence has been a consideration of the psychodynamics, both conscious and unconscious, underlying the group conflicts. An examination of this sort might be of interest only to specialists were it not for the peculiar and unlikely behaviors exhibited on all sides during a campus crisis. Many observers of such incidents have noted, though few have put

367

into print, the number of surprising, illogical actions which disfigure the behavior of previously collaborating groups — and of individuals within such groups — whenever activist students use militant or disruptive techniques to satisfy their demands for change.

Low boiling points and trigger-happy responses, frequently based on the imagery of cowboy films and television programs, occur at the highest levels of official responsibility. During his 1966 gubernatorial campaign, Ronald Reagan, now the Governor of California, said that the student leaders of the 1964 Free Speech Movement at the Berkeley campus of the University of California "should have been taken by the scruff of the neck and thrown out of the university." Testifying in May 1969 before the McClellan Committee hearings on "Riots, Civil and Criminal Disorders," Eric Hoffer, the longshoreman philosopher who has delineated the fanatical "True Believer," said about violence:

> Take Grayson Kirk [President of Columbia University during the spring, 1968 campus disturbance]. Here they got into his room. They burglarized his files. They smoked his cigars. They used his shaving kit. Grayson Kirk didn't forget himself . . . I think it would have been a wonderful thing if Grayson Kirk got mad, grabbed a gun and went out there and gunned them down. I think maybe he would have gotten killed, maybe he would have killed two of them when they were jumping up, but I think he would have saved Columbia. *(Hoffer 1951)*

Hoffer's attitude may seem somewhat blood-thirsty, but the irritability underlying his response is shared by more sophisticated commentators. Irritation with student rebels colors the comments of at least two of the scholars who have recently employed psychoanalytic ideas in accounting for the problematic behavior of the dissidents: Lewis Feuer and Bruno Bettelheim. In *The Conflict of Generations: The Character and Significance of Student Movements,* historian Lewis Feuer reviews student movements in various countries over the past two hundred years. He concludes that student movements have been basically destructive except for the rare occasions when their goals have been taken over by the adult world. The mainly undesirable outcomes, according to Feuer, are logical results of the students' unconscious and irrational motivations: oedipal hostility toward the fathers, castration fears stimulating overcompensatory aggression, and homosexual longings stimulating overcompensatory masculinity. As a result of these motives and

368

no others (for example, intellectual or political motives), the sons develop an attitude which Feuer calls "de-authorization" of the parents. *(Feuer 1969)*

In a similar tone, but with a different list of pathological factors, Bruno Bettelheim, the expert on childhood and adolescent disturbances, told the McClellan Committee that student rebel leaders are (partially concealed) paranoid characters. Their followers are adolescents who have been deprived of emotional gratifications and warmth by their parents, and who are looking both for an object on which to vent their rage and for a cause of sufficient intensity to generate the warm group feelings they have missed since earliest childhood. According to Bettelheim, these grievances, left over from childhood, are much more important than the actual issues about which students currently protest.

The positions of Feuer and Bettelheim suffer, in my opinion, from two kinds of errors. First, they both attribute the behavior of activist students almost wholly to pre-existing neurotic motives, although it is not at all clear to the neutral observer what is cause and what is effect. It is at least possible that the behavior of dissident students is a response to irrational and excessively disturbing external conditions. Shortly after the conclusion of World War II, Dr. Will Menninger, reacting to his experience as chief of psychiatric services for the Army, dealt with this problem by posing the question. He wrote:

> During the war, we had frequent occasions to contrast the psychiatrist's job in civilian life with his job in combat. In civilian life he attempted to understand and treat the abnormal reactions of persons to normal situations. In military life he attempted to understand and treat the normal reactions to an abnormal situation. One might seriously question if our world condition does not now place many of us in a continuously abnormal situation to which we are having normal reactions, even though these by all previous standards are pathological. To such a turbulent world, one might legitimately ask, what is a normal reaction? *(Menninger 1967)*

Although the contrast between the reactions to combat and civilian life is somewhat overdrawn, the question is as pertinent now as it was in 1947, perhaps more so. Any attempt to answer it requires the help of method and theory — a matter to which we shall return when considering the transactional approach toward the end of this inquiry.

The second error arises from the exclusive focus on just one party to a complex interaction. It is simply not reasonable to raise questions about the irrational, unconscious motives of students while ignoring the similar implications of the behavior of those members of the faculty and administration who oppose them. Such a procedure prejudges the question as to where the pathology lies, thereby limiting the inquiry to such a degree as to be misleading. By the same token, it raises questions as to the "blind spots" of the observer. When groups find themselves in conflict, it is difficult enough to determine which group is right or wrong on the ostensible issues, much less which of the groups is "healthy" and which "disturbed."

It was under the condition of maximum intergroup conflict that Freud first turned his attention to group psychology and asked what unconscious processes led individuals to associate in groups, to conform to group norms, to create new forms of behavior, and to involve themselves in adversary relations. *Group Psychology and the Analysis of the Ego,* published in 1921, was prompted by the experiences of psychoanalysts in World War I, as military psychiatrists. Freud's approach was not based upon the attribution of sin, evil, or psychopathology to any one group or society as against another. He was interested in the human condition, in the way in which conflicts operating below the surface of consciousness interacted, for all concerned individuals in groups, with external social reality, distorting that reality and thereby rendering it even worse, even more limiting and traumatic than it had to be, given the economic and technological situation of man vis-à-vis nature.

It is in connection with the problems posed by group-formation and the unconscious origins of intergroup hostility that this inquiry approaches its more immediate aim: to describe in rather general terms the phenomenology of campus disorders and to examine the psychological processes which lead individuals to join one or another of the contending groups in the course of these disturbances.

My colleagues and I at the Lemberg Center for the Study of Violence have had the opportunity to observe campus crises at several American universities, and we have been repeatedly impressed with the speed and intensity with which aggression and hostility are released among all parties connected with these affairs. The extreme and seemingly unreasonable behavior evoked by such disturbances has been deplored, condemned, and praised. Although such judgments are one way of dealing with human problems, there is much to be said for a more neutral examination of the

370

elicitation of aggressive behavior in reaction to group conflict. At any rate, what the observer faces at the outset is a dramatic and kaleidoscopic series of events featuring the sudden use of physical force, threats of more serious violence, warnings of punishment, cries of outrage, abusive language, and gaudy exhibitions of contempt, insult, and calumny.

It would be easy to ascribe such sudden releases of inhibition to contagion, feelings being notably infectious when released at high levels of intensity. Although it is undoubtedly a part of the phenomenon, contagion is too global an explanation. Besides, it affords no leverage on the behavior aside from the usual admonitions to "keep cool."

Rather than remaining satisfied with a theory of random release of hostile energies automatically triggered by the illegal acts of rebellious students, I shall argue that, once the stage is set, the suddenly appearing antagonisms and the associated formation of groups in opposition to each other break out along previously determined lines of cleavage in accordance with certain ego mechanisms which are largely outside the awareness of the individual. This line of argument will not ignore the social and political issues so important to the setting of the stage for conflict. On the contrary, my procedure shall be to begin with the psychological factors and then to examine their interplay with the social structural factors.

Since our observations have been drawn from participating in or observing the process of angry polarization within and between groups, rather than clinical or standard research situations, we must be cautious about any formulations of unconscious motivations. But the existence of unconscious factors at work in campus disorders is supported by two easily observable aspects of the response of those concerned in the conflict: (1) the irrationality, often bordering on the bizarre, displayed by persons whose usual behavior toward each other was characterized by good humor, even in disagreement; and (2) the forgetting, denial, or discounting of the irrational behavior once the crisis has passed.

THE FOUR PHASES

Campus polarization is a crisis which occurs in four stages, each characterized by a sequence of actions and reactions. Given the variations in actual disorder from campus to campus, there is a risk of overgeneralization or unwarranted stereotyping in such an approach. Still, whether or not the four stages actually fit all situations is not as important as the advantage gained through imposing some clarity and order on the dynamics of the arousal, escalation, and decline of group hostilities.

Premonitions

The *premonitory phase* is characterized by slowly mounting resentment within a number of students whom I shall call, for the sake of generalization, the "aggrieved" group. Their anger is aroused by the failure of the administration to respond rapidly enough, or at all, to their expressed desire for change within the institution. The desired changes vary from school to school, but in general they revolve around administrative policy with respect to three substantive issues: (1) the quality and pertinence of the curriculum and other institutional arrangements for students of various ethnic backgrounds; (2) policies related to the conduct of the war in Vietnam and the involvement of the university with military research and training; and (3) the rights of students to have a part in the determination of institutional policy of all sorts.

In the minds of the aggrieved group there is no question of the legitimacy of and the pressing need for the desired changes. Within the student body as a whole, however, there is a spectrum of opinion ranging from active support through apathy to opposition. For this reason, among others, the first administrative response to the proposals of the aggrieved group is likely to be perfunctory. Meetings between representatives of the aggrieved students and the administration, if they occur at all, are viewed by the administration largely as opportunities for "abreaction" — for the expression of feelings and opinions, in the hope that this will satisfy them. No real change is expected nor envisioned by the authorities.

After a certain lapse of time without progress or change, the aggrieved students begin increasingly to see themselves in an adversary role vis-à-vis the administration. The current of the times, laden with scenarios of dissent, asserts itself in the thinking of the aggrieved group, sometimes aided by visits from activist students at other universities. Ideas originally defined as suggestions or proposals become talked about as "demands." This hardening of attitudes and the growing spirit of militancy within the aggrieved group lead to changes both in the general student body and in the administration. An increasing number of previously indifferent students identify themselves with the goals of the aggrieved students, though not necessarily with their activities, mainly because these additional students share the resentment at the failure

372

of the administration to consider requests for change with the proper seriousness. A large proportion of the student body, in other words, feels vicariously slighted.

Representatives of the administration are usually aware of the changing attitudes of the students, but they tend to misinterpret them because of their stake in avoiding rapid or abrupt change. The aggrieved students are now seen as threats to the tranquility and maintenance of order within the school. Their supporters are perceived as misled, easily attracted through romantic impulses or merely youthful exuberance to the inflammatory language in which unrealistic or illegitimate goals are clothed. Since the goals of change are still not taken seriously, administrators discount or dismiss the entire effort through a process of labeling designed to split the student body and to rally outside support for the policy of resistance to change. Leaders of the aggrieved group are called "radicals," "anarchists," and a variety of other names. In private conversation they are often identified as spoiled, pampered offspring of well-to-do, permissive parents or as disturbed persons in need of psychiatric attention. Their followers among the more moderate students are regarded as essentially fair-minded and well-intentioned (though temporarily infatuated) dupes. This labeling process reflects the growth on both sides of the mistrust and disrespect whose unconscious origins we are about to trace.

Toward the end of the premonitory phase some subtle cleavages begin to appear, both within the administration and among the faculty, though they are still papered over with politeness. Some faculty, usually from the social sciences or counseling services, adopt a sympathetic, liberal attitude toward the changes requested by the students. They then urge, to the distress of others that the college president, the deans, or whoever stands for "officialdom" modify the rigid policy of resistance. These persons have usually been in face-to-face contact with some of the dissident students and believe themselves to be "honest brokers" presenting the students' case with intense sincerity and urgency. As a result of the advocate role of the "sympathizers," the spokesmen for the university now shift their tactics to some degree. Representatives of the aggrieved group are seen and listened to more attentively. Some of their demands are accepted as potentially legitimate. The administrators promise to channel these requests for change through the bureaucratic machinery with which every institution of any size is encumbered.

The crisis process at this point is in a paradoxical state. A temporary relaxation occurs because the aggrieved students believe they are finally making progress, while the administrators think they have with some luck defused a potentially dangerous situation. Actually, this is the calm before the storm. On both sides the inevitable disappointment of unrealistically raised hopes is a guarantee of disaster. On the administrative side, the "channeling" procedure, at best a clumsy business, tends to get stalled because of uncertainties and disagreements about the appropriate manner of solving the problem or about whether it should be solved at all. In the students' view, the delays, mixed messages about what is taking place, and the intimations of implacable rigidity behind a surface mask of acceptance all add up to a dead end: no possibility of progress.

Initial Disorder

At this point, the crisis process moves toward the second phase: the *initial disorder*. Disillusioned, convinced that only the force of a dramatic act of protest can alter the situation in their favor, the aggrieved group begins to plan some form of disruption. At the same time, they elaborate and firm up previously (though tentatively) held hostile beliefs about the character and motives of the administration, and of the social system it represents. The resulting ideological creed — for example, that the administration is authoritarian, bigoted, and hypocritical, and that the social system is racist, exploitive, and oppressive — is used to overcome moral scruples about the legal and ethical justification of the disruption being planned. (In saying this, I am not passing any judgment on the validity of the web of beliefs but am merely describing a continuing process.)

So far all is prologue. The actual disorder that opens the second phase may begin with a series of small but increasingly disruptive demonstrations or with a major act such as seizing and occupying a building. The students usually display contradictory moods which nevertheless fit together. They are excited and aggressive, even abusive, but fairly well disciplined; exhibitionistic but secretive; happy because they are finally taking action but fearful of what it may lead to; defiant and uncommunicative yet letting it be known that they would accept communication. An aura of unity and determination expressed in publicly stated "non-negotiable demands" masks privately felt uncertainties and divisions of opinions. Despite the disagreements, the aggrieved group is, at that moment, unified through the sharing of norm-violating behavior: they are all in the same boat.

The usual administrative response is shock. Under the impression that the new policy of bureaucratic openness to complaints has mollified the dissident students and reassured the moderates, the administration is unprepared for serious trouble. But neither the realization that they have misjudged the mood of the aggrieved students nor the deeply felt indignation serves any useful purpose. Some action must be taken, if only to relieve frustration and anger. Unfortunately, the administrators are faced simultaneously with two types of decisions, neither of which is easy to make: what to do about the "non-negotiable demands" and how to deal with the norm-violating behavior. Nor can the two be easily separated, since the message contained in both the illegal behavior and the "non-negotiable" label is the same: no more stalling; the students mean business!

Faced with this threat, the administrators have only a limited number of clear-cut options. They can:

1. Accept all the demands and ignore the norm-violating behavior. This capitulation by the administration promptly resolves the current situation. It is the least common solution.

2. Ignore the demands and throw out the offenders with the help of the police and other law enforcement agencies. Although this approach has been used, it brings about so many additional problems, especially strong support for the militants by the moderates, that many administrators are reluctant to use it.

3. Ignore the norm-violating behavior while offering to negotiate the demands. Since this technique can easily be seen by the students as a "put-on" (with punishment to follow later), and since, from the side of the administration, it does not meet the challenge of illegal threat by the students, it is likely to result in a protracted stalemate.

4. Meet threat with threat by promising disciplinary procedures and punishments for the future while avoiding a confrontation and ignoring the demands, in the hope that the students will lose the support of their classmates and tire of their unproductive behavior. Since they often do, this method can succeed, at least temporarily.

375

5. Ignore both the norm-violating behavior and the demands by doing nothing and saying nothing. This produces an unsettled ambiguity and frustration for the students and gives the administration freedom to pursue any policy of punishment or non-punishment or to sanction, negotiate, or deny any part of the demands, once the students give up. Any administration choosing this inscrutable policy must be certain of support from its various constituencies (faculty, trustees, alumni, and the general public), not all of whom will understand what the administrators are up to. Because of the exacting conditions for its success, this policy is seldom used but it can be devastatingly effective.

Whether or not these policies exhaust the logical (and legal) possibilities for action afforded by the initial situation, most administrations without a history of previous disorder are unable to proceed immediately toward any one policy based upon such an abstract calculus of means and ends.[1] Clear-cut as these policies may be, there is usually too much confusion and emotion and too little prior experience within the administration to permit the straightforward implementation of any one of them; also there are too many audiences to be taken into account. Instead, a seesaw struggle takes place around three more intuitively developed positions. (1) A desire to support the goals of the aggrieved students while minimizing any loss of face to the institution for what may be interpreted as surrender. This position is usually called the "soft line" advocated by the "doves." (2) A desire to defeat and punish the students while minimizing any loss of face to the institution for what may be interpreted as callousness or cruelty. This policy is the "hard line" pursued by the "hawks." (3) A middle ground, or temporizing position, which attempts to placate both the hawks and the doves, in part, while also partially satisfying the demands of the students — a balancing act which requires great skill, diplomacy, flexibility and inventiveness, plus some Machiavellian sleight of hand.

---

[1] Some administrators dealing for the first time with an initial disorder base their strategy on the correction of an error presumably committed at another university. Thus, remembering Columbia's experience, the Harvard administration in the spring of 1969 called in the police a few hours after the students had seized the administration building. Supposedly Columbia in the spring of 1968 had waited too long before summoning the police and so had allowed time for support to build up among the moderates for the student rebels. But the Harvard policy worked no better than Columbia's.

Within a university of any size and complexity, it takes some time for these positions to become crystallized in explicit policy. Since this occurs in the context of relentless political in-fighting, the administration is for the time being unable to promote any coherent policy. It is usually forced to delay action while contenting itself with ritualistic statements for public consumption, usually condemning the students' methods ("We can neither condone nor excuse violence . . .") while expressing cautious sympathy for some of their goals ("The students' demands have been under consideration by the Committee on . . ."). It is this period of delay that ushers in the third phase of the crisis.

Mounting Polarization

The atmosphere of events now becomes increasingly hectic, acrimonious, and conspiratorial. A state of emergency exists. Ad hoc committees proliferate. Sudden summonses to meetings arrive at all hours. Secret emissaries mediate between rival factions, while rumors, counter-rumors, and corridor gossip spread. Student manifestoes circulate, and the ever-present television crews and newspaper reporters are on the lookout for interesting stories, unexpected confrontations, pitched battles, or worse.

Though activities at this point are almost "round-the-clock" and administrators are getting little sleep, the passage of time and the way time is used form the superficial stimuli to the lines of cleavage which now develop. Time is somehow always involved in the justifications which advocates make for their preferred solutions. The "hard line" advocated by the hawks maintains that every day that passes without the implementation of their "realistic" policy consolidates the position of the dissident students, encourages them in their unlawful behavior, and affords opportunity for the growth of extra-campus support by sympathizers in other schools and in the community. The doves fear that the passage of time without an accommodation being worked out will force the students to create some new manifestation of disorder, thus impelling the administration to "crack down," perhaps by calling the police. The "temporizers" though uncomfortable about the passage of time, generally feel that time plays into their hands by wearing down the opposition on all sides to their middle-of-the-road policy. For the aggrieved students, whether occupying a building, maintaining a strike, or staging forbidden rallies, time is a more ambiguous matter. It may exhaust their energies before bringing the administration around.

From attitudes toward time, further polarizations grow by wild leaps into increasingly extreme positions. For the hawks, any attempts to negotiate with the students *before* those "troublemakers" yield to punishment is anathema — a betrayal of everything the school stands for as an intellectual establishment. It is the end of reasoned inquiry, the death of scholarly detachment, the beginning of the politicalization of the school and thus the finis of academic freedom and the dispassionate search for *the truth.* For them, any decision taken under the threat of force is tantamount to accepting a fascist dictatorship. Nevertheless, they have no compunctions about intimidating doves and temporizers with dire predictions. In thundering tones and with the visionary fervor of the prophet, they foresee doom in general and schedule deadlines for specific catastrophes. Since, as they say, it is impossible to appease the students' hunger for violence and revolution, they guarantee that, should their policy lose out, in a few days, weeks, or months another building will be seized, then another and another; next, the students will be running the institution, and in a year it will have collapsed altogether. To buttress the argument, analogies are summoned from all corners of history, with special emphasis on the Nazi and Communist movements.

In addition to such fulminations, the hawks can scarcely conceal their contempt for the doves — those "bleeding hearts," those "masochists" who, perhaps unconsciously, are out to wreck the university. On their side, the doves show a mild but persistent abhorrence of the wrath and, in their eyes, "sadism" of the hawks. Privately, they tend to believe, for the moment at least, that most of the hawks are paranoid personalities. In meetings and public discussions, however, they try to appeal to what remains of the hawk sense of reality by portraying in detail the way the aggrieved students have experienced the institution: its irrelevance, its arbitrary rules and regulations, and its unresponsiveness to student needs and especially to the need for shared communication. Such attempts to explain are, nevertheless, perceived by the hawks both as attacks upon the virtue of the academy and as apologies for deviant behavior — just what one would expect from such sentimental fools. And, in fact, in their attempt to find some means to penetrate the heavy hawk defenses, the doves do at times resort to illustrations based on troubled family relations productive of deviant or psychotic behavior in a child. This is a gambit which, predictably, fails with the hawks though it may impress the "temporizers."

378

Being men of the middle, the temporizers are not much persuaded by the logic of either the hawks or the doves. More realistic than the hawks about the extent of political influence endemic to the university, they are not so afraid of the loss of an already restricted academic freedom. Unlike the doves, they are worried by rapid social change of any sort, with its turbulence, its constant overhauling of bureaucratic procedures, and its threat of loss of support from conservatives in the outside community. Moreover, they are drawn to the hawks position by a shared sense of indignation, though it is based on a different calculation. The temporizers had been impressed by the amount of movement shown by the school prior to the outbreak of the initial disorder. They had shared, vicariously or actually, the "liberalization" of American life in recent decades, the partial transformation of habitual "racist," "anti-student," or indifferent attitudes which this "liberal" movement entailed. Accordingly, they feel offended by the ingratitude of the aggrieved students, who, in their perception, are "biting the hand that feeds them." This feeling is not shared by the hawks, who feel that too much attention has been given to the students all along; nor by the doves, who feel that students have had too little attention. The function of this "betrayal reaction," then, is to diminish the willingness of the temporizers to listen sympathetically to the students in the course of any negotiations — an effect in line anyway with their go-slow policy.

The sense of betrayal is shared by many persons in the general public who ask, with genuine annoyance and uncomprehension, "What do these students want, anyway?" or who write to college authorities demanding that no more concessions be granted the students. Naturally enough, the conservative publications provide ample fuel for such sentiments, but even the "liberal" press is apt to respond with the dismay provoked by feelings of betrayal. For example, in an editorial on December 6, 1968, the *New York Times* said, "Recent episodes at Fordham University, New York University, and San Francisco State College mark a new upsurge in the recurrent effort of a tiny minority to disrupt academic life. College and university officials should have learned by now that it is useless and dangerous to appease or compromise with such disruptive tactics. There is no place and no excuse for violence on the Campus." On March 18, 1969, an editorial in the *Christian Science Monitor,* indulging in the classical phraseology of outrage, said, "There is no longer any excuse — social, political, pedagogical, or theoretical — for college authorities, city officials, or the police

379

to allow rioting, vandalism, terrorism or just plain nastiness to continue on campuses of higher learning." The *Monitor's* fit of indignation seems to have swept its editorial staff off its feet; no matter how firm the regime, nor how many college authorities, city officials, and police officers are brought to bear on the situation, it seems doubtful that "just plain nastiness" can be banished from the campus, or anywhere else.

The polarization of the third phase is painful for most participants. Old friends find themselves unable to converse; people who have scarcely met fall into shouting matches; alliances hastily set up come crashing down, often aided by gossip communicated with the best of intentions. Faculty meetings based on *Robert's Rules of Order* become travesties of rational discussion, with members heatedly declaring each other out of order or throwing other monkey wrenches into the parliamentary machinery.[2] Peacemakers by the dozen offer their own special formulas for solving everything. The intensity of the frustration of concerted action, the apparent reality of institutional chaos combined with the exhaustion of sleepless nights, produces a sense of "executive fatigue," a state in which no decision seems well considered or objectively arrived at. The temptation to avoid or withdraw from the struggle is very strong. It is not unusual for some administrators or faculty to threaten to resign in the heat of controversy, though actual resignations are ordinarily reserved for the soberer and more reflective mood of the aftermath of the crisis.[3]

Despite the appearance of chaos, the group process is actually moving toward resolution, the fourth phase of the crisis. The manner in which the crisis is resolved varies so much from institution to institution that no general description can be offered. The

---

[2] An amusing description (for those not attending it) of a typically frustrating faculty meeting during the height of a crisis is to be found in Orrick 1969, pp. 52-53.

[3] The "walk-out" and the "walk-in" ("sit-in," "sleep-in," "study-in," etc.) appear to be two of the most effective weapons in the whole armamentarium of nonviolent techniques of disruption. To fail to appear at a meeting or to leave in the middle puts an effective stop to action. To appear when not wanted can be equally effective. Seizing a building combines both techniques and is, thus, doubly effective. "Intrusion" and "exclusion," the action bases of these techniques, are universal attention-getting devices, whether used legally or illegally. This is what makes the "we cannot excuse or condone" approach so weak and ineffective as a policy and so hypocritical or comical as a posture.

resolution can be "hawkish," "dovish," or in line with the middle ground of the "temporizers." No matter which method resolves the crisis, there is likely to be some effort made to establish negotiations with the dissident students. The students, of course, do not acknowledge that such an event is occurring, their demands being "non-negotiable." Similarly, the university authorities must officially deny that any such thing is taking place since they will "not negotiate" under threat or force. If not held in secret, such conversations are called "explorations" or "clarification of demands." The function of labeling continues to be prominent throughout the crisis.

If efforts are actually established to end the struggle without using external force, severe dissension occurs within the student group about how much or little to settle for. Hard-liners, often women adept at shaming the men, remind the group that *none* of the demands are negotiable.[4] Moderates, arguing for a policy of realism, urge settling for what they regard as the administration's best possible offer. Extreme activists suggest escalating the disorder, while those with less taste for prolonged struggle indicate a reluctance to go on much longer. In the course of the prolonged discussions aimed at resolving these differences, attitudes and arguments frequently harden. The bitterness underlying such affairs seems to be an example of what Freud called "the narcissism of small differences." In the atmosphere of emergency, small differences in tactics or goals assume huge proportions and are then used to separate the strong from the weak, the "good guys" from the "bad guys," or the true revolutionary from the phony reformist. Here again, labeling and emotionalism rather than precise political or sociological analysis seem the preferred ways of solving a problem.

An important aspect of the negotiations, once they start, is the degree to which administration and student representatives at the negotiating sessions miscommunicate. Identical words and expressions mean different things to the two parties. To the extent that this is the case, such sessions really *are* more for the sake of clarification than negotiation. In part, misunderstanding occurs

---

[4] The intransigent attitude of the female leaders seems to arise less from a purely competitive urge than from having abandoned the more traditional feminine role of peacemaker. Such a role would undermine the whole position of the women within the aggrieved group. But having given it up, the women appear to be particularly sensitized to the possibility of its being taken over by any of the men.

because of the gap in values, beliefs and experience separating the two groups. In part, the failure of communication results from the novelty of such occasions and the absence of any traditional or agreed upon style of conduct for the procedures (conventions such as those that characterize labor bargaining, for example). But in large part, the communication failures are also the product of unconscious psychological processes, which will be discussed subsequently.

Aftermath

The last phase of the crisis process, the aftermath, is formally not a part of the crisis itself. However, there are two related aspects of the aftermath that are relevant to our purposes. The first is the "Rashomon effect," the varying and often incompatible stories that are told of what transpired during the crisis. Interviewers from the media and committees appointed to review the events are frequently surprised by the conflicting narrations of supposedly the same incident obtained from different persons. Certainly this is not a new finding in the history of psychology. The surprise occurs because the discrepancies are so blatant and the witnesses so credible.

The second matter has to do not with inconsistencies in what people remember but with what they "forget." To be sure, with so much happening from hour to hour, no one can witness, much less recall, the whole spectrum of events. What stands out, however, is the inability of people to remember things that they themselves have said and done and that others retain vividly in mind.

For example, after a particularly frustrating faculty meeting during the height of one campus crisis, a junior faculty member, who was a dove, engaged a senior colleague in the same department in a corridor conversation. The young man was attempting to defend the legitimacy of the students' occupation of a campus building by drawing an analogy to the labor movement, especially its earlier phases when strikes, picketing, and sit-ins were still matters of controversy. During the faculty meeting, the senior professor had vigorously attacked the seizure of the building, warning of the fatal consequences to the university if it were allowed to continue. During the corridor conversation, he repeated these arguments and, with some asperity, denied the merits of the labor analogy. When the junior colleague continued to press his argument, the hawk grew red with rage, advised the younger man not to address him by his first name, told him he didn't know what he was talking about, then, with a certain dignified, almost classical flourish, turned on his heel (just as in 19th-century novels), and abruptly departed. After the crisis had died down, this incident was mentioned to the older man. He had no memory of it, denied that it had ever occurred, and showed mild irritation at the suggestion that he could have behaved in such a fashion.

A similar blank wall was encountered at another university when a journalist attempted to interview a high administrative official about the events of the campus crisis. The interview had started in a jovial, friendly atmosphere and continued for some time in this vein. Through others, the journalist had learned that the president had made vacillating statements on the subject of disciplining the rebellious students, at times threatening severe punishment, at other times suggesting that only mild procedures would be used if the students left the building they were occupying. When the journalist brought this up, without revealing his sources, the atmosphere suddenly cooled. Uncertainty was categorically interpreted by the official as "weakness," and its existence in this instance was denied, to the surprise of the journalist, who thought there must be good reasons on both sides of the ticklish question of punishment versus amnesty. When he pursued the point, he was accused of being hostile to the university and oversympathetic to the line adopted by the radical students. The journalist was amazed at the situation he found himself in but was unable to extricate himself. The encounter terminated on a note of muted tension and bitterness. The journalist found the whole episode bizarre and difficult to fathom. He was still quite shaken by it when, soon afterward, he reported the incident to one of our staff members.

EGO MECHANISMS

We have now come to the point where we can ask: what is it about the crisis that accounts for the forgetting, the exaggerations, and the distorted, hostile interpersonal relations in which participants become involved?

Let us begin with the dissident students who provide the apparent stimulus for the crisis. Since they constitute a group — an aggrieved group — we must examine the identifications that hold the group together and apart from the usual student groups. Obviously an extensive transformation of both the object and the nature of identifications has taken place. In the past, and for many students still, faculty and administrative figures are accepted as persons with whose values, if not personalities, the student can identify. There is among most students a generally positive orientation toward scholarship, research, and teaching; this is one factor in the large number of undergraduates who apply for graduate training. And in the past, at any rate, students have been able to overlook the paternalistic behavior of their mentors, sorting out in their own minds and discriminating between the best and worst aspects of university life. They usually accept their student leaders as substitutes, junior partners or intermediate figures in a ladder of positive images pointing toward their own futures. Now comes a gradual but traumatic disillusionment with the university, deep suspicion of its good faith and essential benevolence, and bitterness over the failure of their petition for the relief of grievances. Hence the previously positive side of the identification process is put to severe strain.

In his original discussion of the role of identification in the process of group formation Freud said, "Identification is ambivalent from the very first; it can turn into an expression of tenderness as easily as into a wish for someone's removal." In the same work, *Group Psychology and the Analysis of the Ego,* he said, "The leader or the leading idea might also, so to speak, be negative; hatred against a particular person or institution might operate in just the same unifying way and might call up the same kind of emotional ties as positive attachment."[5] Though Freud never commented in any detail on the transformation of group identification from primarily positive to primarily negative shared attitudes toward the leader of the institution, we can perhaps employ an observation he made in another context as the intervening link in this process. In the first of the two essays included in *Thoughts for the Times on War and Death,* when speaking of the effects upon the intellectual community of the outbreak of World War I, he said, "Then the war in which we had refused to believe broke out, and brought — disillusionment . . . . The individual in any given nation has in this war a terrible opportunity to convince himself of what would occasionally strike him in peace time — that the state has forbidden to the individual the practice of wrongdoing, not because it desired to abolish it, but because it desires to monopolize it, like salt and tobacco." *(S. Freud 1915, pp. 292-93)*

---

[5] S. Freud 1921. Freud repeated this observation in his letter to Einstein *Why War?* and again in *Civilization and Its Discontents*; but in neither instance did he subject the matter to any further discussion or analysis, except insofar as he joined it to the notion of the "narcissism of minor differences."

384

This sentiment, uttered fifty-odd years ago, was widely shared by intellectuals steeped in the humanist tradition and wholly alienated from the militaristic and patriotic fervor which swept the warring nations. In England, Bertrand Russell went to jail for his pacifist, anti-government writings. Lytton Strachey told the Hampstead Tribunal (the equivalent of a contemporary draft board), "This objection [to the war] is not based upon religious belief, but upon moral considerations, at which I have arrived after long and painful thought. I do not wish to assert the extremely general proposition that I should never, in any circumstances, be justified in taking part in any conceivable war; to dogmatize so absolutely upon a point so abstract would appear to me to be unreasonable. At the same time, my feeling is directed not simply against the present war; I am convinced that the system by which it is sought to settle international disputes by force is profoundly evil; and that, so far as I am concerned, I should be doing wrong to take part in it." *(Holroyd 1968, II, p. 177)*

Such reactions to government policy during World War I appear as pale precursors to the convictions of dissident students today concerning the evils of the war in Vietnam. If we remember that such students are self-selected among the general student body on the basis of their intellectuality, awareness of social trends throughout the world, and high standards for political morality, then their sense of disillusion follows logically from the expectations based upon their previous schooling. The germ of the hostile belief system embedded in Freud's and Strachey's comments is, of course, enormously elaborated in the dissident students' "thoughts for the times," in ways that need not be reviewed here. But it seems plausible to assume that the hostile attitude toward the authority of the state and toward all who cooperate with it, including the universities, follows upon the disillusionment. The withdrawal of respect and admiration replaces love with hate and releases super-ego constraints where most authority figures are concerned.

As a result, most authorities, intellectual or administrative, are seen in accordance with the model of the state as oppressive, manipulative, and corrupting. Although this perception is magnified by the newly formed negative identifications, it is also close to the truth. Jails and the armed forces aside, schools, colleges and universities are among the most irrationally authoritarian of American institutions. More precisely, so far as formal organizations are concerned, they are characterized to an unusual degree by decentralized oligarchies: many faculty members are responsible to one departmental chairman, surrounded by his clique of "inner circle" confidants; many departmental chairmen are responsible to one dean who is more loyal, on the whole, to the president and the various governing boards than to the intimate concerns of the departments. The decentralization of oligarchies guarantees feeble communication of mutual concerns. The various departments and their chairmen know or care little about other departments; and the higher administration, erroneously persuaded that departmental freedom and independence are being encouraged, receive scant information about the needs of the department except where their own, usually fiscal, interests are concerned. Thus, despite (or because of) the misleading slogan of "academic freedom" (which literally means freedom to hold and teach unpopular views) the most important policy decisions are made at the top by boards which have little or no contact with staff and line personnel.

The role of the student is beset by similar anomalies. A school shares incompatible features of a hospital, a jail, a retail commercial outlet, and a club. Like a patient in a hospital, it will do the student little good to complain about the service and he must follow orders. Like an inmate in a jail, the student can be put on probation or punished in other ways for infractions of rules. But, like the customer, he can shop around for consumer products, hoping to accumulate an education with which to impress future employers. Finally, as a club member, he can be granted or denied admission, and he is expected to contribute to and take pride in the elite status of his membership.[6]

As a result of these singular institutional arrangements, until the advent of the student power movement, students had few rights and little control over their lives.

With the attainment of the partially realistic perception of the administration as the "oppressor," the student's ego is suddenly assailed with anxiety from three sides.[7] From the environment, the

---

[6] There are only a few studies of the forms and effects of authoritarian structure in the universities. Riesman and Jencks 1968 touch upon the effects. Newcomb 1969 has summarized studies comparing universities with industrial organizations in this regard, adding cogent observations of his own. A more general analysis of the authoritarian structure of American society, and of localized rebellion as a way of democratization, is presented by Walzer 1969.

[7] To call this perception "partially realistic" is not to say that administrators explicitly intend to oppress students. On the contrary, administrators

ego must face the real possibility of punishment for the loss of respect toward authorities. From the id there is the possibility of being overwhelmed with rage, including the resurrection of long-repressed oedipal hostilities. And from the superego there still remains the possibility of guilt. The loss of positive identification is not as deep or thoroughgoing as it may seem at first glance. In fact, the negative side of the identification is like a thin, protective armor that requires constant reinforcement. Therefore guilt feelings must be constantly warded off.

Under these circumstances the ego must be protected. Two defenses are available for this purpose, and used together, they prove fairly serviceable. The first is identification with the aggressor — or, as one might say in this instance, with the oppressor. Anxiety is dispelled in the fashion described by Anna Freud, not through a general identification but by means of an imitation of the aggressor's behavior as perceived by the victim. *(A. Freud 1946, pp. 117-31)* Are the authorities insensitive, unresponsive, willing to use force (the brutal police, the narrow-minded lower courts) to get their way? Yes. Then so are the students. Is the aggressor frustrating and evasive? The list could be extended, but the point is clear.[8]

That this process is unconscious and not well controlled by reality is revealed in a variety of ways. The hostile, disrespectful, impatient attitudes demonstrated toward administrators is apt to be

---

often feel themselves caught up in a system which they are powerless to change and duty-bound to uphold, despite their own dissatisfactions with it. A study carried out by the staff of the Center for Research and Development in Higher Education, University of California at Berkeley, and reported in their newsletter *The Research Reporter* (Vol. IV, No. 1, 1969), reflects such feelings. Thirty percent of all administrators, and fifty percent of the academic vice-presidents, disagreed with the statement, "Open flouting of the university rules is always wrong." Sixty-three percent of all administrators (in each of sixty-nine of the largest and most prestigious universities in the United States) agreed that "A show of 'student power' is sometimes necessary."

[8] The process is complicated by the presence of "projective identification." Students' perceptions of the administrators are exaggerated by the attribution to the administrators of unconscious hostility felt within the self. Thus what is copied is not faithful to the original model. Once the process is initiated, however, the behavior of the students may instigate behavior by the administrators which brings out the very qualities students had assumed to be present, if concealed, from the beginning.

exhibited by student protestors in their behavior toward each other. Since the behavior is defensive rather than a spontaneous release of instinctual energy, it is rarely satisfying, and on this account, prompts a continuous search for new objects. It tends to be ritualized — that is, automatically displayed in the presence of any member of the administration. As reality testing is reduced, the students tend to misjudge clues of receptivity and change in their opponents. Opportunities for successfully pressing their advantage are frequently passed up on this account.

Because of the novelty of the defense, it is always in danger of breaking down. The second defense is then brought to the rescue: the principle of negative justice. Each member of the aggrieved group must be known to the others as equally deserving of the retributions of the oppressor, lest group solidarity weaken. Thus each must provoke in the same way and to the same degree. To maintain such conduct in the face of the positive feelings being warded off — to say nothing of long standing habits — is difficult. To be on the safe side, the aggrieved group needs to keep away from frequent contacts with the administration and to be sure that, when contacts are made, at least three members are together, watching each other and helping each other to continue to display the requisite degree of distance and scorn.

In *The Strawberry Statement: Notes of a College Revolutionary,* James S. Kunen, who participated in the Columbia uprising, cites an amusing example of this sort of ambiguity in student attitudes. In his role as commentator on the local scene, Kunen had made an appointment to interview Dean Herbert Deane of Columbia, a confrontation to which he looked forward with a certain degree of malice, as well as curiosity. Herbert Deane had provided Kunen with the title of his book. In April 1967, a year before the campus crisis, Deane had made the comment, "A university is definitely not a democratic institution. When decisions begin to be made democratically around here, I will not be here any longer. Whether students vote 'yes' or 'no' on an issue is like telling me they like strawberries." After a long, friendly and candid conversation with this paragon of academic paternalism in July 1968, Kunen wrote in his diary, "God, what am I going to do? I *liked* Dean Deane." *(Kunen 1969, p. 116)*

Nevertheless, at the height of the crisis, the students' defenses produce a rigidly maintained and often affected hostile manner. This is not to say that the behavior is insincere; rather, it is out of control because of the conflicting inner feelings. This is one of the

388

reasons for the poor communication during negotiating sessions, noted above. It is also one of the conscious reasons for the activity of the doves, who perceive that the students are not presenting their case in the best light and therefore need an advocate.

Despite their defensiveness in the presence of authority figures and the sometimes inappropriate behavior toward each other evoked by the identification with the aggressors, the students generally display warm relations within the group. The libidinal component which has been detached from authority figures is now directed toward the group as a whole. The resulting increase in available affectionate energy and the closeness of personal relations leads to a rise in group morale. Throughout much of the crisis the students' ability to display wit, humor, and creative activity reaches unusual heights. The occasion becomes memorable in their eyes, and even in the eyes of some outside observers, because of the exuberant energies it releases, and because of some of the comic scenes acted out on all sides.

In *The Strawberry Statement,* for example, James Kunen describes an incident which occurred when the Columbia students arrested in the April 29, 1968, bust were taken to the 24th Precinct Station to be booked: " 'Up against the wall,' we are told. I can't get over how they really use the term. We turn and lean on the wall with our hands high, because that's what we've seen in the movies. We are told to can that shit and sit down." The police, it turned out, merely wanted the students to sit on the chairs along the walls.

The doves within the faculty and administration are among those favorably impressed with the novel, creative aspects of student activity. Anxious as they are to be of help, they, too, are under the influence of an unconscious, defensive process: a variant of what Anna Freud has called "altruistic surrender." In their face-off with the hawks they are not asking for anything for themselves, as are the hawks and the students. Their motives are purely altruistic in that they want to see the students obtain a "fair shake" from the administration. For this reason they undertake, at great cost of energy and possible risk of their security, a strenuous defense of the students' cause. The unconscious motive for this position, however, is envy of the students' aggressiveness. They would like to have the role of the young students for themselves, defying the established authorities, bringing them to heel, and reaping the rewards of victory in the manner of David over Goliath. The oedipal background of such an identification with the challengers, is, again, a part of the constellation of motives. But in the foreground is the problem of envy too productive of guilt-feeling to be directly acknowledged. Accordingly, to back the challengers, to take the risks without reaping the rewards, to offer themselves up to the wrath of the hawks as sacrificial lambs — all these behaviors neutralize the claims of the superego.

Although the voice of the doves exerts a strong influence on the outcome of the crisis, it generates severe antagonisms. Its defensive quality is perceived by both students and hawks. Students feel that doves are defending them for the wrong reasons, that is, for their own narcissistic (or "liberal") reasons and not because of a realistic understanding of the students' position. Hawks, on the other hand, immediately assume that behind the even-tempered and apparently reasonable arguments of the doves there lies an intense desire to humble them.[9]

This sensitivity on the part of the hawks, which to the dovish mind looks so paranoid, is based upon a strong, narcissistic defense. Although hawks show a good deal of variation in personality and background factors, the largest number of them are men who have climbed up the academic ladder from humble origins. They have obtained positions of some power and influence through hard work and the sacrifice of pleasure, exemplifying in the process the individualistic, achievement values of American culture. Not only have pleasures been postponed, but, in addition, such men have had to endure narcissistic wounds and humiliation in the struggle to rise from an inferior status to one of relative superiority. At last they are in a position to enjoy their hard-won privileges — that is, to have power over others, to make the decisions they have accepted from others on the way up. Moreover, in their view, they have been fairer in the exercise of power than have their predecessors. Now, just at this moment, they suddenly find themselves challenged. They are being asked to share their power with the young, with student usurpers who lack self-discipline and are completely callow about the difficulties of obtaining power and the responsibilities of

---

[9] Abrasive behavior between hawks and doves is not confined to the campus. It can break out anywhere and often disrupts cocktail and dinner parties. At the May 1969 annual meeting of the American Association of University Professors, in Minneapolis, a stormy session, punctuated by several angry shouting matches, followed a panel discussion of "confrontation tactics." In the general heat and din one professor accused a colleague of being a "cop-out" and "coward," and another asked in shocked tones, "Are you confronting me, sir?"

exercising it. To add insult to injury, though they deem themselves to be defending liberal principles, their behavior is called reactionary or authoritarian by their opponents.[10]

Under these circumstances, with pride so largely dependent on their careers and the prerogatives of office, the demands and behavior of the dissident students represent direct assaults upon their self-esteem. It is as if they were being forced to return to their humble origins. The narcissistic defense then enlarges the ego by identifying its fate with that of the institution, or even with the country as a whole. If they are to be destroyed, then so is the school and the nation. The view is, after all, not so irrational as it may seem. For the attack upon the hawks is an attack upon the structure of power and the hierarchical values of superiority and inferiority concealed behind the individualism that is supposedly the mainspring of our democracy.[11]

So far as the temporizers are concerned, their unconscious motives are more varied and more difficult to discern. Some are merely timid and cautious, defending themselves against anxiety through watchfulness and delay of action. Others are really emotionally uninvolved in the struggle, denying their unconscious feel-

---

[10] Here we meet the problem with labels again. The word, "liberal," is beginning to lose its meaning. For example, in an article in the July 1969 *Atlantic Monthly,* entitled "The Campus Crucible," Nathan Glazer, traditionally a liberal, but hawkish on the subject of student rebellions, speaks about "the failure of the liberals." By this expression he means faculty members whose sympathy with the goals of the students prevents them from subjecting the tactics of the students to a sufficiently penetrating (and disapproving) critique. If we are forced to make a distinction between hawkish and dovish brands of liberalism, we might as well give up using the word altogether. Of course, the words hawk and dove are labels too, but they have the advantage of being issue-oriented.

[11] Some of the academic hawks are refugees from European communist or fascist regimes, or from left-wing parties in this country. Their experience, either in universities or in other contexts, has been so traumatic, their responses to political intransigence so conditioned and stigmatized, as to render them incapable of making any distinctions where goals of political activity are concerned. For them, any extreme position, whether of the right or the left, is devastating. Still, behind their fears lurks the authoritarianism and elitism of their country of origin, which the regime or party, whether communist or fascist, has exploited. Thus, both reality and fantasy contribute to their responses. The sign of their inability to test reality on this score is their impatience. They cannot wait to find out how far or where student rebelliousness will go. It must be crushed immediately, regardless of its emergent goals and of its constantly changing tactics.

391

ings through isolation. Still others are convinced that compromise and a Hegelian synthesis of opposites are the only effective methods of conflict resolution, techniques that always require time. Because their motives are obscure or undefined, temporizers are apt to be made into scapegoats for the frustrations felt by all. Their delaying tactics and shillyshallying policies are seen as the reasons why the crisis lasts so long.

TRANSACTION, INTERACTION, AND SELF-ACTION

This review of the ego mechanisms and defenses elicited by the crisis is not very satisfactory. It is far from a complete inventory of unconscious ego mechanisms, and it leaves many problems unresolved. It produces the impression that no group comes off very well in the struggle. If there are no very obvious villains, neither are there any heroes. Moreover, it places me in an awkward position since I have not explicitly aligned myself with any group. Can the investigator of such situations really remain above the fray, analyzing everyone's motives except his own? Especially if the investigator is also an academician?

The pressure to take sides is intense. Not only one's inner promptings are at work, but also the expectations of others. As has been repeatedly (and regretfully) observed, in the current heated atmosphere it is difficult to maintain a dispassionate, objective position. Moreover, in some quarters, notably among the students, lack of passion is suspect; it is regarded as indicating insincerity or evasiveness.

Despite these pressures, I should like to postpone stating my position till the conclusion. Rather, I would ask whether there is not a line of argument capable of avoiding an emotional but somewhat arbitrary commitment, on the one hand, and an intellectual withdrawal, on the other. Is there not some mode of analysis which can bring the goals of change desired by the students and their tactics — as well as the goals and tactics of their opponents — into the same frame of reference? Can we devise some language capable of displaying pathology, either within the individual or within the structure of the university, as the outcome of a larger process? Finally, can such an approach indicate the direction in which a possible solution might lie?

I believe that answers to these questions can be found in the transactional mode of analysis proposed by Dewey and Bentley (Chapters One and Two). These writers, one a philosopher, the other a political economic analyst, started with a critique of theories of knowledge, but, like Whitehead, they ended up with a new formulation of process. *(Whitehead 1929.)* Process, they said, has been explained as the operation of self-acting entities or as the result of interaction between entities. They suggested that a more appropriate description would refer to transaction among systems. *Self-action* describes a pre-set entity, like a clock, all wound up and ready to go at a given activation. All the elements of the process are within the entity — the star, the gene, the plant, the personality, the institution — and will simply unfold themselves over time, at least under the right circumstances.

Interaction describes a process in which entities are connected with entities in a sequence of action and reaction, like billiard balls. The patient unburdens herself to her therapist; the therapist makes an interpretation; the patient goes home and for the first time tells her husband what she really thinks of him; the husband calls the therapist in a rage; the therapist notes that the patient is losing some of her inhibitions but, in the process, may be acting out too much. The focus is on the behavior of each entity rather than on the interplay of all as a system.

Transaction refers to a web of complex, interwoven systems within a total field such as the metabolic, endocrine, and neuro-physiological processes that maintain blood sugar at a steady level. Because of the chain-like and reverberating effects, with constant, mutual adjustment of subsystems to each other, such processes cannot be appropriately described by reference to the activity of any one organ or structure. All systems are involved in the behavior of all. On this view, structure (an organ, an institution) becomes both the product of the systems which maintain it and the source (if one is needed) of the activity of some of the systems. The choice of cause or effect is up to the observer — a product of *his* activity — rather than a fixed principle given in the nature of "reality." What is found when the scientist publishes a finding is what he had arranged to look at, because nature consists merely of processes of exchange — that is, of transactions.[12]

To place the processes of campus disorders within this framework, I should like to argue that the description offered by Bettelheim and Feuer and discussed above are examples of cause

---

[12] These views are quite similar to those labeled "general systems theory," though the two bodies of ideas developed independently. Transaction theory is more philosophical in orientation, general systems theory more empirical, but otherwise there is no fundamental inconsistency between the two.

attributed to self-action. In response to the stimulus of a general wave of protest sentiment, with a stylized list of complaints, the pre-existing neurotic problems of the activist students are externalized into a movement whose supporters see it as interaction. If it is self-actional, then the critiques of Bettelheim and Feuer are the logical correctives.

The description which I have just given, on the other hand, is mainly interactional, specifying the conditions to which the "aggrieved" group respond, the initial reactions back and forth in ping-pong manner. While less biased and mechanical than self-action descriptions, it is still selective and thus arbitrary.[13] Omitting some factors from consideration may have unduly biased the explanation. But, since any scientific approach is based on the selection of some variables and the omission of others, how can this deficiency be repaired?

In struggling with the problem in the past, I have proposed for consideration a *field of transacting systems* composed of six foci: the Universe (physico-chemical and cosmic systems), the Soma (biological systems), the Psyche (cognitive and emotional systems), the Group (small face-to-face organizations), the Society (governmental, economic, educational, religious, recreational, intellectual-aesthetic, and family systems), and the Culture (language, technological, value and belief systems). (Chapter Two) The foci are arranged, for graphic and representational purposes, in a circle so that all are interconnected. Processes within and between foci are assumed to run in either direction around the periphery, eliminating the need to specify "cause and effect" except for the aims of a particular investigation. Although all foci are assumed to be operative at all times in the smallest or largest phenomena, as many foci (or parts of foci) as one wishes can be disregarded, provided one allows for the probability of error as a result of the exclusion.

In the interactional analysis presented above, parts of three

---

[13] Dewey and Bentley maintained that self-actional and interactional descriptions were always wrong—anachronistic and misleading. It can be argued, however, that though they are incomplete, they are not on that account necessarily wrong. All behaviorist theories of learning based on the stimulus-response model, for example, are self-actional. They are extremely incomplete. In most, only the unconditioned response repertoire of the organism is observed and worked with. The processes within the organism which are correlated with such responses are mainly ignored (the "little black box" approach). Nevertheless, the observed effects of the experimenter's conditioning procedures are valid within the highly restricted area of his operations and have useful applications.

foci within the transactional field were considered: the Psyche (including unconscious processes), the Group, and Society, at least as represented by educational institutions.[14] Although parts of several other foci could have been plugged into the aggregate of processes, what is conspicuously missing is any consideration of the cultural focus, especially the cultural values governing decision-making processes within the society as a whole and within the university.[15] Bringing this system of values into the analysis is crucial because it is the key to the conflict within the institution as well as to the related conflict within the larger society. To introduce the topic, I shall use the language and concepts proposed by Florence R. Kluckhohn in her analysis of variation in cultural value orientations. *(F. Kluckhohn 1961.)*

The Kluckhohn theory assumes that all cultures (and sub-cultures) find the same solutions to the problem of group relations and decision-making; they vary, however, in the rank-ordering or patterning of the solutions. With respect to authority and decisions, the solutions discoverable in every culture are: (1) the Lineal, in which group relations are arranged vertically, accenting the dominance of the superior over the inferior, with decisions made at the top; (2) the Collateral, in which horizontal group relations are stressed, with decisions made by prolonged discussion to reach group consensus; and (3) the Individual, in which each person is equal to any other and thus is free, indeed obligated, to make up his own mind and to choose his own affiliations, with group decisions taken by majority vote.

The pattern of preference promulgated under the aegis of American democracy is first the Individual; second the Collateral; and third the Lineal solution. We are all educated in accordance with this pattern: Americans should be independent and unsubmissive but in an emergency or for team efforts we should all pull together within the collateral group. While authoritarian hierarchies might be necessary evils, our sympathies are with the little man at the bottom and against the bosses.

Despite the widespread acceptance of this pattern as official

---

[14] The exclusion of economic systems from the previous discussion and from what follows, is a bias which, unfortunately, I am not in a position to control, though I hope to repair the omission in future studies.

[15] For example, somatic factors such as fatigue and the effects of youth and such physical factors as weather (winter being unfavorable to, though not necessarily preventing, campus disorders) could obviously have been given extended consideration.

ideology, if one inspects the actual functioning of our major institutions, one comes across a paradox. Government, schools, most commercial organizations, the economy, the relations between ethnic groups and social classes — all are oriented to a different pattern: the Individual is still first, but Lineality is in the second position, with Collaterality a poor third. The vertical structuring of power is at times so prominent — for example, in our foreign policy generally and particularly in Vietnam — as to assume a virtual first-order position. The accompanying elitism is usually hidden beneath a mask of individualism, as in the notion of a "meritocracy" (the best float to the top).[16] But, in fact, one finds rule by oligarchy, whether carried out by big city "machines," university boards and deans, or congressional committees dominated by Southern conservatives.

As a result of this paradox, our values (cultural beliefs about the way things should be) do not correspond to our practices (the way things really are). Or, to put the matter more precisely, the value orientations which support our institutions are in conflict with the values represented in our official ideology and, accordingly, in our ideal self-concept. Such a conflict in values cannot exist without generating some groups organized to expose it and to change the structure of the social system. Nor can it exist without giving rise to intrapsychic conflict, especially to problems of identity and more especially where the young are concerned. Which way is the student to direct himself: toward power and success ("making it") or toward fulfillment for the self and others?

Whenever groups are beset by a basic conflict in values, there are only a limited number of ways in which chaos and disintegration can be avoided. The conflict can be denied, concealed, or explained away, in which case all concerned are expected to buy the formula which buries the conflict. If such techniques of persuasion fail, then coercion, involving the use of force and punishment, can be used for those who resist the more "reasonable" methods of suppressing the conflict. For example, those who are older, who are in authority, and whose life-style was formed by somehow successfully getting around the conflict (and who therefore feel threatened by being brought to face it again) are likely to start off with some

---

[16] A cynic might say that they do not float to the top; they claw their way up! A cynic is a person who recognizes rather than denies a value conflict but does not propose to do anything about it. However, many students, perhaps a majority, still want nothing more than the opportunity to fight their way up the ladder of achievement.

dissembling technique if challenged. They will say that America is the freest country in the world (denial of conflict), or that the challenger has to recognize the difference between ideals and reality (rationalization of conflict), or that the challenger is right, but things are slowly getting better, and he should be patient (delay as a method of conflict avoidance).

Conflicts act like pain or any other irritant. They must either be avoided or resolved. In the past, and to a large degree still, American students have tended to accept the conflict-avoiding explanations proposed by their wiser and more experienced elders. If they no longer accept conflict-avoidance as readily as in the past, it is because the chances for actual resolution now seem better, and accordingly, the value conflict stands out in sharper relief.[17] Once convinced that the time is ripe, students discover that for each conflict-avoiding technique there exists a "neutralizer" capable of exposing the conflict. *(See Spiegel 1957.)* For example, denial can be met by assertion (the poor, the draftees, the blacks, the Spanish-Americans, the Indians are oppressed); rationalization can be countered by *unmasking* ("reality" doesn't require that poor people be thrown out of their homes by university expansion), and delay can be interrupted by *provocation,* which moves forward the timetable for facing conflicts. Even coercion, the last resort of the powerful, can be met by *counter-coercion* — by sabotage or defiance, the last weapons of the weak.

Of all these methods for exposing the basic conflict of values, "provoking," "unmasking," and "counter-coercing" are the most disruptive. When dissident students sit in as uninvited guests at a faculty meeting, break up a lecture by seizing the microphone, or occupy a building, they gain nothing for themselves. Their actions are effective only because they are norm-violating — an outrage which, like personal insult or injury, can scarcely be disregarded. Any tendency by officialdom to postpone facing the conflict is dealt a severe blow. When students raid the personal files of university officials and publish letters exposing the discrepancy between the public and private views of these officials, they inflict similar injury

---

[17] Each of the upsurges of student protest described by Lewis Feuer occurred at a time when the prospects for social change seemed excellent, given a push by a resolute minority. Despite its self-actional theory, Feuer's book contains many pertinent interactional descriptions, including precise accounts of the value conflict associated with each cycle of the movement. *(Feuer 1969.)*

to convention and public morality. But, on the other hand, the value conflict can no longer be explained away.

We are now in a position to examine the three-way struggle between hawks, doves, and dissident students from a transactional point of view. The neutralizing techniques of the students lay bare the value conflict which has so long been concealed and denied. Every one of the specific "issues" brought up by the students — whether concerned with race, with capitalist exploitation, with the war in Vietnam, with the institution's complicity in the military-industrial complex, with the curriculum or other "student power" issues — all are reflections of the conflict between individualistic, democratic ideals and authoritarian, elitist practices.

Faced with the exposure of the conflict in all its native crudeness, administrators have three choices. They can acknowledge the conflict and embrace Lineality openly, as did Dean Herbert Deane of Columbia: "When decisions begin to be made democratically around here, I will not be here any longer." They can admit the conflict and endorse the official American pattern, usually through implementing some of the students' demands after a thorough discussion. The third option is to continue rationalizing and denying the conflict while describing the students' provocations as representing the very essence of that arbitrary and authoritarian style which the students attribute to the administration. It is this third position which becomes the core of the hawks' opposition to the students' behavior.

Confronted with this situation, the doves face a difficult choice. It is hard to deny the sincerity, even the possible validity of the hawks' fear that student provocation imperils the very "justice" they seek. On the other hand, doves are well aware of the unwillingness of the hawks to face these issues without student pressure. Weighing these two risks, they come to the conclusion that the danger of supporting the students is not as great as claimed by the hawks, while supporting the hawks would guarantee preservation of the status quo.

The doves and the student leaders of the "aggrieved" groups are on the side of change. If the above analysis is correct, then the advocates of change are also advocating that the value conflict be brought out into the open. It is in connection with the transactional implications of this process that I should like to state my own position. I have felt it necessary to make the case for my position carefully, and at length, because it does not conform precisely to any of the standard positions and because, as a student of violence, I am expected to pursue the matter to whatever lengths, pleasant or unpleasant, the evidence seems to lead.

My position is that of a therapist. All therapists have the experience of dealing with conflict wherever they find it, within the person, within the family, or within the culture. Their experience tells them that a concealed conflict almost always has unfortunate effects. It also tells them that in the process of therapy, if it is to be effective, the forces that hide the conflict are loosened, and that, as the conflict erupts into the open, the patient or the family undergoes considerable pain and discomfiture. It is a time for fastening the seat belts. But only by undergoing this exposure can the systems in conflict be brought into a better state of mutual accommodation. This does not mean that the conflict vanishes but only that the person, the family or the afflicted organization of whatever type is able to make a better choice between the two sides of the conflict. Resolution of the conflict means that there is knowledge of what is to be lost and gained by promoting one side of the conflict and demoting the other and that this knowledge can be put into action.

Holding these views, I can reach no other conclusion than that the student leaders are performing a therapeutic function by forcing the value conflict into the open. Of course, there is the danger that some students may become fixated on provoking as an end rather than a means. But this risk does not seem to me to be greater than those encountered in any therapeutic "working through" of conflict.

As in any therapeutic situation, exactly how the conflict of values will be resolved, or even whether it will be resolved, cannot now be foretold. We are too much in the early stages of the struggle. In addition, the universities are merely one focal point of a conflict that cannot be resolved until the exposure spreads to all parts of the social system. If past cycles of disorder are any clue to the future, the chances of a real resolution of conflict are not too good.[18] But it is at least possible that this time around the American people will ultimately choose to demote Lineality to the last and least honored position specified by our official values, provided the students and the young everywhere keep up their pressure.

---

[18] The greatest risk is that the intensity of the identification with the aggressor will result in a fixation on the use of force and violence so strong that the students must constantly seek new objects on which to discharge hostility. Under these circumstances, failure to find a suitable object may end in the turning of the hostility on the self, accompanied by depression or even by attempts at self-destruction.

Does this position make me a dove? Perhaps, but a dove bearing a scalpel rather than an olive branch.

FOURTEEN

Value Conflicts in the University

Discussion of student protest involves the question of social change. Students would not be protesting with such vigor were they not intensely eager for fundamental and difficult transformations, both within the university and in the society as a whole. These changes are presumed to be difficult to achieve because they run counter to some of the basic values which are accepted by most Americans and which are firmly embedded in university practice. Accordingly, the protests and demands of the students meet considerable resistance. The resistance, so it is held, vastly increases the militance and force with which students push their protest, giving rise to techniques of generating change which tend to feature violence.

If these assumptions are correct, then any discussion of the consequences of student protest for the university must be divided into three parts. (1) What changes are the students attempting to bring about, and what effects would flow from these changes? (2) What are the consequences of the methods students use to bring about change? (3) What are the consequences of the methods used by faculty and administration to deal with both the techniques of protest and with the demands for change?

Despite the accumulating body of writings on the subject, it is obviously difficult to discuss the topic of desired social changes because of the tremendous amount of variation in goals of student groups, both between universities and on any one campus. Nevertheless, there is a potential solution to the problem. The variability exists principally at the level of concrete issues. There appears to be much more consensus about the changes in general value orientations which students would like to have instituted. In current studies of this sphere of belief and behavior, the staff of the Lemberg Center for the Study of Violence has been using the theory of variations in cultural value orientations proposed by Florence Kluckhohn. This theory has been expounded and applied to several subjects in previous chapters. I would now like to extend its use to the matter of student protest.

As we have seen, the prevailing pattern of preference for standard American culture is Future in the first position, Present second, and Past in the weak, third-order position. The degree to which Americans ordinarily plan for a far-flung future conceived in terms of something bigger and better needs no spelling out here. This emphasis is, of course, especially pressing in the educational area because of the need for parents and children to plan ahead for school, college, and career in the usual lock-step progression. Present-time concerns are saved mainly for recreational situations — for entertainment, eating, and sex. The Past, in accordance with anti-traditional bias, receives rather short shrift. Americans generally are too busy looking ahead to care about the past, tending to deal with both national and personal history in terms of superficial stereotypes.

Universities and colleges are somewhat variant with respect to this pattern of preference. So far as the usual curriculum is concerned, the Past receives a heavy emphasis in departments of history, classics, archeology, and language. The Past is also represented in a variety of quaint academic rituals and labels reaching back to the medieval origins of the university, as well as in the traditional songs, Latin mottoes, heraldic symbols, and other decorative mementoes which distinguish one university from another. The Future is represented by the sciences with their stressing of research, change, and problem-solving. Quite aside from specific teaching programs, students are continually reminded that undergraduate or graduate studies are preparations for something that lies ahead — future examinations, other goals to be reached, jobs to be obtained, failures to be avoided. Thus the overall pattern of preference for the time dimension in the university is Future, Past, Present.

402

To this pattern of value choices students have responded with demands for more attention to Present time. The "Tune In, Turn On, Drop Out" slogan proposed by Timothy Leary in the early sixties for drug users represented a cry for the rearrangement of time values which has now been institutionalized in the drug and hippie culture. It is not within the scope of this chapter to inquire deeply into the underlying motives for the switch to the Present. That it is connected with fear of the draft, horror of the war in Vietnam, anxieties about the hydrogen bomb, and general doubts about survival in a polluted world have all been commented on by others. For our purposes, we are confronted with the more difficult question: how is the university to deal with the re-ordered time dimension — Present, Future, Past — incorporated in the student protest movement? What are the political and academic consequences of accepting or rejecting this revision of values? How is one to cope with the problem that dominant American middle-class culture, the university, and the student protest movement, each stress a different and seemingly incompatible value pattern in this area?

With regard to man's place in nature, the order of preference in mainstream America is first Mastery over Nature; second, Subjugation to Nature; and third, Harmony with Nature. The first and most popular choice, Mastery over Nature, is consonant with our desired (and demonstrated) technological mastery of problems. Technical competence has fulfilled most of the dreams of antiquity as well as the fantasies of science fiction. For the few problems that remain unsolved, such as chronic illness and death (overlooking war, weather, and overpopulation, which remain on the agenda for technical mastery), the second choice, Subjugation to Nature plugs the gap. In this case, man can recognize his weakness and, in accordance with Judeo-Christian or other religious traditions, pray for deliverance from pain and misery. The third-order, Harmony with Nature, avoids the concept of a struggle between man and nature. Rather, it emphasizes, somewhat on the pattern of the pre-Christian, polytheistic cults, that nature is herself full of contending forces loosely orchestrated through a grand but rather mysterious plan with which mankind must try to stay on good terms in order to avoid misfortune.

The Harmony with Nature position has, until recently, seemed at best charming and anacronistic, at worst magical and threatening, at any rate unrealistic to a science-oriented culture. The student protest movement, however, is attempting to elevate Harmony with

Nature into the first-order position. Students involved in protest have become disillusioned with the first two value choices. Mastery over Nature has been used for evil purposes as exemplified in war, and the computerized invasion of privacy. In addition our vaunted technology has filled the firmament and our one and only planet, Earth, with waste products which it is incapable of disposing of in a safe and sane way. So much for technology. Finally, Mastery over Nature leaves no room for tragedy. A tragic event occurs when somebody goofs, pulls the wrong switch, prescribes the wrong medicine, fails to fasten his seat belt, takes an overdose of drugs, or foolishly falls into some other avoidable mishap. Aside from blaming the experts, there is no psychological relief available, since religion and the whole Subjugation to Nature orientation fails to carry conviction.

To many students born and raised in the Age of Aquarius the rationalism of science and technology appears pretentious and somewhat menacing. Its failures loom as large, if not larger than its triumphs. On the other hand, the peculiar irrationalism of organized religion with its singularly remote and unhelpful deity and its self-serving puritanical morality seems even more objectionable. That a confused adult world should continue to honor a religion it does not and cannot use effectively tends to undermine the credibility of non-protesting adults who offer themselves as models for the young. Thus, a Harmony with Nature position, however expressed, through astrology, magic, ecology, "humanistic" psychology, hostility to research, or to reason itself, tends to capture the imagination of those involved in protest. Given the traditional values of the university, this switch in values presents a problem of staggering dimensions.

The order of solutions for Americans in Activity orientation is first, Doing; second, Being; and third, Being-in-becoming. Doing represents the success theme in American life — the externally made judgment that a person has "made it," has achieved in the eyes of others. Being, on the other hand, places chief value on spontaneity, on the expression of feeling, and on revealing the inner man in a straightforward way. Being-in-becoming places its emphasis on the rounded development of the personality over time. The aim is to bring all aspects of the person together and into fruition, overlooking both the nose-to-the-grindstone pressures of Doing and the impulsiveness of Being.

The student protest movement has rejected this typical rank-order of activity values in favor of the sequence: Being-in-becoming, Being, and Doing. The emphasis on achievement for its own sake, on hard work for success, is relegated to the third place, probably because it has been so over-emphasized to date and because it is not seen as leading to personal satisfaction or happiness. On the contrary, it is perceived as forcing people ruthlessly into career lines and personal conduct which falsify the individuality and inner meaning of a person to himself, somewhat along the lines of the theme expressed in "Death of a Salesman." For this undesirable outcome, Being-in-becoming is proposed as a corrective. For young people especially it offers opportunity to explore themselves and their world(s), to avoid being pushed into premature career choices, to take time out from the "rat race," in the interests of finding for themselves a satisfactory niche and a happy combination of roles in the domestic, occupational, and recreational areas of life.

To the university, this re-ordering of values is not as troublesome as it may seem at first glance. Being is retained in the second position where it has always been. To be sure, its range is now broadened. When Being follows Doing, as in the typical American sequence, its range is restricted because of the need to suppress inner feeling for the sake of success in whatever terms are laid down by "the establishment." If Being follows Being-in-becoming, there is more room for spontaneity and the honest expression of inner feelings, often brought out with sufficient vehemence to unsettle the traditional calm and reserve of the academic mind. Nevertheless, academia has always honored, though it has not sufficiently emphasized, the Being-in-becoming value orientation. With the exception of occasional publish-or-perish overkill, universities have always made room for teachers and scholars not particularly interested in the external success market. Though a heavier investment in the Being-in-becoming value choice would require some readjustments in university programs, the strains would not be overwhelming.

The Relational value orientation is the most sensitive and problematic of all the value dimensions for the structure of universities and is most highly involved in issues of dissent and protest. The preferred American pattern is Individualism first, Collateral second, and Lineal third. In most American groups, the individual is expected to behave in an independent fashion, to make up his own mind about what he wants, and to feel that he is as good as the next person. Tough group decisions are settled by majority vote. Collaterality, the second choice, emphasizes the horizontal, team-like structure of the group. Everyone is considered to be on the same plane, but group harmony is more important than the individual wishes and opinions of a group member. Decisions are therefore made by consensus, a process that requires a good deal of prolonged discussion in order to overcome disagreements. The Lineal choice refers to group arrangements based on a vertical hierarchy. Decisions are made by a boss and are handed down the ladder of authority. Attention is paid to status within the group, to power issues, and to ranking in terms of superiority and inferiority.

There is much empirical evidence at our disposal that the Individual, Collateral, Lineal sequence is heavily endorsed by most Americans. It represents the national egalitarian ethos. The fact that most middle-class families are run on the basis of the Individual, Collateral, Lineal pattern often gives rise to the criticism that today's parents are too permissive. The fact that the criticism is made at all suggests that some parents, particularly among working-class ethnic groups, still give considerable weight to a Lineal, authoritarian value system which is in conflict with middle-class culture. The Collateral aspects of groups are emphasized in all sorts of recreational and informal activities where the maintenance of group harmony and loyalty to the group is more important than recognition of individual rights. The lowly position of Lineality is expressed in resentment toward overweening authority and in sympathy for the underdog.

Nevertheless, despite the evidence that the Individual, Collateral, Lineal rank-order is representative of American ideals and that it is institutionalized within the middle-class family structure, most large-scale bureaucracies in the areas of business, government, education, and health are based on a variant pattern. Such organizations emphasize the Lineal, vertical structuring of relational values to a degree that is inconsistent with the ideal rank order. They are characterized by stratification, superior-inferior status relations, one-way communications (from the top down) which impose excessive impersonality on human relations, and massive control over decision-making in the hands of those at the top of the bureaucracy. This is not to say that the elitism of such organizations thoroughly invalidates the principle of individualism, but merely that individualism is much weakened by the heavy emphasis on Lineality. Thus the operating sequence of Relational values in many large-scale business organizations is Individual, Lineal, Collateral. And, in some organizations such as the military, the police, city governments, federal agencies, hospitals and universities, the Lineal choice emerges in the first-order position, so that the resulting rank-order is Lineal, Individual, Collateral.

The discrepancy between the ideal and the operative Relational values is nowhere more apparent than in the areas of race relations and foreign policy. The elitist principle that holds down blacks, Spanish-Americans, Indians, and other minority groups and the "World Power" principle that governs our international relations are both similarly evolved from a Lineal perspective on human relations. The word "perspective" is used advisedly in this connection, for values pertain not to the nature of reality but to the way reality is viewed. Clearly, there are many persons who would see no justification in reality for racial oppression but who would still view the war in Vietnam as justified by the world power struggle between democracy and communism. But, there are a growing number of persons who would regard this justification as unreal — as a disguise for a policy of economic domination of foreign markets.

To students involved in the protest movement, the connection between racism and war is quite real, and the implication of the universities in both issues is equally real. Universities are viewed as having actively endorsed our military policies by participating in generously financed war-related research and as having implicitly subscribed to racism by the exclusion of blacks, their history, and their culture from any significant role in campus life. Reinforcing these conjoined issues is the students' view of the structure of the university itself as excessively Lineal. To university administrators impressed with the very real limitations on their authority and power, this view of the university often comes as a shock. It is true that power in the university is decentralized and that college presidents, deans, and department heads cannot have their way simply by issuing commands. But the fact that universities are not dictatorships does not mean that they are democracies. Possibly the most appropriate label for the political structure of the average university would be "decentralized oligarchy." Power is both stratified and divided. Influence is commanded by informal cliques of "advisors" or "insiders" surrounding each center of power. From the Board through Chancellors, Presidents and Provosts, Deans and Department Heads, power trickles down the ladder of prestige to layers of faculty and teaching assistants, and on to students, with service employees at the bottom. As a result of the division of power, the oligarchies compete with and often neutralize each other, universities are not run very efficiently, and administrators often feel frustrated. As a result of the informal nature of the decision-making clique at each center of power, the designated "head" is often a "figurehead," and it is important but difficult to know whom to cultivate in order to influence decisions. As a result of both the stratification of elites and of the obscure nature of decision-making, students have felt themselves to be without power and without knowledge of how to communicate effectively in regard to their needs and complaints, the more so since formal student governing bodies have been viewed as a part of the democratic facade covering the essentially oligarchic character of university structure.

Since many of the students who become involved in protest have entered the university already strongly opposed to the Lineal values manifested in the racist and military policies of the nation, it is not surprising that this opposition should be strengthened when they discover that the university is itself organized on Lineal lines. When a student learns that he is expected to know his place in the hierarchy, comply with a complicated network of rules and regulations about which students have generally not been consulted, and suffer without complaint the punishment of probation or expulsion for breaking the rules, he is confronted with a system of human relations greatly at variance from those he learned within his family. The response to this value conflict, around which protest is organized, consists of promoting the Collateral value choice into the first-order position. The protesting students would like to see the university function as a community, on the order of a vastly extended family. Members of such a community would not be overly concerned with prestige or status. Decisions would be made by taking into account the wishes and feelings of all community groups in order to arrive at a reasonable consensus. Given the implications of such a horizontal, egalitarian triumph over traditional, hierarchical decision-making, one could assume that such ill-fitting anomalies as racism and wars in defense of puppet governments or client states could no longer be tolerated within the university. For the image of the university as a consensually responsive, intercommunicating, and conflict-resolving community is meant to be a model for the nation as a whole — or even for the whole world. The Relational profile incorporated into this model is Collateral, Individual, Lineal.

If we are correct in assuming that the concrete needs and complaints articulated in the various student protests and "demands" are responsive to value strains within and without the university, then we should try to inventory the discrepancies cited above in order to pinpoint the dilemma in which the universities find them-

408

selves as a result of the protest movement. Table 5 is designed for this purpose. It compares the ideal value patterns which are actualized in the American middle-class family with the value patterns represented in the structure of the university and in the forms of student protest. The relational patterns associated with large-scale organizations (Ind > Lin > Col or Lin > Ind > Col) tend to be at variance with both student protesters and middle-class family values. This contrast is also a reminder that the problems of the university in a time of value transition are merely special cases of problems facing the whole society.

Despite this across-the-board sharing of value conflicts, the fact remains that universities have been singled out for attack. Protesting students have, in effect, declared that it is within the university that these problems of social change must be identified, confronted, fought out, resolved. Many persons within the univer-

TABLE 5

Family, University, and Student Value Preferences

Orientations	Middle-Class Family	Typical University	Student Protester
Nature	Over > Sub > Har	Over > Sub > Har	Har > Over > Sub
Time	Fu > Pr > Pa	Fu > Pa > Pr	Pr > Fu > Pa
Activity	Doing > Being > Bib	Doing > Bib > Being	Bib > Being > Doing
Relational	Ind > Col > Lin	Lin > Ind > Col	Col > Ind > Lin

sity complain that this strategy is unfair, that colleges and universities cannot be expected to solve all the problems of the nation or of the world. Such complaints are probably based upon a false premise. Student protesters, in all likelihood, do not expect the university to come up with instant solutions. Rather, they hope that the university will function as a model for the way social problems are to be approached. The expectation assumes that since universities prepare the young for the future, and since that future is already heavily implicated in the current value conflicts, it is the special obligation of the university to face up to the associated political problems both on and off the campus and to make a determined attempt to deal with them.

A glance at Table 5 shows immediately that this expectation presents the university with an immensely complicated task. At the simplest level, no large, traditional organization can undergo structural change without tremendous strain and discomfort being imposed upon its incumbents. For those who have been in office for any length of time, the change in habits and role expectations generates much personal stress, reduces efficiency, and often leads to psychosomatic illness, death, or premature termination of employment. But, this universally disabling effect of organizational change could be more easily accepted and overcome were the direction of change to be clearcut and the scheduling of change accomplishable on an easily understood plan. Employees and other members of the academic community could respond more easily to a "Like it or not, this is what's going to happen" policy than to the current situation of ambiguity and uncertainty.

Ambiguity, unfortunately, is built into the current value snarls illustrated in Table 5. The values representative of the university fit neither with the idealized values of the middle-class family nor with the patterns being promoted by the student protest movement. To be sure, with the exception of the Relational orientation, university values are closer to middle-class family values than to those of the student movement. In this respect, the student movement is radical in more than the political connotations of this word. It is radical in substance — that is, in the degree to which it alters traditional views of human relations and the meaning of life. If its aims were to be realized, the norms for behavior within the university and, subsequently, within the social system as a whole would have to undergo extensive transformation.

It is obvious that the university, caught in the middle between two extremely different value patterns, is in trouble. No matter which way it moves it will be in trouble, and if it stands still without change, it will remain in trouble. Nevertheless, the university is a self-directed organization. No matter how battered it may be for some time to come, it will have no choice but to cope with its problems in its own time and in its own way, unwilling and unable to respond passively or mechanically to pulls from either (or any)

410

direction. In the intervening time, however, during which it is undergoing intense internal turmoil and confusion sometimes bordering on paralysis, it cannot respond rapidly enough nor appropriately to pressure for change. The stress is too great and the insight into the appropriate response too dim.

Despite these difficulties, many universities have been attempting to experiment with new structural and functional arrangements. Such efforts, however, are difficult to analyze and to assess because they are so intricately interwoven with the implications of the second question we asked at the beginning of this chapter: what are the political consequences of the methods students use to bring about change? And the question itself is not a simple one. The methods of student protest have ranged from nonviolent techniques such as polls and boycotts, through disruptions of classes and take-overs of buildings, and on to violent attacks on people and property. To complicate matters further, the methods used by protesting students are usually responsive to previous administrative reactions to a set of prior demands for change put forth by some of the more radicalized students. In the immediately preceding chapter this escalation of conflict leading toward disorder was described as a process of action and reaction occurring in four phases. I postulated that, despite the presence of small groups of students (such as the various SDS factions) fixated on violence and disruption as the only effective technique for reaching their revolutionary goals, large-scale, persistent disorder within the university was usually the product of a series of errors on the part of the administration. Most of these mistakes consisted of failures of communication: the invisibility and inaccessibility of top administrative figures for both students and faculty; failure to take early requests for change with sufficient seriousness; neglect or mismanagement of the negotiating process; and carelessness and misjudgment in the use of police, National Guard, and other law enforcement agencies.

It is not within the scope of the present chapter to discuss the process of escalation of disorder. For the university, the political consequences of student protest and disorder are fairly well known. They have tended to divide the American public into sharply polarized groups: (1) a very small group who sympathize both with the aims and the methods of radical protest; (2) a somewhat larger but still minority group who sympathize with some or all of their aims but disapprove of their methods; and (3) a much larger group, probably a majority, who disapprove of both their aims and their methods. This external, public response has produced

411

an acute problem for university administrators. How are they to deal with the negative attitudes toward student protest outside the university while still maintaining a reasonable stance toward the considerable pressure for change within the student body and within much of the faculty?

There are three possible ways of coping with this situation: (1) the Conflict-Resolving Response; (2) the Conflict-Deterring Response; (3) the Mixed Response. The Conflict-Resolving Response is a strategy based on anticipating student demands whenever possible so that they can be made the subject of university-wide discussion. Such early discovery of potential sore-spots, so the strategy goes, leads to a diffusion of tension and toward a potential consensus on which the administration can take action without too much backlash from whatever quarter. Although it is resented by some of the more radical students as co-opting the movement, such a strategy tends to avoid disorder and the need to call in external law enforcement agencies. To be successful, it requires an inordinate amount of communication, meetings, trial-and-error, feedback, correction of mistakes, and just plain hard work on the part of all concerned. The time consumed in all the necessary work may prevent ordinary tasks from being completed and may easily wear out those who have responsibility. Since it does not provide an ironclad guarantee that there will be no disruptions at all, it may be seen as too "soft," leading to loss of support from large donors, alumni, and state legislators, who disapprove of any departure from the traditional Lineal structure of the university.

The Conflict-Deterring Response is less inclined to anticipate the *content* of student protest, more inclined to plan for dealing with the method of protest on a tough, law-and-order, "no-nonsense" basis. It relies on the infiltration of dissident student groups so as to have maximum information on plans for disruptions. Students are warned of exactly what will happen to them if they should break university rules in carrying out protest, and the warnings are backed up by prompt action by the police and disciplinary committees within the university and by court action off campus. Various divide-and-conquer techniques are applied for the sake of breaking up refractory student organizations. Disorder is deterred by intimidation. The firm thrust of this response may earn the university the praise of Lineally-minded segments of the public, but the conflict management technique severely limits student freedom while anger seethes, however well concealed. Aside from repressive vigilance, no change in the structure of the university is likely to take place under these circumstances. Oddly enough, despite the approval of "hardline" segments of the public, universities using this approach seem not to reap any particular financial benefits as a reward, either from state legislators or from wealthy private donors.

Although the facts are not certain, it would appear that only a handful of universities employ either a pure Conflict-Resolving or Conflict-Deterring strategy. Most prefer to try some resolving methods, for as long as possible, using deterrence when the situation threatens to or actually does get out of hand. This Mixed Response seems less rigid and arbitrary. Perhaps it is more adaptive than the other two, but without more experience and comparative research no final conclusions can be drawn. The Mixed Response has the possible disadvantage of appearing, under certain circumstances, as vacillating, contradictory, or weak, thus stimulating distrust among students and disgust in the ranks of the disaffected public. At the present time, the actual proportions and sequencing of conflict-resolving and conflict-deterring procedures in the mix varies considerably from campus to campus. The mix seems to be a product of many factors: the personal style of the president of the university, the previous history of the university within its community, the region or state in which the university is located, private versus public and rural versus urban contrasts, and probably other considerations difficult to discern at present.

Because of our ignorance and the absence of a body of comparative research, any generalizations about the consequences of the various techniques of conflict management seems risky. It has been suggested that ill-conceived conflict deterrence, employing badly trained personnel such as the use of the National Guard at Kent State and of the police at Orangeburg, South Carolina, and Jackson, Mississippi, leads to the unnecessary and tragic killing and injury of students. This is probably true, but it is necessary to await the outcome of various official investigations before coming to firm conclusions. At the present time, the only generalization in which one can have confidence is that, whatever the technique of conflict management, its purpose (as opposed to its effects) is to keep the university relatively stable and free of inordinate turbulence so that the needed changes can be worked out with care.

This situation, interestingly enough, cuts both ways. Many university administrators complain that they are so busy coping with protest and its consequences that they do not have the time to concern themselves with educational reform. On the other hand, many persons, particularly students and reform-minded faculty, believe that it is only because of the protest activity that universities have become interested in making changes in the first place. Both views are probably correct *in part;* though the facts would seem to indicate that, no matter how busy the administration, most universities are currently undergoing change of some sort. The chief obstacles to change would appear to lie not in the areas of time and technique but in the realm of values and value conflicts. This consideration suggests that we should not conclude this chapter without giving some thought to the options open to the university for solving the value problems illustrated in Table 5.

The statements which follow are based on an interpretation of changes already in process plus deductions from the logic of value conflict. However, they are at best informed guesses. For the sake of avoiding repeated qualification they are expressed in positive terms, but they are not meant to be considered as guidelines or recommendations.

The key position of the Relational values as the point of attack of student protest suggests that this area receive top priority in any consideration of structural change. In addition, Relational values are more highly implicated in contradiction and confusion than are the other value dimensions. They are the source of that "hypocrisy" to which the student protest movement is so sensitized. How can the university escape from the contradiction between the ideal Individual, Collateral, Lineal sequence, which it is presumably promoting at the level of belief, and the operative Lineal, Individual, Collateral pattern which it so vigorously practices?

The solution proposed by protesting students is to promote the Collateral choice into first-order position and to demote the Lineal to the third-order position. At first blush this may seem a good solution. It is true that in most large universities fragmentation and isolation of individuals and groups is severe. Except in the course of a crisis there is little overall community feeling. But the effort to highlight and maintain Collaterality in the first position suffers from several inherent weaknesses. As the experience of student militant organizations demonstrates, collaterally organized groups easily undergo fission, particularly in the context of crisis situations when consensus about difficult decisions is hard to reach. Furthermore, in such emergencies, after collateral fission takes place, the split groups usually adopt a fiercely competitive, rivalrous stance toward each other. Under these circumstances, with the survival

414

of the groups at stake, the submerged Lineality tends to reassert itself in an intense and anomalous form. Group leaders begin to behave in an authoritarian manner quite in contradiction to the official ideology of the group. The fact is that emergencies featuring dangerous inter-group rivalry require a Lineal organization of decision making. In threatening fast-moving circumstances, there is simply not time for Collateral or Individual decision making to take place. This is why military and quasi-military organizations are structured on a Lineal basis. A strong authority must make the decision quickly and see that it is executed lest he be outmaneuvered and his cause lost.

Radical student organizations are frequently accused of being "fascist" because of the unexpected prominence of Lineality. It would seem, however, that the term is in error in that the authoritarianism of such groups is a matter not of ideology but of group dynamics. The attempt to cope with the problem by the constant rotation of leaders is of some help. But there is always the danger that, having been driven into authoritarian practices, the group members will, unconsciously at least, begin to place some value on Lineality for its own sake as the means by which they are able to be successful. Examples of this outcome in history are not hard to find.

If the first-order Lineality of the university system is inappropriately elitist and not particularly efficient and the first-order Collaterality of the student protest movement is unstable, then perhaps a better arrangement would be represented by the ideal American pattern of Individual, Collateral, Lineal. If this pattern could be instituted, the gap between ideal and operative Relational values would disappear and the problem of "hypocrisy" would be eliminated. Current structural changes directed at dealing with this problem, however, would not be sufficient. The placing of a few students on various university committees and boards, whether as voting or non-voting members, does not materially alter the Lineal structure of the bureaucracy, though it may result in better feedback from below to the top. In order to preserve Individualism in the first-order position, an arrangement featuring both representation of constituencies and participation in university governance must be found. The format recently installed at the Free University of Berlin constitutes one such arrangement. Governance is in the hands of a tripartite elected University Council composed equally of students, faculty, and administration, with Council decisions being taken by vote. Since this format constitutes a real rather than a *pro forma* distribution of power, students and faculty tend to vote in larger numbers than previously in order to elect members who will represent their views. However, this is only one model, and it may not be suitable for American universities. Some other format capable of reaching the same goals may have to be invented and tried out. What is important is change in the profile of values rather than the particular structures in which the change is embodied.

Once the relational problem is resolved, the other value dimensions should be easier to handle. In my opinion, it would be best to leave the time orientation open. Instead of attempting to create a new rank-ordering of time values, why not let each choice have equal weight? Clearly, Present time considerations have received insufficient attention in the university, and they now require heavier accenting. But the Future and the Past are also of great importance. If each choice were to be equal to the other two, then students and other members of the university community could create their own patterns rather than being forced into a fixed time mold.

In Man-nature orientation, the Harmony with Nature, Mastery over Nature, Subjugation to Nature profile being sponsored by the student movement seems a wise choice. Mastery over Nature has been stretched out of all relationship to the ability of man to attain this position. If it is retained in the second position, the Harmony with Nature choice, divested of its magical overtones, would represent a more rounded, humanistic approach. The demotion of the Subjugation to Nature choice is in line with changes already taking place — even within divinity schools, where theology tends more and more to be taught within a comparative, historical frame of reference.

In Activity orientation, the university profile places too much emphasis on Doing, while the student protest sequence gives it too little stress. At the present time, Doing — that is, hard work for the sake of achievement — is so little honored among dissident students that they often cannot maintain protest over sustained periods of time. After a crisis, their attention is likely to be diverted to some other activity that captures their interest as they follow their Being-in-Becoming explorations or become involved in the spontaneity of Being, perhaps with the aid of drugs. On the other hand, the university's emphasis on Doing stimulates an excessive amount of competitiveness, anxiety about grades, and about performance in general. For both student and junior faculty the worry about whether one will be able to "make it" are pervasive. This is one of

416

the reasons that junior faculty are prone to associate themselves with student causes.

A possible solution to this value conflict would be the sequence, Being-in-Becoming, Doing, Being. With Doing in the second position, the exploratory and relaxed character of Being-in-Becoming would reduce the harsh compulsiveness of the "success theme," while the demotion of Being would screen expressiveness for its own sake, holding it to those areas of emotional behavior in which a safety valve function is important.

TABLE 6

Comparison of Actual and Proposed Values for the University

Orientation	Actual	Proposed
Man-nature	Over $>$ Sub $>$ Har	Har $>$ Over $>$ Sub
Time	Fu $>$ Pa $>$ Pr	Fu $=$ Pa $=$ Pr
Activity	Doing $>$ Bib $>$ Being	Bib $>$ Doing $>$ Being
Relational	Lin $>$ Ind $>$ Col	Ind $>$ Col $>$ Lin

Table 6 summarizes these suggested changes by comparing the actual value profiles characteristic of the university at present with those proposed in the preceding discussion. Whether the suggested value changes are appropriate and helpful cannot be determined at this stage of the ongoing value transitions. It is hoped, however, that they will contribute to an objective discussion of a topic often loaded with emotion and controversy.

Bibliography

Ackerman, Nathan. 1958. *The Psychodynamics of Family Life: Diagnosis and Treatment of Family Relationships.* New York: Basic Books.

Adams, J. K. 1957. "Laboratory Studies of Behavior Without Awareness." *Psychological Bulletin* 54:384-405.

Allport, Floyd H. 1955. *Theories of Perception and the Concept of Structures.* New York: Wiley.

Behan, Robert C., and Hirschfeld, Alexander H. 1963. "The Accident Process II: Toward a More Rational Treatment of Industrial Injuries." *Journal of the American Medical Association* 176:300-306.

Benedek, Therese. 1949. "The Psychosomatic Implications of the Primary Unit: Mother-Child." *American Journal of Orthopsychiatry* 19:642-654.

Bentley, Arthur F. 1950. "Kinetic Inquiry." *Science.* 112:775-783. See also Dewey and Bentley 1949.

Bettelheim, Bruno. 1947. "The Dynamics of Anti-Semitism in Gentile and Jew." *Journal of Abnormal and Social Psychology* 42:153-168.

Blitsten, Dorothy R. 1953. *The Social Theories of Harry Stack Sullivan.* New York: William-Frederick.

Bott, Elizabeth. 1957. *Family and Social Network: Roles, Norms, and External Relationships in Ordinary Urban Families.* London: Tavistock Publications.

419

Campbell, Angus, and Shuman, Howard. 1968. "Racial Attitudes in Fifteen American Cities." In *Supplemental Studies for the National Advisory Commission on Civil Disorders*. Washington, D.C.: Government Printing Office.

Cantril, Hadley. 1950a. "An Inquiry Concerning the Nature of Man." *Journal of Abnormal and Social Psychology* 40:490-503.

———. 1950b. *The "Why" of Man's Experience*. New York: Macmillan.

———. 1954. "The Qualities of Being Human." *American Quarterly* (Spring): 3-18.

———. 1955. "Ethical Relativity from the Transactional Point of View." *Journal of Philosophy* 52:677-687.

———. 1955. "Toward a Humanistic Psychology." *Etc.: A Review of General Semantics* 12.

———. 1958. *The Politics of Despair*. New York: Basic Books.

———. 1962. "A Transactional Inquiry Concerning Mind." In *Theories of the Mind*, edited by Jordan Scher. New York: Free Press.

Cantril, Hadley, and Hastorf, A. H. 1954. "They Saw a Game: A Case Study." *Journal of Abnormal and Social Psychology* 49: 129-134.

Cantril, Hadley, and Ittelson, W. H. 1954. *Perception: A Transactional Approach*. Garden City: Doubleday.

Cantril, Hadley, *et al.* 1949. "Psychology and Scientific Research." *Science* 110:461.

Canty, Donald. 1969. *One Year Later*. Washington, D.C.: Urban America.

Clifford, Roy A. 1955. *The Rio Grande Flood: A Comparative Study of Border Communities in Disaster*. N.p.: National Research Council.

Cloward, Richard A., and Priven, Frances Fox. 1969. "The Urban Crisis and Consolidation of National Power." In *Urban Riots: Violence and Social Change*, edited by Robert Connery. New York: Vintage Books.

Conant, Ralph W., Levy, Sheldon, and Lewis, Ralph. 1969. "Mass Polarization: Negro Attitudes on the Pace of Integration." *American Behaviorist Scientist*, 13, 2 (November-December).

Dahrendorf, Ralph. 1969. *Essays in the Theory of Society*. Stanford: Stanford University Press.

Dewey, John, and Bentley, Arthur F. 1949. *Knowing and the Known*. Boston: Beacon Press.
See also Bentley 1950.

Dunham, H. W. 1955. "The Field of Social Psychiatry." In *Mental Health and Mental Disorder,* edited by A. M. Rose. New York: Norton.

Eliot, Thomas D. 1955. "Interactions of Psychiatric and Social Theory Prior to 1940." In *Mental Health and Mental Disorder,* edited by A. M. Rose. New York: Norton.

Erikson, Erik H. 1950. *Childhood and Society.* New York: Norton.

———. 1958. *Young Man Luther.* New York: Norton.

———. 1969. *Gandhi's Truth: On the Origins of Militant Non-Violence.* New York: Norton.

Fanon, Franz. 1965. *The Wretched of the Earth.* New York: Grove Press.

Faris, Robert E. L., and Dunham, H. Warren. 1939. *Mental Disorders in Urban Areas.* Chicago: University of Chicago Press.

Federal Bureau of Investigation. 1967. *Prevention and Control of Mobs and Riots.* Washington, D.C.: U.S. Department of Justice.

Feuer, Lewis S. 1969. *The Conflict of Generations: The Character and Significance of Student Movements.* New York: Basic Books.

Fogelson, Robert M. 1969. "Violence as Protest." In *Urban Riots: Violence and Social Change,* edited by Robert Connery. New York: Vintage Books.

Frank, Lawrence K. 1948. *Personality and Culture: The Psychocultural Approach.* New York: Hinds, Hayden & Eldridge.

Freud, Anna. 1946. *The Ego and the Mechanisms of Defense.* New York: International Universities Press.

———. 1954. "Discussion of the Widening Scope of Indications for Psychoanalysis." *Journal of the American Psychoanalytic Association* 2:607-620.

Freud, Sigmund. 1900. *The Interpretation of Dreams,* trans. by James Strachey. In *The Complete Psychological Works of Sigmund Freud,* edited by James Strachey and Alix Strachey, vols. IV-V. London: Hogarth, 1964.

———. 1905. *Jokes and Their Relation to the Unconscious,* trans. by James Strachey. New York: Norton, 1961.

———. 1913. *Totem and Taboo,* trans. by James Strachey. In *The Complete Psychological Works of Sigmund Freud,* edited by James Strachey and Alix Strachey, vol. XIII. London: Hogarth, 1964.

———. 1915. "Thoughts for the Times on War and Death," trans. by E. Colburn Mayne. In *Collected Papers,* edited by Joan Riviere, vol. IV. New York: Basic Books, 1959.

———. 1921. *Group Psychology and the Analysis of the Ego,*

trans. by James Strachey. In *The Complete Works of Sigmund Freud,* edited by James Strachey and Alix Strachey, vol. XVIII. London: Hogarth, 1964.

Fromm, Erich, 1941. *Escape from Freedom.* New York: Holt, Rinehart, and Winston.

Genet, Jean. 1963. *Our Lady of the Flowers,* trans. by B. Frechtman. New York: Grove Press.

Goode, William J. 1960. "A Theory of Role Strain." *American Social Review* 25:483-496.

Graham, Hugh D., and Gurr, Ted R. *Violence in America: Historical and Comparative Perspectives,* vols. 1 and 2. Washington, D.C.: Government Printing Office.

Greenblatt, Milton; Levison, Daniel J.; and Williams, Richard H., eds. 1957. *The Patient and the Mental Hospital.* Glencoe, Ill.: Free Press.

Grimshaw, Allen D. 1968. "Three Views of Urban Violence: Civil Disturbances, Racial Revolt, Class Assault." In *Riots and Rebellion: Civil Violence in the Urban Community,* edited by L. H. Masotti and D. R. Bowen. Beverly Hills, California: Sage Publications.

Grinker, Roy R. 1953. *Psychosomatic Research.* New York: Norton.

————. 1961. "A Transactional Model for Psychotherapy" and "A Demonstration of the Transactional Model." In *Contemporary Psychotherapies,* edited by Morris I. Stein. New York: Free Press.

Grinker, Roy R., and Spiegel, John P. 1945. *Men Under Stress.* Philadelphia: Blakiston.

Grinker, Roy R., *et al.* 1961. *Psychiatric Social Work: A Transactional Case Book.* New York: Basic Books.

Hayakawa, Samuel I., *et al.* 1950. *Language in Thought and Action.* New York: Harcourt, Brace.

Hoffer, Eric, 1951. *The True Believer.* New York: Harper & Row.

Hollingshead, August B., and Redlich, Fredrich C. 1958. *Social Class and Mental Illness.* New York: Wiley.

Holroyd, Michael. 1968. *Lytton Strachey: A Critical Biography,* 2 vols. New York: Holt, Rinehart & Winston.

Homans, George C. 1961. *Social Behavior: Its Elementary Forms.* New York: Harcourt, Brace, Jovanovich.

Horney, Karen. 1937. *The Neurotic Personality of Our Time.* New York: Norton.

Ittelson, William H. 1952. *The Ames Demonstrations in Perception*. Princeton: Princeton University Press. See also Cantril and Ittelson 1954.

Jackson, Donald D. 1957. "The Question of Family Homeostasius. part 1." *Psychiatric Orderly Supplement* 31:79-90.

Jammer, Max. 1957a. *Concepts of Space: The History of Theories of Space in Physics*. Cambridge, Mass.: Harvard University Press.

———. 1957b. *Concepts of Force: A Study in the Foundations of Dynamics*. Cambridge, Mass.: Harvard University Press.

Kardiner, Abram, *et al.* 1945. *The Psychological Frontiers of Society*. New York: Columbia University Press.

Kardiner, Abram, and Spiegel, Herbert X. 1947. *War Stress and Neurotic Illness*. New York: Hoeber. See also Linton and Kardiner 1939.

Kenniston, Kenneth. 1968. *Young Radicals: Notes on Committed Youth*. New York. Harcourt, Brace, Jovanovich.

Kilpatrick, Franklin P. 1961. *Explorations in Transactional Psychology*. New York: New York University Press.

Kluckhohn, Clyde. 1951. "Values and Value Orientations." In *Toward a General Theory of Action*, edited by Talcott Parsons and Edward Shils. Cambridge, Mass.: Harvard University Press.

Kluckhohn, Clyde, and Murray, Henry A., eds. 1953. *Personality in Nature, Society, and Culture*, rev. ed. New York: Knopf.

Kluckhohn, Florence R. 1940. "The Participant-Observer Technique in Small Communities." *American Journal of Sociology* 46:331-343.

———. 1950. "Dominant and Substitute Profiles of Cultural Orientations: Their Significance for the Analysis of Social Stratification." *Social Forces* 28:376-393.

———. 1952. "The American Family Past and Present." In *Patterns for Modern Living: Psychological Patterns*, edited by O. H. Mowrer. Chicago: Delphian Society.

———. 1953. "Dominant and Variant Value Orientations." In *Personality in Nature, Society, and Culture*, edited by C. Kluckhohn and H. A. Murray. New York: Knopf.

———. 1958. "Variations in the Basic Values of Family Systems." *Social Casework* 39:63-72.

Kluckhohn, Florence, and Strodtbeck, F. L. 1961. *Variations in Value Orientations*. Evanston: Row Peterson.

Knopf, Terry Ann. 1969. "Sniping—A New Pattern of Violence?" *Trans-Action* (July-August).

Korzybski, Alfred. 1958. *Science and Sanity: An Introduction to Non-Aristotelian Systems and General Semantics*. 4th ed. Lakeville, Conn.: Institute of General Semantics.

Kunen, James Simon. 1969. *The Strawberry Statement: Notes of a College Revolutionist*. New York: Random House.

Leighton, Alexander H., *et al.* 1957. *Exploration in Social Psychiatry*. New York: Basic Books.

Lidz, T. 1958. "The Intrafamilial Environment of the Schizophrenic Patient, part IV: Parental Personalities and Family Interaction." *American Journal of Orthopsychiatry* 27:764-776.

Lidz, T., *et al.* 1957. "The Intrafamilial Environment of the Schizophrenic Patient, part II: Marital Schism and Marital Skew." *American Journal of Orthopsychiatry* 27:241-248.

Lifton, Robert J. 1961. *Thought Reform and the Psychology of Totalism*. New York: Norton.

Lindemann, Erich. 1950. *Life Stress and Bodily Disease*. Baltimore: Williams and Wilkins.

Linton, Ralph. 1936. *The Study of Man*. New York: Appleton-Century.

———. 1945. *The Cultural Background of Personality*. New York: Appleton-Century.

Linton, Ralph, and Kardiner, Abram. 1939. *The Individual and His Society*. New York: Columbia University Press.

Malinowski, Bronislaw. 1930. "Parenthood the Basis of Social Structure." In *The New Generation*, edited by V. F. Calverton. New York: Macaulay.

Masotti, Louis H., and Bowen, Don R., eds. 1968. *Riots and Rebellion: Civil Violence in the Urban Community*. Beverly Hills, Calif.: Sage Publications.

See also Grimshaw 1968.

Maxwell, J. Clerk. 1877. *Matter and Motion*. New York: Dover (reprint).

Mead, Margaret. 1949. *Male and Female*. New York: Morrow.

Mead, Margaret, and Metraux, Rhoda, eds. 1953. *The Studies of Culture at a Distance*. Chicago: University of Chicago Press.

Menninger, W. C. 1967. "The Role of Psychiatry in the World Today." In *A Psychiatrist for a Troubled World: Selected Papers of William C. Menninger, M.D.*, edited by B. H. Hall. New York: Viking Press.

Moore, Barrington, Jr. 1969. "Thoughts on Violence and Democracy." In *Urban Riots: Violence and Social Change*, edited by Robert H. Connery. New York: Vintage Books.

424

Murdock, George P. 1949. *Social Structure*. New York: Macmillan.

Murray, Henry A. See Kluckhohn and Murray 1953.

National Advisory Committee on Civil Disorders. 1968. *Report of the National Advisory Committee on Civil Disorders*. New York: Bantam Books.

Newcomb, Theodore. 1969. "University, Heal Thyself." *Political Science Quarterly* (June).

Neiman, Lionel J., and Hughes, James W. 1951. "The Problem of the Concept of Role: A Re-survey of the Literature." *Social Forces* 30:141-149.

Northrup, F. S. C., and Gross, Mason W., eds. 1953. *Alfred North Whitehead: An Anthology*. New York: Macmillan.
See also Whitehead 1948.

Orr, Douglas W. 1954. "Transference and Countertransference: A Historical Survey." *Journal of the American Psychoanalytic Association* 2:567-594.

Orrick, William, 1969. *Shut It Down! A College in Crisis. San Francisco State College, October 1968—April 1969*. A report to the National Commission on the Causes and Prevention of Violence. Washington, D.C.: U.S. Government Printing Office. 52-53.

Parsons, Talcott. 1949. *Essays in Sociological Theory Pure and Applied*. Glencoe, Ill.: Free Press.

———. 1951. *The Social System*. Glencoe, Ill.: Free Press.

———. 1958. "Social Structure and the Development of Personality: Freud's Contribution to the Integration of Psychology and Sociology." *Psychiatry* 21:321-340.

Parsons, Talcott, and Fox, R. 1950. "Illness, Therapy, and the Modern Urban American Family." *Journal of Social Issues* 8:31-44.

Parsons, Talcott, and Shils, Edward A., eds. 1951. *Toward a General Theory of Action*. Cambridge, Mass.: Harvard University Press.

Parsons, Talcott, *et al.* 1954a. *Family Socialization and Interaction Process*. Glencoe, Ill.: Free Press.

Parsons, Talcott, *et al.* eds. 1954b. *Working Papers in the Theory of Action*. Glencoe, Ill.: Free Press.

Pollak, Otto. 1956. *Integrating Sociological and Psychoanalytic Concepts: An Exploration in Child Psychotherapy*. New York: Russell Sage Foundation.

425

Rainwater, Lee, and Yancey, William L. 1967. *The Moynihan Report and the Politics of Controversy*. Cambridge, Mass.: M.I.T. Press.

Riesman, David. 1950. "The Themes of Work and Play in the Structure of Freud's Thought." *Psychiatry* 13:1-16.

Riesman, David, and Jencks, Christopher. 1968. *The Academic Revolution*. New York: Doubleday.

Rubenstein, Richard E. 1970. *Rebels in Eden: Mass Political Violence in the United States*. Boston: Little Brown.

Runciman, W. G. 1966. *Relative Deprivation and Social Justice*. University of California Press.

Sears, David D., and McConahy, John B. 1969. "Participation in the Los Angeles Riot." *Social Problems* 17:3-20.

Skinner, B. F. Personal Communication.

———. 1957. *Verbal Behavior*. New York: Appleton, Century, Crofts.

Skolnick, Jerome H. 1969. *The Politics of Protest*. New York: Ballantine Books.

Sorel, Georges. 1908. *Réflexions sur la Violence. (Reflections on Violence*. New York: Macmillan, 1961.)

Spiegel, John P. 1954. "The Social Role of Doctor and Patient in Psychoanalysis and Psychotherapy." *Psychiatry* 37:369-376.

———. 1956a. "Interpersonal Influences Within the Family." In *Group Processes,* edited by Bertram Schaffner. New York: Josiah Macy Foundation.

———. 1956b. "A Model for Relationships Among Systems" and "Comparison of Psychological and Group Foci." In *Toward a Unified Theory of Human Behavior,* edited by Roy R. Grinker. New York: Basic Books.

———. 1957. "The Resolution of Role Conflict Within the Family." *Psychiatry* 20:1-60.

———. 1968. "Psychosocial Factors in Riots—Old and New." *American Journal of Psychiatry* 125:281-285.

Spiegel, John P., and Kluckhohn, Florence R. 1954. *Integration and Conflict in Family Behavior,* report no. 27. Topeka: Group for the Advancement of Psychiatry.

Spiegel, John P., et al. 1955. *The Problem of Panic*. Bulletin TB-19-2. Washington, D.C.: Federal Civil Defense Administration.

See also Grinker and Spiegel 1945.

Stanton, Alfred H., and Schwartz, Morris S. 1954. *The Mental Hospital: A Study of Institutional Participation in Psychiatric Illness and Treatment*. New York: Basic Books.

Stone, Leo. 1954. "The Widening Scope of Indications for Psychoanalysis." *Journal of the American Psychoanalytic Association* 2:567-594.

See also A. Freud 1954.

Sullivan, Harry Stack. 1965. *The Collected Works*, vols. 1 and 2. New York: Norton.

See also Blitsten 1953.

Sullivan, Harry Stack. 1953. *The Interpersonal Theory of Psychiatry*, edited by Helen Perry and Mary Gawel. New York: Norton.

Takagi, Paul, *et al.* 1970. *The Reconstruction of a Riot: A Case Study of Community Tension and Civil Disorder*. Waltham, Mass.: Lemberg Center for the Study of Violence, Brandeis University.

Tomlinson, T. M. 1968. "Riot Ideology Among Urban Negroes." In *Riots and Rebellions: Civil Violence in the Urban Community*, edited by Louis Masotti, and Don R. Bowen. Beverly Hills, Calif.: Sage Publications.

Walker, Daniel. 1968: *Rights in Conflict: The Walker Report on Violence in Chicago to the National Commission on the Causes and Prevention of Violence*. New York: Bantam Books.

Waller, Willard, and Hill, Reuben. 1951. *The Family: A Dynamic Interpretation*. New York: Dryden Press.

Walzer, Michael. 1969. "Corporate Authority and Civil Disobedience." *Dissent* (September-October) :395-406.

Whitehead, Alfred North. 1929. *Process and Reality: An Essay in Cosmology*. New York: Macmillan.

———. 1948. *Science and Philosophy*. New York: Philosophical Library.

Whorf, B. L. 1941. "The Relation of a Habitual Thought and Behavior to Language." In *Language, Culture, and Personality: Essays in Memory of Edward Sapir*, edited by L. Speer, *et al.* Menoska, Wisc.: Sapir Memorial Publication Fund.

Wynne, L. C., *et al.* 1958. "Pseudo-Mutuality in the Family Relations of Schizophrenics." *Psychiatry* 21:205-220.

Zetzel, Elizabeth R. 1956. "Current Concepts of Transference." *International Journal of Psychoanalysis* 36:369-376.

Publications of John Spiegel

1947. "Neuroses," In *Progress in Neurology and Psychiatry*, edited by E. A. Spiegel. New York: Grune & Stratton.

1952. "The Psychosomatic Patient." *Medical Social Work Journal* (October).

1953a. "Critique of Symposium." In *Mid-Century Psychiatry*, edited by Roy R. Grinker. Springfield, Ill.: Charles C. Thomas.

1953b. "Discussion of 'Psychoanalysis and the Social Sciences,' by Talcott Parsons." In *Twenty Years of Psychoanalysis*, edited by F. Alexander and Helen Ross. New York: Norton.

1953c. "Psychological Transactions in Situations of Acute Stress." In *Symposium on Stress*. Washington, D.C.: Army Medical Service Graduate School.

1954a. "Cry Wolf, Cry Havoc." *Bulletin of the Atomic Scientists* (April).

1954b. "New Perspectives in the Study of the Family." *New England Journal of Medicine* (November).

1954c. "Emotional Reactions to Catastrophe," *American Practitioner and Digest of Treatment* (November).

1955a. "Emotional Reactions to Catastrophe." In *Stress Situations*, edited by S. Liebman. Philadelphia: Lippincott.

429

1955b. "Factors in the Growth and Development of the Psycho-
        therapist." *Journal of the American Psychoanalytic
        Association* 4:2.
1956a. "A Model for Relationships Among Systems," and "Com-
        parison of Psychological and Group Foci." In *Toward
        a Unified Theory of Human Behavior,* edited by Roy
        R. Grinker. New York: Basic Books.
1956b. "Psychiatric Subject Matter — Some Troublesome Con-
        siderations." In *Psychiatry, the Press, and the Public,*
        edited by W. B. Bloomberg. Washington, D.C.: Ameri-
        can Psychiatric Association.
1957a. Article I in *Integrating the Approaches to Mental Disease,*
        edited by H. D. Kruse. New York: Hoeber-Harper.
1957b. "The English Flood of 1953." *Human Organization* vol.
        16, no. 2.
1958a. "Homeostatic Mechanisms within the Family." In *The
        Family in Contemporary Society,* edited by Iago Glad-
        ston. New York: International Universities Press.
1958b. "Patterns of Typical and Varying Values in the American
        Family." In *N.A.E.B. Seminar on Children's Television
        Programs,* edited by Harold E. Hill. Urbana, Ill.:
        National Association of Educational Broadcasters.
1960.   "The Resolution of Role Conflict within the Family." In
        A Modern Introduction to the Family, edited by Norman
        W. Bell and Ezra F. Vogel. Glencoe, Ill.: Free Press.
        This article originally appeared in *Psychiatry,* Feb. 1957.
1961a. "Applications of Psychoanalysis in Sociology." *Science and
        Psychoanalysis: Psychoanalysis and Social Process,* vol.
        4, edited by Jules H. Masserman. New York: Grune &
        Stratton.
1961b. "Application of Role and Learning Theories to the Study
        of the Development of Aggression in Children." *Psycho-
        logical Reports,* monograph supplement 2-V9.
1962.   "Education in Social Concepts for Psychoanalysis." In
        Science and Psychoanalysis, Psychoanalytic Education,
        vol. 5, edited by Jules H. Masserman. New York: Grune
        & Stratton.
1963.   "The Social Role of Doctor and Patient in Psychoanalysis
        and Psychotherapy." In *Personality and Social Systems,*
        edited by Neil J. Smelser and William T. Smelser. New
        York: Wiley. This article originally appeared in *Psy-
        chiatry,* XVII (Nov. 1954), 369-76.

1964a. "Cultural Variations in Attitudes Toward Death and Disease." In *The Threat of Impending Disaster: Contributions to the Psychology of Stress,* edited by George H. Grosser, *et al.* Cambridge, Mass.: MIT Press.

1964b. "Conflicting Formal and Informal Roles in Newly Acculturated Families." In *Disorders of Communication,* Research Publications, ARNMD vol. 42, edited by David McK. Rioch. New York: Association for Research in Nervous and Mental Disease.

1964c. "Interpersonal Influences within the Family." In *Interpersonal Dynamics,* edited by Warren C. Bennis, *et al.* Homewood, Ill.: Dorsey Press. This article originally appeared in *Group Processes,* edited by Bertram Schaffner. New York: Josiah Macy, Jr., 1956.

1964d. "Some Cultural Aspects of Transference and Countertransference." In *Mental Health of the Poor,* edited by Frank Riessman and Jerome Cohn. Glencoe, Ill.: Free Press. This article originally appeared in *Science and Psychoanalysis: Individual and Family Dynamics,* vol. 2, edited by Jules Masserman. New York: Grune & Stratton, 1959.

1967. "Classification of Body Messages." *Archives of General Psychiatry* (September).

1968a. "Cultural Strain, Family Role Patterns, and Intrapsychic Conflict." In *Illustrations of Theory and Practice of Family Psychiatry,* edited by John G. Howells. New York: W. A. Benjamin.

1968b. "The Nature of the Riot Process." *Psychiatric Opinion* (June).

1968c. *"Die Beziehungen Zwischen Psychoanalyse Und Soziologie Aus Der Sicht Der Psychoanalyse,"* Jahrbuch der Psychoanalyse, Band V.

1968d. "Psychosocial Factors in Riots—Old and New." *American Journal of Psychiatry* (September).

1968e. "The Tradition of Violence in Our Society." (Reprint Series, Lemberg Center for the Study of Violence, Brandeis University.) Reprinted from *The Washington Star,* 13 October, 1968.

1968f. "Responses of the Theorists to E. G. Mishler and N. E. Waxler's 'Family Interaction and Schizophrenia: A Review of Current Theories.'" In *Family Process and Schizophrenia,* edited by Elliott Mishler and Nancy Waxler. New York: Science House.

431

1968g. "The Social and Psychological Dynamics of Militant Negro Activism: A Preliminary Report." In *Science and Psychoanalysis: The Dynamics of Dissent* vol. 12, edited by Jules H. Masserman. New York: Grune & Stratton.

1969a. "Hostility, Aggression and Violence." In *Racial Violence in the United States*, edited by Allen D. Grimshaw. Chicago: Aldine.

1969b. "Social Change and Unrest: The Responsibility of the Psychiatrist." *American Journal of Psychiatry*, 125:11.

1969c. "Environmental Corrections as a Systems Process." In *General Systems Theory and Psychiatry*, edited by William Gray, *et al*. Boston: Little, Brown.

1969d. "Campus Conflict and Professional Egos." *Trans-Action* (October).

1971a. "Theories of Violence—An Integrated Approach." *International Journal of Group Tensions* (January-March).

1971b. "The Age of Incoherence." *The Boston Globe*, 8 May.

In press. "Cultural Value Orientations and Student Protest: An Interpretation." In *Collective Violence*, edited by Marvin Wolfgang and James Short. Chicago: Aldine-Atherton.

——. "Changing Values and Family Conflict in a Time of Political Disorders." In *Progress in Group and Family Therapy*, edited by Clifford J. Sager and Helen S. Kaplan. New York: Brunner-Mazel.

——. "Toward a Theory of Collective Violence." In *The Dynamics of Violence*, edited by Jan Fawcett. Chicago: American Medical Association. This article originally appeared under the title "Violence and Social Order" in *ZYGON/Journal of Religion and Science*, 4:3 (Sept. 1969).

With Bell, Norman

1959. "The Family of the Psychiatric Patient." In *The Handbook of American Psychiatry*, edited by Silvano Arieti. New York: Basic Books.

1966. "Social Psychiatry: Vagaries of a Term." *Archives of General Psychiatry* (April).

With Gillin, J. P., et al.

1955. "The Problem of Panic." *Civil Defense Technical Bulletin* (June). A report of the Committee on Disaster Studies, National Research Council.

432

With Grinker, Roy R.
1943. *War Neuroses in North Africa: The Tunisian Campaign (January-May, 1943).* New York: Josiah Macy Foundation.
1944a. "Narcosynthesis: A Psychotherapeutic Method for Acute War Neuroses." *Air Surgeons Bulletin* (February).
1944b. "Brief Psychotherapy in War Neuroses." *Journal of Psychosomatic Medicine* (April).
1944c. *The Management of Neuropsychiatric Casualties in the Zone of Combat.* Philadelphia: Saunders Manual of Military Neuropsychiatry.
1945a. "War Neuroses in Flying Personnel Overseas and After Return to the U.S.A." *American Journal of Psychiatry* 101:619.
1945b. *War Neuroses.* Philadelphia: Blakiston.
1945c. *Men Under Stress.* Philadelphia: Blakiston.
1946a. "War Neuroses." In *Progress in Neuropsychiatry,* edited by E. A. Spiegel. New York: Grune & Stratton.
1946b. "The Returning Soldier: A Dissent." *Hollywood Quarterly* 1:321.

With Hacker, Frederick J., et al.
1967. "Individuelle und Soziale Psychopathologie und ihre Wechselwirkungen." *Jahrbuch der Psychoanalyse* band 5. Bern and Stuttgart: Verlag Hans Huber.

With Kluckhohn, Florence R.
1954. *Integration and Conflict in Family Behavior,* report no. 27. Topeka, Kan.: Group for the Advancement of Psychiatry.
1968. *Integration and Conflict in Family Behavior* vol. 6, report no. 27A. New York: Group for the Advancement of Psychiatry. Reissued June, 1968.

With Machotka, Pavel
In press. *The Messages of the Body.* New York: Free Press.
———. *Body Presentation: The Visual Aspects of Human Communication,* abridged from *The Messages of the Body.* New York: Free Press.

With Papajohn, J.

1971. "The Relationship of Cultural Value Orientation Change and Rorschach Indices of Psychological Development." *Journal of Cross-Cultural Psychology,* 2:3, 257-272.

Index

Abdication in role repudiation, 133-34

Abreaction and campus disorders, 372

"Academic freedom" as slogan, 386

Acceptance, emotional, 158

Acculturation, 192, 199, 201, 277

Achievement: as perceived by students, 405; valued by Sirrentis, 284, 298, 306

Act, function of, 115-17

Action: in Dewey, 26; in Maxwell, 22; and polarization, 29; and thought, as related forms of behavior, 11-13

Actions, reciprocal, and cultural patterning, 316

Activitists, social, and definition of violence, 341

Activity, interaction and transaction in terms of, 25

Activity orientation: discussed, 165-67; of students, 404-06, 416; of Sirrenti family, 277-78, 298

Adaptation, organizational: definition, 307; in Sirrenti family, 305-8, 314

Adjustment, term explained, 314

Administrators, college, 372-83, 407, 412-14

Affection, need for in socialization, 152-53

Affective component of value orientations, 190

Aftermath phase of campus crises, 382-83

Age groups in U.S. power structure, 347

Agein, 18

Aggression: definition, 341-42; and positive therapeutic position, 344; and student protests, 368, 370. *See also* Frustration-aggression hypothesis.

Aggressive behavior: envy of, 389-90; and role conflict, 364-65; since *1960,* 340; types of, 342

Aggressor, identification with, 387

Aggrieved group: ego mechanisms of, 383-92; and phases of student protests, 372-75; role of women in, 381n; seen as interactional, 394; transactional view of, 398

Allocative response and imaginary roles, 107-8

435

Allocative Structure, 97, 106, 108

Allport, Floyd, 31-32

"Altruistic surrender," 389

Ambiguity, 204, 256, 388, 411

Ambivalence, 204, 279-80

American: activity orientations, 166-67, 405-6; approach to Fictive roles, 256; culture, pattern of preference in, 230, 233, 395-96, 402, 404; individualism, 163, 199, 221; Man-nature orientation, 163-64, 404-5; society, value conflicts in, 395-400; time orientation, 164-65, 402. *See also* American family

American family: adolescence, 179-80; dominant pattern stressed, 176-77; role of father, 180-81; sibling relations, 177-78; situation of older people, 178-79; value orientations described, 190-200; wife-mother role, 181-85

American Revolution, 347

Ames demonstrations, 31

Anthropology, 59-60, 63, 325

Anticipatory responses, 307

Anxiety: Anna Freud on, 387; in clinical situation, 322-23; and nature, 115; of protesting students, 386-87

Apocalyptic fantasies, 61

Approach, 19; transactional, to fantasy formation, 80

Approval, need of child, 157-58

Aristotle, 8, 17

Aspect: part of system appears as, 26, psychological, of behavior, 6

Assertion as counter to denial, 397

Assumptions, set of, 31, 32

Attention of patient, and therapist, 333-34

Attention-getting devices in student protests, 380

Atraction, 22; mutual, acted out, 274-75

Attrition in role attenuation, 138

Authoritarian: practices vs. democratic ideals, 347, 350, 351-54; structure and universities, 385-86

Authoritarianism: of campus hawks, 391n; democratic ideals vs. U.S. social system, 347-50

Authority: and justification of repression, 360; Spanish-American authority relations, 172; of therapist and patient's cultural orientation, 330

Authority figure: Italian-American father as, 287; and student protests, 369, 383-84, 384-86, 389

Autistic withdrawal, 208

Automatons, intra-cerebral, 79

Autonomy, 79

Axiom, 18

Axios, 18

Bateson, Gregory, 160n

Behavior: and academic conflicts, 390n; aggressive, and role conflict, 364-65; disturbed, social theory of, 92, 93; human, self-actional description of, 79; human, way of viewing, 146; human, unified theory of, 33; norm-violating, and student protests, 375-76; norm-violating, effectiveness of, 397-98; reciprocal, and equilibrium, 359; related to position, 14; sex role, in Sirrenti family, 299-301; sexual, 152; social, motivation expressed in, 320; and substance, 115; systems of, 3; systems of, for analysis of family process, 33; of therapist, and Man-Nature orientation, 328; thought and action, related forms of, 11-13; without awareness, defined, 325

Behavioral: norms and radical movement, 411; patterns, need for analytical dissection of, 153; research and techniques of change, 354; response, 65; sciences and language problems, 112-13; system and complementary roles, 319; system, pattern of and condition of, 28-29

Behaviorist theories, 65, 394n

Being-in-becoming orientation; defined, 166, 405; student view of, 405, 417

436

Being orientation: and Celia Tondi, 196; defined, 165-66, 405; and Fictive roles, 256; as Irish-American value, 332, 335; and Mexican society, 166; preferred by Italians, 191, 256; and Sirrentis, 277, 278, 284, 299; student view of, 405, 417; and therapy for Irish-American patient, 331

Belief systems, and visible world, 54, 69

Benedict, Ruth, 160n

Benevolent neutrality: expected of therapist, 327-36; internalization of, 330; and Irish-American patient, 331, 335-36

Bentley, Arthur, 29n, 30n, 392-93, 394n; and Dewey, 14-30, 33, 76, 313

Berkowitz, Leonard, 356n

Betrayal reaction to student protests, 379

Bettelheim, Bruno, 368-69, 393-94

Binomial system, 100

Biological: limitations, 200; structure defined, 99-100

Blacks: and riots, 346-47; and theories of collective violence, 355-65 *passim*

Body management roles and Sirrenti family, 299

California, 19th century riots in, 346

California, University of, 368, 387n

"Campus Crucible, The" (Glazer), 391n

Campus disorders. *See* Student protests

Cantril, Hadley, 30, 31, 32, 34

Cardiovascular disease, 62

Carnegie Corporation, 33n

Carnegie, Phipps and Co., 346

Casework, theory of, 91

Castration fears, and student protests, 368

Catastrophe, extensive, 56

CAT cards, 207, 208

Catharsis, Celia and Timmie Tondi, 257

Celia. *See* Tondi family: Celia

Change, organizational, stress induced by, 410-11

Change, social. *See* Social change

Channeling procedure in student protests, 374

"Character," defined, 318

Chesterton, G. K., 100

Children's Medical Center (Boston, Mass.), 188, 194

Chinese-Americans, riots against, 346

Chinese camps, interdisciplinary studies on, 89, 89n

Chinese society, orientations, 163, 164

Christian Science Monitor, 379-80

Church, teachings of, 222. *See also* Roman Catholics

Circularity, 26

Circular transactions, 247

Civil disorder, 347, 350

Civilization and Its Discontents (Freud), 384n

Classification of personality, components, 165

Class position, 150

Clues; for initial management of Celia Tondi's symptom, 247-48; of receptivity, misjudged by students, 388

Coaxing: by Ben Sirrenti, 303; role induction technique, 128

The Cocktail Party (Eliot), 130

Coercion: and conflict suppression, 396-97; role induction technique, 127-28

Coercive hostility, and Connie Sirrenti, 303

Collaborative relationship established between Celia Tondi and therapist, 249

Collaterality: American preference patterns, 175, 176, 178, 395-96; defined, 167-68, 395; in early U.S. history, 353; in group decision-making, 351-54; Italian preference, 192; as Jewish-American value, 332; and integrated theory of violence, 359-61; in Sirrenti family, 278, 284, 294, 299-302, 308; Spanish-American preference, 173;

and structural change in universities, 415-16; and student value preferences, 406-10; in Tondi family, 195, 196, 213, 233, 247-48, 252-54, 259-60, 262; and wife-mother role, 182

Collateral: relatives, 144; structures, and resistance, 354; systems, tensions in, 302

Collective disorder compared to previous protests, 347

Columbia University, 368-70, 376n, 388, 389

Committee on the Family, 33

Communication: benefits to patient, 327; compromise attained by, 262; flow of, in doctor-patient relationship, 314-16; by indirection, 236; about race relations, 363; in role playing, 154; and student protests, 381-82, 412, 413; verbal, and cultural patterning, 316; in well group, 199. *See also* Media

Communication processes, 57, 194, 315

Communication systems, 68, 316

Communications theory, 3n

Community, image of university as, 409, 415; possible intermediate focus, 46n

"Community Control," 354

Comparative analysis, four general findings, 199-200

Complementarity: in analysis and therapy, 319-21; defined, 118-19; of roles and equilibrium state, 316-17; in Tondis, 234-35

Completeness, 39n

Complexity, reduction in, 65

Compliance, in Tony Tondi, 210

Component, 165

Compromise: attainment of, 262; and role modification, 125-26; in well group, 199

Concealment in Irish-American culture, 335

Concreteness, misplaced, fallacy of, 4, 8, 13

Conditioned responses, 65

Conditions, 28

Conference, multidisciplinary, 33

Conflict: defined, 119; diversion of, 302; inner, and student protests, 388-89; institutionalized, 360; interaction and, 29; intrapsychic, and American values, 396; polarization of, *See* Polarization of conflict; psychodynamics of group conflict, 368-99 *passim*; and relative integration in Sirrenti family, 308-9; in role system, 189-90; social, 54; and recurrent disorder, 350; sources of, in role system, 121-22; stimulation of, 45; of therapist, original vs. therapeutic values, 332, 333; in Tondis, 200, 234-35. *See also* value conflicts

Conflict-avoidance, and young people, 397

Conflict-Deterring Response, 412, 413

Conflict of Generations, The (Feuer), 368

Conflict-resolution, 45; compromising is basis, 125-26; methods of, and campus violence, 383-90 *passim*, 412-14; new mode of, in Tondis, 262-64; processes of, and critics, 126; in Sirrenti family, 294-98, 301-9; and symptomatic episodes, 294; theories on, 357; and therapist's position, 399

Conflict-Resolving Response, 412-13

Conflict theory, diversity of, 357-58

Conformity, in Tony Tondi, 210

Confrontation and compromise, 262

Confusion and relational values, 415

Congressional committees and student protests, 367, 368, 369

Conscious communication in well group, 199

Conscription Act, 346

Conservative aspect of therapist's role, 328

Constipation: Angela Succi suffered from, 218; as seen by Celia Tondi, 195; in Sonny Tondi, 194, 202, 226, 237, 249

Constitutional Convention of *1787*, 347

Consultant, type of, 124n

438

"Contagion theory," 356, 371
Continuity, importance of, 168
Contradiction, and relational values, 414
Control groups, 70
Core culture, 160n
Correlation studies, 88
Counter coercion, technique of, 397
Countertransference, 80, 324-26, 329, 330, 336
Covert rebellion, 210
Cross-cultural comparison, 255
Cues: ambiguous set of, 31; for change, 276-77; cross-cultural comparison, 255; in role playing, 154
Cultural: analysis, 333, 336; anthropologists, 325; change and Sirrentis, 276-77; dynamics, need for consideration of, 336; influences in non-classical framework, 324-25; inquiry, 52; orientations, 64; patterning and symbolic gestures, 316; patterns, variability noted, 160; processes, 48; relation, in family system, 145, 150-51; sanctions, 53-54; strain, 198; themes, 160n; traditions and Sirrenti value orientation, 298-309; transition and point of vulnerability, 199; value orientations, 159, 315-16, 395, 402-17; values, 92, 160, 322; variations, investigation of, 324
Culture, 61, 64, 69; collapsed into personality, 63; as focus, 45-46, 394; as an organism, 13; and psychology, 160; transmission without intervening foci, 63. See also Value orientations, cultural
Curriculum and campus disorders, 372
Cynicism, 396n

Dangerous Corner (Priestley), 130
D'Annunzio, Gabriele, 343
Dating, attitudes toward, Italian vs. American, 96-97
Deane, Herbert, 388, 398
Death of a Salesman (Miller), 405
Decision-making: by student protesters, 414-415; and individualism

in group, 351-54; patterns of, in theory of violence, 359, 360; within universities, 407-409
Deduction, induction and, 18
Defenses: organizational, 307; of student protesters, 387-91
Defensive reaction-formation, 252-53
Defiance, in psychotherapy, 128
Delay, and conflict avoidance, 397
Demands: how to deal with, 375, 381; "non-negotiable," as public mask, 374; and student protests, 372
Democratic: ideals vs. authoritarian practices, 347-50; institution, university as, 388, 389, 407; values, conflict with authoritarian values, 351-54
Demography, and role adoption, 363-64
Denial: of affect, 251; of conflict, as American defense, 397; in Irish-American culture, 335; neutralizing technique, 129; renounced, 335-36; and student protests, 371
Depression, 50; resolved by Sirrentis, 296, 298; and student protests, 399n
Deprivation, and riot theory, 356
Descartes, 40n
Description: dividing point between types of, 79-80; of event, self-action required, 35; interactional, effects on research design, 74; interactional, 32, 80; interaction and transaction in terms of, 24-25; patient's reaction to description of role, 320; self-actional, 76, 79, 80, 81; transactional, 26, 31-32
Dewey and Bentley, 14-30, 33, 76, 313
Dewey, John, 29n, 41n, 392-93, 394n. See also Dewey and Bentley
Diagnostic procedure, 194, 207-10
Differentiation, 52, 271
Disasters, natural, interdisciplinary studies of, 89
Disease and social factors, 87
Disequilibrium, transference as mechanism to locate, 315

Disobedience, in Sonny Tondi, 195

Disorder, escalation of, 411-12

Disorganization, within Spanish-American family structure, 174-75

Dissident students, transactional view of, 398

Disturbed behavior, social theory of, 92, 93

Doctor-patient relationship, 313-15, 318-20, 321

Doing orientation: and American father, 181; and American mother, 183; and American Society, 166, 175, 191; defined, 166-67, 404-405; and Tony Tondi, 253; as Jewish-American value, 332; and Sirrenti family, 278; student view of, 405, 416

Dominant and Variant Value Orientations (Florence Kluckhohn), 161n

"Don Juan in Hell" (Shaw), 318, 319

Double-blind procedures, 70

Doves: role in campus negotiations, 389-90; and student protests, 376-79, 381; transactional view of, 398

Draft Riot of *1863*, 346, 348

Drive, 49, 157n

Drive state, somatic, 65

Drug therapy, 69

Dunham, 88

Dynamic interactions, and campus violence, 367

East St. Louis riots, 346

Eating problems, Timmie Tondi, 194

Ecological studies, 88

Education, 18

Educative activity of therapist, 327-28

Effects, interactional, 80

Ego: alien, 197; defenses of Connie Sirrenti, 305; distress responses, 306-7; ideals, 261; mechanisms of aggrieved group, 383-89; mechanisms and group psychology, Freud on, 370; and sudden antagonisms, 371; mechanisms in student protests, 383-92; protection, identification with aggressor as, 387; psycho-logical problems, 238-39; support of, and doctor's role, 322, 323; syntonic, 197

Einstein, Albert, 8, 21, 40, 115

Electro-magnetic radiation, 21

Elements, 24

Eliot, T. S., 130

Elitism: and American values, 347-48, 350, 396; and integrated theory of violence, 360; and student protests, 391n, 407, 408. *See also* Linearity

Empirical observations on causes of violence, 357-58

Emotionalism and campus crises, 381

Enculturation without intervening foci, 63

English language, scientific limitations of, 112, 114, 125

English patient, value orientation, 316

English society, 164, 168

Energy exchanges, 44

Entity: 27, 28, 42, 74, 81, 143; self-acting, 32; and transactional inquiry, 43; unique or autonomous, 78-79

Environment: interaction and transaction in, 25-26; and value orientations, 298-309

Environmental controls, 342, 343-54

Envy: and Sirrenti family, 279, 282; as unconscious motivation, 389-90

Epidemiological questions, 88

Epistemology, 10, 16, 19

Equilibrium: and Age of Anxiety, 340; and complementarity, 316-17; and reciprocal behavior, 359; and transference, 314-15

Equivocal roles, defined, 121

Erikson, Erik, 89, 180, 362

Essences, 24, 27

Ethics, 343-54

Ethnic groups: and civil disorder, 350; in family system, 150, 151; and student protests, 372, 407; in U.S. power structure, 347, 348. *See also* specific names

Ethnographies, 63

Evaluating, role induction mechanism, 128-29

Foreign policy, and student protests, 407
Form, defined, 114
Formulation, 27
Founding Fathers, value goals of, 352-53
Frank, Lawrence K., 33n, 160n
Free association, 50n
Free Speech Movement, 368
Free University of Berlin, 415
Free will, 79
Freud, Anna, 332n, 387, 389
Freud, Sigmund, 330; *Civilization and Its Discontents*, 384n; on death, 104; on effects of war, 384, 385; and fictive roles, 106; *Group Psychology and the Analysis of the Ego*, 370, 384; on humor, 122-23; on narcissism, 381, 384n
Fromm, Erich, 166, 167
Frustration: studies on, 356n; of therapist, 332
Frustration-aggression hypothesis, 356, 357, 358, 362
Function, 96; as dynamic aspect, 113-14
Functional change, in wartime, 56
Future time orientation: and American middle-class values, 164-65, 175, 183, 191, 402; and Irish-Americans, 335; and Italian-Americans, 277-78, 284; and Jewish-Americans, 332; valued by students, 416

Gardner, Dr. George, 188
General systems theory, 3n, 78
Genet, Jean, 6n
Gente, la, 172
Geographical setting, point of reference in family, 148
Glazer, Nathan, 391n
Goals: and choice of role systems, 119; of student protests, 372-73, 376, 402, 411; goal structure defined, 97
Grimshaw, Allen, 356
Grinker, Roy, 33, 34, 35, 78
Group, 62-69 *passim*; defined as focus, 45; as focus of transactional

field, 394, 395; cohesion, 45; conflicts, psychodynamics of, 367-68; decision making, 45, 351-54; feelings and student activists, 369, 389; formation and role of identification, 384; norms, 92; processes, 48, 308-9, 368-99 *passim*; psychology, Freud on, 370; psychotherapy, research limitations, 119; solidarity, of Sirrenti family, 288; violence, theories of, 355-66
Group for the Advancement of Psychiatry, 33, 143
Group Psychology and the Analysis of the Ego (Freud), 370, 384
Guilt feelings, and campus crises, 387

Hampstead Tribunal, 385
Harmony-with-nature orientation, 163, 404, 416
Harvard University, student protests, 376n
"Hawks" in student protests, 376-79, 381, 389-91, 398
Head-rocking, Timmie Tondi, 202, 223
Hegal, Georg, 29
Hitches, 30
Hobbes, Thomas, 13
Hodos, 19
Hoffer, Eric, 368
Hollingshead, August, 88
Homeostatic mechanisms, 117, 316
Homosexual longings, and student protests, 368
Hospitals, mental, 68-69, 89
Hostility, and student protests, 370, 385, 387
Humor: and role conflict, 122-23; use of, as denial, 336
Hypocrisy, as perceived by young, 352, 360, 414, 415
Hypothesis, 16
Hypotithenai, 16

Idea, 10, 11, 17, 18
Idealists, 7, 13
Identification: as ego protection, 387-88; Freud on, 384; in learning social role behavior, 153; in posi-

tive therapeutic position, 344; among student protesters, 383-84, 387, 387n
Ideology: discrepancy with reality, 352-53; and moral scruples, 374
Image, uni-dimensional, 16
Imagery, travelogue, 18
Imitation, in learning social role behavior, 153
Inclusion, principle of, 347
Indefiniteness, 10
Indeterminateness, 9
Individual and family, 147
Individualism: concealed values of, 391; in group decision-making, 351-54; and integrated theory of violence, 359-61; Spanish-American view of, 171; and structural change in universities, 414-15; and student value preferences, 405-10
Individualistic orientation, 166, 213; and American pattern, 175, 176, 192, 352-53, 395-96; in Sirrentis, 271, 278, 294; suited to industrial society, 185; in Tondis, 233-34, 247-48, 252-54
Individual needs, 159
Induction and deduction, 18
Information processes, 57
Inhibition, sudden release of, 371
Inhibitors, environmental, 343-54
Inquiry: continuum of methods of, 50n; cultural, 52; interdisciplinary, 57; organization of, 23; process of, 19, 38; transactional vs. interactional, 24-25, 75-76
Inside-outside problem, 32
Instigators, environmental, 343-54
Institute for Psychosomatic and Psychiatric Research and Training, 33n
Instrumental Structure, 100
Integration: conflict and, within systems, 29; mechanisms of, 152; during Age of Anxiety, 340; relative, of group processes in conflict-controlled field of behavior, 308-9; and role expectations, 301; in role system, 119
Intellectual defense, 250

Interaction: to conflict, 29; defined, 23, 96, 393; and description of systems, 32; and student protests, 394; and transaction, 24-26, 314
Interactional inquiry: approach to sociological theory, 34n; as description of psychotherapy, 80; details of observations seen as, 76; in therapy, 75-76; and transactional inquiry, 42-43
Interconnection: causal, 23; concept of, 1
Interdependence of foci in field, 60
Interdisciplinary research, 57-58, 89
Interpersonal security, 153
Interpretation, recognition of Allocative Structure in, 110
Interruption pattern, in Tondis, 236-39
Intrapsychic defense and value orientation, 252
Introspection, 50n
Irish-American patient, 330-36
Irish-Americans: attacks on, 345-46, 361; and dominant values, 334; in family study, 188; and subjugation-to-nature, 331, 332, 333; in U.S. power structure, 347, 348
Irrationality and student protests, 371, 404
Italian-American: community, 213, 255; family, 188, 213, 244; fathers, 287; marriages, 221; mothers, 216
Italian-Americans in U.S. power structure, 348
Italian values, 230, 238; and American values, 192; and Celia Tondi, 197; and Fictive roles, 255-56; and languages, 278; and present time orientation, 191; strain between Collateral and Being orientation, 199; and Subjugation-to-nature orientation, 191. See also Sirrenti family; Tondi family

James, William, 16, 37
Jammer, Max, 112-13
Japanese, Lineal preference, 167
Jealousy, sexual, and Sirrentis, 275-76
Jefferson, Thomas, 352, 353

Material system, 21
Matter, 13, 27
Matter and Motion (Maxwell), 21-23, 38
Maturation, plasticity diminishes with, 152
Maxwell, J. Clerk, 8, 21-23, 38, 39, 40
Meade, George Herbert, 136
Mead, Margaret, 90, 160n, 184-85
Means, ends and, 18
Mechanics: classical, 8; Newtonian, 23
Mechanisms: of biological arousal, 342; of control in Sirrenti family, 298-309 *passim;* integrative, 152; projective, 68; regulative, 316; re-integrating, 119, 121-22; for solutions in adolescent peer group, 180
Media: distortion and objectivity, 365; and student protests, 367, 368, 377, 379-80; and theories about riots, 356, 365
Memory, inconsistencies in, and student protests, 382
Menninger, William, 369
Mental health, 308, 327
Mental illness: as Soma-Psyche strain, 50; as transactional effect, 308
Merton, Robert, 118
Metaphor, implicit, 16
Method, 19
Mexican society and Being orientation, 166
Michael Reese Hospital, 33, 33n
Middle-class values: and American family, 177-78; and Mastery-over-nature orientation, 190-91; and official value patterns, 352; and Sirrenti family, 271, 278; and the university, 402-10; in U.S. power structure, 347
Migration of peoples, 56
Milieu, use of word in studies of mental hospitals, 68-69
Military pressures, interdisciplinary studies of, 89
Mind, 13

"Misplaced Concreteness, The Fallacy of," 4, 8, 13
Mixed Response, 413
Mode of Abstraction, 4
Moderates: and role response to social change, 362; and student protests, 381
Modifications: in research, 336; within role systems, 117, 119; and transference problems, 334
Modifications in the Course of Ulcerative Colitis in Relationship to Changes in Life Situations and Reaction Patterns (Lindemann), 144n
Morality, 52; as prescientific form of social control, 345
Morris, Charles, 165
Mother-child patterns of transaction, 158
Motherhood and maladjustment, 184-85
Mother's Day, 178
Motivation, 95; irrational, and student protests, 368-69; of patient, and optimum disequilibrium, 321; and social roles, 320
Motivational processes, distinguished from cultural value orientations, 315-16
Murray, Henry, 160n
Mythological roles, Allocative Structure, 106

Names and naming, 15, 20, 25, 26
Narcissism: Freud on, 381, 384n; of small differences, 2; and student protests, 390, 391
National Advisory Commission on Civil Disorders, 357n, 358n
National Commission on the Causes and Prevention of Violence, 358n
National Labor Relations Act, 346
Native American Party, 345, 349, 361
Nativism, 350; and reconstructionism, 348-49; as response to social change, 360-63
Nature and anxiety, 115. *See also* Man-nature orientation

445

Physical contact, in Tondis, 236
Physical sciences, language problems, 112-13
Physics, pre-Galilean, 23
Physiological processes, 65
Pierce, Charles, 16, 37
Place, in family system, 150
Plasticity, 152
Plato, 10, 17
Pluralism, and integrated theory of violence, 360
Polarization of conflict: described, 29, 54, 121-22; and group violence, 357; in integrated theory of violence, 363; mounting polarization phase of student protest, 377-82; role of expert in, 124-25; of public, by student protests, 411
Poscere, 19n
Positive absolutism, 343, 344
Positive evaluating, 302
Postponing, as induction technique, 131-32
Postulare, 19n
Postulations, 19
Postulatum, 19n
Power structure: fragmentation of, 357; in integrated theory of violence, 360; operation of, in U.S., 347-48, 353
Prehension, 6, 10-11, 27
Premonitory phase of student protest, 372-74
Present percept, 32
Present time orientation as Irish-American value, 331, 332, 335; as Italian value, 191, 277-78, 284; of Spanish-Americans, 164, 173; use of, in therapy, 328; valued in American culture, 402; valued by students, 403, 416
Press. *See* Media
Pressure, 22
Prestige systems, 68
Priestley, J. B., 130
Primary group, 147
Procedures, transactional, 32
Process: and analysis of family, 33; concept of, 9, 11, 393; of conflict resolution, 126; communication as

information, 57; and interdisciplinary studies, 89; and language, 113; motivational, 315-16; psychodynamic, 196; reciprocal, 74; regulative, 314; science as, 38; somatic, 43, 47, 48, 50, 65, 116; of student protests, 393-94; and study of family, 143; and time scale, 113-14; and transactional inquiry, 23, 27-30; types of, 43-45, 47n, 48, 65-66, 68; Whitehead on, 16
Projection, 306
Protest function and symptomatic behavior, 307
Protest reactions, and pathological equilibrium, 254
Protestants, 243, 345-46, 347
Provocation: as counter to delay, 397; as neutralizing technique, 132
Psyche, 59, 62-66, 68; as focus, 44-45, 304, 394, 395
Psychiatric social workers, 33, 91
Psychiatrists, role in wartime, 369, 370
Psychiatry: diagnostic study recommended, 201; testing of theories of, 92; view of Connie Sirrenti, 304-5
Psychoanalysis: claim to uniqueness, 59; concepts of, 35, 49, 50n, 116-17; distinguished from psychotherapy, 313, 318-23; and experimental demonstrations, 31; and family study, 188, 196; interactional descriptions of, 34; and negative evaluating, 130; Neo-Freudian, 88; and role theory, 120
Psychobiological rhythms, 236-39
Psychodynamics: of families, 196, 304-9 *passim*; of group conflicts, 367-68; inner, 66, 198; and role theory, 323
Psychogenetic data, 68
Psychogenic factor, 201
Psychological: changes, 47, 56; factors in student protests, 371, 382, 386-88; processes, 48, 50; sciences, and social sciences, 94-95; tests, 67
Psychopharmacology, 69

Psychosexual timetable, 83
Psychosomatic studies, 33, 49, 50
Psychotherapy, 34, 66, 69, 203; distinguished from psychoanalysis, 313, 318-23; flow of communication in, 314; reality in context of, 326; roles in, 106-8, 110-11, 139, 321-23; and self-actional description, 80; settings for, 324-25; transference in, 324, 325-26, 334; and value of cultural analysis, 336. *See also* Therapist
Pullman Strike, 346

Quakers, 343
Questionnaires to determine ranking pattern of group decision-making, 351-52

Race relations: communication about, 363; discrimination, 57, 347; and student protests, 407. *See also* Blacks
Radicalism, 362, 411, 415-16
Rashomon effect, 82, 382
Rationalization, 397, 404-5
Reaction, 22, 29; and abnormal circumstances, 369; reaction-formation, 252-54
Reagan, Ronald, 368
Reassurance and doctor's role, 322, 323
Reality: and adjustment *vs.* change, 340-41; concepts of, 8, 9, 10; defined, 14; discrepancy with ideology, 352-53; and labeling, 365; as perceived by Irish-American patient, 331-32; in psychotherapeutic context, 323, 326, 328, 345; social, distortions of, 370; students' perceptions of, 386-87; testing, 328, 388, 391n
Reconstructivists, 348-50, 361-63
Redetermination, 25
Redlich, Frederick, 88
Reduction in complexity, 65
Reductionism, 59
Reference points in family, 147-48
Reflections on Violence (Sorel), 343

Reform, educational, and student protests, 414
Refusal, and role repudiation, 135-36
Regions, principle of interdependence of, 41; as foci, 42
Reification, fear of, 115
Reinforcement, 65
Relational value orientations: and behavior of therapist, 328; democratic-authoritarian conflict, 351-52; discussed, 167-69; and integrated theory of violence, 359-61; of Italian families, 230, 298; preference patterns, 353; and race relations, 407; Spanish-American, 171-73; and university structure, 405-11 *passim*
"Relations;" and role structuring, 318; and transaction, 24
Relativist principles, as ethical position, 343-44
Relativity, theory of, 8
Religion: and American values, 403, 404; as Sirrenti family value, 288-90; in U.S. power structure, 347, 348
Renaming, 25
Replacement and role repudiation, 135-36
Repressed memory and aims of treatment, 326
Repression: by Connie Sirrenti, 305; justification of, 360; masking role system equivalent of, 130; of riots, 356
Reproduction, as function of family, 151-52
Repulsion, 22
Research: during Age of Anxiety and Age of Violence, 339-40; on aggression, need for, 342; behaviorial, and techniques of change, 354; on conflict theory, 356-58; design, 66; results of modifications in, 336; sample of family study, 188-89; on social psychology, 119; therapeutic practices analysed, 70-74
Reservation and role attenuation, 137-38

Residential institutions, 156
Residential patterns and family structure, 150-51
Resignation and role repudiation, 134-35
Resistance, emotional, 327, 332, 333, 354
Retinal sensory functioning, 32
Revenge behavior, 342
"Revolutionary" as role response to social change, 361-63
Riesman, David, 175
"Riff-raff theory" of riots, 355-56
Riots: integrated theory of, 358-65; nineteenth-century, 345-46, 348; popular theories of, 355-56; scientific theories of, 356-57. *See also* Student protests
Rising expectations, collapse of, 356
Ritualization by student protesters, 387-88
Ritual visiting, 261
Robert's Rules of Order, 380
Rohrschach cards, 207, 208, 210
Role adoption, 359, 362-65
Role analysis, 33, 34, 35, 95-111, 120, 139
Role assignment, 125, 318, 323
Role attenuation, 137-38
Role behavior, 53, 153, 154
Role commitment, 120
Role conflicts: and aggressive behavior, 364-65; displaced, 262; formal, 190, 194; and humor, 122-23; informal, 190; and pathology, 189; showed by all families, 199; in Sirrenti family, 307; and visits to family, 324
Role discrepancy, 123
Role dislocation, 132-38
Role displacement, 136-37
Role exchange, 136
Role expectations, 153-54, 301, 410-11
Role induction, 126-32, 235, 302-3
Role manipulation, 117, 119, 126
Role modifications, 117, 119, 122-26, 303, 307
Role partners, 80, 118, 120, 136, 359; defined, 189-90

Role-playing: and cultural value orientation, 316-17; interplay between explicit and implicit roles, 317-23; and socialization, 154-55
Role relations: doctor-patient, 320, 321; family network, 198; and therapeutic stalemate, 251-52
Role repudiation, 133-36
Role responses, 154, 360-63
Role reversal: defined, 122, 125; distinguished from role exchange, 136; and Sirrentis, 303; and Tondis, 194, 245-46
Role satisfactions, defining, 321
Role segregation, 253
Role set, 118
Role structure, 108-11, 115, 304, 318, 319
Role systems, 56, 130, 153-54, 321, 359; discussed, 115-22
Role theory, 155, 157, 198, 320-23
Role transposition, 136
Roles: adversary, 372; of advocate, 373; age roles, 192, 298-99; of appreciator, 322; biological, 101-3, 235; character roles, 104-5, 110-11, 135, 193, 239-42; complementary, 319, 321; concept discussed, 153-57; and cultural patterning, 255, 315-17; domestic, 192; explicit, 121, 317, 320, 321; expressive, 317; family, 159, 192; female, 172-73, 181-85, 282, 291; Fictive, 106-8, 193-94, 255-57, 274-75, 303; formal, 101-3, 108, 110, 190-92, 197, 199, 229-35, 298-309; general and specific, 155; imaginary, 106-8, 110-11; implicit, 105, 121, 317-23 *passim;* informal, 104-5, 108, 193, 195, 235-36, 303; institutional, 103, 111; instrumental, 317, 321; male, 172, 255, 283, 287, 290; and motivational processes, 315; occupational, 193; patient's, 319-21; peer group, 180; reciprocal, 153-54, 321; recreational, 193; religious, 193; sex, 192, 274-75, 290, 300; sick, 193, 235; students', 386; supernatural, 106, wife, 181-85. *See also* Social roles

Roman-Catholics, 211, 222, 243; and Italian-American values, 268, 269-70, 288-90; Protestant attacks on, 345-46, 348, 349, 361; in U.S. power structure, 347, 348
Ruesch, Jurgen, 33n
Russell, Bertrand, 385

San Francisco State College, 379
Sapir, Edward, 113, 160n
Scale, problem of, 93
Schizophrenia, 28, 66
School phobia, 194
Sciences: organization and outlook of, 2, 38, 57; social *vs.* psychological, 94-95
Scorn, example of, Whitehead, 3n
Scoundrel, 245
Security, need for, 158
Selectivity, issue of, 82
Self-action: contrasted to transaction, 32, 314; defined, 23, 393; Dewey and Bentley on, 23-24; need for self-actional description, 35, 76, 78-81; and student protests, 394
Self-destruction and student protests, 399n
Self-inquiry, 50
Semantics, dangers of, 114
Sensory inputs, 44
Sex: Sirrenti family value, 289-90; and needs of parents, 158; Tondi family value, 218-19, 221-22
Shakow, David, 33n
Shared norms, breakdown of, 357
Shays, Daniel, 345
Shays' Rebellion, 345, 348
Shaw, George Bernard, 319
Sinning: admission of, 335-36; as way of getting attention, 333
Sirrenti family: nuclear, described, 265-67; environment, 267-68; extended families, 268-73; relationships and value preferences, 273-91; crises and resolutions, 291-98; integrative processes, 298-309; man-nature orientation, 298
    Benito, Sr. (Ben): described, 265, 271; and parents and siblings, 268-

71, 281, 283-84; jobs, 271, 278-80, 297; marriage relationship, 273-75, 276, 291, 296-97, 300-3, 307-8; value preferences, 277-81, 288, 299; as father, 287; courtship, 291-94; relationship with mother, 293, 297; trip to Canada, 295-96
    Benito, Jr. (Benny), 265, 295; described, 266-67; relationship with mother, 284, 285, 286-87, 296; with father, 287; with brothers, 288
    Carlo, Father (priest), 281, 283, 295; described, 269-70, 271; and Ben, 284; as peacemaker, 296, 303, 307
    Consuelo (Connie), 265; described, 266; and mother and sisters, 268, 271-73, 293, 305; and Ben's brothers, 270, 283, 284; concept of marriage and sex, 273-75, 276, 289-90, 296-97, 300-3, 307-8; hospitality of, 275-76; value preferences, 277-278, 299; relationship with Ben's mother, 281-83, 291, 293-94, 295, 303, 307-8, with Ben's father, 283, with her children, 284-87, 288, 296, 297-98, 299, 306; and religion, 288-90; response to suffering, 290-91; courtship, 291-94; emotional crisis, 295-96; personality structure, 304-8
    Dominic (Dom), 270, 271, 283, 295
    Eduardo (Dr. Ed), 270, 271, 283, 284, 295, 297
    Grandma (Maria Gondo), 274; described, 268-69, 270-71; language problem, 278; and Connie, 281-83, 291, 293-94, 295, 303, 307-8; as healer, 290; and Ben, 293, 297; opposes marriage, 293-94; trip to Canada, 295
    Grandpa (Rudolpho), 267-71 *passim*, 275, 281, 283, 297
    Louisa, 272
    Louise, 269
    Natale (Nat), 265, 277, 284, 295; described, 266; relationship with mother, 285, 286, 290, with father,

450

287, with brothers, 288; injury, 291; emotional crisis, 297-98

Rudolphe (Rudy), 265, 284, 295; described, 266; relationship with mother, 284-85, 285-86, with father, 287, with brothers, 288; injury, 290-91

Vito, 269, 271, 283-84, 295

Situation, definition of, 365

Skinner, B. F., 21n

Skolnick, Jerome, 356

"Sky King," 254

Social backgrounds and role adoption, 362-63

Social change: during Age of Anxiety, 339-40; during Age of Violence, 340; direction of, and research, 354; and student protests, 397n, 401-2; and theories of riots, 357-65 *passim;* university as model for, 409-10

Social Class and Mental Illness (Hollingshead and Redlich), 88

Social factors and disease, 87

Social institutions, reciprocal effects with cultural value orientations, 350-54

Social mobility, 229-30

Social psychiatry, 87-88, 91

Social psychology, research limitations, 119

Social roles: classification of, 100-2; in conceptualizing behavioral processes, 156-57; defined, 94-97, 189, 315, 359; and describing transactions, 33; and doctor-patient relations, 313-15; and family study, 188; and linguistic problems, 112-15; and motivation, 320; structure of, 115-17; and theory of violence, 358-65. *See also* Roles

Social system: point of reference in family, 147; U.S. power structure, 347-50

Social theory, 35; of disturbed behavior, 92, 93

Socialization of children, 151-53, 157-58

Society, defined as focus, 45, 394, 395

Socioeconomic situation and procedure with patient, 323

Sociology, 59, 119

"Soft line" and student protests, 376-79, 412

Soma, 59, 61, 65, 66; defined as focus, 44, 394

Somatic: needs, 66; pain, 50, 61; paradox, 43; response to physical hardships, 56; transactional processes, 313-14

Sorel, Georges, 343

Space, 93

Space-time continuum, 8, 12, 13, 14, 16, 44

Spanish-American value orientations, 163, 164, 169-74 *passim*

Spanking card, 207

"Standpatters," as role response to social change, 361-63

Stanford-Binet test, 208

State, authority of, challenged by students, 384-86

Status relations, 151-52, 238

Stimuli, interpretations of visual, 31

Stone, Leo, 332n

Stone object, described in self-actional terms, 77

Strachey, Lytton, 385

Strain: definition and types of, 49-55; in Sirrenti family, 291-98, 301-8; among Spanish-Americans, 174

Strategy of illusory completeness, 39n

Strawberry Statement, The (Kunen), 388, 389

Stress, 22, 49; defined, 340; and organizational change, 410-11

Structure: of ego, and method of treatment, 323; and function, 114-15; and interdisciplinary studies, 89; organizational, and therapist, 328; self-consistent, 32, 35; as static aspect, 113-14; structural change in universities, 414-17; and transactional processes, 28

Student protests: advocate role in, 373; and anxiety, 386-87; and authority figure, 369, 384-86, 389; and

451

Robert, 212, 229

Ruth, 212, 215

Timothy (Timmie), 195, 222; described, 194, 202, 206-7; fantasy, 254-57; head-rocking, 202, 223, 237; health problems, 225, 227; school progress, 257-58; stuttering, 205, 227, 254; testing procedure, 208-9; unconscious determinants, 255; victim role, 242

Widow (Tony's mother), 212-13, 214

Traditional value profile and Sirrenti choices, 294

Training, 18

Transaction: adaptation as system of, 314; contrasted with interaction, 24-26, 314; defined, 22-24, 27, 38, 313, 393; Dewey and Bentley on, 20, 23-26, 30; and energy exchanges, 44; implicit roles and explicit roles in, 319-20; mother-child patterns of, 158; observed through sets of interactions, 76

Transactional approach, 34, 36; and envisionment, 76; and fantasy formation, 80; and Sirrentis, 304-9; and somatic processes, 313-14; and student protests, 392-99

Transactional description, 26, 31-34

Transactional field, 30, 36, 48, 61; and built-in complexities, 64; foci within, 33, 41-42; and interdisciplinary research, 186

Transactional inquiry: confined to one foci, 55; and interactional inquiry, 42-43; process of, 30, 31, 36; and research designs, 70; in therapy, 75-76

Transactional system: analyzing state of, 155; at optimum disequilibrium, 321

Transactionism, 30, 33, 34

Transference: cultural aspects of, 324, 329, 336; explained, 314, 321, 325-26; interactional effects described in terms of, 80; management of, in doctor-patient relationship, 313-15, 321, 333-34; and neurosis,

imaginary role structure, 111, problems and modifications, 334

Transformation process, 48, 49, 53, 61

Transitional: forms, 49; roles, 104, 108, 109-11, 124-25, 193

Truth, 26

Unconscious: canons of choice, 160n; determinants, 255

Uniqueness, 78-79

Universe: as focus, 43-44, 394; as system of transaction, 38, 59, 61, 65, 69

Universities: as model for social change, 410; protest movements in, 346-47, 350 (see also Student protests); structure of, 385-86, 405-12, 414-17; value conflicts in, 401-17

Unmasking, 130-31, 397

Ursuline convent, attack on, 345

Value conflicts: in American society, 395-400; democratic-authoritarian, 351-54; and Formal roles, 194, 199-200; methods for exposing, 397-98; and obstacles to change, 414-17; as reinforcement, 197-98; and social change, 355-65 passim; and student leaders, 399; in universities, 401-17

Value orientations, cultural: of American family, 190-200; categories of, 351; defined, 53-54, 161-62; incongruent, 241; and intrapsychic defence, 252; middle-class Americans, 169-70, 327, 328-29; and motivational processes, 315-16; patterning of, 64, 69, 73, 192, 251, 252, 304, 359, 360; as point of reference, 147-48; profiles of, 192, 231, 298-309; and rearrangement of priorities, 354; and role discrepancy, 123; and social institutions, 350; and strain, 199; theory of, 90, 99, 161n, 188, 190, 351-52, 359-60, 395, 402; and therapeutic relationship, 251-52, 325, 328-33

Values: academic, 384; ambiguity of communicated, 192; breakdown of shared, 357; defined, 53; dominant,

454

161; institutionalized, 360; preferences, 277-81, 288, 299, 405-10; tenacity of assumptions, 31, 190; Value Structure defined, 97-99; variant, 161, 168-69

Variations in technique, and cultural analysis, 336

Veblen, Thorstein, 182

Vietnam war and student protests, 372, 385, 407, 408

Violence: defined, 341; ethic of, 343-54; integrated theory of, 358-65; and student protests, 368, 371, 378, 399n, 411-12; theories of collective, 355-66

WAMPAM structure, 347

Whitehead, Alfred North, 35, 40n, 393; theories of, 3-10 *passim*, 13, 15, 16, 21, 27, 38

Whorf, Benjamin, 113

Why War? (Freud), 384n

Wish and aims of treatment, 326

Withholding as neutralizing mechanism, 128

Women: as aggrieved students, 381n; confusion of expectation, 185; and segregation of sexes, 182-83

"Working through," 31

"World Power" principle, 407

World War I, 384, 385

Wretched of the Earth, The (Fanon), 344

Wynne, Lyman, 138

Yankee working-class family, 188, 199

Youth, American accent on, 176

Zetzel, Elizabeth, 325n